In Memory of My Father
William Griffith Thomas (1939–2020)

All of the author's royalties earned from sales of this book will be donated to the National Association for the Advancement of Colored People Legal Defense and Educational Fund, Inc.

The NAACP's Legal Defense and Educational Fund is a 501(c)(3) nonprofit organization dedicated to the pursuit of racial justice through litigation, advocacy, and public education.

Contents

A Question of Freedom

Prologue
Georgetown, April 2017

It was early morning when I crossed the Francis Scott Key Bridge from Virginia into Georgetown. College spires loomed in the distance, gray in the dawn light. I was headed to a religious service at Georgetown University that would acknowledge the trauma of a massive slave sale in 1838, a deal that shored up the finances of the struggling college and sent more than two hundred men, women, and children into the cane fields of Louisiana. Most of the families torn apart in the sale could trace their lineage to White Marsh, one of the Jesuit-owned plantations located in Prince George's County, Maryland.

I had been researching the history of the White Marsh families for nearly a decade, uncovering the lawsuits they had brought against the Jesuits and other prominent Maryland slaveholders long before the 1838 sale. Some won their freedom. Others didn't—but each of their cases challenged the legitimacy of slavery in American law. Together they counted among the most significant freedom suits in U.S. history. And there were hundreds of others. Yet their particular stories would lead me, like the Georgetown Jesuits, to reckon with what I did not know about my own family and its role in this story.

More than a hundred descendants, a dozen university officials, and a cluster of Jesuit priests assembled inside Healy Hall for the liturgy and slowly processed into an ornate, wood-paneled auditorium on the third floor. After the opening prayer Sandra Green Thomas rose to address the congregation. Thomas, a descendant of the Hawkins family and president of the GU272 Descendants Association, waited a long moment before speaking. "My people were humble," she began. "They provided for their families. They tried to protect their children as best they could from the cruelties of this world, but given what the world is and what people can be, they were not always as successful as they would have hoped." The anguish and fortitude of her ancestors echoed in the firmness of her tone. "Their pain was unparalleled," she observed. "Their pain is still here. It burns in the soul of every person of

1

African descent in the United States. It lives in people, some of whom have no knowledge of its origins but cope with the ever-present longing and lack it causes."[1]

I had met Thomas in New Orleans for the first time a few weeks before the ceremony. I had asked her then what slavery meant to her family, and she had said that slavery was quite simply one thing: theft. To understand American history required dealing with the fact that slavery was premised on a series of lies. The slaveholders, whether Jesuit priests or English tobacco planters, saw themselves differently, of course. We had talked about how they rationalized slavery on the basis of race, religion, law, science, and history and with myriad other prejudices, doctrines, sentiments, and myths.

Now, I wondered how Thomas would broach the lies that slaveholders told and the theft that slavery was. She turned to the heart of the matter, and to the Jesuits whose predecessors had enslaved her ancestors. "I know it is difficult to honestly look at yourself, the way you operate in the world, and your true motivations and priorities." Americans face an uncomfortable truth, she noted. History demanded "self-revelation" about the stories we accept without questioning, about the narratives we use without thinking. She offered forgiveness to the Jesuits, but she sought justice. Thomas spoke for all of the descendants who thirsted for an acknowledgment of their family's particular enslavement, and after she finished thunderous applause erupted in the room.

An expectant hush fell across the auditorium as the Reverend Tim Kesicki, a Jesuit priest and president of the Jesuit Conference of Canada and the United States, rose to address the descendants. He wore a plain black business suit and Roman clerical collar. With an air of earnestness, he spoke slowly, like a pastor to his flock. The long shadow of enslavement, Kesicki said, "remains with us to this day, trapping us in an historic truth." The truth, he admitted, was that the Jesuits had "betrayed the very name of Jesus." Kesicki offered a sweeping apology, confessed the sin of enslavement, and sought "on bended knee" forgiveness for the Jesuits' entire participation in slavery.

But he did not kneel. The remarks, sincere and heartfelt as they were, seemed strangely inadequate. Kesicki wished to acknowledge the sins of the past but was unprepared to deal with the real trauma the Church had caused and offered no meaningful pathway forward. His apology and the request for forgiveness fell flat. Descendants turned their heads away.

In this uncomfortable moment, something more than a Jesuit failure came into view—Kesicki's words symbolized an American failure to deal with a hurtful history. He had not referred to a single descendant or ancestor by name; he had directed his apology to his "sisters and brothers." For hundreds of years the Jesuits had spoken to the enslaved families on similar occasions without addressing them individually, and here at Georgetown the particularity of their enslavement appeared again to be disregarded. Kesicki's apology, nonetheless, marked a subtle but decisive departure in the Jesuits' acknowledgment of their role in slavery. Even the most recent Jesuit histories had failed to fully acknowledge the Society of Jesus's complicity. Indeed, until Kesicki spoke, most attempts to come to terms with this history had downplayed the Jesuit slaveholders' actions: decisions explained, rationalized, and inspected, all pointing to something called "slavery" but not to the families they enslaved. The same vagueness could describe how Americans more generally regard slavery.[2]

But America's founding, like Georgetown University's, cannot be disentangled from its enslavement of *particular* families. Our national imagination still sees slavery as an aberration, a detour, from the true story of the country. Many Americans see enslaved people in history as faceless and nameless, victims of a long-ago system that has now disappeared. In such a situation, the nation needs to experience what we at the liturgy experienced: a confrontation, a reckoning, with real people, with real histories, with real families whose descendants live among us. Until such encounters happen more widely, Americans will continue to live in separate historical spheres of understanding, a condition that more than anything limits our ability to come to terms with the past. We cannot, of course, do anything to change what happened long ago, but we can change the way we understand what happened and what it means to us in the present.[3]

One of the wealthiest black majority counties in the United States today, Prince George's County held more than 60 percent of its total population in bondage at the nation's founding. In May 1789 a small group of Jesuits met at White Marsh plantation and decided to found a college at Georgetown. They also resolved, for the first time, to start systematically selling people they thought were too old to work.[4]

Edward Queen, Charles Mahoney, and others who were enslaved at White Marsh sued the Jesuits for their freedom in 1791. Thirty-five years old, Edward Queen said in his initial petition that he was entitled to his freedom because he was "descended from a freewoman."[5] With a handful of depositions and three generations of family lore about his grandmother, Queen expected to prove that she was a free person. He had real evidence to show that he and everyone in his family had been illegally held in bondage.[6]

The eastern United States, ca. 1840 (M. Roy Cartography).

Queen's lawsuit opened the floodgates. For at least seventy years and five generations, from the 1780s right up to the Civil War, the enslaved families of Prince George's County staged more than a thousand legal actions against hundreds of slaveholding families who found themselves defending slavery in court.[7]

The lawsuits extended well beyond the Jesuits. Thousands of individuals, from the highest ranks of society to the lowest, were involved in these trials. And the suits spread into other counties as more and more of the enslaved families sought freedom in the courts. At a pivotal point in 1813 the Queen family appealed their freedom suits to the U.S. Supreme Court in *Queen v. Hepburn*. The Queens' lawyer on that occasion was none other than

Francis Scott Key, one of the capital's most sought-after attorneys. And among the sitting justices on the Supreme Court was Gabriel Duvall, who had previously represented Edward Queen in the family's first freedom suit. Despite a string of Maryland decisions in favor of the family's claim to freedom, the Queens lost their case in the Supreme Court.[8]

The decision had far-reaching repercussions for the family and the nation. *Queen v. Hepburn* closed off an avenue of freedom for the Queens, but it also raised the evidentiary standard for freedom suits more generally so that future claims would be as unlikely to succeed. Chief Justice John Marshall used the hearsay rule as a bright-line standard, a means to arrest the procedural unraveling of slavery. The rule privileged the kinds of evidence slaveholders could control (documentary records and direct testimony) at the expense of the kinds of evidence the enslaved persons could produce (old depositions and family lore). Faced with the direct words of the Queen ancestor, the lower-court judges effectively silenced her. "The declarations of an ancestor, while held as a slave, cannot be given in evidence." The ruling kept the family histories and genealogies of the enslaved people in the shadows for decades, even centuries, afterward.[9]

Queen v. Hepburn raises questions about the motivations of everyone involved. Why did the Jesuits and other slaveholders fight so ferociously in court to hold on to the people they enslaved? What did people like Edward Queen hope to achieve, and what did they think was within their reach? Why did lawyers like Francis Scott Key take these cases, and how did judges, even those with moderate antislavery convictions, end up advancing legal principles in the trials that would ultimately uphold slavery? What's more, how did the Duvall, Key, and Queen families know one another long before the case was argued in the Supreme Court in February 1813? A year and a half later, Key witnessed the British bombardment of Ft. McHenry in Baltimore, and he wrote the poem that would become "The Star-Spangled Banner." Did the Queen case leave any lasting impression on his thinking, on his conscience?[10]

I set out initially to understand what happened to the families from White Marsh in Prince George's County and found to my surprise that their freedom suits exposed a central myth of American slavery: the idea that slavery rested on a solid, fundamentally legitimate, legal basis in Anglo-American law and constitutionalism.

To a shocking degree it did not.

The freedom suits that erupted in Maryland probed a glaring vulnerability in the law of slavery. Maryland's 1776 constitution made no mention of slavery or slaveholding and declared that all "inhabitants . . . are entitled to the common law of England." The common law of England included at a minimum a baseline presumption of personal freedom. But it also encompassed precedents that called slavery itself into question. Indeed, the Maryland constitution specified that all English laws and court decisions through June 1, 1774, applied in the state. As did the acts of assembly up to that date unless they "have been or may be altered" by the constitution's Declaration of Rights. The legislature in the 1780s passed acts that revised aspects of the colonial statutes but never passed a fundamental law sanctioning slavery as a legitimate form of property holding. The difference was potentially significant. Over time, the ambiguities in the law only deepened.[11]

It could be argued that both Maryland statutory law after 1776 and the U.S. Constitution after 1789 presumed the existence of slavery and therefore, however indirectly, assured slavery's legitimacy. Naturally, slaveholders adopted the view that the constitutionality of slavery went without saying. The Constitution protected slaveholders in significant ways, not least by requiring the return of anyone fleeing slavery across state lines. But there was a plausible argument that in the absence of direct authorization for slavery, English common law applied in Maryland—whatever that meant for enslaved people. Here was the third-largest slaveholding state in the nation, with more than a hundred thousand people held in bondage—a third of its population—yet its constitution proclaimed the common law of England as a fundamental right of all inhabitants. Decades later, antislavery lawyers argued that "slavery has no legal foundation" under English common law, and therefore no basis in Maryland and, by extension, the District of Columbia.[12]

Eventually, as we shall see, Maryland slaveholders were so rattled by the freedom suits and abolitionist arguments that they moved to place slavery on a firmer legal and constitutional footing. The state ratified a constitutional amendment in 1837 declaring that "the relation of master and slave, in this State, shall not be abolished" unless by a unanimous vote of the General Assembly and with full compensation to slaveholders. The amendment in effect made slavery unamendable. It was one of the farthest-reaching protections for slavery in the nation. Two years later the General Assembly declared slavery legitimate "from [the colony's] earliest settlement."[13]

Beginning in the 1780s, slaveholders, including the Jesuits, were on a collision course with the enslaved families they held in bondage. The American Revolution set in motion a long, intense struggle over slavery and its place in the new republic. Opponents of slavery made moral, philosophical, and legal arguments against human bondage as a violation of natural law. A broad principle of universal freedom coursed through American politics and led to persistent calls for emancipation and abolition. Slaveholders responded with soulless pronouncements that enslaved people were property and that the right to hold property was inviolable under the law, indeed protected under the U.S. Constitution. In their desperate struggle to defend slavery, slaveholders asserted that blacks because of their race could not be construed as persons with rights under the meaning of the Constitution.[14]

It is natural to wonder how an enslaved person could have the standing to sue in an American court. The simple answer is that these cases were in the first instance civil (that is, private) matters and drew on a long tradition of common-law precedent that no person could be deprived of his or her liberty without cause. Another body of Anglo-American law treated freedom suits like habeas corpus actions, asking the court to determine whether a person was being unjustly detained in bondage. Many states, including Maryland, passed statutes granting enslaved people the right to petition for freedom and governing which courts would hear these cases. In addition, because of manumission and various other contractual and legal mechanisms, some people were enslaved for fixed periods of time, say five or seven or ten years, to be freed at a later date under the terms of a contract, a deed, or a will, whether recorded in the court or not. When slaveholders reneged on these agreements, as they often did, the enslaved persons might bring freedom suits that treated the dispute as a breach of contract.[15]

Petitions for freedom were filed in nearly every colonial state and all across the Atlantic World. Freedom suits brought an end to slavery in Massachusetts in the 1780s and helped lead to gradual emancipation in Brazil a century later. Hundreds of freedom suits were tried in the courts of major American cities, including St. Louis, New Orleans, Charleston, Richmond, Baltimore, Annapolis, and Washington, D.C. Similar lawsuits went through the courts in Cuba, in Jamaica, and across the Caribbean.[16]

Some observers, both at the time and up to today, have dismissed the petitions for freedom as exceptional cases that in no real way challenged slavery. I disagree with this premise, but let's summarize it here: Because petitioners claimed that they were "wrongly" enslaved, because they did not argue that slavery should be abolished for everyone but argued only for themselves, their cases were idiosyncratic, narrowly construed, and of little wider effect. Further, according to this reasoning, the petitions offered a sort of theater in which slaveholders could demonstrate their adherence to the highest ideals of the law and appear at least to themselves to be acting humanely. In this view, the petitions served the slaveholders by covering slave law with a veneer of fairness and therefore were a way for slaveholders to manage slavery and simultaneously assuage their moral conscience. Thus, a legal procedure that permitted freedom in exceptional cases worked so well because it actually justified mass enslavement rather than threatened slavery.[17]

But as the enslaved families knew, the freedom suits were one of the most public and consequential weapons they could use to oppose slavery. Their actions put slaveholders personally on trial in local courtrooms. Crucially, because freedom petitions were civil actions, not criminal cases, *neither* enslaved black plaintiffs *nor* white defendant slaveholders could testify on their own behalf. Just as no man could be a judge in his own case, no person could testify in his or her own interest. The terrain was hardly level, of course. Slaveholders wielded extraordinary power, and statutory law protected their interests. Nevertheless, in freedom suits slaveholding defendants could not take the stand.[18]

There are no transcripts of these trials. We know who testified as witnesses for which side, but we do not know what they said in court. The original case files held at the Maryland State Archives in Annapolis and the National Archives in Washington, D.C., include depositions, exact transcripts of what some witnesses said under oath. The case files also contain various pieces of evidence and attorneys' handwritten notes. These raw documents give us a window into each trial as it unfolded, what arguments were made and who made them, but we have to read these with a critical eye. Legal fictions were commonplace. Attorneys misrepresented or caricatured events and personalities. Defendant slaveholders lied to protect their property. Enslaved families engaged in their own deceptions. Busy lawyers did not always bother to discover all the evidence. Clerks made errors of transcription, garbled names, and wrote down incorrect dates. So, the clues in the case files cannot be the only sources we consult. Family lore, family documents, church records, and other written accounts offer crucial evidence. The odyssey of these families over hundreds of years can be traced through the records of the plantations, the churches, the courts, the state, and the nation. When we combine these different forms of knowing about the past, they work like poles holding up a large tent. On their own, the poles might fall to the ground, but tied together they make a stable structure.[19]

Most of us know the outlines of a tragic outcome: that slaveholders used the law to make slavery ever more secure; that hundreds of thousands of enslaved people were ripped from their families and sold in the domestic slave trade to Georgia, Louisiana, and Mississippi; that slaveholders embraced a racist policy of colonization and removal as the only solution they could imagine; and that the infamous *Dred Scott* decision in 1857 both denied black citizenship and gave slaveholders blanket authorization to take slaves into any state or territory in the United States. When Republicans won the presidential election of 1860, slaveholders seceded from the United States and fought a devastating war to create an independent slaveholders' republic.[20]

And yet we should not lose sight of the fact that the freedom suits were, in effect, a public counterpart of the Underground Railroad. Through them a network of black families waged a desperate battle over freedom through the law. White slaveholding lawyers had their own reasons for entering the fray. Intricate courtroom skirmishes over evidence and procedure exploded into full-scale battles in the advance and retreat of freedom. Arcane procedures like jury instructions could decisively turn a trial one way or the other. Such moments were filled with political drama, tension, and potentially life-altering consequences for families. Slaveholders fought tooth and nail in court to keep their human property. Freedom suits distilled the essence of the freedom struggle into a stark, if clarifying, confrontation between the enslaved person and the enslaver. Blacks wanted freedom. And slaveholders wanted to keep them enslaved.[21]

Slaves sued slaveholders in every court available to them and in every jurisdiction they could reach from the very beginning of the United States. If a slave could sue at all, slavery was not absolute. Long before the 1850s and the Republican Party, African Americans suing for freedom articulated the principle that nation's foundational law guaranteed freedom. These men and women dreamed of a wider emancipation and an end to hereditary enslavement. Beginning in Maryland and then culminating in Washington, D.C., the families in this story took the position that Frederick Douglass would eventually reach in the 1850s: slavery "never was lawful, and never can be made so."[22]

My pursuit of this story has been more than a scholar's. My research uncovered a revelation for which I was unprepared. My grandmother's family, the Ducketts, owned plantations neighboring White Marsh. One family member, Allen Bowie Duckett, had been appointed by Thomas Jefferson as an associate justice to the Circuit Court of the District of Columbia. I did not know that he got his start as a young lawyer defending the Jesuits against the freedom suits by the Queens. Nor did I know that his father was a judge in the Prince

George's County court and that he presided on the day when more than twenty members of the Queen family won their freedom. It was one of the largest emancipations in a single courtroom that I found in the archival records of Maryland.[23]

I tried to piece together what happened to the enslaved Queens in Maryland who did not win their petitions for freedom and who were not sold by the Jesuits. Did they remain in Prince George's County? Did the Jesuits sell them to nearby planters? Did they ever win their freedom in court?

After the Civil War, the Maryland General Assembly vainly hoped that the federal government would compensate former slaveholders. So the state collected sworn affidavits from all slaveholders in each county listing the enslaved people they held in bondage as of November 1864, the moment of emancipation in the state. Each statement by the slaveholders included the full names of the enslaved persons, as well as their term of servitude (if any), age, gender, and physical condition. I reviewed page after page of these specious claims, these unwarranted expectations of compensation. Hundreds of enslaved families were listed. As I combed the records, it was as if the Queen family in Maryland had finally and entirely escaped their enslavement, whether they accomplished this feat through freedom suits, manumission, or negotiation.

But this was not the case. The final and most surprising discovery of all is the hardest for me to reconcile. The last Queens enslaved in Maryland, indeed some of the last slaves legally held in the United States at the very end of the Civil War, were held in bondage by a branch of the Duckett family. Elizabeth M. Duckett claimed the following slaves in her possession: Adeline Queen, age eight; Sam Queen, age five; Louisa Queen, age four; Henry Queen, age two; Daniel Queen, age six months; and their mother, Henny Queen, age thirty-five.[24]

I was stunned. The separation between the past and the present seemed to dissolve, and the sudden lack of critical distance left me raw. I had no way to account for the motivations of my distant relations, for the murky legacy of their actions. I felt the nuances and resonances of the evidence before me in a new, more personal way. It was clear that my family's complicity was not anonymous or indirect; it was explicit and inseparable from the families seeking freedom and from what happened to them. Perhaps this realization was necessary, even inevitable.

My family's narrative, it turned out, did not include any understanding of the Queens or the particular enslavement they experienced. The deeper I dug in the archives, the more the parallel file on my family's history came into view and the more I saw their actions through the lens of another family. Like most people, I had never approached the history of my own family with a critical eye. Myths and silences worked in our family as they do in others. This is not the story I planned to write, and I struggled with whether to write it at all. Perhaps this disclosure will allow others to find the moral imagination to confront the past, no matter what it is, and to face what we find.[25]

The only way to proceed was to approach this history with the methods and perspectives of a professional historian, knowing even as I did that I, too, am in this story. Until I listened to the descendants of the Queens, and others whom the Ducketts enslaved, until I brought these family histories together, the full story, a more complete truth, would not be told. In light of what I was finding in the court records, the stories families like mine have been telling about themselves suddenly appeared as incomplete as they have been dishonest. A haunting question presented itself: Is reconciliation possible? What would it look like?

What happened two hundred years ago in our families, and in the nation, may seem distant, but those events are still with us. They are inseparable from us and bear unavoidable and immediate implications in our world today. Because we all live inside of stories—of family, of community, of nation—and because we blend and shape our stories into mythical narratives, only when our narrative is revealed as broken, as ruptured, as somehow incomplete are we able to interrupt its authority in our lives and form a different narrative drawn from different stories.[26]

This book weaves together three storylines. First, this is an intensely human account of the families whose quest for freedom profoundly shaped the course of American history. Looking closely at White Marsh and at the surrounding networks of families, enslaved and free, we will follow them as they navigated and negotiated the explosive claims of freedom through the web of the law and the courts. Delving into the lives and experiences of the families involved in these trials, and the likely contours of the world they inhabited, this book traces the intricate relationships among everyone involved in the freedom cases, from the tobacco fields of Maryland to the mud-filled streets of Washington, D.C., to the sugar districts of Louisiana.[27]

Second, it offers an attempt to repair American history by piecing together evidence long ago dismissed in courts and buried in archives. This narrative draws on historical imagination, an attempt to reconstruct the situations people faced and to piece together what we can know of their lives. It requires a critical appraisal of the archive itself and how we know what we know, and it burrows into the historical record to discover what we can and cannot glimpse through the sources, with the strategies undertaken in this investigation revealed, described, and shared rather than hidden from view. I have tried to write a narrative history, but from the inside of the freedom trials, so we can see the lives they illuminate, then and now.[28]

Most of all, *A Question of Freedom* is a story of American families, of their struggles, dreams, ideas, actions, choices, shortcomings, and possibilities. While I was researching this book, the parable of the wicked tenants was never far from my mind. The gospel story is about what happens when the master discovers that the tenants he entrusted to manage his vineyard had instead enslaved his servants and killed his son in order to seize the inheritance for themselves. The violence in the vineyard is a metaphor for what happened at White Marsh and at the other plantations in Prince George's County and across the American South. The suffering from it appeared to me to be unanswered for and continuing.[29]

Then while researching and writing this book, I attended the Summer Institute for Reconciliation at Duke Divinity School. In this forum, pastors, community organizers, lawyers, and scholars reckoned with the historical trauma of racism and its consequences. The work was personal, difficult, and necessary. Within families like mine there were widely divergent responses to the question of slavery and freedom from one generation to the next. Their motivations in specific situations varied, but as a whole, the white slaveholding families in this story operated within a narrow range of reaction, well inside the distressingly cramped vision of their class. In particular situations some white slaveholders saw that slavery was immoral and incompatible with natural law and the nation's founding principles. Faced with the moral problem of American slavery, many, including my ancestors, often made selfishly pragmatic decisions. They convinced themselves they were masters of the vineyard.[30]

PART I

The Planting

For the vineyard of the Lord of hosts is the house of Israel, and the people of Judah are his pleasant planting; he expected justice, but saw bloodshed; righteousness but heard a cry!

—ISAIAH 5:7 (RSV)

CHAPTER 1

A Meeting at White Marsh, 1789

Let America cease to exult—she has obtained but partial freedom.

—VOX AFRICANORUM IN THE *MARYLAND GAZETTE,*

MAY 15, 1783

The poplars swayed high above Edward Queen and Charles Mahoney on that May morning. The summer heat crawled up from the Patuxent River, summoned from its slack banks and slow bends, drawing its oppressive punch from the Chesapeake Bay and the Atlantic Ocean beyond. To the east, the Potomac River, a longer, broader, and deeper tributary than the Patuxent, ran almost due south on its course to the bay. The little region between the two great rivers—the Potomac and the Patuxent—produced some of the finest tobacco in the country. In the world, for that matter. The leaf grown in Maryland, called "Brightleaf" Oronoco, was strong in taste, yellow in hue, and coarse in texture, but it was a variety with a steady market in continental Europe. The leaves were cultivated, tended, harvested, packed, and transported by the hands of nearly thirty thousand enslaved men, women, and children. Each enslaved person tended as many as twelve thousand plants on two to three acres of soil.[1]

Every May and June the scent of new tobacco seedlings wafted across the rivers, creeks, marshes, and fields of the Patuxent. For Edward Queen and Charles Mahoney, the aroma was a foretaste of what was to come: the air pungent with sweat. Five hundred hills a day with the hoe. In the late summer and early fall the leaves were hauled in, hung, and cured. For four to six weeks in the spring when the new planting began, the whole country between the great rivers of Maryland smelled of Oronoco leaves. Every day just breathing the air was a reminder of all that had been extracted from the men and their families, and all that would be taken in the years to come.[2]

Edward Queen had just celebrated his thirty-fifth birthday when the Jesuit priests arrived at the plantation they called White Marsh for their annual business meeting on May 11, 1789. Grandson of a free woman, he chafed at his family's enslavement.

Edward was barely five years old when his grandmother died, but she had been taken away long before he was born. In fact, Edward probably never met Mary Queen; the Jesuits sent her with her son Ralph to Bohemia Manor, one of their plantations across the Chesapeake Bay on the Eastern Shore of Maryland. She had died there nearly thirty years earlier, in 1759. Edward's mother, Phillis Queen, would have told him Mary's story: how she was a free woman from New Spain, present-day Ecuador, who lived in London for three years before coming to the Maryland colony as an indentured servant. In addition to his mother and his aunt Nanny Cooper, who was also at White Marsh, Edward was acquainted with several white men and women who remembered Mary Queen. By the late 1780s, Mary Queen's descendants comprised the largest enslaved family at White Marsh and had been trapped in bondage for three generations.

Charles Mahoney was thirty-two. His family was spread out all over Maryland, enslaved for generations not only on the Jesuit farms but also on other big tobacco plantations up and down the Western Shore. Charles Carroll of Carrollton, a signer of the Declaration of Independence and Maryland's leading political figure, enslaved more than forty of Charles Mahoney's relatives.

Mahoney's great-grandmother Ann Joice was said to be a free woman of color from Barbados, a black woman indentured to Lord Baltimore. The Joice family passed down from one generation to the next the story of their family's enslavement. Ann Joice was sold away from her family, her indenture disregarded and "burned," and she was thrown in a basement cellar for six months to keep her from running away. Three of her sons, desperate for their freedom, killed an overseer who mistreated them. Found guilty, the three men were hanged and quartered, their body parts placed on pikes in Prince George's County as a warning to other slaves. Charles had heard these stories, and he knew men and women, white and black, who had met his great-uncles, were at their trial, and watched their execution.

Led by Edward Queen and Charles Mahoney, the enslaved families of White Marsh sued three Jesuit priests and set in motion a momentous legal and social battle over the future of slavery in the new nation.

"Sell to the Best Advantage"

The main complex of White Marsh plantation—a stone basilica, a few frame buildings, a kitchen, and stables—stood on a hill one hundred feet above the Patuxent River and overlooked a broad alluvial plain, where the river's course flattened as it flowed southward toward its junction with the Chesapeake Bay. An overseer's house and the cabins of at least one hundred enslaved people sprawled in the bottomlands below, no more than two hundred yards away. From the vantage point of the church, one could see the low-lying ground along the river, a half-mile wide and a mile and a half long. Livestock grazed in the meadows. Tobacco, some wheat, rye, and "plenty [of] Indian corn" stretched along the river's loamy, sandy bottoms. Rich in mica, the low banks shimmered white in the sunshine, which lent the place its name, "White Marsh." By reputation, experience, and history, the Patuxent soil was "fit only for Tobacco," but the crop's command over the region's economy was waning. Every plantation had already begun diversifying into wheat and cereals, as well as livestock. Most large plantations experimented with weaving and woolens. Others had converted their fields to vineyards and fruits.[3]

Slaveholders tried to adapt slavery in Maryland to every conceivable situation. In fact, the number of enslaved people in the state rose steadily after the American Revolution, climbing between 1790 and 1810 to more than 111,000 men, women, and children. In these years, more than 30 percent of the entire population in the state was enslaved. In the United States, only Virginia and South Carolina held more people in bondage.[4]

At the time, the white slaveholders in Prince George's County could claim to be among the most deeply committed to slavery in the nation. Well over half of the county's total population was enslaved—58 percent—and in no other Maryland county were there fewer free blacks than in Prince George's. In that bastion of enslavement, just 164 free blacks could be counted in 1790.[5]

Despite the depth of slaveholding in the tobacco region, enslaved families had reason by 1790 to anticipate a freer society and to take action where they could to claim their own freedom. In Baltimore one in every five African Americans was already free, and less than 10 percent of Baltimore's total population was enslaved. Ten years later, in 1800, nearly half of all blacks in Baltimore were free. The city was rapidly expanding, its population doubling every ten years. Merchants, shipbuilders, millers, iron foundries, and other large-scale enterprises took off, and skilled black labor filled a ready demand. In Baltimore freedom was more and more common. For decades, freedom had been a virtual impossibility, but in the twenty-five years after the Revolution, free blacks were the fastest-growing segment of the Maryland population.[6]

In the tobacco counties along the Western Shore, though, especially in Prince George's County and Charles County, planters ferociously held on to slavery. As tobacco prices collapsed in the 1790s, they remained tied to the crop, even as they planted more and more wheat, raised livestock, and employed slave labor in skilled crafts, including weaving, spinning, tallow making, and tanning. There was no increase in the rate of manumission following the economic downturn. These slaveholders did not free enslaved people because they thought that slavery was no longer especially profitable or necessary. Instead, in the midst of the depression, tobacco planters tried with every means at their disposal to hold on to slaves and to keep them in place. In many cases enslaved people were the slaveholders' largest financial assets, worth more than real estate or crops. Slaveholders in the 1790s in Maryland speculated that they could sell surplus slaves. The cotton planters in some of the more southern states were already buying in Maryland. A brisk business developed. Slave traders were making offers.[7]

Among this landscape of slaveholding tobacco planters, how the Jesuits came to own White Marsh and enslave so many people there deserves some explanation. The priests in Maryland played a more active role in the acquisition and accumulation of property than they ever wished to admit. By the middle of the eighteenth century the Jesuit order had become the single largest slaveholder in South America, with more than seventeen thousand enslaved people on their estates in the Spanish Empire. At the time of their expulsion from South America in 1767, the Jesuits owned more slaves than any other person or organization in the Western Hemisphere.[8]

In Maryland the pattern was similar. Through "headrights," property purchases, patrimonies, and generous benefactors, the Jesuits accumulated significant landholdings in seventeenth-century Maryland. At first, the priests held these properties individually, but by the 1720s they had established a means to pool their holdings even though Maryland's colonial law barred the order from holding property. Gradually, priests executed wills that named only the superior of the Maryland mission as their beneficiary. So, the Reverend William Hunter, S.J., bequeathed to the Reverend George Thorold, S.J., the properties he held in St. Mary's County. Meanwhile, the Reverend Thomas Mansell, S.J., consolidated holdings on the Eastern Shore in Cecil County. In 1726 Thorold conveyed all of the plantations on the Western Shore to the Reverend Peter Attwood, S.J., totaling 7,990 acres, including,

In St. Mary's County:

> St. Inigoes Manor: 2,000 acres
> St. George's Island: 1,000 acres
> Chapel lands: 40 acres

In Charles County:

> St. Thomas Manor: 3,500 acres
> Port Tobacco Creek: 500 acres
> Splittfield: 30 acres
> Piercefield: 20 acres
> Hazard: 100 acres
> Bretton's Neck: 700 acres
> The Outlet: 100 acres

Bohemia Manor and related properties in Cecil County on the Eastern Shore comprised another 1,143 acres. In total, the Jesuits owned 9,133 acres in 1727 and held dozens of enslaved men, women, and children.

Then James Carroll, a methodical and land-hungry Catholic planter in Anne Arundel County, died in 1729 without heirs, leaving the Jesuit Superior the Reverend George Thorold 2,000 acres at Carrollsburg (that is, White Marsh) and numerous other properties. Carroll also set up trusts for two of his nephews at the Jesuit seminary in Belgium and gave them land and slaves. Carroll's bequest to the Maryland mission was the "one gift," so singular and unusual that it was celebrated by none other than Pope Benedict VIII in the folios of the papal bullaria. "Bestowed from without the Order," Carroll's legacy was unlike anything the Jesuits had experienced in Maryland. The lands included Carroll's "dwelling place" called Fingaul in Anne Arundel County, as well as unsold portions of "Bright Seat" and "Ayno" in Anne Arundel and the properties in Prince George's County, including

"Carrollsburg," "Cheney's Plantation," and "Ridgeley's and Tyler's Chance." The inventory of his estate in 1729 listed thirty-three slaves. One of them was Mary Queen, Edward Queen's grandmother.[9]

At first, in the wake of James Carroll's largess, the Jesuit priests tried to reconcile slaveholding as a practice consistent with their spiritual mission. One of the superiors wrote a set of guidelines for priests titled "Charity to Negroes." "As they are members of Jesus Christ," he began, "they are to be dealt with in a charitable, Christian, paternal manner, which is at the same time a great means to bring them to do their duty to God, [and] therefore to gain their souls." But he was worried that too many priests were behaving too much like secular slaveholders. He had heard "much talk of temporal [affairs]" and warned that if priests were "too much bent" upon temporal things, such as making money, it would lead to their spiritual corruption. "Our discourse ought to be chiefly of the progress of our missions," he warned, rather than about production or farms or, presumably, slavery and wealth accumulation.[10]

The Jesuits had become some of Maryland's largest slaveholders, though, and their affairs were shot through with the business of enslavement and slaving. The Reverend John Lewis, the manager at White Marsh in the 1760s, started tracking the productivity of the women on the plantation and accounting for their children.[11]

Lewis was the first to record anything about the members of the Queen family who within thirty years would sue the Jesuits for freedom. He began with the daughters of Mary Queen, Nanny Cooper and Phillis Queen. They were "far advanced in age [and] mothers of many children." He listed only the youngest of their children, not bothering to connect them to their older children. Phillis's son Edward "Ned" Queen was nearly ten years old, not yet capable of work but old enough to be living at White Marsh away from his mother. Edward's older sister, Susanna Queen, was twenty-four and apparently without children. His twin brothers Proteus and Gervais were fourteen.[12]

Then, in 1767 the Reverend John Ashton, age twenty-five, arrived at White Marsh as its manager and priest. The Queen family was without question the plantation's largest. Edward "Ned" Queen was thirteen years old, just beginning to work in the fields. His twin brothers were seventeen, young men no doubt yearning for freedom. Their sister, Susanna Queen, was Ashton's contemporary in age.

Armed with Lewis's census, Ashton had access to the names, family groups, and ages of the enslaved inhabitants of White Marsh and Lewis's notes on each person's capabilities. Sarah and Doll were "lame." Tom and Susanna, Betty, John, Nell, Samson, Jenny, and Nanny, in their seventies, were all deemed too old to be of service. Priscilla the "spinster" was "a cripple" (and probably a Queen). The plantation had a cook, Nelly; a shoemaker, Robert; and a carpenter, Isaac. Isaac owned livestock of his own. There were six horses "belonging to the Negroes."[13]

Inexact and approximate, the financial account books of slaveholders provided guidance to their successors as rules of thumb and indicators of past practices. Gradually, slaveholders relied on their account books to track the human beings they enslaved. Their births and deaths. Their monetary "value." The books categorized the enslaved on the basis of value: reproductive mothers, children, working-age men and boys, those too young to work, and those men and women "not capable of work." Even though slaveholders maintained elaborate records, they withheld such information from the enslaved persons, including their birthdays and ages, as well as any other information that would give them a sense of self-possession.[14]

John Ashton took to his position as the manager at White Marsh with unusual zeal. He advocated for more efficient practices on all the farms, especially in the 1780s, when the Jesuits began managing their property collectively in a private trust. Ashton's superior, the Reverend John Carroll, considered him "a most valuable man to our affairs" and praised his "method and economy" in managing what the Jesuits called their "temporalities," meaning all of their plantations, properties, agricultural products, and slaveholding.[15]

Ashton drank up the praise from Carroll, however slight, however indirect, however misplaced. He was Carroll's distant cousin and came to see himself as Carroll's indispensable partner in what both men called "the Religion"—the entire Jesuit effort in the Catholic Church, in the face of the pope's suppression of the Jesuit society in the 1770s. If Carroll was Ashton's Peter, Ashton was Carroll's Paul, industrious and unhesitating in attending to the temporal affairs of the Church while Carroll managed its spiritual ones.[16]

In the wake of the American Revolution, Ashton, Carroll, and the other Jesuits reorganized and regulated the management of their estates. Fearing that "a junto of three or four" making decisions about such large assets would "breed disturbances and disgust," the priests decided to govern the plantations through a corporate constitution, one that they hoped would guard against "abuse of power" and foster "mild and equitable government." The Jesuits created a private trust that was, in effect, a corporation.[17]

Perhaps because of Ashton's seniority, but probably because of his meddlesome persistence, the Jesuits selected him as the so-called procurator general, who would oversee all of the estates and report to the clerical body. Forty-seven years old in 1789, born and educated in Ireland, Ashton had twenty-two years of experience managing White Marsh. His family connections with the powerful Carrolls lent him credibility, and he assumed a leadership role in what the Jesuits called "the general chapter" from its inception.

The Maryland Jesuits crafted a set of specific bylaws for their corporate organization. First, the procurator general would appoint the managers of each estate, and although the managers would have "sole discretion," each in turn would be "accountable" and required to "exhibit his books" if asked. A series of rules followed. No manager could sell any of the real or human property under his purview. Each manager was barred from contracting any debts beyond what "he can speedily pay from the income of the Estate." Nor could any manager file a lawsuit without the authorization of the procurator general, and every manager was required to make an "inventory" and keep books of "credit and debit." These manager priests were allowed to maintain a house and entertain guests according to their "rank" and "station," but they were strictly to avoid making the house a place of "great resort," parties, or extravagant "entertainments."[18]

After paying the estate's expenses, each manager was supposed to send any "surplus money" from his farm to the procurator general to be used for the good of the whole Jesuit chapter or corporation. In sum, the managers were expected to be "actuated by more noble principles than self interest [and] mercenary views."[19]

With Ashton at the helm of the corporation and the expectations for the management of their estates clarified, the Jesuits never fully acknowledged the contradiction between their principles and their self-interest. At the annual meeting of the general chapter held at White Marsh in May 1789, the priests were consumed with practical matters. The questions they faced were those of running large plantations for profit. For days they conferred with one another about what regulations were needed, which accounts required attention, whose pensions to fund, how to distribute the minutes of their proceedings, and how to pay for new buildings on the estates. The priests were, after all, in the tobacco business, and that meant buying and selling on credit and negotiating their debts with merchants who shipped the cured leaf from Annapolis and Georgetown to markets in Britain and continental Europe.[20]

Basilica at White Marsh, April 2017 (courtesy of Letitia Clark).
Over five days in May 1789 the Jesuits met at White Marsh. The original basilica where they held Mass, constructed ca. 1741, still stands.

On May 15, 1789, the fourth day of the annual business meeting at White Marsh, the Jesuits made a pair of fateful decisions. First, they agreed to collect funds to found an academy at Georgetown. Second, they resolved to "dispose of" enslaved men and women too old to work because they were a "great danger" and a "burden" to the estates.

Their plan was simple: sell all people over the age of about forty-five, people they called "supernumeraries." A small committee consisting of the farm managers and Ashton, as procurator, would determine "whether there is a sufficient number of slaves for the use [and] service of the said plantation." Then they were "empowered . . . to sell to the best advantage all that shall exceed such number." Money from the sales would be applied first to the "discharge of all debts due from the plantation on which the said slaves lived," second to "the District to which they belonged," and last to the general fund of the chapter. Ashton was charged to "take an account of all superfluous slaves once every three years" and to "dispose of them in the above manner."[21]

From White Marsh word of Ashton's plan and the looming slave sales would have spread quickly to other Jesuit farms. The families at White Marsh, especially the Queens and the Mahoneys, had reason to expect the worst. Edward was thirty-five years old. His mother, Phillis, was nearly seventy.

"Entitled to Liberty and All the Rights of a Free Man"

Every enslaved person in the county, including Edward Queen and Charles Mahoney, knew that one mixed-race family, the Butlers, had just won their freedom. The Butler family filed more than ninety suits for freedom, winning every single one of them between 1787 and 1791. Suddenly, similar claims of freedom seemed plausible.

In fact, the Butler case exposed a tangle of contradictions in the colonial laws. The family's ancestor Eleanor "Irish Nell" Butler was a free white woman who arrived in the colony in 1681 as an indentured servant of Charles Calvert, Third Lord Baltimore. She married Charles Butler, an enslaved man held by William Boarman, an officer in the provincial militia and an associate of Lord Baltimore. Boarman had obtained a 3,333-acre grant in Charles County from the king and served as justice of the peace, as a delegate to the General Assembly, and as county sheriff. A 1664 act of the Assembly required that when a freeborn woman married an enslaved man, she would become a slave for the duration of her husband's life. Her children would also be enslaved. The children of women already married to enslaved men would be slaves until they were thirty years old. Calling these marriages "shameful matches," the Assembly punished freeborn English women who were "forgetful of their free condition, and to the disgrace of our nation, do intermarry with negro slaves."[22]

According to several accounts, Lord Baltimore confronted Nell Butler about the marriage on her wedding day. One witness said that he "chided" her and "told her she would put a mark by that upon her children." Another said that Baltimore asked her to marry a man "of her own colour." A third person overheard Baltimore observe, "What a pitty [*sic*] so likely a young girl as you are should fling herself away to marry a negro." Warned by Lord Baltimore that the act would apply to her and that she and her children would be enslaved, Nell brazenly responded that she "had rather marry the negro under these circumstances than to marry his Lordship with his country." At this, Baltimore threw up his hands. Go ahead, marry him and "be damned," he allegedly said.[23]

Nell married Charles at the Boarman plantation in a Catholic ceremony presided over by a priest, in front of dozens of witnesses and friends. Sometime after the wedding, Lord Baltimore urged the Maryland Assembly to repeal the 1664 act both because he wished to exempt Nell and Charles from its penalties and because he considered the act an encouragement to slaveholders who might force white women into marriages with enslaved men. There being so few enslaved women in the colony, masters might be tempted to arrange marriages that would bring them even more enslaved laborers in the generations to come. "The instigation, procurement, or connivance" of the slaveholders, the Assembly patronizingly concluded, exacerbated "the lascivious and lustful desires" of the women.[24]

At Baltimore's urging the legislature reversed and repealed the 1664 act in 1681 and declared that both the white women who married slaves and their children would remain free. The new law applied to all such marriages contracted after the last day of that assembly. To prevent further mixed-race marriages, the law fined masters ten thousand pounds of tobacco for allowing such marriages on their plantations.[25]

Joined in matrimony before the new act took effect, the Butlers remained enslaved, and the Boarmans passed them down as property from generation to generation. But the Butlers' children were all born after the 1681 act. Were they free? Or did the 1664 act apply to them because their parents were married under its provisions?[26]

In 1770 the Butlers' grandchildren William and Mary sued for their freedom. They were first cousins once removed. Though married, both were directly descended from Nell Butler, so each had a legitimate claim to freedom. The repercussions of their freedom suit would affect potentially dozens of other slaveholders across the Western Shore of Maryland. One of the witnesses testified that "there was about one hundred and twenty of them [Butlers]" who could be freed if the case were successful. However, he also observed that the enslaved "by their count" said there were as many as three hundred who might claim their freedom. Whites were suspicious that "some saltwater negroes," as they derisively put it, were being counted, using the term to describe those who had come directly from Africa and could not have been descended from white women. Hundreds of other enslaved people in different families caught between the provisions of the 1664 and 1681 acts might make similar claims and bring lawsuits. Thousands might be liberated in the wake of this single decision.[27]

The judges of the provincial court initially ruled in favor of freedom and ordered William and Mary Butler discharged from their enslavement.

But Boarman's attorneys were quick to appeal the case to the highest appellate court in the colony. They argued that Nell and her children were property, and property could not be taken away by legislation "*ex post facto*" unless explicitly stated. A law, they concluded, cannot operate "on events antecedent to its passage."[28]

Within a few months, the court of appeals reversed the lower court's ruling and denied the Butlers their freedom. The justices determined that the assembly of 1681 "knew that [property] rights had been acquired under the law of 1664, and in the course of so many years as that law subsisted, there might have been instances where these rights had been transferred." Although the General Assembly decided to repeal the 1664 act, the judges "thought it would be contrary to public faith to destroy these rights." Plainly speaking, slaveholders had property rights on the lives of children yet unborn, a claim they acquired through the 1664 act. The court would not "strip him [Boarman]" of this property, nor would it interfere with the property rights of slaveholders who might have purchased slaves from Boarman. The right to the unborn children meant all would continue to be enslaved.

After the American Revolution, the next generation of Butlers filed a new round of lawsuits. In Prince George's County twenty-six-year-old Mary Butler sued Adam Craig for her freedom. At the same time another family caught in the provisions of the 1664 law—the Toogoods—brought their own lawsuits claiming descent from a free white woman. Like the Butlers, the Toogoods had lost an earlier freedom suit in the colonial courts. In October 1782 Eleanor Toogood sued Dr. Upton Scott, one of the most prominent physicians in Annapolis. When Eleanor Toogood's case went to trial, the judges of Maryland's general court allowed hearsay testimony about her ancestor and declared her free. Scott appealed the judgment, one of the first freedom suits in Maryland after the Revolution to reach the courts. On appeal Toogood's attorney, Jeremiah Townley Chase, called the 1664 act "highly penal and rigorous, if not inhuman." The Maryland court of appeals agreed and upheld the general court's conclusion that the Toogoods were free.[29]

A few years later, in 1787, Mary Butler's freedom suit followed. Chase made the same argument for her as he had for Eleanor Toogood—that the 1664 act was "highly penal," that its punishment was "unjust and cruel," and that the previous judgment in the colonial court was nonbinding. Neither Eleanor Toogood nor Mary Butler had been named in the lawsuits of their mothers. How could their petition not be heard? Their argument was grounded in the Revolutionary, Enlightenment, and republican skepticism of absolutism, excessive punishment, and inherited status. According to newly discovered evidence, much of it secondhand hearsay, Nell Butler had never been convicted in a court of record for intermarrying with an enslaved man, and therefore neither she nor her descendants could be enslaved.

In June 1791, when Adam Craig appealed the decision freeing Mary Butler, he enlisted a noted authority on colonial law—the lord propriety's attorney general of Maryland—who argued that the colonial decision was "conclusive" and "settled the law." But the Maryland High Court of Appeals was unpersuaded, disregarded the colonial court's earlier decision, and upheld the general court's use of hearsay evidence and its decision in favor of Mary Butler's freedom. Mary Butler's children immediately sued and won. Thirty-five years old, now a free woman, she appeared in the general court and was deposed as a witness for her children. In case after case the defendants simply conceded the matter, and juries in Annapolis awarded the Butlers not only their freedom but also hundreds of pounds of tobacco in damages, lawyer's fees, and court costs.[30]

Slaveholders took notice. Jesuit priest Nicholas Lewis Sewall purchased an enslaved woman in Charles County named Chloe in a creditor's sale. She was "said to be of the Butler Breed." In the bill of sale, the seller noted that he had changed her name to "Suck" and stipulated that if she won "her freedom by courts of law or otherwise," then the seller "shall not be answerable or accountable." The unequivocal warning was *caveat emptor,* buyer beware.[31]

For good reason, it seemed. Chloe Butler sued Sewall in 1791 and won her freedom. A year later all of her adult children—Abraham, Fanny, Bridget, and Henny—won their cases. Nearly every large slaveholder in the Western Shore of Maryland was involved in the Butler lawsuits, either directly as a defendant or indirectly as a witness: the Carrolls, the Boarmans, the Claggetts, the Diggeses, the Darnalls, the Hills, and the Neales, to name a few. In the October 1791 term of the general court, the same session in which Edward Queen and Charles Mahoney filed their suits against John Ashton, the Butler family won every single case they filed. Stephen Butler sued Charles Carroll of Carrollton, the leader of the Maryland Senate, and the jury handed down a verdict that Butler was "entitled to liberty and all the rights of a free man" and "most unjustly and wrongfully deprived of his liberty."[32]

The Butler suits suggested that colonial precedent could be overturned, but they left a core question unanswered: Did Mary Butler, Chloe Butler, Stephen Butler, and all of the others prevail in court because their ancestor was white or because their ancestor was free? If hereditary enslavement for descendants of white women offended juries and judges, would they react the same way to claims by free native and free black descendants?

The Butler cases offered a lesson in how to win freedom suits, one that Edward Queen, Charles Mahoney, and others closely observed and would follow. First, to be successful in court required fierce determination on their part and unrelenting pressure on the slaveholders, who as a class were likely to be as uncooperative as the Boarmans had been before the Revolution and Adam Craig after. Second, the Butlers organized a cascade of lawsuits that were filed in term after term by members of the family far and wide. The Queens and Mahoneys would do the same. Third, to represent them they turned to Mary Butler's lawyer, Jeremiah T. Chase, and his cousin Samuel Chase. Between 1787 and 1789, Samuel Chase orchestrated the Butlers' initial petitions for freedom, gathered depositions, and lined up witnesses in county courts stretching from Baltimore to Annapolis and down the Western Shore.[33]

No political figure in Maryland was more controversial than Samuel Chase, one of Maryland's four signers of the Declaration of Independence. Son of an Anglican minister, educated by his father, and trained in the law at Annapolis, Chase rose to prominence quickly. First elected to the House of Delegates in 1766, he went on to become Speaker of the House and a leading Federalist. In the Revolution he attempted to corner the market on cereal grains and snatched up confiscated loyalist properties. Both earned him a reputation for shameless profiteering. Accused of using his political position for personal gain, Chase came under a cloud and lost his seat in the Continental Congress. During the war he and his associates borrowed heavily to acquire saltworks, ironworks, and lumber businesses seized from British loyalists around Baltimore, including thousands of acres and hundreds of enslaved people. Viewed by his enemies as an opportunist and a social climber, Chase was, according to one historian, "feared by many, respected by some, and loved by very few."[34]

After the war Samuel Chase feuded openly with Charles Carroll of Carrollton, his archconservative counterpart in the state senate, fellow signatory of the Declaration of Independence, and the head of Maryland's leading Catholic family. Carroll at every turn defended the aristocratic gentry elite and guarded against any subversion of "our social order and the rights of property." Although both men became leading Federalists, Carroll considered Chase uncouth and unreliable. In particular, Carroll opposed Chase's advocacy of paper money throughout the depression of the 1780s, a policy that would have benefited the overextended Chase personally.

In the late 1780s, as the Maryland legislature debated debt relief, paper money, and the role of the judiciary in the debt crisis, Samuel Chase began representing enslaved petitioners like the Butlers who were suing for their freedom. That many of them filed their cases against Carroll's extensive family and associates likely incensed Carroll further. Chase convinced the courts to allow secondhand testimony—then called hearsay—not only about the lineage of families but also about the status of specific ancestors, whether they were thought to have been free or enslaved. He worked with the enslaved families to identify white and free black witnesses who would testify to the genealogy of enslaved families, uncovering who was related to whom and who held them in bondage.

Finding such witnesses and filing freedom suits proved possible because of several historically unusual characteristics that shaped the daily experience of the enslaved families in the Chesapeake region. By the 1780s four generations of the Butler family had lived in Maryland. Similarly, Edward Queen was part of his family's third generation in Prince George's County, and Charles Mahoney and his seven brothers were Ann Joice's fifth-generation descendants. Over these generations, deliberately and patiently, the Butlers, the Queens, the Mahoneys, and other enslaved families had achieved a measure of stability and permanence in Maryland. Their families married and raised children, negotiated with those who enslaved them, and extracted accommodations where they could that maintained the integrity of their families. Even through the uncertainties of inheritances, abrupt sales, and property disputes, the enslaved families in the Chesapeake gained more cohesion, not less, over the course of the eighteenth century. This was particularly true on the Jesuit plantations where there had been relatively few sales and the priests recognized slave marriages. Edward Queen may not have seen his grandmother in decades, but he knew her. He lived with his mother, aunts, uncles, cousins, nephews, and nieces at White Marsh, and he communicated with the Queen family members who were living elsewhere. Such networks of family, memory, knowledge, and commitment were rare in the New World plantation societies, and they laid the foundation for a long-term strategy for freedom in the courts.[35]

Second, and equally important, Mary Butler, Edward Queen, and Charles Mahoney could gain ready access to the legal system. Towns, courts, and law offices abounded from Annapolis to the county seats and into the local villages. In the city of Baltimore another set of lawyers serviced the courts. Dense networks of roads and rivers provided a convenient means to travel to these places. Slaveholders regularly hired out enslaved people or sent them on their own to conduct errands and perform all sorts of tasks, and families had a degree of mobility that brought them into contact both with one another and with other families. Across the Patuxent River from White Marsh, fifteen miles to the east, was Annapolis, where the leading lawyers of the state gathered to try cases in the General Court of the Western Shore.[36]

"Blush at the Very Name of Freedom"

Unlike the Butlers, who said they were descended from a white woman, Edward Queen and Charles Mahoney each brought lawsuits based on his ancestor's having been in England. Each of their freedom suits, therefore, argued that because their ancestors set foot on English soil, where the law did not sanction human property, they came to the colonies as free women. The Queen and Mahoney cases presented fundamental questions about slavery. If slavery were unlawful in England under the common law, and their ancestors were free, how was it justifiable in Maryland?

Any answer to this question revealed that slavery was far more contested in the law than slaveholders wished to admit. In the seventeenth and eighteenth centuries, Anglo-American slaveholders had asserted that enslaved people were captured in war in Africa and that their status as slaves could be legitimately conferred and transferred. They had improvised repeatedly to create a patchwork of local statutes for policing a slave regime and perpetuating hereditary slavery. In regulation after regulation colonial laws covered up the essence of enslavement and made inheritable a condition previously reserved for individuals captured in a state of war. American slaveholders in the colonies acted as if the laws governing and policing slavery sufficiently defined the institution, even though they knew that no fundamental a priori law allowing the practice of human bondage was ever passed. The entire edifice of slave law rested uneasily on the king's prerogative powers that sanctioned slavery only in conquered and colonized lands, places beyond the reach of Parliament and not represented in Parliament.[37]

From Barbados to Maryland, English colonial settlers also brought with them a set of assumptions that only non-Britons, only blacks "imported" from Africa, could be enslaved. Only they were subject to enslavement that was inheritable, matrilineal, and permanent. Only they were deemed "slaves for life," as were their children, their children's children, and on through the generations. Slaveholders used wills, deeds, and other everyday legal trans-actions to give slavery a foothold, and a foundation, in the law. Slow to address slavery openly, and fearful of a backlash in Parliament, colonial assemblies passed slave statutes in haphazard, incomplete, and sporadic fashion, mainly in response to the resistance of the enslaved. Slavery materialized in colonial statutes to sanction what slaveholders were already doing in practice. Maryland's colonial assembly passed in 1715 what would become the closest thing to a foundational slave code it would enact. The statute declared that all "negroes and other slaves already imported, or hereafter to be imported in this province, and all children now born, or hereafter to be born, of such negroes and slaves, shall be slaves during their natural lives."[38]

But even this act declared only *who* could be enslaved—"negroes" who had been "imported"—not *what* slavery was. Colonial laws like Maryland's did little to resolve whether slaves were property under the meaning of Anglo-American law. Could enslaved people be bought and sold? Were contracts for their sale enforceable in British courts? Were the enslaved transferable for debts? Were they inheritable like livestock or other personal property? These questions were far from abstract in the late seventeenth century, when the Stuart monarchs promoted hereditary slavery throughout the empire and Charles II chartered the Royal African Company with the exclusive right to ply the slave trade on the African coast. The royal company signed contracts with British slaveholders and imported slaves to the colonies in vast numbers. These and other contracts included collateral held in the form of human property. According to historian Holly Brewer, the Stuart monarchs "legitimated the formal enslavement of Africans" at the same time as they were "suppressing representative government" and establishing a hierarchical social order based exclusively on "inheritable blood." Charles II and James II appointed judges in England favorable to slavery in the expectation that the King's Bench might establish precedents that would legitimate slaveholding throughout the realm, including even in England. These judges sought to accomplish what English law had not yet authorized: the buying and selling of people as property. In a pivotal case, one of the king's judges ruled that a contract to buy and sell black slaves was legally enforceable in England—in other words, that black slaves were lawful property in claims for the recovery of debts or the taking of property.[39]

Liberal members of Parliament viewed these baleful decisions with alarm and appointed judges who would reverse them. In subsequent cases lawyers for the enslaved argued, "It is against the law of nature for one man to be a slave to another." The laws of England, indeed the air and soil of

England, they contended, "make men free." Eventually, judges began ruling that slavery was untenable in the law. In a widely cited case, Sir John Holt, chief judge of the Court of King's Bench, wrote that "[the] common law takes no notice of negroes being different from other men" and concluded, "No man can have property in another." Other cases followed, and Holt issued reports condemning slavery as incompatible with English common law.[40]

Holt's rulings did not go uncontested. Plantation owners and slave trade merchants sought to revive their property rights in African slaves and pushed for guidance from the Crown. Law officers of the Crown responded in 1729 with a joint opinion declaring that slaves brought from the West Indies did not become free in Great Britain and that the slaveholder's "property or right" was not impaired as a consequence of setting foot on English soil. Slaves, the Crown's officers maintained, were property throughout the empire and could be forced to return to the colonies. The thrust of their argument was circular: because the colonies could not have laws repugnant to English law, because colonial law was "subject to" English law, the presence of slavery in the colonies meant that slavery was legitimate in England. There was no distinction in their minds between the colonies and England. Slavery was legal across the empire or it was not legal at all. Parliament avoided the subject of whether slavery was legal in England itself, as did the leading writers and legal philosophers at the Inns of Court in London. Under pressure to protect commercial interests in the colonies and the merchants conducting the slave trade, Parliament declared enslaved people legitimate property for the recovery of all debts in the colonies. The measure was decidedly friendly to slaveholders because, for all practical purposes, it guaranteed that slave property would receive uniform treatment across the empire.[41]

Over the eighteenth century, however, a growing contingent of lawyers, judges, and writers considered slavery suspect. Sir William Blackstone, the leading authority on English law and a professor at the University of Oxford, published his *Commentaries on the Laws of England* in the 1760s in which he laid down the most complete argument up to that point that slavery was incompatible with English common law. Although he admitted that slavery might have a legal basis in Britain's colonial plantation societies, "pure and proper slavery," Blackstone wrote, "does not, nay cannot, subsist in England; such I mean, whereby an absolute and unlimited power is given to the master over the life and fortune of the slave. And indeed it is repugnant to reason, and the principles of natural law, that such a state should subsist any where." Then Great Britain's highest court ruled in *Somerset v. Stewart* in

1772 that slavery had no basis in natural law and could be maintained only through "positive law." As such, slavery did not exist in England, and no person on English soil could be taken forcibly out of England against his or her will. The *Somerset* decision was an ideological turning point, the epicenter of a legal and social earthquake that sent aftershocks reverberating through the Atlantic World.[42]

The facts of the *Somerset* case were straightforward. James Somerset, a Virginia-born enslaved man, had been taken to London by Boston customs official Charles Stewart and had run away from Stewart in the city. Stewart tracked Somerset down, seized him, and imprisoned him in a brig preparing to depart for the colonies, where he would likely be sold as punishment. Antislavery lawyers and black abolitionists heard about Somerset's plight and filed for a writ of habeas corpus to stop Stewart. The King's Bench authorized the writ, ordered Stewart to deliver Somerset to the court, and heard arguments that would decide Somerset's fate.

When Chief Justice Lord Mansfield issued his opinion in *Somerset,* there were more than fourteen thousand enslaved people in England, mostly temporarily, mainly held by West Indies plantation owners. Mansfield's decision did not emancipate them. Instead, his narrow, rather technical ruling prevented Stewart from taking Somerset away by force. Mansfield held that "so high an act of dominion" as to seize a person and haul him away was intolerable. Parliament had passed no law that recognized such sweeping personal authority.

But Mansfield's language in *Somerset* was far less restrained. He implied that human bondage had no authorization or legitimacy in natural law. Slavery, he observed, "is of such a nature, that it is incapable of being introduced on any reasons, moral or political." Slavery was "so odious, that nothing can be suffered to support it, but positive law." Further, Mansfield treated slaves as persons, not property. They were subjects of the realm, not aliens. And slavery was a status, not a form of property holding. Persons might be held to service or labor, but presumably they could not be treated as chattel or property, especially in the absence of a law authorizing such treatment. At a minimum, whatever else slaveholders in England might do to those enslaved, they could not send these persons out of the reach of its courts by force.[43]

The implications were hugely significant. The landmark decision departed from Blackstone's reasoning in important ways. Unlike Blackstone, Lord Mansfield was unwilling to concede that there could be two systems of law, one for England under common law and one for the colonies under the law of conquest, one intolerant of slavery, the other indulgent. Instead, Mansfield argued that now the question was "whether any dominion, authority or coercion can be exercised in this country, on a slave according to American laws." Mansfield's answer was definitive: "The black must be discharged." In the absence of positive law or immemorial usage or custom, freedom was the natural condition. Therefore, the decision treated slave law as purely local in effect, as inoperable outside certain boundaries, and as limited to specific conditions. Mansfield's decision moved slavery entirely out of the reach of the common law and its moral protection. Whatever slavery was, it was not sanctioned by English common law. As a result, *Somerset v. Stewart* wiped out the line of seventeenth-century precedents that had once propped up slavery as a lawful form of property. News of the decision made its way across the Atlantic with surprising speed. Nearly every newspaper in British America carried a report of its outcome. When enslaved people in Virginia and Maryland heard about it, they widely discussed its implications. Rattled slaveholders speculated that word of the decision prompted some to run away.[44]

Somerset, especially Mansfield's description of slavery as "odious," raised doubts about the legitimacy of slavery itself.[45]

The initial legal strategy of the White Marsh families was to use the *Somerset* principle to assert that their ancestors, though black, were free because they had set foot on English soil, and therefore their descendants were free. Their claims could lead to a narrow victory, one that did not question the legitimacy of slavery writ large but merely established that the families were descended from free women. Yet their lawsuits could provide an opening wedge for freedom more broadly, potentially validating the *Somerset* principle in Maryland courts and planting it more firmly in precedent. At the very least, the meaning of Maryland's constitutional commitment to the traditions of English common law for all "inhabitants" would be tested. If *Somerset*'s common-law principles were recognized in a Maryland court, even if only in individual freedom suits, then slavery's constitutionality might come into question.[46]

As early as 1783, a revolutionary call to end slavery appeared in the pages of the *Maryland Gazette.* Vox Africanorum (the Voice of the Africans, a pseudonym) wrote, "Though our bodies differ in colour from yours; yet our souls are similar in a desire for freedom." He warned that stakes for the newly formed republic were great. "Let America cease to exult—she has obtained but partial freedom." Because slavery continued, the American Revolution stopped short and was incomplete. "A people who have fought—who have bled—who have purchased their own freedom by a sacrifice of their choicest heroes, will never continue advocates for slavery," Vox Africanorum asserted. Slavery derived not from "the laws of Nature" but instead from the laws of municipalities and states. Slavery was the product of British "pride, insolence, and avarice." As for differences in color between blacks and whites, they "can never constitute a disparity in rights."[47]

In Maryland antislavery ideas were surprisingly public. Luther Martin, the state's attorney general and one of its preeminent attorneys, walked out of the 1787 Constitutional Convention on the grounds that the Federalist project disfavored small states, centralized the national government, and failed to end the African slave trade. At the convention, Martin, a slaveholder, said that the slave trade "was inconsistent with the principles of the revolution and [it was] dishonorable to the American character to have such a feature in the Constitution." Other prominent political figures had opposed slavery at the convention. Rufus King of Massachusetts and Gouverneur Morris of New Jersey condemned slavery as a "nefarious institution" that violated "the laws of humanity." Elbridge Gerry of Massachusetts insisted that the Constitution have "nothing to do" with slavery so as "not to give sanction to it."[48]

The national government was already taking steps to contain slavery and establish freedom as the norm of republican government. The Confederation Congress barred slavery from the Northwest Territory, except for the punishment of certain crimes. The Northwest Ordinance, as it was called, established a charter of national freedom and a proto–Bill of Rights protecting the basic liberty of individuals. Thomas Jefferson drafted the legislation guaranteeing freedom of worship, trial by jury, and fair representation to all inhabitants. On the eve of the Constitutional Convention, five of the original thirteen states had abolished slavery or their state supreme courts had declared it unconstitutional. Two more states, New York and New Jersey, were debating gradual emancipation acts. The question from the 1780s was not whether slavery was wrong—many patently conceded that it was—but whether slavery might be ended.[49]

When Martin returned to Maryland, he gave an extensive report on the proceedings in Philadelphia, attacking the Constitution for not abolishing the Atlantic slave trade immediately. His speech to the Maryland House of Delegates in 1788 was reprinted and circulated widely. Calling slavery "inconsistent with the genius of republicanism," Martin claimed that the Constitutional Convention should have allowed the federal government to legislate "for the gradual abolition of slavery and the emancipation of the slaves which are already in the States." Martin argued that the twenty-year ban on regulating the African slave trade fatally compromised the Constitution and opened the door to the "nefarious institution." Some slaveholders like Martin opposed the slave trade not principally for humanitarian reasons but because they knew that the value of the enslaved persons they held in bondage would increase if the African trade were closed. Across Virginia and Maryland slaveholders in favor of the Constitution turned Martin's critique on its head, trumpeting the Constitution's protection of slavery in their campaign to convince slaveholders to ratify the Constitution. Decades later abolitionists picked up Martin's words as the clearest evidence they could find that the Philadelphia Convention had produced a proslavery Constitution.[50]

Martin's speech revealed the profound ambiguity on the question of slavery at the core of the Constitution. On the one hand, the Constitution sheltered, and advanced, the interests of slaveholders. Behind the closed doors of the Convention, James Madison maneuvered to defeat the proposal for equal-state suffrage in Congress, an idea that Martin and other delegates from small states vigorously supported. Madison manipulated and exploited the tension between the states that had slaves and those that did not as a strategy to convince delegates from small states to approve a national legislature based on proportional representation. To do so Madison had been willing to protect slavery in the national government. The Three-Fifths Compromise counted "persons held to service" for representation purposes. The importation of slaves from Africa could not be outlawed by the national government for twenty years. Congress was specifically empowered to "suppress insurrections," and states were obligated to return enslaved people "escaping" from one state into another. These provisions were major concessions to slaveholders that gave slavery national protection at a moment when it was most vulnerable to legal and constitutional challenge.[51]

On the other hand, the Constitution did not explicitly sanction the idea of human property, and no fundamental provision in the document authorized slavery under national law. Antislavery delegates to the Constitutional Convention insisted that the Constitution refer to "persons held to service," not "slaves." Following the model of the Northwest Ordinance, the provision in the Constitution for returning fugitives implied that slavery was solely a creature of state and local law. A subtle but potentially powerful legal distinction emerged between national law—framed by the Constitution and based on the principles of freedom—and state law, where the colonial legacy of human bondage persisted.[52]

In the fall of 1789 the Maryland legislature began considering suggestions to abolish slavery. Citizens on the Eastern Shore, where Quakerism was especially strong, sent petitions to the legislature calling for abolition. The Maryland House of Delegates voted to prevent the petitions from being read and heard on the floor. The Society of Friends in Baltimore sent a similar petition, and it, too, was refused a hearing. Then in September 1789 a new organization opposed to slavery formed in Baltimore: the Maryland Society, for Promoting the Abolition of Slavery, and for the Relief of Free Negroes, and Others, Unlawfully Held in Bondage. Nearly three hundred members joined, including such leading citizens as Gerard Hopkins, George Buchanan, Elias Ellicott, and William Trimble. Other leading Federalists spoke publicly in favor of emancipation. Physician and politician James McHenry, one of Maryland's delegates to the Constitutional Convention, supported abolition and widely reprinted a biographical sketch of Benjamin Banneker, the free black author and almanac-maker as an example of racial equality.[53]

The Maryland Society's condemnation of slavery was unambiguous: it constituted a "crisis in the minds of Men" because God "created all Men free and equal." The society not only invoked the Great Commandment to love one's neighbor as oneself but also appealed directly to ideas about natural law: "The human race, however varied in colour or intellects, are all justly entitled to liberty; and it is the duty and the interest of nations and individuals, enjoying every blessing of freedom, to remove this dishonour of the Christian character from amongst them."[54]

The society appointed standing counselors (lawyers) who did not have to be members and therefore could be slaveholders. In 1789 the first honorary counselors of the Maryland Abolition Society were none other than Samuel Chase and Luther Martin, perhaps the most prominent lawyers in the state. Two other lawyers were encouraged to "urge" the "Claims to Freedom" of the enslaved before the "Courts" that were "authorized to decide upon them."[55]

When the society petitioned the House of Delegates in November 1789 for the gradual abolition of slavery, the House referred the proposal to a committee of seven led by a twenty-five-year-old freshman delegate named William Pinkney. Pinkney was a young lawyer with considerable formal training in the classics who had studied law with Samuel Chase in Baltimore. Largely on the basis of his loyalty to Chase, he was elected a delegate to the Maryland convention that ratified the U.S. Constitution. Subsequently, in 1788 he won a seat in the Maryland House of Delegates. His admirers considered his style of speaking "marked by an easy flow of natural eloquence and a happy choice of language." Pinkney's nephew recalled that he dressed with "careless simplicity" in his early years in the legislature and exhibited decidedly informal manners, a sign of his revolutionary idealism and disdain for the trappings of inheritance and aristocracy.[56]

In 1788, during Pinkney's first session, the legislature considered doing away with the law allowing the manumission of slaves. Manumission by deed, but not by last will and testament, had been lawful under Maryland colonial law since 1752. Pinkney rose from his seat in the House, condemned slavery, and argued that manumission ought to be broadened, not restricted. Pinkney stressed the importance of considering the "endless generations yet to come"; if slavery continued, the law would doom millions "to the curse of perpetual bondage." He feared that white Americans failed to see the problem in front of them because they were blinded by racial pride: "When we talk of policy, it would be well for us to reflect whether pride is not at the bottom of it; whether we do not feel our vanity and self-consequence wounded at the idea of a dusky African participating equally with ourselves in the rights of human nature."[57]

Then the bill to eliminate manumission came up for consideration again in 1789 and was referred to Pinkney's committee. Instead of restricting manumission, Pinkney and his colleagues recommended abolishing slavery gradually through manumission "by silent and gradual steps, with the consent of the owner." They objected to "compulsory abolition" because they considered it a "violation of acquired rights," and they objected to "sudden" abolition because they considered it "dangerous." The committee also objected to the exportation of slaves from Maryland, calling the slave trade "a species of traffic inhuman in itself, and disgraceful to the government." So the committee recommended making individual manumission more liberal, not less, and suggested repealing the sections of Maryland's 1715 and 1728 slave codes that penalized "the child for the offence of the parent." These specific provisions had punished the children of white and mulatto women and black men, whether free or enslaved, with thirty-one years of enslavement.[58]

Pinkney's committee, in other words, took aim at an exceedingly narrow but highly significant means of perpetuating hereditary bondage in colonial society. The provisions affected mixed-race families and their children, such as the Butlers, the Queens, and the Mahoneys, trapping generation after generation in slavery. The children of mixed relations would be the opening wedge in a broader effort to dismantle slavery without violat-

ing the individual rights of slaveholders, not only because they were descended from whites but also because they were the most obvious casualty
of the laws upholding hereditary bondage.[59]

Pinkney gave an impassioned speech in the Maryland House. He said
he would not shy away from uncomfortable truths about "perpetuating slavery." Going further than Jefferson, he probed at the justifications that his
contemporaries used to defend slavery and prodded his fellow delegates to
wake up to the tyranny of enslavement and its corruption of free society.
"The door to freedom is fenced about with such barbarous caution, that a
stranger would be naturally led to believe that our statesmen considered the
existence of its opposite among us, as the *sine qua non* of our prosperity," he
warned. Slaveholders proceeded "in the knowledge of moral principles and
an enthusiasm in the cause of general freedom," but they "stooped to become
the purchasers of their fellow-creatures." Pinkney confessed that he and his
contemporaries were as "equally guilty" as their ancestors. "They introduced
the system [of slavery]; *we* enlarge, invigorate, and confirm it." He was astonished at the hypocrisy of those who countenanced slavery and wondered
"that the people of Maryland do not blush at the very name of freedom."[60]

As a matter of public policy, he argued, slavery threatened the very nature of the republic and civil society. "Dangerous consequences" would
come, he predicted, from using the law to support "this system of bondage."
The hypocrisy at the heart of the nation's founding would lead inevitably to
"a contamination of principle." Legislatures were creating a permanent form
of "civil slavery, by legislative acts." Maryland's laws allowing the manumission of slaves, and slaves' gradual emancipation, were consistent with the
principles of freedom, Pinkney pointed out, but "the extension of civil slavery," he argued, "ought to alarm us."

Pinkney had little patience for those who believed in the racial inferiority of blacks. "Gracious God!" he cried. "Can it be supposed that thy al-
mighty providence intended to proscribe these victims of fraud and power,
from the pale of society, because thou hast denied them the delicacy of a European complexion! Is their color, Mr. Speaker, the mark of divine vengeance, or is it only the flimsy pretext upon which we attempt to justify our
treatment of them?" Pinkney disparaged such "holy arguments" because
"they are as convenient for the tyrant as the patriot." Blacks were "men," he
told the House of Delegates, the same as "we are" and "endued with equal
faculties." They are "in all respects our equals by nature."

Nothing like Pinkney's speech had ever been heard in the legislatures
of Maryland or Virginia. Jefferson's doubts about slavery in *Notes on the State*

of Virginia were just that, doubts. He was more concerned with the effect of slavery on white men and women than on the enslaved. Jefferson more than tolerated slavery in American society—he justified it as a necessary evil, as the best possible condition for a race of people he considered "inferior." But the young delegate in Maryland's State House sailed far beyond Jefferson's comfortable shores. He not only exposed the contradiction between slavery and freedom in American society but also laid bare the duplicity of racial ideas like Jefferson's.

Within a week of Pinkney's speech, Charles Carroll of Carrollton introduced a bill in the Maryland Senate "for the gradual abolition of slavery and for preventing the rigorous exportation of negroes and mulattoes" from the state. The bill was tabled. So Carroll called for a conference with the House to discuss the abolition of slavery bill and to have a "candid exchange of sentiments." The House voted thirty-nine to fifteen against having a conference to discuss the bill. Despite his exuberant speech on the floor against slavery, William Pinkney voted with the majority to kill Carroll's proposal, as did several other members of his committee on the grounds that abolition should be granted voluntarily by slaveholders, not coerced by the state.[61]

Carroll eventually put forward another plan that reportedly would have bound all female slave children to be educated until age twenty-eight, when they would become free. All other enslaved people under forty-five would be freed at a fixed date in the future. Carroll's emancipation bill, like Jefferson's 1783 version in Virginia, never made it to the floor of the Maryland legislature for debate.[62]

As late as 1789 the colonial underpinnings of slavery were still codified in Maryland law, operating unrestrained more than a century after their enactment. Only the legislature or the courts could remove these provisions or blunt their force. Maryland, like many other Southern states, passed no immediate postrevolutionary statutes further defining slavery.[63]

Instead, Maryland's legislators left it up to the judiciary to figure out how much of slavery would remain in place after the Constitution was ratified. In large measure this was because in no other state did English common law become as enshrined in the state constitution. In case after case, lawyers and judges drew from its sources and traditions. Maryland's judges pursued a doctrine of "judicial legislation," following parts of English common law that made sense in the particular setting of Maryland and giving judges enormous flexibility, and discretion, in the determination of individual cases.[64]

But the Butlers' successful freedom suits, William Pinkney's provocative speeches, and the seriousness of his committee's proposals in 1789 all indicated another facet of the potential for American freedom: the depth and breadth of the antislavery change under way in American society. It is notable that the debate over gradual abolition in the 1789 Maryland legislature, constrained as it was, focused on colonial law and, in particular, on the problem of hereditary bondage. The Butler family's lawsuits turned on a similarly powerful question: Was hereditary bondage, regardless of race, a legacy of colonial absolutism so offensive to natural law that it ought to be ended?

Pinkney's liberal ideals simultaneously betrayed the deeply conservative view of Maryland slaveholders, who sought above all else to protect the individual rights of slaveholders to do whatever they wanted with their property. Other prominent revolutionaries like Jefferson were beginning to justify slavery with ideas about racial inferiority. In this way they attempted to make the most glaring imperial legacy in American society—slavery—fit within the revolutionary American republic founded on the principles of freedom, however awkward, however contradictory it may be. Meanwhile, Jefferson and his followers also began to view the inherited common law with suspicion, as insufficiently republican because it vested such extraordinary power in judges to shape the outcome of any given case.[65]

So, in the fall of 1789, when William Pinkney moved to liberalize manumission and proposed to repeal the sections of the 1715 and 1728 slave codes related to children of white and black parentage, his proposals were much more than symbolic gestures. The legal possibilities for the enslaved families at White Marsh brightened and gained immediate legitimacy. Politically, a faction in Maryland led by Chase and Pinkney had become uncomfortable with the forms of hereditary slavery that survived intact through the decades of revolution, war, and constitution making. They spoke openly and frankly against color prejudice, and they clearly opposed the expulsion of free black and mulatto persons from the state. As a matter of public policy Pinkney seemed to take the most limited action possible toward abolition, starting with the descendants of white women. Five years later Pinkney helped the Queen family file their freedom suits.[66]

Taken together, these measures posed a potentially radical departure. They were designed first to encourage individual slaveholders to emancipate the enslaved, second to restrict the state from further enslavement of mixed-race people, and third to establish a policy that would prevent the removal of free black and mulatto families from the state. Rather than use state action against individuals, Pinkney relied on the free individual's pursuit of happiness. To men like Pinkney and Chase, this solution appeared entirely consistent with Lockean principles stressing the liberty of individuals in society, upon which much of English and early American law was founded.

The Butler freedom suits showed that Maryland courts would dismantle hereditary enslavement at least for the descendants of free white women. Then William Pinkney and the Maryland legislature openly discussed plans for the gradual abolition of slavery. A group of like-minded antislavery reformers in Baltimore began organizing lawyers and raising money to bring freedom suits across the state, especially ones that might expose hereditary enslavement as a feudal legacy. And word traveled across the Atlantic of the British debates over slavery and the slave trade.[67]

We can only discern the motivations of Edward Queen, Charles Mahoney, the Butlers, and other enslaved families through their actions and through the possibilities open to them in their historical time and place. In January 1791 Samuel Chase, the Butler family's lawyer and the honorary counselor for the Maryland Society for Promoting the Abolition of Slavery, rose to become the chief judge of the Maryland General Court of the Western Shore. Chase handed off the Butler cases to two of his accomplished protégés: his cousin Jeremiah Townley Chase and his friend Gabriel Duvall from Prince George's County. By October 1791 Duvall was working with Edward Queen and Charles Mahoney, who became the lead plaintiffs in a set of lawsuits aimed at the Reverend John Ashton, at the Jesuit corporation, and at the vestiges of colonial slavery in American society.

The recent decisions freeing the Butlers suggested that black plaintiffs could win major victories in the courts, even overturn colonial decisions based on hereditary enslavement. The high-profile debates over slavery and manumission in the Maryland House of Delegates could be seen as the early signs of a new era of freedom. In Baltimore, moreover, and even Annapolis, a free black community was beginning to thrive. These cities were home to more than eight thousand free blacks already in the state. Edward Queen and Charles Mahoney knew full well that their lawsuits could be won. Their freedom suits had the potential to turn the world of the slaveholding tobacco planters in Prince George's County upside down.

Attempting to Poison a Certain Richard Duckett the Younger

PRINCE GEORGE'S COUNTY, MARYLAND, 2015

On a bright November day, I drove through Prince George's County on my way to find Sprigg's Request, a hundred-acre plantation acquired in 1729 by Richard Duckett Jr., who married the granddaughter of Thomas Sprigg. Duckett purchased hundreds of acres of prime tobacco land from his relatives and his neighbors. His ten children married into the leading slaveholding families of Prince George's County, and one of his sons, Thomas Duckett, was named in a deposition as a potential witness in the freedom suit filed by Edward Queen. Richard Duckett Jr. and Thomas Duckett were my ancestors.

I had never been to the corner of Prince George's County near Sprigg's Request, despite growing up across the Potomac River in Alexandria, Virginia. Until researching the Queen family's freedom suit, I knew nothing of Richard Duckett and his plantation. From later maps, I ascertained that the land was located near White Marsh, just a few miles to the south and west of the former Jesuit plantation.

My father's mother descended from Richard Duckett Jr., and I remembered that one of her cousins had spent his retirement in the 1970s piecing together the Duckett family tree. Thick volumes of his research bound in laminated scrapbooks stood on the shelves in his library, their pages festooned with his meticulous hand-painted coats of arms and elaborate charts. Inky black lines of genealogy on sheepskin parchment gave the appearance of authority. Decades later, viewed through my professional, academic eyes, the whole book looked like amateur investigation into matters

43

no one knew how to solve anymore. Pieces were missing and broken. Branches of the family tree included most of the prominent planters of colonial Maryland, including the Bowies, the Magruders, the Contees, the Claggetts, and the Duvalls. Each family in the blue book had its own meticulously hand-painted crest.

Our principal family lore, however, concerned an entirely different line of my ancestors, the Thomas family: all nonslaveholding yeoman farmers, Welsh immigrants who came down from Pennsylvania and settled in Loudoun County, Virginia, where they were surrounded by Quakers. Independent, hard-headed, and intensely driven, by all accounts the Thomas clan scorned slaveholding and kept to themselves. One look at my great-cousin's charts, on the other hand, told me that the Duckett branch of my family from Prince George's County embraced slaveholding. Richard Duckett arrived in the seventeenth century with a king's grant of land on which he grew tobacco.[1]

Just before setting out to find the old place, I had stumbled across a reference to Sprigg's Request in the *Proceedings of the Council of Maryland*, the transcript of the colonial governing authority. The entry in that volume was short but stomach-turning.

An enslaved man named Thomas was convicted of attempting to poison Richard Duckett Jr. at Sprigg's Request in 1755. He was sentenced to hang, only to be mysteriously pardoned. Did Duckett withdraw the accusation? Was evidence of Thomas's innocence discovered? The report does not say. Two men accused of the same crime at the same time against other planters were convicted and hanged. Their bodies were "hung in chains" for weeks on public display at county road crossings.[2]

The poisonings throughout eighteenth-century America, from Maryland to New York, tell us that slavery was nothing less than a state of war between the enslaver and the enslaved in every home, on every plantation, and at every crossroad. Few visible traces of that war remain. I found no markers to memorialize the men whose bodies hung in chains.[3]

Today, subdivisions with large, multimillion-dollar homes line the old road between Annapolis and the outskirts of Washington, D.C. There are no more tobacco fields along the Patuxent River between Bowie and Upper Marlboro, where as recently as the late 1970s, tobacco fields and barns stretched from Prince George's all the way south to St. Mary's County. Historic houses in the area, such as the boyhood home of Johns Hopkins, remain unoccupied. Their brick shells sit in fields of grass, and storm shutters hang precariously off their hinges. Old boxwoods and magnolias stand untended.

In the Waterford Estates subdivision, set back from the entrance, stood Pleasant Prospect, its line of entry still impressive in its arrangement and order, but empty and to all appearances a relic left from a world long ago. Nearby, the real estate developer placed two large signs that described the archaeological history of the Duckett plantation. In 2004 Prince George's County for the first time began requiring developers to undertake full archaeological surveys of historic properties and to document the history of enslaved families in the area. The Register of Historic Places in the 1970s documented the grand plantation homes in the county, but slave cabins, cemeteries, and other sites had been ignored, destroyed, and desecrated. The Duckett plantation, I soon learned, was one of the first properties in Prince George's County to complete a full archaeological survey with the goal of uncovering the history of slavery.

A team of archaeologists uncovered the remains of Duckett's original wood-frame manor house, as well as the kitchen, the meat house, a washhouse, an overseer's house, and the quarters for seventeen enslaved workers who planted, harvested, and cured hundreds of acres of tobacco. More than fifteen thousand artifacts were unearthed. Wine bottles from London inscribed with the initials "RD" were marked for Richard Duckett. He imported the finest silver plate from England and delftware, porcelain, and ceramics from China, as well as English and French firearms, ammunition, and equipment. When he died in 1788, Richard possessed eighty-two cattle, forty-one sheep, forty-four pigs, and sixteen horses, along with scythes, hoes, plows, hand mills, saws, and hatchets. The inventory of his estate included 4,000 pounds of pork, 40,000 pounds of hay, 10,500 nails, 281 bottles, 25 pewter plates, and 12 ivory-handled knives, among other items.[4]

But the principal and most valuable entries in the entire inventory could be found under the headings "Male Negroes" and "Female." The men were listed first. Henry was sixty-eight years old. Ben was sixty. Dick and Hercules were forty-five, James was thirty-four, and Lewis was twenty-eight. Moses and Ignatius were twenty-six, Charles was twenty-three, and Henry was twenty-one. A woman named Theaner was sixty-three years old. There were Rachel and her two children, unnamed; Villender, age twenty; Elizabeth, sixteen; and twelve-year-old Rachel. The slaveholders who compiled the inventory took no notice whatsoever of family relationships. Just a name, age, sex, and price.[5]

Duckett's total estate was appraised at £1,863, and the enslaved men, women, and children on the plantation accounted for nearly half of that sum, valued together at £856. When Duckett died in 1788, revolutionary ideas about human freedom were circulating throughout the Atlantic, Quakers were manumitting their enslaved and petitioning to end slavery in Maryland, and enslaved families like the Butlers were winning their freedom in local courts.

Richard Duckett Jr. did not free anyone.

Richard Duckett Jr. was enslaving seventeen people at his death, ten men and seven women and children. Over the course of his eighty-four years, he likely enslaved, bought, and sold many others. His principal heir, Isaac Duckett, born in 1753, enslaved more than fifty people, abandoned his father's wood-frame home, and in 1798 erected a commodious brick Georgian mansion in its place, one of the four most expensive structures in the county when it was finished. He called it "Pleasant Prospect." By 1800 Richard Duckett Jr.'s five sons together held 163 slaves and thousands of acres.[6]

Looking at Sprigg's Request and its transformation into Pleasant Prospect, I am hard-pressed to find a "turn" toward enslavement, as if slavery happened there somehow unintentionally. Enslavement was a strategy of the Ducketts and other gentry tobacco planters from the moment they arrived in the colony. The brick Georgian mansions and historic homes, with boxwood and periwinkle in well-maintained gardens and groves, could not hide what I had found in the written record. Enslaving. Dismemberment. Separation of families. The question was how the law could sanction such terrible things.[7]

CHAPTER 2

Ought to Be Free

I have known the Defendant ever since I was a boy.

—WILLIAM HILL, OCTOBER 23, 1792,

DEPOSITION AGAINST HENRY ROZIER

On October 17, 1791, the sheriff arrived at the Reverend John Ashton's residence in eastern Prince George's County and delivered a summons from Samuel Chase, the chief judge of the general court. Chase commanded the Jesuit priest to appear in Annapolis without delay to answer a petition filed by Edward Queen saying that he should be free.

Queen's attorney, Gabriel Duvall, lived on one of the plantations next to White Marsh. The Duvalls were among the first to settle in Prince George's County in the seventeenth century, and Gabriel, thirty-nine years old and a member of the House of Delegates, was one of the most active lawyers at the bar in Annapolis. He was successful and knowledgeable, and a lawyer of his capabilities could not be underestimated.

Edward Queen's lawsuit was not the only one under way against either the Jesuits or Maryland's wealthiest families. Duvall already represented another family, the Shorters, with an equally explosive claim to freedom. The Shorters claimed descent from a free white woman and had begun lodging dozens of lawsuits in the general court. Depositions were being taken, witnesses contacted, and defendant slaveholders summoned to Annapolis.[1]

A narrative map of the freedom suits, encompassing the
Western Shore of Maryland, parts of the Eastern Shore of Maryland,
and Washington, D.C., ca. 1790–1838 (M. Roy Cartography).

Bohemia Manor

■ Fingaul—James Carroll bequeathed this plantation as well as White Marsh to the Jesuits in 1729, including enslaved people.

■✝ Bohemia Manor—In the 1750s, the Jesuits sent Mary Queen and her son Ralph away from White Marsh to work at this Jesuit plantation. White residents there later testified that Mary told them she was a free woman from New Spain.

■✝ Newtown—In the 1770s and 1780s, the Jesuit manager at Newtown accused the enslaved women of promiscuity, sold their children, and broke up the families.

■✝ White Marsh—The Queen and Mahoney families lived for over six generations on this Jesuit plantation. Jesuit trustees met here in 1789 and decided to sell some of the enslaved. The families sued for their freedom in 1791.

■ Roswell Neale's Mill—Jenny Shorter, enslaved, was well known as a skilled "Doctress." The Shorter family descended from her mother Elizabeth, a free white woman. Some won their freedom in the 1790s.

▲ Maryland State House—Until 1804 the General Court of the Western Shore met here, where the jury ruled in favor of Edward Queen's freedom in May 1794 and Charles Mahoney's freedom in May 1799.

O Free Queen Neighborhood—Following Edward Queen's case, dozens of Queens won their freedom in court. Most remained close to White Marsh. Some rented land from antislavery Quaker planters.

▲ Charles Co. Court—In August 1796, both the Queen and the Thomas families suffered decisive reversals in this court, losing a pair of freedom suits against the Jesuits.

■✝ St. Thomas Manor—Removed from his position at White Marsh, Rev. John Ashton retired here in Port Tobacco. Rev. Charles Neale refused to hear confession from either Ashton or Susanna Queen.

▲ U.S. Supreme Court—In *Mima Queen v. John Hepburn* (1813), the court sustained the verdict against her freedom and ruled hearsay evidence inadmissible.

◆ Litchfield Enlarged at Hilltop—In 1815, Susanna Queen's two eldest children inherited Rev. John Ashton's property including several slaves.

☐ Miller's Tavern—The notorious tavern on F St. doubled as a secure "slave pen." In 1815 Ann "Anna" Williams leapt from the third-floor window. A congressional inquiry followed. She won her freedom case in 1832.

● St. Inigoes—On Easter Day 1817, over 150 enslaved and free black men and women gathered at the St. Inigoes "dram shop" and staged a rebellion. Some said they "meant to be free."

▲ D.C. Circuit Court—Enslaved men and women brought more than 450 freedom suits against slaveholders in the District. In the 1820s the families sued high-profile political figures.

O Middle River Station—Michael Queen, a free black man, purchased over 20 acres of property in the 1840s along the Philadelphia, Wilmington, and Baltimore Railroad, a main corridor of the Underground Railroad.

O Queenstown—By the 1850s free Queen family members acquired property in this area and established an independent free black community.

39

38

A veteran of numerous property battles in the courts and within the Jesuit order, Ashton was not easily cowed, but Queen's lawsuit threatened to unravel the entire Jesuit plantation system, expose Ashton's mismanagement of their premier estate, and affect the future of slavery in Maryland—perhaps even in the United States. But the Reverend Ashton faced a still more nauseating prospect: Edward Queen's freedom suit could easily make public what had become an open secret on the plantation.

Just a few years earlier, Ashton had been accused of carrying on an illicit relationship with Susanna "Sucky" Queen, who was likely Edward Queen's niece. Sometime in 1785 or 1786 she had had a child, and rumor in the White Marsh neighborhood spread that the child was Ashton's. A white indentured servant on the plantation named Edward Kelly filed a formal charge of paternity against Ashton with the Prince George's County magistrate. Later, Ashton would privately accuse Kelly of fathering the child. Meanwhile, however, a fellow Jesuit, the Reverend Bernard Diderick, swore an affidavit in court charging Ashton and Queen with fornication. Diderick's account was specific and damning but entirely based on hearsay, and the county magistrate refused to pursue the case.

Undeterred, Diderick filed a formal complaint with the Superior Reverend John Carroll, who had just been nominated by his fellow Jesuits to be the first bishop in the United States. Carroll brushed off Diderick's accusations and defended Ashton as a reliable priest unjustly accused. Still, Carroll decided to open an internal informal investigation, probably to head off any public scandal that might erupt around a court case. In due course he identified a former Jesuit who had converted to Anglicanism as the source of the "imputation" against Ashton. Carroll came to the predictable conclusion that the salacious rumors were false and "are sometimes circulated" against Jesuits because of "Protestant prejudices."[2]

Carroll complained to his superior in England that Diderick made it a point "to oppose Mr. Ashton" at every turn. He privately hoped that Diderick "would return to Europe." All he required was Diderick's apology for making public what should have remained confidential. No apology came. By late 1787, unsatisfied with the lack of resolution, Ashton went on the offensive and filed a formal complaint inside the Society of Jesus, accusing Diderick of defaming him. He asked for Carroll's direct, immediate intervention.

Carroll's perfunctory investigation again cleared Ashton of all charges. The result could not have been surprising, since Ashton was one of his strongest allies within the society and a distant cousin. Carroll met with Diderick in January 1788 and informed him that he had found no evidence that Ashton had taken advantage of his position at White Marsh or carried on a sexual relationship with Susanna Queen. He insisted that Diderick issue a written apology to Ashton and his fellow Jesuits as penance. Grudgingly, Diderick complied. In language designed to substantiate the charges against Ashton, Diderick's self-serving apology went on for thirty-three pages, an elaborate diatribe without a hint of remorse, constructed more to explain the righteousness of his position than to admit any error of his ways.

Incensed, Carroll required Diderick to "retract the exceptionable passages" of his apology. When Diderick reluctantly agreed, Carroll felt compelled to write the stubborn priest again to rebut his various assertions. Point by point, Carroll cataloged the "reprehensible passages" in Diderick's conniving apology. He said, "The erroneous statements" were "too many for a letter." He could not even bring himself to repeat in writing what Diderick had written about Ashton. Instead he wrote in a coded shorthand, referring to Diderick's "obnoxious" accusations about Ashton's relationship with Susanna Queen as "&c"—a catch-all phrase specifically referring to the accusation of a sexual relationship. Carroll was so concerned that his letter might one day be used to further the scandal that he mentioned the principal actors only by their initials, "Mr. A" for Ashton, "K" for the indentured servant Kelly, and "Mr. C" for himself.[3]

But like a Russian nesting doll, Carroll's letter revealed a story within the story. Somewhere at the center of the bundle was a complete account, a truth waiting to come out. For the first and only time in his long career, the Reverend Carroll, the Jesuit superior, mentioned a member of the Queen family by name in writing: "You yourself told me that the adventure of Phillis being seen &c, was at the very time that one of the parties was entirely deprived by the violence of a burning fever. Now, as you knew this, how can you justify yourself for concealing that circumstances when you related the tale told by Duval & the Negro-man? Did it contribute to yr. vindication to tell all our Brethren & some seculars the hearsay?"

Carroll's references to Phillis and her "adventure" were meant to discredit Diderick's account, but they revealed a hidden axiom at the center of the controversy. The only Phillis at White Marsh was Edward Queen's mother, who was in her midsixties. Did Carroll mistakenly write "Phillis" when he meant to write "Sucky"? Or did Diderick mistakenly accuse Phillis Queen of a relationship with Ashton when he meant to write Sucky Queen instead? If so, did Carroll decide not to clarify the mistake because it would only lend credence to Kelly's original accusation? In either case, one of the

Queen women was the subject of Diderick's testimony—that she was "seen," that her "adventure" was witnessed, and that she was the protagonist of a "tale" told by one of the Duvalls, possibly Gabriel Duvall, and a "Negro-man," probably Edward Queen.

When the sheriff arrived at White Marsh on October 17, 1791, John Ashton was the one Jesuit who personally oversaw White Marsh and collectively represented the private trust that would soon be called the Corporation of Roman Catholic Clergymen of Maryland (or "the corporation"). Edward Queen named John Ashton as the defendant slaveholder not only because Ashton held him individually as a slave but also because he was the procurator general of the Jesuit trust that held Queen's entire family as slaves. As such, Ashton offered an inviting target in court. He was a potential embarrassment for his superiors, and perversely, because of his alleged relationship with Susanna Queen and alienation from the Jesuits, he was also unpredictable, a possible renegade who might advance the Queen family's freedom for his own reasons.[4]

"The Spirit of the Law"

As Edward Queen began his freedom suit, a curious debate erupted in the Maryland legislature. Delegates proposed to censure the Maryland Society for Promoting the Abolition of Slavery. The charge against the society was that it was bringing specious lawsuits for freedom. Because the attorneys took these matters seriously and courts offered freedom cases a hearing, each petition proceeded through legitimate discovery, evidence gathering, and eventual trial by jury; naysayers charged that these cases were drummed up on false pretenses, and many white slaveholders began to greet every petition for freedom with more than a whiff of disbelief.

Outraged by the very notion of Edward Queen's petition for freedom, a group of Maryland slaveholders filed a formal complaint in the legislature before the Committee on Grievances and Courts of Justice. They said that the freedom suits were expensive and time-consuming, and constituted "improper interference" in their domestic affairs. The House committee agreed and recommended that the legislature consider measures to restrict petitions for freedom, so the Maryland Society replied with a lengthy memorial calling the committee ex parte (outside of its proper jurisdiction) and defended the suits as reasonable and well founded. "The truth really is, that, on the part of the petitioners," the society's vice president wrote, "there never has been an attempt to prevent the fullest investigation of the question . . . truth being the only object sought by those who have conducted the suit on their part, whereas the defendants have uniformly strove, by every artifice in their power, and by the most unremitted exertions, whenever they thought the state of evidence was favorable to them, to urge on a hearing, and preclude all further inquiry."[5]

Seeking to rein in spurious freedom suits, the House of Delegates over-whelmingly voted to condemn the Maryland Society for taking part in what the House deemed "unjustifiable, uncandid, and oppressive conduct." Even William Pinkney and Gabriel Duvall voted for this measure. The so-ciety's memorial was branded "indecent, illiberal, and highly reprehensible, and moreover . . . as untrue as it is illiberal."

Unsatisfied with this rebuke, some legislators tried to pass an even more censorious resolution. They argued that the Maryland courts were "abundantly sufficient" to protect "people in the enjoyment of their rights and privileges, without the intervention of any association of men whatever." On this point perhaps a majority could have been found, but the proposed resolution did not end there. The conduct of the Maryland Society was char-acterized as "oppressive and subversive of the rights of our citizens," and the principles of the society were held to be "repugnant to the laws and con-stitution of the State." Thirty-one delegates voted in the affirmative, thirty-three against. Neither Pinkney nor Duvall could stomach the caustic language in the resolution, and their nay votes helped kill the measure once and for all.

Afterward, the Maryland Society issued a public statement, saying that it regretted that the House felt "impelled *by the circumstances of the moment*" to make such serious charges. Content to leave the matter "to the public mind," the society defended its course of action in the freedom suits. "The petitions were *originally proferred* [sic] from the strongest impressions that the petitioners were unjustly deprived of their freedom:—they were *prose-cuted,* because, upon further investigation, the Society had no reason to be-lieve their first impressions erroneous; on the contrary, many facts appeared which, in their opinion, confirmed them."

In this overheated environment some judges viewed every freedom suit as dubious, if not specious. Enslaved petitioners faced all sorts of obstacles thrown in their path. In May 1792 a lawyer for the Maryland Society in Queen Anne's County informed a county justice that he was bringing a freedom suit against him—the judge. The judge took the lawyer aside and proposed a scheme of collusion to shut down the suits. Would the lawyer bring the case into court with the intention of dropping it for lack of evidence? The lawyer later explained the proffer: "That I should file the petition, tell the court I had been induced to believe the Negroes were entitled to their freedom, but, from the testimony I heard, I was confident the claim could not be supported, and to move them to order a judgment entered up against the negroes. This, Sir, would have been a bar to any future prosecution of their claim, and would have consigned them to the rigours of slavery for life." When the attorney ignored the judge and pursued the case in good faith, the judge intervened again. He offered an outright bribe: "If you will let the petition fall through, and will report to the Society [of Abolition], that you do not believe from the testimony you have heard, that the claim can be supported, I will make you a compliment of four or five guineas, and if that will not be sufficient I will double it."[6]

The dispute spilled out into the newspapers over the summer of 1792. In an open letter to the public the offended lawyer called the judge's clumsy attempt to suborn the freedom suit "a crime against the spirit of our laws and constitution." Federalist leaders, ever protective of their tight grip on Maryland's judicial branch, tried to intervene by quietly proposing that "the affair be referred to gentlemen of candour, honour, and integrity." The accusation against a sitting justice appointed by the governor was a serious matter and could lead to his disbarment. Backed by the chief justice of the district, the county judge offered a thinly veiled excuse for the misunderstanding. Meanwhile, the Maryland Society's lawyer heard from a handful of slaveholders that they planned to retain all of the lawyers at the bar to keep them from representing slaves in freedom suits.

The idea was not far-fetched. Every slaveholder knew that courts were supposed to be forums of "full, fair, and open investigation." Judges were sworn to "observe the strictest neutrality." Lawyers had strong incentives to investigate claims openly and candidly as "the first principle of law" and follow "natural reason," but some judges tried to circumvent claims to freedom, either through the law or outside of it. And lawyers might be convinced quietly, privately, and discreetly to file weak claims for enslaved plaintiffs "without seeing their witnesses, without even hearing their allegations."[7]

Sometimes slaveholders stalled for months or even years by ignoring a summons to appear in court. The courts expected a response from anyone they summoned, at the very least for an attorney to appear on behalf of the defendant and answer the charge. Sometimes, perhaps hoping the matter would go away, slaveholders refused to respond until they were held in contempt. Henry Hill Jr., one of Prince George's most prominent slaveholders, was fined for contempt in 1792 after a petition case against him brought by

Gabriel Duvall went unanswered for just one month. Anne Chunn, another conspicuous slaveholder, ignored the court for three and half years and was held in contempt. Some cases dragged on so long that the enslaved petitioner died. In other cases the slaveholder died, and the enslaved petitioner had to file a new round of petitions against the heirs.[8]

Slaveholders like Henry Hill often tried to discredit the testimony of enslaved petitioners and their free black witnesses. Anne Butler, an eighty-two-year-old free black woman and a descendant of Eleanor "Irish Nell" Butler, testified in a case against Hill. His attorneys rounded up white witnesses to impugn her character. One said she was once caught stealing sheep and punished severely. Another, a priest who had formerly bought her and held her as a slave, called her "infamous" for "thievery." In a fit of anger, he told her after one incident, "Damn your soul, get off my plantation." As if to justify this unchristian outburst, his wife testified that Butler was "a thief and liar." A barrage of other white witnesses made similar statements.[9]

Lawyers sometimes decided that the claims of certain families were unsubstantiated, and they would rush to have them dismissed. When a family in Anne Arundel County claimed to be descended from a "free East India Mulatto woman," William Pinkney, Gabriel Duvall, and Philip Barton Key all defended different slaveholders against the claim. Whenever the leading members of the bar lined up like this, the claim could be snuffed out.[10]

Judges wielded extraordinary power in these cases. They decided what evidence would be admissible and what would be excluded. They gave jury instructions that could determine the outcome, and some judges interpreted state law in creative if dubious ways to defeat claims for freedom.[11]

Seventeen miles east of White Marsh plantation, the General Court of the Western Shore held its sessions in the Maryland State House in Annapolis. The building rose more than two hundred feet to its dramatic spire high above the town. In its architecture and position, the State House was meant to express republican ideals of civic society: balance, proportion, and impartiality.[12]

Edward Queen would have walked into the great rotunda, where plasterers were still stuccoing the interior of the dome 111 feet overhead. Enslaved men probably prepared the stucco that came from St. Mary's County and surely hauled the plaster up the long hill from the docks. Under the rotunda dome, staircases on either side of the hall led to the campanile 135 feet above. According to one contemporary account, "The spectator has one of the most delightful panoramic views to be found in the United States. It commands a view of nature in all the beauty of poetic scenery—the ancient city—its environs—the adjacent country—the noble Chesapeake, and the eastern shore beyond it, for an extent of thirty miles around, breaks upon the view of the delighted eye."[13]

The general court heard its cases in an open chamber that was a continuation of the great hall. Stairs on either side of the bar led up to the bench where the justices sat. The court and the bar, therefore, were positioned in the open, visible from the main entrance at the other end of the State House. Queen could look back from the court, all the way down the hall, through the rotunda, and out the doors to the city of Annapolis. The architecture implied that anyone might approach the court, obtain a hearing, or witness its proceedings.

But the General Court of the Western Shore inherited the jurisdiction, and the reputation, of the colonial provincial court it replaced. Any contest greater than £100 sterling went before the general court; anything less was tried in the county courts. Treasons, murders, felonies, and cases of insurrection, for instance, went to the general court, while all minor offenses and misdemeanors were heard by the courts in the counties where they occurred. The general court had the authority to take appeals from lower county courts and heard nearly all petitions for freedom, in principle because they were cases involving life and potentially large financial damages. All appeals from the general court went to a higher court of appeals. Beginning with the Queens, the court's decisions became so controversial that the Maryland legislature spent most of the 1790s attempting to limit its jurisdiction and ultimately abolished the general court in 1805.[14]

When Edward Queen filed his petition for freedom in 1791, the general court had so many freedom suits under way that the clerk of the court published notices in the *Maryland Gazette* explaining how it planned to hear these cases without disrupting its regular business. The petitions, he noted, would be heard in the first week of the session. Whatever cases were left would be taken up as "opportunity may permit."[15]

With dozens of cases pending, hundreds of people were coming and going. Despite its location in the State House, and its entry through corridors of symbolic authority, this court more than any other forum in American life jumbled together every rank of society. Men and women testified, sued, and were summoned. Free and enslaved were tried one after the other. Artisans, laborers, and wage earners were routinely called upon as witnesses. Although only propertied white men could serve on juries, the jurors were drawn from twelve counties and included nonslaveholding Germans from the western towns, Irish mechanics from Baltimore, and Quaker merchants

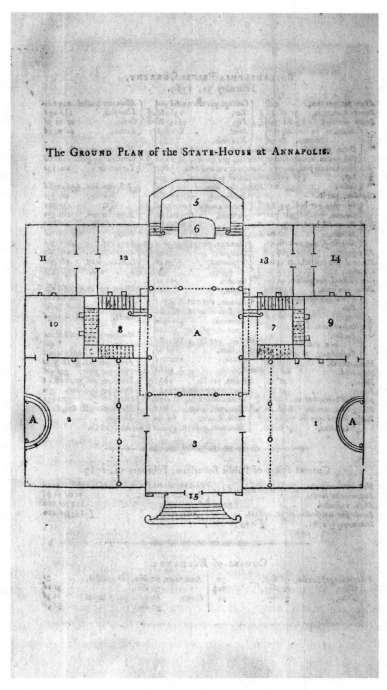

The GROUND PLAN of the STATE-HOUSE at ANNAPOLIS.

Floor plan of first floor of the Maryland State House, 1789, in the *Columbian*.
A small set of stairs led at the end of the great hall to the bench (No. 5), where the
judges sat. The "Bar" (No. 6) was where attorneys stood to make their arguments.
Enslaved plaintiffs and slaveholder defendants crowded behind them in the hall
of the Rotunda (A).

from Annapolis. All of this business took up four large rooms on the first floor of the State House. During the court's monthlong sessions every May and October, thousands of people of all backgrounds moved through its offices and courtrooms.

With so much at stake in the courts, no area of political life in Maryland drew more attention than the judiciary. Political factions coalesced in the 1780s at first around two loosely organized geographic regions: one centered in Baltimore and Annapolis and another based along the Potomac River, including Prince George's County. These regional alignments quickly morphed into political parties, with the Republicans leading in Baltimore and Annapolis and the Federalists dominating the Potomac River counties to the south. Because courts supervised elections, each side tried to gain supremacy in the judiciary. Skirmishes regularly erupted in the legislature over which courts might adjudicate which areas of the law and over which courts were empowered to supervise elections.

The Federalists attempted in 1790 to professionalize the bench by replacing the traditional county courts with higher district courts. Instead of seating untrained judges in the county courts, the Federalist governor would appoint professional lawyers to the district court benches. Their opponents, eventually called Republicans, branded the Federalists as propertied, aristocratic, counterrevolutionary, and undemocratic. The nascent Republicans in Maryland saw the judiciary proposal as a Trojan horse, a political means to qualify Federalists for the bench and exclude Republicans. The act passed and authorized the governor to appoint two justices of "integrity, experience, and legal knowledge" to each county court and a chief justice who would ride a five-county district. Fractious disputes followed over who would be appointed justices to the new district courts, and there were lengthy debates over how much and how often these justices should be paid.[16]

Throughout the 1790s the Republicans sought to take over the courts and wrest control of them from their Federalist adversaries. At a minimum they sought to dampen judicial discretion and empower juries to decide the law and well as the facts of a case. As partisanship intensified across Maryland, the petitions for freedom became more than a local or personal contest. They became a divining rod in the decade-long battle over who would control the courts, an instrument for both parties to discover and tap deeper wells of support as they sought to control the judiciary. No court was more coveted, none more associated with the conservative Federalists, than the General Court of the Western Shore. Holding its sessions right in the middle of the State House, hearing the most controversial freedom suits, taking free black witnesses, the general court had the potential to shape the nation's emerging political parties.[17]

Just days before Edward Queen's freedom case went to trial in May 1794, another case in the general court revealed how quickly revolutionary ideas of freedom were spreading in the Atlantic World. Three years earlier, in August 1791, a slave insurrection had exploded in the French colony of Saint-Domingue, and in September of that same year, John Guiho De Kerlegand, a slaveholding French planter, fled to Maryland. With him he brought enslaved people, including a man named Hector. Since 1783 Maryland law had prohibited the importation of slaves "except by citizens of the United States" who intended in good faith to "reside" permanently in Maryland. Temporary sojourners who were U.S. citizens could bring slaves into Maryland but only for a limited time. American slaveholders moving into Maryland had to certify that all of the enslaved persons and all of the mothers of enslaved children under age three in their possession had resided in the United States for at least three years. This provision was designed to prevent enslavers from using Maryland as a way station in the transatlantic slave trade by arriving in a state that did not bar importation, then moving to Maryland and holding the enslaved persons there for later sale. Slaveholders could obtain an exemption to this provision, but they had to verify that the enslaved people were not intended for sale.[18]

De Kerlegand was neither a temporary sojourner nor a U.S. citizen. By the letter of the law, Hector and any other enslaved people De Kerlegand brought into Maryland should have been free under the 1783 act. A year after he arrived, De Kerlegand applied for and received U.S. citizenship.

Meanwhile in Saint-Domingue, the slave revolt gathered extraordinary momentum, becoming the largest and best-coordinated slave insurrection in modern history. More than a thousand plantations were destroyed in the first few months. In France the revolt prompted a profound and urgent reconsideration of colonial policy. Radicalized revolutionaries dropped distinctions of color in the law, and in the spring of 1792 the French National Assembly granted political equality and citizenship to free men of color. News of the revolt spread through the grapevine around the Caribbean and to North and South America. Black sailors, white refugees, and military forces moved from port to port carrying with them the news of the unprecedented events in Saint-Domingue.[19]

As the revolt in Saint-Domingue widened into a raging civil war, the Maryland legislature, dominated by Catholics and Federalists, loosened the restrictions on importing slaves. In fact, it made an exception in 1792 to allow French subjects to bring slaves with them into Maryland. Then, in the summer of 1793, the republican revolutionaries in Saint-Domingue granted freedom and citizenship to slaves who would fight against the royalists and their allies. The revolutionaries took another step: they abolished slavery by decree, hoping to win the allegiance of the enslaved. Following that, on February 4, 1794, the revolutionary French National Convention shocked slaveholders in the Atlantic World. The French government declared the total abolition of slavery in all French colonies, including Saint-Domingue. The declaration proclaimed, "All men, without distinction of color, will enjoy the rights of French citizens."

That spring, Hector sued for his freedom in Maryland, claiming that John G. De Kerlegand was not a citizen of the United States when he arrived in 1791 and therefore had violated the Maryland nonimportation law. Under that law Hector and any other slaves De Kerlegand brought with him were immediately free. Hector argued that the less restrictive 1792 act did not apply and could not be retroactively enforced. The argument appeared airtight, and indeed a county court jury in Frederick, Maryland, wasted little time finding that Hector was "entitled to his freedom."[20]

De Kerlegand appealed the verdict to the General Court of the Western Shore in Annapolis, where judges led by Samuel Chase reversed the lower court's decision. The French abolition of slavery, like a lightning bolt in the night, illuminated for Federalist-oriented judges the dangers of revolutionary liberty.

Denied his freedom with the reversal, Hector appealed to the High Court of Appeals and enlisted as his lawyers William Pinkney and Arthur Schaff, another successful attorney who had long opposed slavery. "Nothing can be more plain," Schaff argued, than Hector's claim to freedom. If a non-U.S. citizen came into Maryland with an enslaved person, then the slave was immediately free, even if the slaveholder did not originally intend to reside in the state. The object of the 1783 law, after all, was clearly to bar foreigners from bringing slaves into Maryland. The fact was that De Kerlegand came to Maryland with the intention to reside permanently in the state.

De Kerlegand's attorneys responded with a simple analogy. They compared the law to a "nut which has a shell and a kernel." They warned the justices, "If you stick to the shell, which is the words, you will never get to the kernel, which is the spirit of the law." Open the shell of words, look inside the Maryland 1792 law, they argued, and you will find that its kernel, its spirit, was to encourage French subjects to become "citizens or settlers in the state" and to entitle them to keep their slaves. "The spirit of the law," they concluded, "is in favour of De Kerlegand." This argument, thin as it was, had the double virtue of allowing Federalist opponents of the French Revolution to accommodate planters fleeing a slave insurrection even if the letter of the law did not allow it.

The judges of the High Court of Appeals admitted that a strict reading of the law meant Hector was entitled to freedom, but they agreed that the "spirit" of the 1792 act meant that De Kerlegand, as an asylum seeker, could bring slaves into Maryland. The ruling not only reversed Hector's freedom but also upset the traditional legal principle that laws should not be retrospectively applied unless the statute specifically allowed it. Edward Queen certainly would have learned from watching Hector's case how the law could be twisted to mean almost anything that served one party or another. Neither Hector nor Edward Queen could testify in open court, but in petitions for freedom neither could the defendant slaveholders John G. De Kerlegand or John Ashton. He would have observed how the lawyers worked and how their arguments either swayed or failed to sway the juries and the justices.[21]

When Edward Queen arrived at the general court in May 1794 for his own freedom trial, the effects of the Haitian Revolution were palpably felt in Annapolis. Hector's and Edward Queen's cases overlapped for weeks, as witnesses were called and appeals heard. Queen undoubtedly knew that the French had abolished slavery. For him, the lawsuit against John Ashton promised a potential pathway to his whole family's freedom, however uncertain, however negotiated, however mediated through attorneys he did not fully know or perhaps even trust.[22]

To "Stop the Mouth of Lawyer Key"

There comes a point in every trial when a lawyer speaks for the client, but perhaps in no area of the law was this moment more keenly felt than when an enslaved person sued for his or her freedom. Before the court, no enslaved persons could speak directly for themselves, and yet it was their liberty and their freedom on trial, their family genealogies in dispute, their children and children's children who would potentially remain enslaved and considered property. In these cases, more than any others, the attorneys spoke for the enslaved plaintiffs in a form of ventriloquism that was both highly charged and potentially treacherous.

The enslaved clients, no doubt, took full measure of their attorneys, assessing not only their legal acumen but also their willingness to persuade in causes not their own, in social and political circumstances filled with risk. Enslaved plaintiffs such as Edward Queen could see that the courts did not seek the truth so much as set standards. They knew that the rules and procedures, the laws and opinions, the judges and attorneys were all in the hands of slaveholders. The question was: Could they work from within a system created by and for their enslavers? Because the courts established a particular order, a regime of authority based on the interests of those who governed through the mechanism of the law, enslaved people had to read their attorneys for cues, for signs and indications of the stakes in the law beyond their family's particular situation.[23]

Edward Queen's lawyers were Gabriel Duvall and Philip Barton Key. Their initials filled the docket ledgers of both the general court and the Prince George's County Court for years, in appearance after appearance. Although each led the Annapolis bar, they were an unlikely pair, and although they appeared jointly on behalf of the Queens, the Queen case shattered their alliance and split their political pathways.

Duvall was the older of the two by five years, and he grew up in Prince George's County at Darnall's Grove, a plantation nearly contiguous to White Marsh. Nineteen years old in 1771, Duvall left home, studied law in Annapolis, and became the clerk of the general court. Swept up in the American Revolution, he joined the Maryland militia and fought at the Battles of Brandywine and Morristown. Two of his brothers died late in the war in action against the British regulars, one at Camden, New Jersey, and another at Eutaw Springs, South Carolina. "They fell contending for everything, like freemen," he wrote his father. "At times I could almost die to let them live and scarcely have a wish to survive them."[24]

For the rest of his long life, Duvall considered himself a revolutionary, forever living up to the cause for which his brothers had died. After the war Duvall opened a brisk law practice in Annapolis and was elected in 1787 to the House of Delegates. That same year, at age thirty-five, he married Mary Bryce, the daughter of a prominent Annapolis merchant captain. After the birth of their first child in January 1790, Mary died at their home in Prince George's County, and her death broke his heart. He later built a brick mansion on the plantation and named it "Marietta." He wrote his father that his wife had met her death with "fortitude, seldom equaled." Duvall confided that nothing in the world was "more severe" than losing her. "May God of his great goodness and mercy . . . enable me to bear this affliction with fortitude and patience so great was my affection for her."[25]

The law, then, was Gabriel Duvall's life. That much is obvious from the historical record. He was involved in hundreds of cases every year in the 1790s. Duvall sent his son, Edmund, to live with his grandfather at Darnall's Grove when he was selected to fill a vacant seat in Congress. More than any other attorney, Duvall laid the groundwork for the Mahoney, Queen, and Shorter family lawsuits. He may have been motivated by the conviction that the Queens and the Mahoneys had a legitimate claim to freedom.

But lawyers like Duvall had a host of other reasons to take on freedom suits. In Maryland lawyers stood to be paid if their clients won their freedom, and given the large number of successful suits, representing a family like the Queens or the Mahoneys in case after case could mean a steady stream of fees. In addition, the Maryland Society for the Abolition of Slavery paid some lawyers to bring freedom suits for people "unlawfully held in bondage." On the Eastern Shore of Maryland, the local chapter reported that it filed sixty freedom suits in seven years between 1789 and 1796 and lost only one case. The Baltimore chapter reported, "A variety of suits were instituted against the unlawful holders of slaves last year, and in consequence many have been liberated." The Maryland Society's annual reports, however, never mentioned any of the prominent freedom suits on the Western Shore, and there is no evidence that *Queen v. Ashton, Mahoney v. Ashton,* or any of the other freedom suits in Prince George's County were ever sponsored by the Maryland Society in Baltimore. Instead, it is likely that black plaintiffs directed their own legal actions and enlisted local attorneys like Duvall, who took the cases for their own reasons. Some lawyers may have sincerely believed in ending slavery. Some may have been attracted by the legal principles at stake in these cases. Others may have wished to be associated with a humane cause. Whatever the reason, the lawyers also might have used the freedom suits to voice political positions they might not otherwise have taken in politics or in public.[26]

Unlike Duvall, Philip Barton Key remained a loyalist in the Revolutionary War and served actively in the colonial British forces against the Americans. His regiment fought George Washington's Continental Army at the Battle of Monmouth Courthouse. Late in the war his unit was dispatched to defend a British fort at Pensacola, Florida. Spanish forces unleashed a devastating attack and captured more than a thousand men, including Key. As a prisoner of war, Key was sent to Cuba. When the war ended in 1781, back in Maryland the General Court of the Eastern Shore found Philip Barton Key guilty of treason. His property was slated for confiscation.

Released from prison in Cuba after the war, Key went to London, where he studied law at the Middle Temple, Inns of Court. Returning in 1785 to Annapolis, he read law with Gabriel Duvall and was admitted to the bar in 1787. After a few years practicing in the county courts of the Western Shore, at thirty-three years old Key moved back to Annapolis and married Ann Plater, the sixteen-year-old daughter of George Plater, a leading planter and lawyer from St. Mary's County who was elected governor of Maryland in 1791.[27]

So, in the fall of 1791, when Edward Queen's attorneys first took on his case, they possessed extraordinary political connections. Duvall was a member of the House of Delegates and had been handpicked by Samuel Chase to take over some of the freedom suits for enslaved families. Meanwhile, Chase was chief judge of the general court where Queen's case would be heard. Despite Key's loyalist background, he was the son-in-law of the newly elected governor of Maryland. His cousin Philip Key, moreover, served in the House of Delegates alongside Gabriel Duvall, and in 1791 he was one of the few legislators who voted against each of the three proposals to censure the Maryland Society for bringing freedom suits in the courts. That autumn Philip Key was elected to Congress. In fact, Philip Key, Philip Barton Key, Samuel Chase, Luther Martin, and William Pinkney had all aligned themselves for the time being with the emerging Federalist political faction. Of all prominent lawyers in Maryland at the time, only the widower Duvall remained aloof from the growing Federalist consensus.

In May 1792 Duvall and Key began collecting depositions for Edward Queen's case. The first witness they interviewed, Richard Disney, testified that his mother was the midwife who delivered Mary Queen's daughter Nan. Although his testimony was secondhand hearsay, Disney's account possessed extraordinary credibility. White midwives were in a position to know and verify black genealogies even though they were paid by slaveholders. Disney's mother knew Mary Queen and was "well acquainted" with James Carroll and his family. According to Disney, his mother said, "It was a shame that the mother of Phillis and Nanny was kept in Slavery." She said that if James Carroll "would be false in one thing, he would be false in another." The biblical turn of phrase came from Luke 16:10: "Whoever is faithful in a very little is faithful also in much, and whoever is dishonest in a very little is dishonest also in much." The reference was especially damning and implied that James Carroll had followed Mammon, not God, by enslaving the children of a free woman through force and deception.[28]

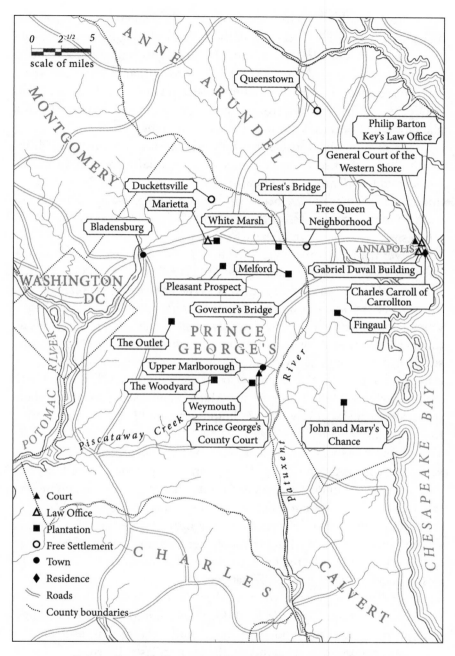

Prince George's County and surrounding principal sites
(M. Roy Cartography).

Disney also testified to several specific details about Mary Queen that he had heard from his mother and others. First, Mary Queen was brought to Maryland by Captain Larkin, and "she had a great many fine Cloathes." Second, she was taken ashore for a while by "old William Chapman," and it was "noised about that there was a fine lady from London and nobody wants to buy her." Third, he heard from several other sources close to the Carroll plantation that Edward's mother "Phillis ought to be free."[29]

It seems highly probable that Edward Queen and his mother, Phillis Queen, had identified Richard Disney as a potential witness and directed Duvall and Key to him. They knew that Disney's mother was Mary Queen's midwife, and she may have been Phillis's, too, and probably delivered Edward on May 3, 1754, as well as the rest of Phillis's children. If so, then Richard Disney's testimony would have had great value before a jury.

Over the next three years Duvall and Key gathered more witnesses. Each provided further corroboration of Disney's statement. One witness heard that Phillis "was as free as he was." When asked why, he replied, "Her Mother was free and was brought into this Country by Captain Larkin and was sold for seven years." He said she was sold to one of the Chapmans and that her name was Mary Queen. Later, she was sold to James Carroll, who sent her to his remote plantation on the Patuxent River called Fingaul. Another person testified that twenty years earlier he noticed "how many mulattoes there were at the priests' [White Marsh]" and decided to inquire about them. He learned that Edward "ought to be free for his grandmother was a free woman."[30]

Another witness was in some ways the most surprising—Gabriel Duvall's first cousin Caleb Clarke. Three years younger than Duvall, he, too, grew up and lived in Prince George's County. Clarke testified that his mother said that "a yellow woman called Mary Queen was brought into the Country by Captain Larkin." His mother often heard James Carroll and Mary Queen "quarrelling and wrangling about her freedom." Mary asked him for a legal document declaring her freedom, a concern Carroll allegedly dismissed, saying, "Pah! Law. Have patience you will be free by and by." According to this story, Carroll promised her, "You will get your freedom," but Carroll died without signing a legal document that Mary Queen was free. Instead, she remained in bondage on Carroll's plantations, and she was passed as property into the hands of the Jesuit priests. Based on this testimony, Edward Queen contended that his grandmother came from New Spain, not Africa, and that she was sold as an indentured servant, not a slave.

Her complexion, her clothes, and her time in London were all evidence of her status and her origins.[31]

When Edward Queen's case finally went to trial in May 1794, the Reverend Ashton's attorneys had spent three years attempting to delay the proceedings while Key and Duvall filed deposition after deposition. In that time Ashton's attorneys lined up witnesses who would testify that Mary Queen was always considered a slave and that they had never heard either her or her daughters make any claim to freedom. They also introduced an extract of James Carroll's will, purporting to show that Carroll bequeathed a woman named Mary to his nephew Anthony Carroll, a Jesuit priest who left Maryland for England. The court entered this extract into evidence, but the transcribed copy had a serious and undetected error. Carroll bequeathed a woman named "Margaret" to his nephew Anthony, and at some point a transcription error changed "Mag^t"to "Mary." This crucial piece of evidence, whether fabricated or not, was the only documentary record Ashton's attorneys produced.[32]

In fact, Ashton's defense was weak and disorganized, and his attorneys seemed to be counting on the general court's slaveholding jurors to deny Edward Queen's petition regardless of the evidence.

Nothing of the sort happened.

Improbably, Ashton's attorneys failed to strike one of the jurors, Archibald Robinson, who was the legal counsel for the Maryland Society in 1791 when Queen filed his case. Perhaps led by Robinson, the all-white jury reached a stunning verdict on May 23, 1794. They decided that "Mary Queen . . . was not a slave." Edward Queen was therefore freed, and John Ashton was ordered to pay 1,997 pounds of tobacco to him in damages and legal costs. Based on prevailing tobacco prices, the award was minimal, probably between $50 and $125 in contemporary currency. Lawyers' fees in Maryland courts were fixed by law at 400 pounds of tobacco for an appearance in the general court. At least one-third, possibly half, of Queen's award, in other words, went to his lawyers.[33]

Despite the paucity of the financial award, the verdict for Edward Queen's freedom, coming as it did in the wake of the Butler suits, raised the distinct possibility that thousands of enslaved people from other families might also win their freedom. Even before Queen's case went to trial, the Maryland legislature had drastically altered the legal procedure for freedom suits because enslaved plaintiffs were winning them. The Butlers won case after case between 1791 and 1793 in the General Court of the Western Shore, its jury pool coming from many counties with nonslaveholding majorities. Dozens of cases were pending, including more Queen cases.

But in December 1793 the legislature changed the law, stripping the general court of its jurisdiction over petitions for freedom. Going forward, all petitions for freedom had to originate in the lower district courts of the county where the petitioner and the slaveholder lived. Jurors and witnesses, therefore, would all be local and therefore liable to influence and intimidation in ways that they might not be in the general court. Judges of these courts were appointed by the governor. All were slaveholders. Clearly determined to clamp down on freedom petitions, the legislators considered the general court "inconvenient to the citizens" who had to travel back and forth to Annapolis from up and down the Western Shore. Furthermore, petitions for freedom verdicts could be appealed to a higher court only on matters of law, not evidence. In other words, the findings of fact in the lower court, whatever they were, could not be challenged on appeal. The changes benefited slaveholders and were potentially chilling, altering the calculus any enslaved person would have to make before he or she took the step of filing a petition.[34]

Slaveholders, including the Jesuits, scrambled to shut down further lawsuits. The Corporation of Roman Catholic Clergymen of Maryland, Bishop John Carroll, and the directors of the nascent Georgetown College were alarmed that the Queen case and other pending cases could potentially dismantle part of their plantation operations and, with the wrong verdict or judicial decision, wipe away as much as half of their property. The Jesuits were paying traveling expenses for lawyers to take depositions "against freedom of negroes." The costs were mounting. Three months after the judgment in Queen's favor, Philip Barton Key struck a confidential agreement with the Jesuits. The entry in the Jesuit account book noted: "To . . . retain or stop the mouth of lawyer Key from speaking in favor of the Negroes who have sued for their freedom." The Jesuits paid Key £4 17s 6d to stop representing enslaved families on their plantations.[35]

Philip Barton Key accepted the retainer, broke off his brief alliance with Gabriel Duvall, and forswore any further lawsuits against the Jesuits. He continued to represent members of the Queen family in individual cases that he had already filed in April 1794 in Prince George's County, all against the Reverend Ashton, and he continued, as we will see, to represent Edward Queen. However, he moved over to the Jesuits' defense team in Charles Mahoney's pending lawsuit against Ashton.

The Butlers and the Queens were not the only families to garner successful freedom suits. Two other large families—the Shorters and the

Thomases—followed Edward Queen and began suing slaveholders. The Shorters came from St. Mary's County. Their ancestor Elizabeth "Betty" Shorter, a free white indentured servant, married an enslaved man named Robin in 1681. Her daughters, Moll, Jenny, and Patty, remained enslaved under Maryland law. They had numerous children, and like the descendants of Eleanor "Irish Nell" Butler, they continued to be held as slaves far beyond their terms of enslavement despite the repeal of the 1664 law that initially bound them. Basil Shorter, the eldest great-grandchild of Elizabeth Shorter, coordinated dozens of her descendants across southern Maryland. His attorney, Gabriel Duvall, collected scores of depositions. Because the Shorters filed their cases before the 1793 act took effect, their suits would be heard in the General Court of the Western Shore.

The Shorter family took on Maryland's luminary politicians, priests, and Catholic slaveholding families: Charles Carroll of Carrollton, Daniel Carroll of Duddington, Notley Young, the Neales, the Boarmans, and the Roziers. Philip Barton Key represented nearly all of the defendants. When the sheriff arrived at some of these plantations with subpoenas ordering them to make the petitioners available for trial, the slaveholders ignored the court orders and sold the enslaved petitioners or tried to send them to remote plantations. Raphael Boarman heard that Anne Shorter had sued him, and before the sheriff arrived, he sold Shorter and sent her to Havana, Cuba.[36]

Every deposition became a crucial battleground. With Key as opposing counsel attempting to discredit every story about their claim to freedom, the enslaved families realized that they needed to shape their stories *as* the witnesses were being deposed. What happened in a deposition governed what could happen in trial. What was said or not said in a deposition affected what juries would hear or not hear. The questions each lawyer asked became more elaborate and specific, but free black witnesses who had already won their freedom in the general court sometimes ignored the questions, spun long answers to the initial queries, and filled their statements with descriptions of the Shorters' complex lineage. Henny Butler's rendering of the Shorter history in southern Maryland overflowed with specificity. It was a full genealogy of the family. In a powerful and memorable vignette, she explained that the one of the Shorter women "would always talk about her freedom" whenever someone made her mad.[37]

Most of the compelling evidence in the Shorter cases came from the testimony of free blacks who had previously won their freedom in the general court. William Hill's mother was a white woman who married an enslaved man, and Hill "served his time" and became free. A bricklayer by trade, Hill said that the Shorters "had as much right" to be free as he did because they were descended from a free woman. When he was called back for a third deposition, Hill was bombarded with fifteen highly specific questions from Philip Barton Key designed to trip up the Shorter witnesses and expose their claim as fraudulent. Sixty-seven years old, Hill responded to the first question, "Do you know the Parties, the Petitioner and the Defendant, and how long have you known them?" with an uninterrupted account of the family's history (presented here in the first person):

> I have seen Basil Shorter, and I have known the Defendant ever since I was a boy. When I was about twelve or thirteen years old, I knew a mulatto woman named Jenny Shorter who lived at Roswell Neale's on Clement's Bay in St. Mary's County. Jenny Shorter was a Flux Doctor, and she was frequently sent for. To attend the families of old Henry Wharton, Joshua Doyars, and Mr. Sligh when sick with the Flux. Jenny managed a Mill for Mr. Roswell Neale which was called Tomacokin Mill. Jenny Shorter had great liberty in going about, attending people sick with the Flux in the Neighbourhood.[38]

William Hill had masterfully highlighted Jenny's "great liberty," implying that the family's freedom had to have been acknowledged in the neighborhood. Pressed by Philip Barton Key, he was later forced to admit that he had "never heard" whether Jenny was free or entitled to her freedom and that he "never heard her claim her Freedom, nor any other person say that she claimed it." Key's line of questioning was meant to isolate the Shorters. If he could show that their claim to freedom was never public, he might be able to convince the jury that it was not true.

But the enslaved petitioners took control of the depositions in another way: they asked their own questions. Clement Shorter sued one of the most prominent slaveholders in Charles County, James Neale. Both Shorter and Neale were in the little courtroom in Port Tobacco when a white witness named John Lancaster was being deposed. Lancaster said that none of the Shorters ever said anything about their freedom until the Butler family began winning their freedom suits in the general court. At this point the slaveholder James Neale interrupted Lancaster, asking him a series of questions about one of Jenny Shorter's sisters. When Neale was finished, Clement Shorter spoke up.

"Do you know the mother of Patt?" Shorter asked.

"I do not," Lancaster replied.

The exchange was brief but significant. An enslaved man directly questioned a white witness, in the presence of the slaveholder, no less.

The Shorter family won more cases more quickly than any other family besides the Butlers: twenty-eight freedom suits in the General Court of the Western Shore in May and October 1795 and several more in the local county courts. Their success generated considerable opposition. Men like Lancaster refused to answer their questions. Some white witnesses said that the Shorters only made their claims after the Butlers won their freedom, that they invented the story about Elizabeth Shorter, that even their name was merely a description of their diminutive size rather than an inherited legacy from a free white woman. Among the strongest deniers of the Shorter claim was the Reverend Leonard Neale, a Jesuit priest whose brothers were also Jesuits—the Reverends Francis Neale and Charles Neale. He was forty-five years old when he was deposed, so his memory would have been fresh. Although other white witnesses including his uncle confirmed that Neale's father enslaved one of Jenny the Flux Doctor's daughters, Leonard Neale said he knew nothing about the family at all. "I have simply heard," he remarked, "that the Negroes under that denomination [Shorter] pretended to such a descent" and that their claims as a consequence were a "pretense," "perfectly groundless."[39]

Under Key's direction, the slaveholders in southern Maryland closed ranks. At the first word of a lawsuit, some sold and transported petitioners out of the reach of the courts in a concerted scheme to shut the petitions down. Free black witnesses like William Hill were brought back in for further questioning. White witnesses for the slaveholders stonewalled every claim. They insinuated that the enslaved families made up their claims after the Butlers won their freedom, and when prompted by the slaveholders' attorneys, they attacked the reputation of any white woman who gave the freedom claims credit if they were poor or of lower status.[40]

But Edward Queen's success in May 1794 strengthened the hand of the enslaved families. He won his freedom without any free black testimony. The white jurors in the general court handed down dozens of verdicts for the Shorters against the slaveholders. Unless new information came forward, the Queens would continue to win their lawsuits.

The "Poppaw Queen"

Edward Queen was a free man, but technically his mother, Phillis, and his siblings, nephews, and nieces were all still enslaved at White Marsh. Their individual petitions for freedom had been filed in the lower court in Prince George's County, where more than twenty Queen family cases were pending in 1794. Other members of the Queen family who had been taken to Harford County, north of Baltimore, heard about Edward's case. They enlisted William Pinkney as their counsel and filed their own petitions for freedom against another Jesuit priest. All of their cases awaited trial. Because Edward won his freedom in the higher general court, the descendants of Mary Queen, whether living at White Marsh or not, understandably considered themselves free.

The Queens at White Marsh did not wait for any further court decisions. They began leaving the plantation, some moving to Baltimore, others to plantations nearby, where they hired themselves out.

Meanwhile, Edward Queen, still represented by the duplicitous Philip Barton Key, filed another, even more surprising lawsuit against John Ashton, charging him with unlawful imprisonment and assault. It appears that Queen wanted damages for the time he should have been free, at minimum for the three and half years since the time he had filed his petition in October 1791. He brought the suit in Prince George's County Court before the local judges, and Ashton found himself ordered by the court to appear and answer whether he "did beat and evilly treat and imprison" Edward Queen. The language was standard in a civil charge of trespass, the only pleading that seemed to fit Queen's case, but it surely gave him some perverse satisfaction.

His civil suit may be one of the first attempts by an enslaved person in the United States to secure reparations for the time lost by his enslavement. The trespass charge against Ashton was a daring act of provocation. If Queen succeeded, others could seek similar damages for time they had been enslaved.[41]

Ashton responded by taking out a runaway slave ad in the *Maryland Gazette,* in what was the first and only public mention of the Queen family's quest for freedom. Ashton disparaged the runaways as "NEGROES, calling themselves Queens." Edward's cousin Simon Queen was listed first, then "Billy, Jack, Lewis, Isaac, Paul, Matthew, and Tom, very black negroes, and Tom, Billy, Nick, and Fanny, of a brown complexion." Ashton petulantly complained that they "quitted me for no other reason but because they were not set free at the last court." This was misleading at best. He knew that although the lower court had not yet ruled on the Queen cases, the higher general court had already decided in favor of Edward Queen. Ashton maintained that until the lower court ruled, he was within his rights to keep

Twelve Pounds Reward.

Prince-George's county, May 1, 1795.

ABSENTED themselves from my service since the late Prince-George's and Anne-Arundel county courts, the following twelve NEGROES, calling themselves QUEENS; *Simon, Billy, Jack, Lewis, Ifaa:, Paul, Matthew,* and *Tom,* very black negroes, and *Tom, Billy, Nick,* and *Fanny,* of a brown complexion; they are all young, hearty, and well made negroes, and quitted me for no other reason but because they were not set free at the last court. As I have recognised for the said negroes I conceive that I do not forfeit their services, nor lose any share of my authority over them, before trial; I do therefore promise the above reward to any person who will inform me where the aforesaid negroes may be found, and be witness against such persons as harbour or employ them, or TWENTY SHILLINGS for each one. I likewise forewarn all persons from harbouring or employing the said negroes at their peril, as I am determined to prosecute every such person agreeably to law.

JOHN ASHTON.

John Ashton advertisement for Queen family,
Maryland Gazette, May 7, 1795.

every Queen except Edward enslaved. "I conceive that I do not forfeit their services, nor lose any share of my authority over them." He offered a £12 reward for their capture and return.[42]

Within months Ashton found himself once again on the defensive, his relationship with his bishop uncertain, his reputation among the Jesuits weakened because the enslaved families at White Marsh were leaving the plantation. In January 1796, with all of the Queen freedom suits still pending, a disgruntled priest dredged up Ashton's alleged liaison with Susanna Queen and wrote an angry and accusatory letter to Bishop John Carroll. The accusing priest, the Reverend Dennis Cahill, lashed out at the entire Jesuit order in Maryland. Cahill saw himself as "a penniless stranger" from Ireland who despite his hard work was treated as an outsider and had never been given due consideration for his "labors at the Marsh." He thought that Carroll and his "junto," including Ashton, had confined him to "the dung cart" of unimportant assignments. Cahill considered it galling that he once asked to borrow several slaves from White Marsh and was rebuffed. Excluded from the benefits of Jesuit slaveholding, he was furious at Carroll. "You [kept] me out," he raged.[43]

Leaving White Marsh, nursing his wounded ambition, Cahill issued an extraordinary ultimatum to his bishop. He warned Carroll that rumors of Ashton's "tasty arrangmt. with his doll, Sucky," were spreading far and wide. Worse, he said that Ashton, perhaps after too much to drink, told him that Carroll had fathered two children "by a hussy" in Virginia and that the bishop had paid "hush money" to keep her quiet. According to Cahill, Ashton boasted that Carroll's "predicament" explained why Carroll threw "Cold Water" on the accusations about Susanna "Sucky" Queen. Cahill could not conceal his disgust with Carroll or Ashton. He sneered that he had left White Marsh because one of them might "name [him] a father for a mollato child." Without a hint of subtlety Cahill then demanded £300 in "reparation" from Carroll in exchange for him to "remain silent" on the whole matter. The offer was nothing short of blackmail.[44]

A few months later Cahill wrote Carroll again because Carroll had not responded. He accused Carroll of attempting to destroy his character. Weeks and months passed, and still Carroll did not reply.[45]

When Carroll finally responded, he was pointedly restrained. He wrote that "an almost invincible reluctance to push matters to an extremity" had delayed his response. "If . . . the nature of the offence really required it, you would see your letters in their true light and offer an apology for them," Carroll reprimanded the priest. With no apology forthcoming, Carroll informed Cahill that he would file formal charges against him under canon law for having "falsely reproached" his bishop (Carroll), for spreading "infamous imputations on the Bishop's character," for traducing his position "in an outrageous manner," and for attempting to coerce Carroll into purchasing his silence by way of "a large sum of money."[46]

The salacious accusations against the Jesuits remained shrouded in canon law, where they might never see the light of day, but the verdict in Edward Queen's freedom trial and his subsequent civil suit against Ashton created vulnerabilities that were much more public. With more than twenty pending freedom suits led by Edward's mother, Phillis, in the Prince George's County Court, the confidential affairs of the Jesuit slaveholders might come out into the open. The lower courts were supposed to be more favorable to the slaveholders. That was why, after all, the Maryland legislature removed the freedom suits from the general court and gave the local county courts original jurisdiction over them.

In April 1796 the Prince George's County Court finally heard Phillis Queen's freedom suit. The judge of the local court was Thomas Duckett, the son of Richard Duckett Jr., and one of the principal slaveholders in the area, whose properties bordered White Marsh. He was a planter, not a professional lawyer, appointed to the judiciary by the governor. Duckett could be reliably counted on to represent the slaveholding class. Moreover, the jury included some of the largest slaveholders in the state. Five of the twelve jurors enslaved more than thirty people apiece. Just one juror was a nonslaveholder, while another of the jurors, Samuel Judson Coolidge, was the son of a merchant captain who imported slaves. Undoubtedly, the legislators who voted to move freedom suits from the general court to the local courts would have been pleased. In Prince George's County the Queens faced a legal system run almost exclusively by slaveholders.[47]

In the years since Edward Queen's trial in the general court, Ashton's lawyers had looked for more witnesses to discredit the stories about Mary Queen. Philip Barton Key used this tactic against the Shorters, and Ashton's lawyers followed it, too. They found one of the few witnesses in Prince George's County to have met and spoken with Mary Queen personally. Surprisingly, he was Benjamin Duvall, Gabriel Duvall's eighty-three-year-old great-uncle. He testified that Mary Queen came from Africa, not New Spain. He called her a "Poppaw Queen," a "Queen in her own country," who wore beads on her arms. Her hair was twisted around, and "when dressed near a yard long and on the top she had a knot of beads." She was James Carroll's slave, he said, and "always treated by her Master as a Slave." In vivid detail Duvall noted that she spoke English "in a broken manner"; that she lost two brothers on the Middle Passage who were thrown overboard to the sharks; and that she and her sister survived the ordeal only because they were "allowed to be on deck and washing for the sailors," a euphemism for sexual assault. Duvall claimed they were from the Popo region of the Gold Coast, but he also admitted that Mary's complexion was "very yellow." Duvall may have confused Mary Queen with another woman. No one else remembered her hair and the beads, nor did anyone else recall such a distinctive accent.[48]

Because Benjamin Duvall lived next to White Marsh, and because he had met and remembered Mary Queen, his testimony carried considerable weight. He claimed that he was "frequently at Fingaul" and never heard James Carroll or anyone else say Mary Queen should have been free. He recalled that Mary had a son named Ralph with Thomas Barm, the white overseer at Fingaul, "who kept her as a Mistress." Duvall offered another important detail: it was James Carroll who "commonly called her his

Poppaw Queen." Duvall's story crafted an alternative history of Mary Queen as an African and therefore unmistakably as a slave.

His account fit neatly within the prevailing experience of eighteenth-century Maryland, when thousands of enslaved Africans were brought into the colony, including via a well-known voyage in 1717 financed in part by James Carroll. Carroll had helped commission a slave ship, the *Margaret,* built in London and outfitted for the slave trade on the West African coast. The *Margaret* sailed to Sierra Leone, where its captain traded rum, guns, tobacco, and textiles for 136 enslaved people, packed them in the hold, and set off for Annapolis. Thirty-one died in the Middle Passage, a devastating mortality rate of 23 percent. Each of the 105 people who survived would have known people who died on the voyage. Seventy percent of those on board the *Margaret* were men, but there were at least 13 adult women. Once the *Margaret* arrived in Annapolis, James Carroll personally handled the sales of the enslaved Africans to local planters, and he purchased some of the enslaved people for himself. Because the story of the *Margaret* was so widely known in the Carroll family and subsequently among their neighbors, it was not surprising that Benjamin Duvall remembered Mary the "Poppaw Queen" as an African.[49]

Yet the county court, dominated by slaveholders, came to a surprising verdict.

Judge Thomas Duckett allowed all manner of evidence, including hearsay, into his courtroom, perhaps because he was untrained in the law or perhaps because the general court under Samuel Chase had done so in every freedom suit to that point. The jurors in Duckett's court therefore heard the testimony of those who said Mary Queen was a free woman from New Spain, the same depositions Edward Queen used. All of them were full of hearsay. And they ignored Benjamin Duvall, whose account of Mary Queen as an African from the Popo region did not align with the details provided by other witnesses. The all-white, slaveholding jury gave greater weight to the testimony of the Queen witnesses, followed the ruling of the general court in Edward's case, and rendered a verdict in favor of freedom for Phillis Queen. The decision made sense. A higher court determined Edward Queen was free, so surely his mother, Phillis, should be also. Since Edward's grandmother Mary Queen was "not a slave," surely her daughter could not be a slave either.

Like dominoes, all twenty remaining Queen cases in Prince George's County fell the family's way. Edward's sister Susanna and her daughter were declared free. Then his twin brothers, Gervais and Proteus. Then the children of Nanny Cooper. Simon Queen. Mary Queen and her children. Then Phillis's and Nanny's grandchildren. Charity Queen and her son. Sucky Queen and her daughter. All of the Queens who had ever filed a freedom suit in Prince George's County were free. Nine of the twenty lawsuits freed an untold number of children and grandchildren, making the total count of people freed in April 1796 possibly upward of fifty or more. It was one of the largest single court-ordered emancipations in Maryland's history.[50]

The trials cost John Ashton and the Jesuits 6,795 pounds of tobacco in damages, court costs, and fees. A large sum by any measure, the amount was as much as White Marsh plantation produced in tobacco in a single year. The Queen family members freed in April 1796 represented more than a quarter of the people the Jesuits enslaved at White Marsh: twenty-four men, women, and children along with numerous others not named. Their immediate freedom constituted one of the largest single financial losses in the annals of the Jesuit corporation.[51]

And more Queen family members had suits pending in other counties along the Western Shore. Just a few months later, in August 1796, Nancy Queen's case went to trial against the Reverend Charles Sewall, one of the Jesuits who had attended the meeting at White Marsh in May 1789. Sewall's attorneys brought in the deposition of Benjamin Duvall, and the jury in Charles County gave it much greater weight and credit than did the jury in Prince George's. Persuaded that Mary Queen was an African slave from the Popo region of the Gold Coast, they ruled against Nancy's freedom. In the wake of the verdict against Nancy Queen, most of the other cases were dropped or dismissed. Until new evidence could be found, the Queen family faced an insurmountable roadblock: Benjamin Duvall's vibrant, exhaustive, and specific firsthand testimony was a story that white jurors were strongly inclined to find credible.[52]

It is curious that Benjamin Duvall's deposition was taken just one month after Philip Barton Key accepted the Jesuits' retainer. The timing raises questions about how and why Benjamin Duvall was not identified for deposition by either side in the three and half years of discovery for Edward Queen's case but was suddenly discovered in September 1794 in preparation for Phillis's case. Clearly, Edward's attorneys led by Gabriel Duvall would have avoided deposing Benjamin Duvall, knowing what he was likely to say. In 1794 one of the Jesuit's lawyers in Phillis Queen's case was Allen Bowie Duckett, the nineteen-year-old son of Thomas Duckett, the judge of the Prince George's County District Court, where Phillis's freedom suit would go to trial. A recent graduate of Princeton who was freshly admitted to the bar, Duckett grew up a stone's throw from White Marsh, next door to the Duvalls, and he may have identified Benjamin Duvall for the Jesuits. Or it is possible that Philip Barton Key hinted to the Jesuits that Benjamin Duvall should be deposed. The deposition was entered in the court record on September 23, 1795, a year after Key was retained by the Jesuits to stop the freedom suits.

Five months later, in February 1796, however, Gabriel Duvall deposed a witness on the Eastern Shore who claimed to have met Mary Queen and spoken with her before she died. Fredus Ryland's testimony included Mary Queen's own words and would potentially counter Benjamin Duvall's tale of the "Poppaw Queen."

It is implausible that Key did not know about Ryland's deposition, and yet Ryland's deposition was never introduced in Phillis Queen's freedom suit. Perhaps Philip Barton Key did not consider the deposition necessary. Perhaps he did not consider it admissible. Perhaps he never received it from Duvall, who went on the general court bench that month. After all, it was one of Duvall's last depositions as an attorney for the Queens. But a more disturbing inference can be drawn. It is possible that Philip Barton Key, retained by the Jesuits even as he represented the Queens, chose to disregard the Ryland deposition.

Duvall, however, did not ignore it. He entered Ryland's explosive deposition in two cases being heard in 1796 alongside Phillis Queen's. Both were pending in the Anne Arundel lower court. One was titled *Charles Queen v. John Ashton.* A jury probably never heard the case. Charles, like the other Queens, appears to have been freed after the verdict in Phillis Queen's trial.[53]

The Ryland deposition offered the strongest proof yet obtained that Mary Queen came from London and was a free woman. But Ryland's testimony was never introduced as evidence in a Maryland court or shown to a jury. It remained on file in the Anne Arundel courthouse and presumably in Gabriel Duvall's law office. Would a jury ever hear it?

Two days after Edward Queen's mother, Phillis, won her freedom, Queen's brazen suit against John Ashton for false imprisonment went to trial in Judge Duckett's court in Prince George's County. Both sides tried to persuade the judges to issue jury instructions in their favor. Queen argued that the suit was proper, that a trespass charge could be sustained against a slaveholder who robbed a man of years of his working life. Ashton argued that the premise of the trespass charge was specious, that slaveholders could not be held accountable for enslaving people regardless of the circumstances. Judges David Crawford and Thomas Duckett, however, offered the jury no instructions about whether such a suit was proper. With little guidance, the jury ruled in favor of Ashton and ordered Edward Queen to pay the slave-holding priest 433 pounds of tobacco for "false clamour" and to cover attorney's fees (200 pounds of tobacco each), clerk's fees, court costs, and charges Ashton bore in defending himself.[54]

We can gauge something of the force of Edward Queen's character in these actions. His attorney, Philip Barton Key, would not have relished bringing the trespass and unlawful imprisonment charges against Ashton. Key had already agreed to represent the Jesuits going forward and was working behind the scenes on Ashton's defense team against Charles Mahoney. He may have sabotaged Nancy Queen's freedom suit in Charles County. All the while, Edward Queen probably knew about the secret arrangement Key had with the Jesuits.

Determined to fight Ashton to the end, though, Queen filed an appeal in the General Court of the Western Shore arguing that the justices should have instructed the jury that the suit was "proper" as a matter of law for recovering damages for being held as slave. Queen may have believed that the jury ruled against him because, not otherwise instructed, it was allowed to consider the suit improper. What would happen, jurors probably wondered, if plaintiffs who won their freedom were able to recover civil damages for the time they were enslaved?[55]

After the Queen family won its series of cases in both the general court and the Prince George's County Court, the Maryland Assembly updated the code on slavery and clamped down on petitions for freedom yet again. The major changes concerned the laws related to manumission and had been in the works following William Pinkney's speech advocating for a more liberal policy. Ever since 1752, no Maryland slaveholder had been legally able to free slaves through a last will and testament. Manumission by a deed, however, was lawful for those enslaved persons under the age of fifty and in good health. In 1796 the legislature moved to allow manumission by last will and testament but to restrict all manumission to individuals under the age of forty-five who were in good health and able to work to support themselves. With the opening of a new avenue of freedom through last will and testament, the act had immediate and dramatic effects as the enslaved persons bargained for their families and slaveholders rewrote wills.[56]

Ostensibly to cut down on frivolous claims, the 1796 act required that the plaintiff's attorneys had to pay the court costs if a petition for freedom were dismissed, unless the judges found "probable cause" for the case. As a result, enslaved petitioners and their lawyers would presumably think twice before filing a lawsuit. No one manumitted under the act was entitled to vote in elections, serve on juries, give evidence against any white person, or give evidence in freedom suits.[57]

The neighboring Commonwealth of Virginia also hardened its laws regarding freedom suits. Beginning in 1795, enslaved Virginian petitioners could no longer choose their own attorneys. The court would appoint counsel, who would serve without "fee or reward" of any kind. Virginia imposed a $100 fine on anyone who aided an unsuccessful petition and barred abolitionists from sitting on juries in freedom suits.[58]

Charles Mahoney's petition against John Ashton was still pending. His, too, had been filed before the 1793 act and therefore like Edward Queen's would be tried in the General Court of the Western Shore in Annapolis. After the Queen verdicts, the Mahoneys had good reason to expect a decision in their favor.

Edward Queen, like his mother and siblings, left Prince George's County and may have moved across the river to Anne Arundel County. From there he probably moved north, closer to Baltimore. He continued to press his civil suit against John Ashton, claiming damages for his years of imprisonment as a slave. The appeal was never heard. Forty-four years old, Edward Queen died on February 23, 1798. The following day he was buried at St. Peter's Pro-Cathedral in Baltimore, the seat of the diocese, a church where Ashton had performed the first mass.

Queen had been a free man for barely four years.[59]

The Nine Ninety-Nine

Any investigation into slavery in the United States usually begins with the interviews of men and women formerly enslaved, taken during the New Deal by the Federal Writers' Project. In Maryland there were twenty-two such interviewees. Just two were born in Prince George's County.

Dennis Simms described a system of enslavement on the Contee plantation, his birthplace, that was as brutal, capricious, and repressive as any farther south. "When we behaved, we were not whipped, but the overseer kept a pretty close eye on us," Simms recalled. The overseers watched their every move. If caught out of their cabins after dark, "we would be unmercifully whipped." They were never allowed to congregate after work, "never went to church," and were never taught to read or write. Simms said he "thought of running off to Canada or to Washington but feared the patrollers."[1]

Simms spoke of a particularly, horrifyingly cruel punishment in Maryland reserved for disobedient or defiant enslaved persons. "We all hated what we called 'nine ninety-nine,'" he recalled. "Usually a flogging until [the victim] fell over unconscious or begged for mercy." The term "nine ninety-nine" does not appear in any other slave narratives in the United States, but in Prince George's County the colloquialism was widely used and well understood by the enslaved families who lived there. "Parson" Rezin Williams, a free man born in Prince George's who became one of the best-known preachers in the nineteenth century, described the nine ninety-nine as a whipping until unconscious. "Some cruel masters believed that Negroes had no souls," he observed by way of explanation.

The very fact that a term existed for such a punishment and that no historians had ever mentioned it stopped me in my tracks as I read the narratives of former slaves from Prince George's County.

How was it possible that I had never heard of this?

The "nine ninety-nine"?

Could it be ninety-nine lashes with a cat o' nine tails?

What's more, reading Dennis Simms's account of the nine ninety-nine, I experienced a sinking and sickening glimmer of recognition. There was something about the Contee family. Like a lighthouse beacon in the night, the afterglow lit up my memory long after the sweep of its beam. Simms said he was born on the plantation of Charles Contee. My records confirmed my suspicions. The Contees married into the Duckett family, and Charles Contee inherited the Duckett plantation Pleasant Prospect. It dawned on me that Dennis Simms was born at Pleasant Prospect in Prince George's County on June 17, 1841.

He had endured the nine ninety-nine there, on Duckett ground.

Rezin Williams was the only other man interviewed from Prince George's County. I found that he, too, had been born on a Duckett plantation— Fairview. His father, a free man born in Prince George's Country, worked for George Washington at Mt. Vernon as a hostler, and his mother was descended from a Native American woman. Williams was freeborn and hired himself out to the Ducketts and their successors. Interviewed in 1937, when he was 116 years old, Williams broke into a spiritual he had written at Fairview on the eve of the Civil War:

> I'm now embarked for yonder shore
> There a man's a man by law;
> The iron horse will bear me o'er
> To shake de lion's paw.
> Oh, righteous Father, will thou not pity me
> And aid me on to Canada, where all the slaves are free.

Williams told his white interviewer a parable about his own awakening to slavery's many levels of deception. As a young man, Williams said, he sometimes accompanied the Ducketts to the Baltimore slave market because he thought they considered him "a good judge of slaves." Perhaps they had said these exact words to him many times. On one occasion, ordered to walk ahead of the coffle through the city, Williams led the enslaved through "a dark and dirty tunnel" into the market pen, "where they were placed on the auction block." Williams was ashamed to discover that he was no more than a "decoy." Only then did he realize that no one would ever ask for his assessment of the character or quality of the enslaved, that his presence had no purpose other than to deceive the thirty or forty men, women, and children who were about to be sold. Worse, he was told "to sort of pacify the black women who set up a wail when they were separated from their husbands and children. It was a pitiful sight to see them, half naked, some whipped into submission, cast into slave pens surmounted by iron bars."

Was his self-deprecating tale a subversive message to whites who were blind to the central deceit of slavery—that it hid the complicity of free people as easily as it laid bare the subjugation of the enslaved? That anyone could become a decoy unknowingly? That enslavers attempted to manipulate the self-worth of everyone they encountered?[2]

Williams's experience was more common across the Chesapeake plantations than is generally recognized. Torture and cruelty were the prevailing techniques of enslavement in the early United States. The deception, treachery, and violence of enslavement respected no boundaries. State law gave enslavers all the sanction necessary to punish enslaved men, women, and children by any means up to and including death. On one plantation in Charles County, one enslaved woman struck back when the mistress "slapped her." She was sold and taken south. "We never saw or heard of her afterwards," her nephew explained. Another ex-slave named Silas Jackson recalled, "I have seen men beaten until they dropped in their tracks or knocked over by clubs, women stripped down to their waist[s] and cowhided." What he did not see, what was hidden from view, was equally terrifying. Jackson never personally saw a slave sold.

Instead, he witnessed them taken away in chains. What happened to them, how they had been sold, what fate awaited them, were questions unanswered. Every New Year's Day, he and others feared that they might be next, taken without notice, and disappeared into the slave trade. Like many other plantations, the place where he was born, a nine-thousand-acre plantation, had a jail, a stone building with iron bars, where "the whipping was done." Enslaved workers were "driven at top speed and whipped at the snap of the finger by the overseers." One night, the master crept down to the cabins and overheard a secret prayer meeting. A man named Zeek stood before the group and fervently asked God to "change the heart of his master and deliver him from slavery." Within twenty-four hours Zeek had "disappeared, no one ever seeing him again." Rumors circulated that Zeek's prayer could be heard for years after his death "down in the swamp at certain times of the moon." Years later, Jackson heard that the master confessed on his death-bed to killing Zeek and was convinced he would go to hell for the murder.[3]

Offering a prayer for freedom could get a man killed in the night or disappeared and sold south. Ex-slave Mary James had only a "faint recol-lection" of her grandparents because her grandfather was sold to the rice plantations in South Carolina and her grandmother "drowned herself in the river when she heard that [G]rand-[P]ap was going away." She found out that her grandfather was sold because he "got religious" and said God would set the enslaved free.[4]

Incidents of staggering cruelty were routine in Maryland. Josiah Henson, born in 1789 in Charles County near Port Tobacco, experienced the depravity of slavery before he was old enough to comprehend its full implications. He recalled that one of his earliest memories was seeing his father come home one day, bleeding from one hundred lashes and missing his right ear. Henson was three years old. The sight of his father in this con-dition proved unforgettable:

> He was beside himself with mingled rage and suffering. The ex-planation I picked up from the conversation of others only par-tially explained the matter to my mind; but as I grew older I understood it all. It seemed the overseer had sent my mother away from the other field hands to a retired place, and after trying per-suasion in vain, had resorted to force to accomplish a brutal purpose. Her screams aroused my father at his distant work, and running up, he found his wife struggling with the man. Furious at the sight, he sprung upon him like a tiger. In a moment the overseer was down, and, mastered by rage, my father would have killed him but for the entreaties of my mother, and the overseer's own promise that nothing should ever be said of the matter. The promise was kept—like most promises of the cowardly and debased—as long as the danger lasted.[5]

After his brutal punishment, Henson's father was "utterly changed." He had been a jovial, banjo-playing "ringleader," a "good-humoured and light-hearted man." He was a man "of amiable temper and of considerable energy of character." But after "such cruelty and injustice under the sanc-tion of law," he turned inward, and "the milk of human kindness in his heart was turned to gall." Morose, sullen, insolent, and disobedient, his father was sold to the cotton frontier in Alabama. "Furious at such treatment," Henson recalled, "my father became a different man." Neither Henson nor his mother ever heard from him again. Within a few years Henson—age five or six—was put on the auction block, sold, and separated from his mother.

Josiah Henson remembered the sale this way: "The crowd collected round the stand, the huddling group of negroes, the examination of muscle, teeth, the exhibition of agility, the look of the auctioneer, the agony of my mother—I can shut my eyes and see them all."[6]

Free and enslaved blacks could see that slaveholders would not hesitate to use the slave trade to control the enslaved. Born on the Eastern Shore of Maryland, Frederick Douglass was separated from his mother before his first birthday. He recalled, "Frequently, before the child has reached its twelfth month, its mother is taken from it, and hired out on some farm a considerable distance off, and the child is placed under the care of an old woman, too old for field labor." When Douglass's mother could, she traveled twelve miles on foot each way to see him at night. She had to be back before sunrise. Douglass could not remember ever seeing his mother "by the light of day."[7]

We should have no illusions. The families of Prince George's County faced the full spectrum of slaving's merciless techniques—uprooting, forced migration, isolation, violence, and deception. At the dawn of the nineteenth century, enslavers did not need a court of law in Maryland to sanction the nine ninety-nine. They could act as jury, judge, and jailor on their plantations, where law placed few discernible limits on their power and authority.

CHAPTER 3

Charles Mahoney Is a Free Man

Slavery is incompatible with every principle of religion and
morality. It is unnatural, and contrary to the maxims of political
law more especially in this country, where "we hold these truths to
be self-evident, that all men are created equal."

—RICHARD RIDGELY, ATTORNEY
FOR CHARLES MAHONEY, MAY 1799

On May 25, 1792, the grandson of Ann Joice walked into the Prince George's
County courthouse in Upper Marlboro and gave a riveting account of his
family's claim to freedom. Seventy-seven years old and a free man, Peter Harbard swore out his deposition in front of Charles Mahoney, Gabriel Duvall,
and the justice of the peace. Free blacks had testified in the Butler freedom
suits. But they were descended from a white woman. This was different. Ann
Joice was a black woman who claimed she was free because she had been in
England, where slavery was unlawful. White witnesses up to that moment,
one after another, had discredited her story. As Charles Mahoney listened
to his great-uncle, he must have realized that Peter Harbard's testimony
would utterly recast the story of Ann Joice and her claim to freedom.[1]

Harbard had been born in 1719. Enslaved at the Woodyard when Colonel Henry Darnall owned the plantation, he lived there until he was twenty-

two. There can be little doubt that Harbard was present at the Woodyard in 1770 when his uncles killed the overseer in a bid for freedom and were tried and publicly executed. At some point, probably after 1770, Harbard managed to purchase his freedom from Stephen West, a prominent merchant who bought the Woodyard.

Harbard's account contained an unexpected and shocking revelation, one that would likely sway jurors from modest backgrounds. He said that Ann Joice, his grandmother, was a "dark mulatto woman" and that he frequently heard her say that she came into Maryland as "an Indentured Servant for four years." Harbard explained that Lord Baltimore sold Joice's indenture to Henry Darnall, and she served the Darnall family at the Woodyard as a cook. When her term of servitude expired, however, Darnall "burnt her indentures" and sent her out of the county to Benjamin Hall's plantation, "where she was kept in a kitchen celler for five or six months."[2]

At this moment, Charles Mahoney must have felt a flood of emotions: relief that a great silence had been breached, indignation at Ann Joice's extralegal imprisonment, anger at the injustice his family bore, appreciation for his great-uncle's equanimity, and renewed determination to press ahead. Harbard pointed out that he personally heard his grandmother Ann Joice say that "if she had her just right that she ought to be free and all her children." Because depositions were taken in the third person, we might turn his statement into its more likely original construction: "My grandmother Nanny Joice said, 'If I had my just right, I ought to be free and all my children.'"[3]

The statement was powerful and direct. Even though it was hearsay, the courts had allowed similar statements in the Butler and Queen cases. The words of Ann Joice, if the jury were allowed to hear them, would be hard to ignore. Sensing that the family lore about Ann Joice's time in England had merit, Gabriel Duvall requested in October 1793 that the court authorize a special commission in London to gather any relevant documents about Ann Joice and her indenture to Lord Baltimore. It took more than three years for the commission to reply.

Charles Mahoney and his brothers Daniel and Patrick had sued the Reverend John Ashton in October 1791 just days after Edward Queen. And like the Queens, members of the Mahoney family had been enslaved by the Darnalls and the Carrolls and dispersed across Maryland. Although Edward Queen and Charles Mahoney shared Ashton as the object of their lawsuits, and although they petitioned the courts nearly simultaneously, their cases could not have been more different. In less than four years, Edward Queen gained his freedom in the courts and more than twenty close relatives followed, but for Charles Mahoney the trials would take more than a decade and would not resolve so clearly the question of his family's freedom.

We know little about what Charles Mahoney looked like or how he carried himself. The court records indicate that he attended several depositions rather than leave them to his lawyers. One of the witnesses described the sons of Ann Joice, including Charles's great-uncles, as "the strongest men he ever knew to come from one woman." Light-skinned and powerful, they worked as carpenters and skilled craftsmen at the Woodyard, one of the largest and earliest plantations in colonial Maryland. Charles probably inherited these qualities and may have carried the same of air of determination. Later he would be described as "yellow" in complexion and five feet, six inches in height. Although he could neither read nor write—he signed all of his court documents with an "X"—he spoke with authority and grace in later legal records.[4]

In its length and complexity, *Mahoney v. Ashton* was like almost no other petition for freedom in American history. The proceedings spanned the decade of the 1790s. Nineteen depositions were filed, and at least eight witnesses took the stand. The Maryland General Court dispatched a commission to London to gather evidence. Three years transpired before the commission reported back, so much time that Mahoney's lead counsel, Gabriel Duvall, had been appointed a judge on the general court that would hear the case. He recused himself. There were three jury trials and two appeals. Eventually, ten prominent attorneys were involved, as both sides pulled in advocates from powerful families and enlisted supporters with political weight. In a final, desperate attempt to secure a verdict in their favor, Ashton's attorneys appear to have manufactured evidence favorable to their version of events. White planters all over the state observed these affairs, knowing that more than fifteen hundred descendants of Ann Joice, all relatives of Charles Mahoney, stood to gain their freedom if he and his brothers won. The political and financial stakes in *Mahoney v. Ashton* were dizzying.

When individually held to account, slaveholders responded with immediate countermoves to blunt the freedom suits. And as these cases wound their way through the Maryland courts, a more collective, if desultory, response developed from the slaveholding class. The slaveholders told themselves that no individual case would undo all of American slavery. But black petitioners thought differently because each case for them could become a transcendent moment in the cause of liberty. Each case advanced freedom on the ground. Each opened up spaces of freedom deep inside American slavery. Gradually, the true nature of the freedom suits dawned on the slaveholders. When black petitioners began filing a staggering number of suits, proslavery lawmakers attempted to put a chokehold on freedom in the courts. The slaveholders found out they were locked in a momentous struggle on terrain they assumed favored them.

Mahoney v. Ashton constituted a much broader legal challenge to the institution of slavery in Maryland than slaveholders at first realized. The Mahoneys set out to prove that Ann Joice was a free woman because she had been in England in the 1680s. As such, their lawyer, Gabriel Duvall, thought that the *Somerset* principle might apply. If it did, and Ann Joice was considered free, the ruling in Charles Mahoney's case might establish a precedent for *Somerset* in the Maryland courts. Two points assumed paramount significance: first, that she was a black indentured servant from Barbados who spent time in England before coming to the colony; and second, that she was entitled to her freedom after her indenture but was enslaved because of her color. Gabriel Duvall was joined by his fellow lawyers Jonathan Roberts Wilmer, John Johnson, Thomas Jenings, and Richard Ridgely, well-connected, slaveholding, Jeffersonian Democratic-Republicans. Despite their slaveholding, these Republicans celebrated individual liberty with a degree of enthusiasm that led them to question hereditary enslavement, especially for individuals with legitimate claims to freedom. The Mahoney case gave them an opportunity to demonstrate their fidelity to liberty and at the same time confer some legitimacy to slaveholding by setting legal boundaries around slavery—as inapplicable to certain people and conditions, as a vestige of imperial policy that would eventually, somehow, be ended. For the Mahoneys, it seemed as if the ideals of the American Revolution and the political realignment in Maryland might do much more than secure their own family's freedom.

On the other side, the dyspeptic Reverend Ashton accumulated an all-star cast of attorneys led by Philip Barton Key, all prominent Federalists intent on safeguarding the right of property who saw themselves as protectors of the natural order of society. More than anything, these conservatives were in the tradition of Edmund Burke, the English statesman who opposed the French Revolution. They feared a messy unraveling of slavery or, worse, a social revolution that might accompany emancipation. They saw slavery as natural and sanctioned throughout history. They rallied behind a series of English court cases in the seventeenth century that treated black slaves as property under common law in disputes over debts. And they took a dim view of the *Somerset* decision, straining to give it the narrowest interpretation they could.

But Ashton's vulnerability as a defendant jeopardized all the slaveholders ever associated with the Jesuits, including the most prominent conservative in the state, Charles Carroll of Carrollton. Leader of the Maryland Senate, signer of the Declaration of Independence, Carroll held more than 60 Joice descendants in bondage. In 1790 he enslaved 365 people. Carroll once referred to the Reverend Ashton as "a silly, peevish, disagreeable man," but when Charles Mahoney sued Ashton for his freedom, the aristocratic senator and the irascible priest shared a common predicament: together they faced the unattractive prospect of freeing hundreds of people they preferred to keep enslaved.[5]

Others also stood to lose a fortune if the courts determined that the Mahoney claim to freedom was valid. Simultaneous with the Mahoney lawsuit, Eleanor Joice brought a case against Notley Young in the local court in Prince George's County. Like Carroll, Young was among the wealthiest planters in Maryland, with 265 people he enslaved on plantations throughout Prince George's County. Eleanor Joice summoned fourteen witnesses, including members of the Carroll, Darnall, and West families. All three white families had deep connections to the Woodyard, where Ann Joice was first enslaved and where her children were born and raised. Gabriel Duvall's cousin was Eleanor Joice's attorney, and her case was not the only one under way at the county level. Jack Joice, Catherine Joice, Thomas Joice, and Michael Joice all sued for their freedom at the same time.

A consistent string of victories for enslaved families in the general court and in the Prince George's County Court made these questions especially pressing. The verdicts in favor of freedom for the Butlers and the Queens extended the idea of freedom under the common law much further than conservative, aristocratic gentry families were willing to tolerate. And freedom opened the possibility of citizenship for African Americans in Maryland just as political parties were beginning to take shape. In *Mahoney v. Ashton*, the loose alignments of Federalists and Jeffersonian Republicans collided and became more cohesive. *Mahoney v. Ashton* became a political contest over whether slavery could be reconciled with the ideals of the law and the Revolution. More than any other freedom suit, this one had the potential to become an American *Somerset*.[6]

"She May Have Never Set Her Foot in England"

Mahoney v. Ashton finally came to trial in October 1797 before a jury that would have to weigh the contradictory histories of Ann Joice. The parties had both stipulated that Charles, Daniel, and Patrick Mahoney were in fact descended matrilineally from a woman named Ann Joice who had lived at the Woodyard. These facts were beyond dispute. So the case turned in essence on whether Ann Joice was a free woman and, if she were, exactly how she had become free.

At first the justices of the Maryland court seemed to follow the logic of Duvall's *Somerset* strategy. They restricted the jury to an exceedingly narrow question: Was Ann Joice ever in England? Yes or no?

If yes, then the court could apply the *Somerset* principle and decide that Ann Joice was a free woman.

If no, then the *Somerset* principle was irrelevant and Joice likely a slave because of her color.

Framed this way, Charles Mahoney possessed a substantial advantage.

Because the general court's jurors were drawn from eleven counties stretching from Baltimore to Annapolis and west to the mountains, there was a real possibility to shape the jury and mitigate the number of jurors friendly to slaveholding. Jurors came from places such as Frederick County, where German immigrants settled and actively avoided slaveholding. Parts of Anne Arundel County held a growing contingent of Quakers, who were manumitting all enslaved people they held. In Baltimore and Harford County, near Pennsylvania, smaller farmers and urban dwellers might lean in favor of freedom in petition-for-freedom cases. Eight of the first twelve jurors were eliminated. Eight more names were called, and four of these were struck. Then five more jurors were called, and four of them were struck. Three called and two struck. Two called and one struck. The process took several more rounds. The final jury in October 1797 was made up almost entirely of slaveholders who held fewer than five slaves. Only one held more than twenty slaves.

But after hearing the evidence, the jury issued a special verdict that satisfied no one. They determined that Ann Joice was a "black woman" who lived as a slave at Henry Darnall's plantation the Woodyard, but they did not find any evidence that she or her children ever claimed that they were entitled to their freedom. The jury determined, furthermore, that Ann Joice came into Maryland with Lord Baltimore "from England." As if to confuse all parties, the special verdict concluded, "If . . . the court shall be of opinion that the Petitioner's entitled to freedom then the Jurors aforesaid find the issue in this cause for the Petitioner but if the court upon the matter aforesaid shall be of opinion that the Petitioner is not entitled to freedom then the Jurors aforesaid find the issue aforesaid for the Defendant."[7]

The verdict settled nothing. Jurors issued special verdicts like this to protect themselves from being prosecuted later for an erroneous verdict. Even if the law pointed in different directions, juries could be held responsible if their findings were grossly wrong, so they often issued verdicts confined to specific facts and put the responsibility for the final interpretation of the law back on the judges. In the 1780s and 1790s special verdicts proliferated in American courtrooms. Some judges considered the men called for jury duty incompetent, unqualified, and possibly biased, often motivated merely by the per diem payment for serving on a jury and unequipped to decide complicated legal questions. Judges increasingly assumed responsibility for especially complex trials. They examined witnesses, interrupted attorneys, pronounced verdicts, and directed juries with ever more narrow instructions to establish facts, all the while reserving the power of judgment on matters of law. In *Mahoney v. Ashton* the justices had attempted to steer the jury to a verdict on the facts that would isolate the legal question they desired to answer for themselves: Did the common law of England and Lord Mansfield's antislavery decision in *Somerset v. Stewart* apply to anyone in Maryland?[8]

So the question before the court, it appeared, was whether Ann Joice's coming from England proved her status as a free woman. A jury instruction one way or the other would determine the outcome. If the court decided that her presence in England conferred freedom, on the basis of English law and precedent, then the justices could instruct the jury to find for the Mahoneys. If, on the other hand, the court determined that English law and precedent were insufficient to confer freedom, then the jury would have to find in favor of Ashton. The judges postponed the argument for a year while both sides combed through old depositions, looked for new witnesses, and searched for precedents in English law that would define Ann Joice's status.

At some point after the 1797 special verdict, Charles Mahoney and his brother Patrick left White Marsh and decided to live as free men. John Ashton did little to retrieve the Mahoneys or keep them at White Marsh other than place a single runaway advertisement in the *Maryland Gazette* in January 1798. He offered a $16 reward for the return of "two mulatto fellows called Charles and Patrick Mahoney." Ashton sneered that they "pretend that they are set free by the verdict of a jury in the last general court." The court had ordered them to remain in service at "home" until the judges ruled on the special verdict, but according to Ashton, "This they refuse to do."[9]

Meanwhile, Charles Mahoney retained two of the best lawyers in Maryland to argue his case, John Johnson and Richard Ridgely. At twenty-

Sixteen Dollars Reward.

RAN away from the fubfcriber, living in Prince-George's county, two mulatto fellows called CHARLES and PATRICK MAHONEY; they have been away about three weeks; they pretend that they are fet free by the verdict of a jury in the laft general court, but were ordered by the court to return home till a point of law fhould be fettled relating to their cafe; this they refufe to do. As they are well known in and about Annapolis and the foreft of Prince George's, where I fufpect they muft be, I do hereby forewarn all perfons from harbouring or employing them, and will give any perfon EIGHT DOLLARS reward for fecuring either of them in gaol.   ⅜ w
    January 8, 1798.   JOHN ASHTON.

John Ashton advertisement for Charles and
Patrick Mahoney, *Maryland Gazette*, January 8, 1798.

eight, Johnson was the younger of the two by fifteen years and just beginning his practice. He had already represented the Queen family in a pair of freedom suits against a Jesuit priest in Baltimore. He would make a name for himself with his arguments in *Mahoney v. Ashton*. Ridgely had already made a name for himself. He served in the Continental Congress from 1784 to 1786 and in the Maryland Senate from 1786 to 1791. His main law practice was in Baltimore, where his distant cousin, Charles Ridgely of Hampton, operated one of the largest iron foundries in the United States and a four-thousand-acre plantation with more than three hundred enslaved people. The Baltimore Ridgelys were among the largest slaveholders in the United States in the 1790s. Three decades later, in 1829, Charles Ridgely would initiate one of the largest manumissions in American history.

Richard Ridgely and John Johnson expected the Maryland court to free Charles Mahoney, since their reading of the special verdict was "self-evident": Ann Joice came from England and could be nothing other than a free woman.

When the court reconvened in October 1798, Ridgely and Johnson's argument was interrupted. The judges "expressed a wish" that they would "confine their observations to the question, whether the jury have found that Joice was *in* England [emphasis added]." This stunning announcement, the lawyers realized, meant that without establishing that single fact, "the petitioner could not succeed." Practically speechless, Johnson stood before the judges and said that this ruling would "destroy their train of reflection" (that is, their argument).[10]

"At a loss," Johnson set out to convince the judges that the special verdict meant that Joice "was in England." It appeared to him "self evident" that "unless she was there, it was impossible to prove that she came from thence." How could she come "from England" without having been in England? What "stronger words" could there be than these?

In response Philip Barton Key proposed a devastating, if brilliant, answer. "Every word in the special verdict may be true, yet she may have never set her foot in England," he replied. "For if a ship had anchored in the River Thames, and this Joice had been taken thence, in common parlance, she would have been said to have come from England." Key argued that the court could not make deductions based on any fact from the special verdict. The verdict meant only what it explicitly said: that Ann Joice came *from* England, nothing more. The verdict, according to Key, said nothing about whether Ann Joice was ever *in* England.

At this point Key's co-counsel, Luther Martin, added his considerable authority to Ashton's defense. Martin was the sitting attorney general of Maryland and one of the most successful lawyers in the United States. He had served as a delegate to the Constitutional Convention at Philadelphia, where he denounced the slave trade as an "odious bargain with sin" and "inconsistent with the principles of the revolution and dishonorable to the American character." But since the 1780s, when Martin, alongside Key, had defended the slaveholders in the Butler and Toogood freedom suits, his views had tempered considerably, and he had gravitated toward conservative positions on slavery, property, and social restraint. Martin dressed like a Federalist and wore wigs and fancy, ruffled shirtsleeves "richly edged with lace" long after the costume had gone out of fashion. Despite his record of distinction and success, Martin possessed serious failings. Among the worst was that he regularly came to court intoxicated. Roger B. Taney recalled of Martin that his fancy shirts were constantly soiled, his dress was unkempt, and his manners were coarse and undignified. "His argument was full of digressions and irrelevant or unimportant matter, and his points were mixed up together and argued without order, with much repetition." Yet, even with all these "defects," Taney admitted, Martin was "a profound lawyer."[11]

Martin proceeded to parse the word "from" in the special verdict, arguing that "no evidence" was given that Ann Joice was "in" England. He compared the principle to that found in an indictment for not repairing a road from point A *to* point B. With pedantic precision, Martin concluded that coming "*from* a place excludes that place."[12]

John Johnson could not believe what he was hearing. Clearly exasperated, Johnson contended that to come from a place implied that a person was *in* that place. He suggested that the distinction was one without a difference. In a clever analogy, he concluded, "Our act of assembly says, that negroes imported *from* Africa shall be slaves. This certainly means that they should come out of Africa."[13]

After these arguments about prepositions and their implications, the two judges for the Maryland General Court reached a unanimous decision. They pointedly noted, "The sole question at present . . . is, have the jury found, that Joice . . . was in England? . . . The jury must find the facts. It is the province of the court to declare the law arising upon those facts." They repeated Philip Barton Key's summary that "every word of this verdict may be true, yet Joice may never have been in England." The special verdict, they decided, did not find whether Ann Joice had been "in England." Therefore, the verdict was "insufficient," and they dismissed the case and ordered a new trial.[14]

"Slavery Is Incompatible with Every Principle of Religion and Morality"

In May 1799 Charles Mahoney's second trial for his freedom got under way. Eight years had passed since he filed his original petition. Seven years had passed since he sat in the Prince George's County courthouse when his uncle Peter Harbard gave his deposition. Five years had passed since Edward Queen won his freedom in the same court. The first trial must have been agonizing for Mahoney and his brothers, as their great quest for freedom was whittled down to seemingly ridiculous semantic questions, its jury never asked to render a verdict on their claim of freedom.

Yet *Mahoney v. Ashton* only became more contentious in the second round, its logic even more circuitous.

A new jury was called, and its selection was just as arduous as the first. Johnson and Ridgely wasted no time moving to strike jurors with ties to large slaveholders. They immediately removed Samuel Chew, a slaveholder who had inherited more than thirty slaves from his father, Samuel Lloyd Chew. The latter had a petition-for-freedom suit brought against him in 1794. The

Chew family had deep connections to Charles Carroll of Carrolton, having mortgaged property to Carroll over the years. Other potential jurors were equally implicated in the slaveholding families. Mahoney's lawyers struck Patrick Sim from the jury, a prominent citizen of Upper Marlboro active in Prince George's County government. His first wife was the great-niece of Charles Carroll. On the verge of bankruptcy in 1799, Sim had already sold off most of his land and enslaved property. Although a few years earlier Sim had served on a jury that rendered a not-guilty verdict in a rape case against an enslaved man, he had also previously served on a jury that denied a petition for freedom in Prince George's County. Similarly, Mahoney's lawyers targeted James Neale from Charles County, whose family members included four Jesuit priests in Maryland.[15]

Ashton's attorneys were equally aggressive. They systematically challenged as many small slaveholders who lived outside of the plantation districts as they could. They removed two men from Harford County who held fewer than three slaves each. They nixed a physician from Allegany County who held one. Then they struck a tailor who once held five slaves but now held one and had a record of manumitting slaves. An immigrant cabinetmaker from western Maryland who did not hold any slaves was similarly removed.

On the face of it, the final jury could not have been more favorable for Charles Mahoney. At least two were nonslaveholders. There were four ethnic Germans. Four jurors held one or two enslaved people. Two were tavern keepers; one was a tailor. One of the largest slaveholders on the jury was Samuel Judson Coolidge. Coolidge's father had partnered with Stephen West, importing large numbers of enslaved people into Annapolis before the American Revolution. A well-known planter from Upper Marlboro, the young Coolidge purchased Strawberry Hill from the estate of one of the county's wealthiest planters, John Hepburn, and married Hepburn's granddaughter. They held nine slaves, but unlike his father, Samuel Coolidge may have harbored sentiments more in favor of freedom. Within a year of the trial, he would manumit one woman named Susanna. He sold another person on a contract that required manumission after ten years. Within a decade he would no longer hold anyone in bondage. Moreover, Coolidge had already served on the county court jury that freed Edward Queen's mother, Phillis Queen, in 1796, rendering a verdict that led to the liberation of more than twenty other Queen family members. Mahoney's attorneys undoubtedly recognized his name. Ashton's attorneys did not try to strike him, a serious oversight based on either an utter miscalculation of Coolidge's sympathies or an overreliance on the logic of slaveholding.[16]

When the trial opened, the court entered into evidence a list of indentured servants apparently retrieved from London by the commissioners dispatched six years earlier. The list of servants on the ship *John and Christian* out of Bristol in 1688 included a woman named "Mary Joyce" who appeared on a list of headrights assigned to Lord Baltimore. No one could say with any confidence that Mary Joyce was Ann Joice, so the trial proceeded along the same lines of argument from the first trial. In fact, the justices allowed the special verdict from 1797 to be read into evidence in the case.

Each side called a few new witnesses in addition to the depositions already entered in the record. Mahoney's attorneys called Philip Baker to the stand. Son of a prominent Maryland physician and a large slaveholder who lived in Prince George's County, Baker had been a student at St. John's College in Annapolis in the early 1790s. Baker's father conducted business with Gabriel Duvall, and his sister married into the family of Overton Carr, who had already begun manumitting enslaved families on his plantation. There are no transcripts of Baker's testimony, so what he could say about the Joice family remains entirely unclear, but like several of Mahoney's witnesses, he fit a particular type: he was in his twenties, and his family showed evidence of leaning in favor of freedom. Three such men testified for Charles Mahoney.

Ashton's witnesses, by contrast, were predictably conservative. One had a long-standing freedom suit against him pending in Prince George's County Circuit Court. Another was the son of Stephen West, who lived at the Woodyard with his mother and more than 150 people they enslaved.

In the closing arguments Richard Ridgely began with drama and precision. "If Joice was a slave before (which we do not admit)," Ridgely said, "the moment she set her foot upon the soil of England she became free, no matter where she was born or whence she came." Mahoney's case would certainly depend on whether the justices would apply the *Somerset* principle and consider his ancestor a free woman, but their argument went much further. "Slavery is incompatible with every principle of religion and morality. It is unnatural, and contrary to the maxims of political law, more especially in this country, where 'we hold these truths to be self evident, that all men are created equal'; and that liberty is an 'inalienable right.'"[17]

Mahoney's lawyer made the argument in court, but the argument was Mahoney's. His voice, his perspective, his claim to freedom guided the case from the beginning, and he may have insisted that Ridgely make this wider appeal, that he denounce slavery as incompatible with the Declaration of Independence and condemn slavery in open court as a violation of "every principle of religion and morality."

The gambit was an inspired one. Ridgely appealed to American ideals of liberty and equality, but he hitched the entire legal argument to English common law and its basis in natural law. The question he wanted the court to wrestle with was whether Mahoney's ancestor could be anything other than free in England, given the *Somerset* decision and the principles embedded in English common law at the time. He reviewed the long line of prominent legal writers who held that no man was "naturally" a slave, that slavery was in fact unnatural, and that under common law no man can have "a property" in another. Ridgely reminded the Maryland justices of the "abhorrence with which slavery was regarded" in English law, and he quoted Blackstone at length as the leading authority on the subject: "The spirit of liberty is so deeply implanted in our constitution, and rooted even in our soil, that a slave or a negro, the moment he lands in England, falls under the protection of the laws, and so far becomes a freeman; though the master's right to his services may possibly still continue." As for Maryland's 1715 law declaring "all Negroes and other Slaves Already Imported . . . shall be Slaves during their natural lives," it was moot. "The act does not say *all negroes* brought into Maryland shall be slaves," Ridgely argued. Only those "imported" from Africa directly were subject to enslavement under the 1715 law. The term "imported" could not have applied to anyone who came from Great Britain. But Ridgely went further. He condemned the 1715 Maryland slave code as "highly penal," indeed fundamentally unrepublican, one that should be "construed strictly, and not extended beyond the letter of the law."[18]

Ridgley concluded with the principle that Maryland should take notice of "the law of England" and recognize in U.S. court that "the act of *Joice's* landing in England, operated as an emancipation of her from the bonds of slavery, even if she were a slave before." Mahoney's second counsel was Thomas Jenings, a young lawyer from Baltimore. Jenings closed the argument with a sweeping denunciation of slavery itself. The question, he said, "is to be decided upon the principles and maxims of the law of England." And English law abhorred slavery. "Slavery cannot be justified on any principles whatever." The only foundation for enslavement was "captivity" in a just war. "None of these reasons exist as to the natives of Africa," Jenings pointed out. The slave trade itself was unlawful. And hereditary racial slavery was entirely without legal foundation in England. Jenings laid the groundwork for an entirely abolitionist antislavery constitutionalism: "No where can we find in the history of its [England's] jurisprudence, or in the writings of the various authors who have commented upon its constitution and laws a single passage which justifies slavery." He concluded, "If there is any injustice, any hardship in this case, the petitioner [Mahoney], and his ancestors, have suffered it; they have been held in thraldom when they were entitled to their freedom; they have been the victims; they have been the only sufferers."[19]

Charles Mahoney's entire argument eroded the legal foundation for slavery in Anglo-American law. If slavery had no basis in English law, how could it be justified in Maryland? *Somerset* was the culmination in a line of precedents that Mahoney's lawyers cited back to the seventeenth century that "there is no such thing as a slave by the law of England." The chief justice of the general court Jeremiah Townley Chase seemed to agree. He concluded, "This question, in the apprehension of the court, depends on the common law of England. The common law of England is founded on the *principles of natural justice* . . . slavery is not tolerated by the common law [in England]." If Ann Joice went to England and came to Maryland from England, she was free. And Chase instructed the jury in these terms.[20]

On May 12, 1799, the jury returned an unambiguous verdict: "Charles Mahoney is a free man." The jurors found that he was descended from "a free woman named Ann Joice" and that he must be "freed and discharged of and from the service of the said Reverend John Ashton." Ashton was ordered to pay Mahoney's court costs and legal fees of $159 and, as compensatory damages, 8,929 pounds of tobacco. The amount was itself stunning—over $650 in eighteenth-century currency—the largest award made in a petition for freedom case in the General Court of the Western Shore. Despite the plunging prices for tobacco throughout the 1790s, even after payment to his attorneys Mahoney's award would have been worth enough to buy a small piece of property or a large herd of prime livestock.[21]

After May 12, 1799, and for the foreseeable future, Charles Mahoney was indeed a free man. So was his family. Long before the trial, Senator Charles Carroll of Carrollton had struck an agreement with the Mahoneys he enslaved that he would abide by the court decision if they would refrain from launching freedom suits against him. He wished to avoid the court costs. So Carroll made a list of twenty-three people on his home plantation at Doughoregan Manor who had "obtained their freedom" based on the court decision in *Mahoney v. Ashton*. He calculated their total value at £527.04 and made a notation for each individual of the diverse, highly valuable skills they possessed—John a shoemaker, Nanny a nurse, Fanny a cook, Moses a miller, Daniel a carpenter, and Cate a spinner. All, as well as Cate's six young children, were free unless the court of appeals reversed the verdict for Charles Mahoney.[22]

Ashton's legal team immediately appealed the case. They contended that the judges had allowed improper hearsay testimony into evidence, as well as the 1797 special verdict, arguing that the latter had been set aside and overruled, and should not have been given to the jury to consider. Most of all, they objected to Jeremiah Townley Chase's jury instructions. They had proposed to sidestep the *Somerset* question as irrelevant because if the jury found Ann Joice was treated as a slave, carried to England, and afterward brought into Maryland and held as a slave, then the jury should find for Ashton.

With the May 1799 verdict in his favor, Charles Mahoney and his family picked up and left White Marsh and the other plantations. They took work where they could get it, hired themselves out, lived as free people, and waited for the final and momentous appeal before the Maryland High Court of Appeals. The court, however, postponed the hearing on *Mahoney v. Ashton* for almost four years, from one term to the next, until June 1802. When the justices at last convened for the case, they heard one of the most sustained, searching, and serious arguments about freedom and the law in an American court.

"The Aristocrats Mustered All Their Force"

With the stunning decision in 1799 in favor of Charles Mahoney's freedom temporarily in place, hundreds of other petitions for freedom stood waiting to be heard in the Prince George's County Court, most filed on the heels of Edward Queen's success in 1794. At least initially, the lower county courts appeared surprisingly favorable to enslaved petitioners, no less so than the general court in Annapolis had been. The general court decided case after case for enslaved petitioners, in part because it drew its jurors from a pool of nonslaveholding counties, and because its leading justices, Samuel Chase and Jeremiah Townley Chase, devised the legal strategies first used in these cases.

The Queens were not the only successful plaintiffs. In September 1797 a Prince George's County jury made up of large slaveholders issued a verdict for Ignatius Butler's freedom. At the same time, "Negro Patience" and eight others sued one of the descendants of Henry Darnall. Although the jury did not award them freedom, the Darnall heir quickly manumitted Patience and the others. Dozens of petition cases were continued from one session to the next. Nearly all of the prominent white families of the county had at least one suit against them. The juries, therefore, included numerous men who were from these same families. In April 1800 and September 1801 three more cases in Prince George's County were decided in favor of black plaintiffs, each with a jury dominated by large planters, each with large numbers of witnesses summoned from the county.[23]

Meanwhile, in 1799, New York passed an emancipation act that would end slavery gradually over time in the state. The Jeffersonian Republicans in Maryland, led by Gabriel Duvall, seemed poised to take over the state assembly and even win the governorship. The Federalists, led by Philip Barton Key, rallied to defend hereditary enslavement in *Mahoney v. Ashton*, assert a common-law argument legitimating slavery, and protect property qualifications for voting. The presidential election of 1800 loomed on the horizon. Would Charles Mahoney's freedom lead to a wider liberation?

The White Marsh families knew that freedom, in fact, had immediate political significance. Nothing barred free black men from voting in Maryland, and having been freed by the courts, the men of the Queen, Butler, Shorter, Joice, and Thomas families cast ballots in the state and federal elections in 1800. They did so at a moment of intense political rivalry in Maryland, when their votes, though small in number, might be enough to tip the balance in local elections. In the counties the property qualification was 50 acres or £30 current money. In Annapolis a man could vote if he owned a whole lot with a house, or £20 sterling, or had five years' service in a trade. As for the prospect of black voting, the Federalists quickly codified a distinction in voter eligibility between freeborn African Americans and those who had been freed or manumitted from enslavement, barring the latter from voting if they were manumitted after 1783. Under the new law, men like the Queens who won their freedom in the courts after 1783 were ineligible to vote. Even on this basis many black men could still vote, and it remained unclear exactly how these provisions would be enforced at the polls.

Expecting to win support from laborers and artisans in the upcoming presidential election, the Democratic-Republicans proposed dropping all property qualifications for voting and holding office. The measure passed the Maryland House but failed in the Senate in 1799. When the jury of small slaveholders and artisans in *Mahoney v. Ashton* decided in favor of Charles Mahoney's freedom, therefore, their verdict contained a political message aimed at the great planters and Federalists: a restive spirit was stirring in these lower ranks against the political supremacy of the large slaveholders, their pretensions, their authority, and the deference they blithely expected from the lower orders. The story of the burning of Ann Joice's indenture and of how the great planters trapped her in slavery may have hit an especially raw nerve with jurors in the spring of 1799.

With so many of the Democratic-Republican attorneys on Mahoney's side and so many of the Federalist attorneys on Ashton's side, the political overtones could not be ignored. The Jeffersonians entrusted republican government to the juries of common men and distrusted the high-minded Federalist justices wedded to colonial precedent. In both Virginia and Maryland, the Democratic-Republicans wanted to revise criminal and civil codes to reduce, if not eliminate, judicial discretion. They thought that judges had become profoundly antidemocratic, wielding obscure common-law precedents found only in rare treatises and reports, instead of relying on juries or, for that matter, statutes passed by the legislature. As a result, the battle in *Mahoney v. Ashton* over whether slavery had any legitimate basis in English common law became one front in a widening contest over making the law republican in the 1790s. Democratic-Republicans like Duvall, Ridgely, Johnson, and Jenings argued that the basis for slavery in English common law was illegitimate and that those seventeenth-century precedents held no authority in a republican society premised on natural rights. They trusted juries to protect individual liberty, perhaps especially for the wrongfully enslaved. However ironic it may seem in retrospect, the freedom suits sharpened republican ideology.[24]

Federalists like Martin, Harper, and Key, in contrast, dredged up feudal concepts of villeinage, an ancient form of bondage tied to real estate. They revived dim precedents approving hereditary enslavement of Africans and allowing property in human beings for the collection of debts. Their argument relied on decisions made by judges appointed under the sway of Stuart monarchs who wanted English law to justify slavery. They classified certain people—Africans who had been "imported"—as a legitimate form of property. On the defensive in the late 1790s, Federalists turned to the judiciary as a bulwark against what they saw as the undisciplined, democratic urges of the mob.[25]

In November 1799 the Democratic-Republicans gained control of the Maryland House for the first time and immediately sought to repeal the property qualifications for voting. The measure failed because the Federalists barely held the Senate and refused to let the property qualification disappear. Still, no other restrictions kept free black men from the ballot. They could vote in Maryland alongside white men, if they could meet the same property, age, and residence requirements.[26]

The stage was set for a dramatic presidential election in 1800 that pitted the Democratic-Republicans in Maryland, led by Gabriel Duvall, against the Federalists, led by Philip Barton Key. The freedom suits, especially

Mahoney v. Ashton, structured the political division between the emerging parties. The questions of freedom and the terms of enslavement in the colonial world had to be reconciled with the political and ideological conditions of the post-colonial, Revolutionary republic. By 1800, when Gabriel Duvall declared himself a candidate for the Electoral College in support of Thomas Jefferson, each side had already taken its position in the decade-long Mahoney case. The lawyers and judges aligned with the Jesuits and the Carrolls came out openly as Federalists against Jefferson. According to Duvall, "The aristocrats mustered all their force" to oppose Jefferson and everything he stood for. In the heated public exchange that followed, John Johnson and Gabriel Duvall, both of whom represented Charles Mahoney, spoke for Jefferson. On the other side, Robert Goodloe Harper and Philip Barton Key defended the Federalists and opposed Jefferson.[27]

For election to the Electoral College in 1800 the Jeffersonian Duvall, associate judge of the Maryland Court of the Western Shore, opposed the Federalist Jeremiah Townley Chase, the chief judge of the Maryland Court of the Western Shore. Duvall wrote to James Madison in April that Chase was the "most popular man on their side, and every exertion will be made to obtain success." He warned Madison that there would be "controversy" in the newspapers over Jefferson's purported atheism. When Philip Barton Key published an anonymous handbill calling Duvall a tool of the Virginians and Jefferson a "Frenchified" tyrant, Duvall defended Jefferson's character and turned the tables, reminding voters that Key could not be trusted because he was a loyalist in the Revolution who donned a British uniform and fought against the Americans. Key responded that the "insinuations" amounted to a personal attack. Perhaps because they were former partners on so many cases, Duvall considered the mudslinging in the election "the depravity of the times" and regretted that the charges "so often descend to the meanness" of petty personal criticism. Whatever the misgivings, the campaign turned ugly.[28]

A crucial battleground in the partisan contest of 1800 emerged in Anne Arundel County. Charles Mahoney's lawyer John Johnson was on the ballot, challenging Ashton's lawyer Philip Barton Key and Allen Quynn, Federalists who had served as delegates for the previous six years together. Key had taken Gabriel Duvall's seat in 1794 when he went into the U.S. Congress and was reelected each year thereafter along with Quynn, the long-serving mayor of Annapolis who had been a delegate since 1791.

In the October balloting at least twenty black voters appeared at the polls in Annapolis, many of them clearly motivated to vote for Johnson because he had won Charles Mahoney's freedom. Four, including Ralph Joice, were disqualified on the grounds that they were not freeborn but had obtained their freedom in petition suits after 1783. Six black voters overcame challenges to their eligibility, and in all, sixteen black voters, including members of the Shorter, Joice, Mahoney, Thomas, and Butler families, cast ballots for John Johnson, while only five voted for Philip Barton Key. Key lost his seat in the House of Delegates by a handful of votes. He contested the election in the House, arguing that some voters were ineligible and others who were barred were in fact eligible. He did not prevail, and Johnson was seated in the House.[29]

Philip Barton Key's unpopularity with black voters, so widely evident in the October 1800 election for the Maryland House, stemmed in all likelihood from his representing slaveholders in one petition case after another, especially the Reverend Ashton. Key defended more than twenty slaveholders in petition cases in Prince George's County between 1794 and 1796. On the docket books, the initials "PBK" appear beside nearly every slaveholder facing a freedom suit. Although he had represented the Queen family against Ashton in earlier cases, his sudden appearance alongside Ashton probably alienated the Queens as well.

John Johnson in effect owed his seat to the black voters whose families he helped free in the courts. Once in office, given the opportunity, he did not hesitate to recognize the debt. When the General Assembly in 1800 took up a proposed constitutional amendment to abolish all property qualifications but did so with a clause restricting the vote to "white" men only, Johnson voted in favor of striking the word "white" from the proposed measure, one of just sixteen delegates to do so. Quynn and fifty other delegates voted to keep the provision restricting the vote to whites. Just six black men had voted for Quynn in 1800. The Maryland Senate, controlled by the Federalists, opposed removing the property qualification, and the proposed constitutional amendment failed to pass.

A year later, with Democratic-Republicans in control of the Senate for the first time, they moved to eliminate the property qualification once and for all. The conservatives in the Senate balked again and remained skeptical of widening the franchise. Maintaining a property qualification, they argued, would be crucial to avoid mob rule in the future. As the population grew from immigration and natural increase, they feared that "a considerable proportion of that population will probably be . . . destitute of property, and without sufficient virtue and knowledge to resist the arts, corruptions, and impositions of ambitious men, desiring of raising themselves to power, even on the ruins of public liberty and happiness." The Federalists in the Senate conceded that "liberty is the common and natural right of all men" but made a distinction between liberty and the right of suffrage. "Admitting all men to be equally free by nature," the Senate proclaimed, "it does not follow, that in all circumstances they should equally participate in the affairs of government." In exchange for broadening the franchise to men without property, the Democratic-Republicans proposed restricting the franchise to whites. There was little debate on the floor about these measures, and eventually in 1801 the Senate agreed to drop the property qualification and restrict the vote to "free white male citizens" over the age of twenty-one. The law stripped Maryland's free black citizens of the vote and went into effect in 1802 just as the second jury trial in Charles Mahoney's freedom suit got under way.[30]

The timing was not a coincidence. The free blacks who had won their freedom in the courts were proving a political force to be reckoned with, and a majority of conservative white slaveholders exemplified by Philip Barton Key had concluded that freedom brought dangerous, even unacceptable, consequences. Within months, because of *Mahoney v. Ashton,* these powerful political figures would take another more extraordinary step to stop the freedom suits: they would abolish the General Court of the Western Shore.

Meanwhile, the Jesuits, the Carrolls, and many others feared the unraveling of slavery on their respective plantations, as well as the potential financial losses if hundreds of Mahoney family members went free. Neither the Jesuit trustees nor Bishop John Carroll trusted John Ashton to defend their interests against the Mahoneys. Ashton's propensity for engaging in expensive lawsuits increasingly appeared to jeopardize both their financial stability and their public reputation with neighbors in Prince George's County. Clearly straining to avoid further legal costs, and to rein in John Ashton, the trustees decided in 1801 that the managers of the Jesuit plantations could not enter "any lawsuit of any consequence" without prior permission of the trustees.[31]

As if these entanglements were not embarrassing and expensive enough, Ashton had the audacity to appear at the May 1801 meeting with a fifteen-year-old mixed-race boy as his personal servant. Slaveholders often traveled with young boys as their valets, and so did the Jesuit priests, but the public appearance of this young man sparked an explosion of renewed controversy among the Jesuits over Ashton's relationship with Susanna Queen. Could this young man be his son? Susanna Queen had won her freedom on April 15, 1796. Ashton had not seen her since that day. But in the summer of 1800 Susanna Queen returned to White Marsh. She had married an enslaved man held by the Jesuits in June 1799. And Ashton, still the manager, appeared to treat her so favorably as to renew the suspicions of his antagonists. She built her own cabin at White Marsh with Ashton's consent. Her presence and that of her two mixed-race children led to more speculation that Ashton was their father. Suddenly, Ashton faced the possibility that he would be removed from his position as the manager of White Marsh. He might even be defrocked.

Ashton heard from his friend the Reverend Charles Sewall, one of the Jesuit priests sued by the Queen family, that another priest, probably Francis Neale, refused to hear Susanna's confession and began to pressure "the poor unfortunate girl" to answer whether she had sworn to false statements when Bishop Carroll investigated the rumors of their relationship thirteen years earlier. Ashton responded, "I will be ready to make oath on my death bed that to the best of my knowledge she swore true."[32]

His explanation only seemed to raise more doubt about what he might be hiding. Did he mean that Sucky Queen answered Carroll's questions, as far as they went, yet imply that she still may have had a child with him? Ashton maintained that he was under no obligation to make a "public confession" of all the sins of his life, no more so than Carroll was. Did this mean that Ashton would confess to his paternity in private, in the confessional booth, but not in public, in a court of law? He would not say. All he would say was that "these reports are propagated by the Mahoneys who have all run away from me & are now dispersed through the country & irritated, because they see me the obstacle to their freedom."[33]

No doubt pressured by John Ashton's adversaries within the Jesuit corporation and worried about a public scandal, Bishop John Carroll agreed to remove Ashton from his post as the manager at White Marsh plantation. Ashton's response was immediate and furious. "What authority has John of Balt. to dispossess me of the White Marsh, which I have held under lawful authority twenty-four years?" he bellowed. Rambling like a drunken sailor, speaking about himself in the third person, Ashton warned that Carroll had no more power to "appoint a cook wench to John Ashton's kitchen" than to "turn him out of doors [and] appoint him a successor." Provoked and increasingly unrestrained, Ashton did not hesitate to threaten Carroll. "Let me eat my bread in peace or I will disturb the peace with a vengeance," he chided. "Do not provoke me or I will be a match for you. I do not value your purple robes or glittering ornaments."[34]

Ashton's dismissal from White Marsh struck him "like a thunderbolt." Fueled by resentment and probably by alcohol, he lurched from defiance to incredulity. The tenor of his correspondence with Carroll led the bishop to place Ashton's letters in a folder marked "Special." Carroll kept the separate file for scandalous behavior by priests, and he probably burned or destroyed the most incriminating pieces. For the most part Carroll's special file concerned drunken priests, and Ashton clearly had a drinking problem. "You mentioned to me when I was last in Baltimore," Ashton protested, "something about drinking & keeping a woman in the house [who] had the misfortune to have a child." Ashton reminded Carroll of their many nights at Liège, Belgium, together and objected that no one had ever seen him "in the least disordered." As for the woman, Ashton steadfastly denied any impropriety. She was a "good & necessary servant & as free from all communication with me as the woman that sleeps under the same roof with you & immediately over your head."[35]

Ashton speculated that the rumors in 1801 about them could have come from only one source: his fellow Jesuit, and nemesis, Bishop Leonard Neale. Ashton had opposed Neale's appointment as president of Georgetown College, and as a result, he concluded, "old sores" have been "ripped open." Neale, he said, was motivated by "revenge, envy, and ambition." It was Neale, Ashton suspected, who maneuvered to oust him from his post at White Marsh.

Rather than wait to be censured or removed from the Jesuits entirely, Ashton decided to resign his "faculties" as a priest in 1801 and step down as a trustee of Georgetown College. Then he told Carroll that he would "dismiss" the pending freedom suits against him, presumably leaving the corporation in the lurch and potentially freeing some of the Mahoneys in one dramatic act. For the first but not the last time, Ashton threatened to use the enslaved families as pawns in a raging internecine battle within the Jesuit society.

On the one hand, Ashton's vehement protests that he was not the father of Susanna Queen's first child were consistent with his early career in Maryland when he condemned the Carroll men for forcing enslaved women to have sex. If he did father a child with Susanna Queen, then he lied under oath and in direct correspondence with his bishop, John Carroll. Ashton may have been a drunk, but the consistency of his statements that he was not the father of Queen's child never wavered. As if to suggest how wrong the Jesuits were about the nature of the whole Queen affair, Ashton told Carroll, "She is no more to me than a broom stick."[36]

But Ashton's self-serving explanations defy what we know about slaveholders; they also appear to contradict the special interest he took in Susanna Queen for years afterward. In fact, their relationship spanned three decades. Susanna Queen's first child was born in 1786 or 1787, when she was about fifteen years old. Ashton would have been forty-four at the time, and after eighteen years in Maryland he clearly considered himself as much a slaveholding planter as a Jesuit priest—so much so that when the U.S. census began its survey in Prince George's County, Ashton listed himself, not the Church, as the slaveholder of the ninety-two people held in bondage at White Marsh. Nothing in the written historical record directly pinpoints the character of their relationship, but psychological coercion, rape, and sexual assault were common. Other slaveholders sexually assaulted fifteen-year-old girls. In light of his later actions and what we know about the proclivities of slaveholders in that time and place, Ashton's denials ring hollow. Moreover, we know that Susanna Queen extracted various promises from Ashton over those three decades, agreements that shaped her life and the lives of her descendants. One of his promises was that the house at White Marsh was hers.[37]

Meanwhile, the breach between Ashton and the Jesuit corporation widened into a yawning chasm of ill will, lack of trust, and irreconcilable differences over property and honor, money and duty, temporal and spiritual affairs. Dismissed from his position, his property taken from him, his reputation sullied, John Ashton had all the reasons he needed to deny his archrivals in the Jesuit order any further hold on whatever property he still possessed. John Carroll speculated that after the May 1799 verdict, Ashton sold "some of the family of the Mahonis" and that Ashton never "accounted for" their sale. He offered no proof, but given Ashton's temper, it is equally plausible that Ashton manumitted them without telling the trustees because he considered them to be his property, not the corporation's.[38]

Growing ever more defiant as the July heat settled into the Patuxent River valley, Ashton refused to recognize the authority of the trustees who removed him from White Marsh. The priests who plotted against him were "dogs" and "animals." The case against him, "if it is a moral case," could only be heard by his confessor. "If it is a case of public scandal," it was a matter only for Carroll, his superior. And because Carroll's previous investigation had cleared him of wrongdoing, Ashton felt more than vindicated. "I have been placed here, by lawful authority," he wrote Carroll, "[and] will not surrender it but to lawful authority."[39]

By midsummer 1801 Ashton saw himself as a victim of conniving priests with "intemperate tongues." He directed his wrath at the Neale brothers—Leonard, the ineffectual president of the college, and Francis, the equally inadequate trustee. Even John Carroll thought they were poor man-

agers of the college at Georgetown. Their unpopular program of rote mem-
orization and erratic but harsh discipline had students fleeing in droves.
Ashton reminded Carroll that he had "saved the estates from destruction"
and had been a "principal promoter" of Carroll's projects, including the epis-
copacy, the college, and the incorporation of the Jesuit estates, and then he
refused to turn over his property. In fact, Ashton began to dig in his heels.[40]

Carroll was astounded. He wrote Leonard Neale that Ashton's "violence & abuse & threats have no bounds." He confided to Neale, "I always
foresaw this consequence & the apprehension I had of the lengths to which
he might proceed." The whole subject was filled with "anxiety" and might
possibly become a full-fledged "scandal." Carroll let Neale know that Ashton had resigned his priesthood, his trusteeship of the corporation, and his
directorship of Georgetown College. He also told Neale that he would not
restore Ashton's priesthood under any circumstances.[41]

Eventually, Ashton thought he had traced "the source of all this dis-
turbance" over his alleged paternity of Susanna Queen's children. A young
French priest named William Vergnes in the Maryland diocese told the
Neale brothers what he saw and heard while living at White Marsh in the
summer of 1800, when Susanna Queen and her children returned to White
Marsh to live with her husband. Vergnes told the Neales about Queen's return and that Ashton "was the father of her child & of many children." The
Neale brothers, bolstered by Vergnes, propagated these rumors about Ashton and Susanna Queen so widely throughout the "lower counties" of Charles
and St. Mary's that Ashton informed Carroll that unless he removed Leonard Neale and William Vergnes from their positions, he would go "before
the General Court" and sue "them both & prosecute them for slander & defamation."[42]

The escalation was significant. The General Court in Annapolis met
in the State House and only heard cases with large monetary damages. A
slander case in that court would drag the Jesuits' internal controversies into
the state's most public and political court. Ashton found out that the French
priest now ensconced at White Marsh wanted to persuade Susanna Queen
to make a general confession of her whole life because "his suspicious curi-
osity in the affair was so great." Vergnes tried to trick her into admitting
Ashton's paternity of her children in the confidence of a priestly confession,
but according to Ashton, "she had too much sense for such a Gascone," and
he declared that "she will never go to him again." In a court of law, on the
other hand, Ashton could challenge the rumors in a public setting. He could
summon Leonard Neale to say what the French priest told him, and he could

summon the college's trustees to testify against Neale's reliability. In open court the affair would tarnish the church, the college, and the bishop.[43]

But on November 3, 1801, the trustees of the Jesuit corporation ignored Ashton. In fact, they ordered that the manager of White Marsh pay Vergnes "the usual salary," and they noted in droll meeting minutes that Ashton had "resigned the management of the White Marsh" and would keep his salary as its priest until the summer of 1802, when he would retire. In the meantime, he was directed to give a complete financial accounting and inventory of everything bought, sold, and held as property at White Marsh.[44]

Ashton did no such thing. He packed up furniture and silverware, corralled all livestock he considered his property, appropriated funds to spruce up his private home in Charles County, and left White Marsh with a number of enslaved people.[45]

When the court of appeals finally heard the arguments in *Mahoney v. Ashton,* John Ashton's sympathies had turned. He appeared on the docket, but he may have been the defendant slaveholder in name only. Alienated from his brethren in the Society of Jesus, dismissed from a post he had held for thirty-four years, and stuck with the legal bills from a decade spent defending the freedom suits on behalf of the Jesuit corporation, Ashton had plenty of reasons to want to punish the Jesuit corporation and its trustees. No longer exactly adversaries, John Ashton and Charles Mahoney found, however curiously, that their interests were congruent. Both wanted something from the corporation, if for different reasons. Ashton wanted compensation and respect. Mahoney wanted freedom and his family. One or both of them may have decided that they could help each other attain what they desired.

"Hundreds of Negroes Have Been Let Loose"

On June 21, 1802, the High Court of Appeals heard the arguments in *Mahoney v. Ashton* about whether the May 1799 verdict for Charles Mahoney's freedom would stand. Senator Charles Carroll of Carrollton followed the trial closely and helped orchestrate the defense. In fact, the legal team defending Ashton turned more to the senator than to the priest. Luther Martin and Philip Barton Key were now joined by Arthur Schaff and Robert Goodloe Harper. Schaff was among the most distinguished lawyers at the Maryland bar. Harper was Charles Carroll's son-in-law, as well as a U.S. congressman from South Carolina, and heavily dependent on Carroll's financial largess. He was eager to represent Carroll's interest in the Mahoney claim.

They went on the offensive, asserting that the common law of England sanctioned slavery and that although Blackstone seemed to suggest that slavery was unlawful, nonetheless there *were* slaves in England. Their interpretation of Lord Mansfield's decision in *Somerset* relied on the idea of "attachment." Under this doctrine, even though slaveholders could not compel anyone to be a slave *in* England, if an enslaved person was brought from the colonies, that person's enslaved status continued once he or she left England. Schaff began by stating plainly, "A slave has no rights—even the murder or maiming of one is only an offence against the government." Ann Joice, he argued, was nothing more than "property." She was "not a subject for the law to operate on." According to Schaff, the *Somerset* decision had no bearing because it determined only that slaves cannot be held in England. "There is no reason," he argued, "why a negro brought from England, or any other place, should not be a slave." Furthermore, the Maryland law of 1715 declared that "all negroes" imported "shall be slaves." A case like *Somerset,* decided nearly a century after Ann Joice arrived in Maryland, could not be considered "retrospective."

Robert Goodloe Harper agreed. "The question of freedom was not before the court," he argued. Instead, the issue was whether the master's "right of service" could be enforced. Harper invented an ingenious way around the *Somerset* question, one that would shore up the property rights of slaveholders in Maryland. Because the decision was silent on whether slaves became free once in England, the limited nature of Mansfield's ruling was simply that "the right of the master cannot be enforced in England." Harper maintained, in other words, that in England a slaveholder's right was merely "suspended," not "divested." By this logic, Ann Joice could have been held as a slave before and after her arrival in England.

John Johnson tried to persuade the court that Harper's reasoning grievously misconstrued English law and precedent. "The moment a slave arrives in England," he repeated, "he is as free as if he had been legally manumitted by deed." No person "is naturally a slave," and under English law, "no person could have a property in another."

The final rebuttal went to Luther Martin, Ashton's high-profile, if intemperate, attorney. "Negroes, we contend, are property, a merchandise," he began with blunt force. Picking up Harper's argument, Martin dismissed the *Somerset* decision as inapplicable for two reasons. First, no decision could be retrospectively applied. Second, Martin suggested, *Somerset* meant that the slaveholder's right to hold slaves, though divested when *in* England, revived upon leaving England. Slavery reattached to Ann Joice.

Speaking for a whole class of conservative slaveholders, Luther Martin was convinced that freedom petitions had come to represent a great dis-
turbance in the law and a perversion of social order. He ridiculed the idea
that setting one's foot on English soil could make a slave into a free man,
that he was somehow "instantly changed," and that as if by magic British
air could "electrify the flesh" with freedom. The whole concept of *Somerset*
offended Martin's sense of the right to property and, if allowed in American law, would create "great uncertainty." As for the English judges cited by
Mahoney's attorneys, such as the liberal justice Lord Holt, who said that English soil conferred freedom, Martin dismissed them as having a "revolutionary ebullition of liberty" in the brain. Such rulings, he argued, were
dangerous. So was allowing hearsay into evidence, for a very simple reason,
according to Martin. "It is giving the power to ignorant persons to judge of
rights. In the case of the Butler's, reputation was given in evidence that they
were descended from a white woman; so also in the case of the Toogood's.
In the case of the Queen's, that they were descended from a native Indian of
South America. In all these, and in many other similar cases, hundreds of
negroes have been let loose upon [the] community by the hearsay testimony
of an obscure illiterate individual."[46]

Here was the Burkean nightmare of social chaos laid bare: Liberalism
unchecked. The lower ranks thrust into positions of authority. Masterless
men loose in society. The wisdom of the ages subverted. Martin drew a line
in the sand for the justices. His counterargument to the freedom suits was
that they were the opening wedge in a revolutionary movement that might
turn society upside down, destroy slavery, ruin property, and, like the French
and Haitian Revolutions, replace the law with a form of mob rule. Martin's
comment was racially disparaging but undoubtedly highly effective.

On June 25, 1802, the High Court of Appeals reversed the May 1799
judgment freeing Charles Mahoney. The defeat was total. Even when the
judges upheld the lower court's decision, they did so for reasons damaging
to Mahoney's case. The judges agreed that the general court was correct in
instructing the jury, but only because they thought it left open the possibility that Ann Joice might have been a "white woman or native of England,"
whence the "presumption" should be "in favor of freedom." No one had argued that Joice was a white woman. In freedom suits up to that point the
defendant slaveholders bore the burden of proving that a petitioner's ancestors had always been a "slave for life." Now it appeared that the court of appeal in Maryland might flip the burden to the enslaved, requiring enslaved

petitioners to prove that they were descended from a free, presumptively "white" woman.[47]

To make matters worse for Charles and Patrick Mahoney, and indeed for all future petitioners in Maryland, the judges also ruled that the Maryland colonial law of slavery, not the *Somerset* principle, should prevail in its courts. "Upon the bringing of Ann Joice into this state, then the Province of Maryland, the relation of master and slave," they decided, "continued in its extent as authorised by the laws of this state." The court noted the "collision of individual opinions" in English precedent but decided to rely on the "positive law of the state in 1715." Luther Martin, Robert Goodloe Harper, and Philip Barton Key rendered the *Somerset* principle a dead letter in Maryland law. Charles, Patrick, and Daniel Mahoney would have to find another basis for their freedom suit than that of their black ancestor setting foot in England.[48]

A few weeks later Charles Carroll of Carrollton learned that the Mahoney decision had been reversed and that the case had been sent back to the general court for another jury trial. Carroll wrote to his son-in-law and lead counsel, Robert Goodloe Harper, worried that the Mahoneys might find another way to win their claim of freedom. "What chance can the petitioners have of getting their freedom in a new tryal?" he inquired.[49]

In fact, Carroll heard the news about the new trial directly from Daniel Mahoney (a relative of the Daniel who sued Ashton). Forty-seven, a master carpenter, and a descendant of Ann Joice, Daniel was temporarily freed at least until the court ruled otherwise. Sometime in July Daniel arrived at Carroll's plantation and hand-delivered a letter to Carroll from the Mahoneys' attorney. Richard Ridgely brimmed with confidence that the Mahoneys would prevail. And Daniel carried himself with the self-assurance that his family would ultimately win their case in the next general court.

It must have been a remarkable moment. Carroll, the leader of the Maryland Senate, signer of the Declaration, and one of the largest slaveholders in the state, standing face to face with Daniel Mahoney, a man he had formerly enslaved, a man whose relatives voted for the Republicans, a man whose family was leading a freedom suit that could unravel slavery. What did they say to each other? Daniel Mahoney told Carroll that their lawyer had "proof" that would "put their right to freedom . . . out of all doubt."[50]

In October 1802 the third jury trial in *Mahoney v. Ashton* got under way. Mahoney's lawyer Richard Ridgely was convinced his client would be vindicated. Little seemed to have changed on the fundamentals in the case.

The court of appeals ruling that disallowed the earlier 1797 special verdict required a new trial, but otherwise, he thought, all facts and jury instructions remained in place. A new jury therefore could reasonably be expected to reach the same conclusion. Ridgely had written Charles Carroll to this effect, saying, "If in the new trial to be had in October the jury shall be of the same opinion, the petitioners for freedom will succeed . . . The only material fact existing in the cause at this time is where did Joyce come from to this Country? If from England, Ashton must prove she was carried there as a slave. I think the weight of the testimony in the former trials was contrary to that fact, and so the jury found."[51]

The attorneys for Ashton, however, came to trial not only with a fresh line of argument but also with evidence so recently unearthed that it may have been fabricated. Ann Joice, they argued, was a "Guinea Negro" who never set foot in England. Robert Goodloe Harper, Carroll's son-in-law, introduced witnesses who purported to have seen diaries and other documents from a steward on Lord Baltimore's ship showing that Baltimore purchased Ann as a slave while en route from England to Maryland. No actual documents remained, just the word of two white men. Even Senator Carroll was skeptical.[52]

The jury in 1802 faced a much different set of evidence from that of its counterpart in 1799. With these new facts Carroll and Ashton's attorneys succeeded in shifting the legal questions in the case away from the *Somerset* principle and the long line of antislavery precedents in English law. Evidence, however flimsy, that Ann Joice was a "Guinea Negro," given the jury instructions, forced a jury of small slaveholders and artisans simultaneously swept up in the Democratic-Republican moment to sidestep the question of freedom. The jury concluded, "Charles Mahoney is not free."

As *Mahoney v. Ashton* reached its apogee, the ascendancy of the Democratic-Republicans proved especially contradictory. Emancipation through the courts gained momentum simultaneously and in relation to the Democratic-Republican surge in the emerging two-party competition. Federalist slaveholders like Charles Carroll, who considered slavery a moral evil and had once proposed legislation for gradual emancipation in Maryland, found themselves unable to reconcile their commitment to property rights in slavery with their revolutionary ideals of freedom. Individual blacks might gain their freedom, the Federalists reasoned, because they were exceptional or worthy, but the Federalists defended their slaveholding as a property right based on ancient English precedents.

By the early 1800s, their Democratic-Republican counterparts were equally contradictory, perpetuating slavery on the basis of race while advocating for the freedom of specific individuals. Ashton's lead attorney, Federalist Philip Barton Key, lost his seat in the House of Delegates because black voters who won their freedom in the courts voted for Mahoney's Republican attorney John Johnson instead. But Johnson's allies among the Democratic-Republicans proved more eager than the Federalists to draw a color line in the law. If property no longer served as a threshold for office holding and voting, then color would suffice. Under the Democratic-Republicans Maryland was one of the first states to limit the vote to white men. In subsequent court cases Democratic-Republican judges argued that "color is *prima facie* evidence of slavery" and that anyone "descended from a white woman" was de facto a free person, not a slave.[53]

Only the Quakers took a principled stand. In Anne Arundel County, the Snowden, Thomas, Chew, Parker, and Hopkins families began manumitting hundreds of enslaved people in the 1790s and 1800s. Less than a month after the final Mahoney trial, Samuel Hopkins, a prominent Quaker in Anne Arundel County, purchased the freedom of "Old Shoemaker John," one of the Mahoney relatives enslaved by Charles Carroll. The senator remarked dismissively that he was "now calling himself John Joice." Hopkins paid Carroll $200. Joice then managed to free his wife and child. Philip E. Thomas, a banker, businessman, and leading Quaker in Baltimore, watched the Mahoney case closely and, at the same time, observed a disturbing new phenomenon: the market in Maryland for selling slaves south to the cotton frontier in Georgia. In 1804 Thomas concluded that the Democratic-Republican legislature would do little "to protect the blacks" from kidnapping and the slave trade. Indeed, he thought that the legislature would "take advantage of the subject being brought before them to rivit the chains faster and increase their oppression." The "barbarous cruelties" of the trade and the "shock" of its violence, Thomas hoped, would lead "every feeling mind" to question it. Still, he predicted "an awful day of retribution" and, paraphrasing Jefferson, thought that the oppression of the enslaved ought to make Americans "tremble for our Country."[54]

Despite the verdict in favor of the Jesuits, Charles Mahoney and the Joice family had no intention of giving up their claim to freedom, and boiling with resentment, John Ashton was more than ready to use the Mahoneys against his fellow Jesuits. *Mahoney v. Ashton* began in 1791 as one of dozens of freedom suits designed to take limited steps toward freedom, but over the years, as its delays and reversals multiplied, everyone involved in the case experienced its ironies and contradictions. Under their weight, Ashton's once-respectful relations within the Roman Catholic leadership disintegrated. A Jesuit priest had become the primary defender of slaveholding in Maryland only in the end to consider freeing the men who had sued him.

A few years later, the enslaved families who remained on the Jesuit farms felt the backlash of the Mahoney verdict in a different way. Archbishop John Carroll and the Jesuit corporation were left with a pile of lawyers' bills to pay, but Carroll could not bear to use the corporation's general fund, as it was always on the verge of insolvency. So Carroll and the trustees required the individual Jesuit plantations to foot the bill. White Marsh, St. Inigoes, Newtown—each would be expected to put up cash. Carroll wrote Francis Neale, the corporation's agent, "The sale of a few unnecessary Negroes, three or four, and Stock would replace the money."[55]

The bishop's solution was both tragic and doubly ironic. The enslaved would be sold to pay the legal bills the Jesuits racked up defending slaveholding against an unsuccessful freedom suit.

But *Mahoney v. Ashton* succeeded in a different way. Charles Mahoney and his Democratic-Republican lawyers managed to place into the legal record of Maryland the long history of common-law precedent in English courts declaring slavery unnatural and illegitimate. They were able to do so only because the fact at issue was whether Ann Joice was "in England." On the basis of that fact alone, all of the law questions related to slavery could be debated in a Maryland court. What Charles Mahoney did was show that with a certain set of facts—his ancestor's presence in England—and a claim to freedom that was never based on color, the legal question of whether slavery was unnatural would have to have its day in court. With a different set of facts—that Joice never set foot in England—the court did not have to determine what her presence on English soil meant. The judges could instruct the jury that her color determined her status, since a "Guinea Negro" could be nothing other than enslaved. After *Mahoney v. Ashton* it was patently obvious that another black family, such as the descendants of Mary Queen, might be able to make a similar claim. If they could establish that their ancestor set foot in England and came to Maryland before 1715, then the law questions about the illegitimacy of slavery would come clearly before the court again.

Charles Mahoney's political achievement was immense. More than any other Marylander, he had placed the question of freedom before the state. He had organized a legal challenge to slavery that lasted more than a decade and held the state's leading slaveholders to account. He had orchestrated the testimony of white and black witnesses to show that black persons like his ancestor were in fact free and that slavery was incompatible with the founding principles in the Declaration's guarantee of equality. He had laid bare the fundamental contest over slavery in English common law. And at the end of his eleven-year quest, Charles Mahoney would lead his brothers to exploit the divisions that their suits created among the slaveholders in a final bid to achieve their freedom.

For the mixed-race families closely observing the outcome of *Mahoney v. Ashton,* the final verdict sent a disturbing signal. Since the Revolution, the law had seemed to presume liberty as a natural condition, and local decisions about the status of an individual were usually respected. Juries ruled in favor of freedom in case after case where a white ancestor was claimed, even when those ancestors were black or nonwhite. Now judges were overturning those decisions. The Mahoney case introduced a newly significant presumption: that the facts of one's ancestry did not matter if blackness meant enslavement.

After *Mahoney v. Ashton* the Queen family saw that their history might raise similar legal questions. Their ancestor Mary Queen had spent time in London also, but unlike Ann Joice she was not African. They had testimony in hand that could establish a set of facts about her presence in London. Could they win a second round of freedom suits in the Maryland courts and turn the law more decisively toward the principle of freedom?

Our Ancestors Are Calling Our Names

NEW ORLEANS, 2017

The growing realization that my family bore a close connection to these events, one closer than I ever realized, gnawed at my conscience. The past brushed up against the present. All along I had planned to search for descendants of the families that sued for their freedom in Maryland, but now my investigation took on an unexpected urgency. The documentary record showed unambiguously that my ancestors had enslaved the Queens in Maryland right up until the end of the American Civil War. That revelation felt like the thirteenth stroke of a clock. What did I really know about all that came before?

When Rachel Swarns, a *New York Times* reporter, published a lead story in April 2016 documenting the scope of the Jesuit sale of enslaved families to Louisiana in 1838, the descendants of the Queen and Mahoney families realized their connection to the families in Maryland. The sale had split the families into two distinct branches: one based on Maryland's Western Shore near Annapolis, the other in the parishes upriver from New Orleans. The trauma of the uprooting took a terrible toll, and with each succeeding generation the tributaries grew farther apart. Once in Louisiana, families like the Queens and Mahoneys gradually lost touch with the memory of the freedom suits they had pursued for generations in Maryland against the Jesuit priests and other slaveholders.

Now, in 2016, aided by the nonprofit Georgetown Memory Project, descendants were orchestrating thousands of DNA tests across dozens of families with the goal of tracking down all living descendants of the men,

women, and children sold by the Jesuits. Online communities were springing up around these genealogies. When I went to New Orleans to meet with
the descendants of the Queens and Mahoneys, it felt as if whole family histories were unfolding in present time.

We gathered at the New Orleans Public Library on a warm, humid
afternoon in April 2017. The professional historian in me wanted to know
what their families knew about the Maryland freedom suits, what lore had
been passed down from one generation to the next, what had happened to
the families in Louisiana, and whether they had brought another round of
freedom suits there. I had a list of questions and a script in hand to guide
the conversation, but it was the descendants who patiently and deliberately
led me instead toward the moral reckoning we as American need to even
begin to comprehend this story.

An educator, teacher, and nonprofit leader, Karran Harper Royal found
out through DNA results that she was related to the Queens and the Mahoneys in Maryland, but her family in Louisiana had no memory of the freedom suits they had brought and won in the Maryland courts. For Royal,
the unfolding history of her Queen and Mahoney ancestors had revealed a
powerful counternarrative: the idea that from the very beginning of the
United States, black people had claimed their freedom. "Nowhere was I
taught this," she said. "It would have given me a different perspective on what
people in bondage were able to accomplish . . . if they could win their freedom in the court system."

Sandra Green Thomas, a New Orleans city administrator, learned of
her Queen ancestry from the DNA matches she was receiving, but like
Royal's, her family also did not know about the Maryland lawsuits. She told
me that her family's deep history was "being brought to light." Her ancestors
fought in the Continental Army during the Revolutionary War and sued for
freedom in court. All of this history was confirming for her a conviction she
has held ever since she was a little girl: "This is my country. I am an essential element of this country. My people are an essential element. How could
this country get to where it is in 240 years? That's the blink of an eye when
it comes to nation building. Without an exploited and oppressed people, you
can't get there that fast."

It is impossible to consider the history of American slavery and freedom without such a reckoning, and it seems equally impossible to consider
the history of a single family without reference to the nation's history, without considering how all Americans are implicated in the history of the United
States.

Mélisande Short-Colomb, a professional chef and caterer in New Orleans in her early sixties and a Queen-Mahoney descendant, had carefully studied the complex history of New Orleans, of empires colliding in the Atlantic World, of the French Revolution, the Haitian Revolution, the American Revolution, and of slavery in the United States. World events centered on families that had been written out of history, she told me, yet Short-Colomb's grandmother had always said that her family was "free back in Maryland," that the family had once sued for their freedom in the Maryland courts. This piece of family lore, handed down for generations, seemed inexplicable to Short-Colomb as a child, or at least mysterious, because she knew that the family had been enslaved in Louisiana for as long as anyone could remember. How could they have been free in Maryland if they were slaves in Louisiana? On this question, according to Short-Colomb, the family history was full of "vagaries." She heard that they were enslaved by "Irish Catholics," but she had heard nothing from her family about the history of the Jesuits, the scale of the Georgetown sale, or the pivotal freedom cases in the Maryland and D.C. courts.

The news about the Georgetown sale cast everything in a new light. Short-Colomb, who survived Hurricane Katrina, learned that it was the Jesuits who enslaved her family back in Maryland. "All of the things my grandmother ever told me," she explained, "sort of fell into place with missing pieces." These stories were what her grandmother called "the begats," a reference to the genealogies in the Hebrew and Christian Bible. Stories of ancestors, of their struggles and accomplishments, of memories that reached back all the way to Maryland.

The Queen and Mahoney family lore passed down through the generations, it turned out, contained vital historical truths: that members of the families had in fact won their freedom in court and that some of them had been free. Like Mary Queen or Ann Joice, Short-Colomb's grandmother had carried the threads of her family's history, woven them into stories, and passed them all the way down into the twenty-first century. Across eleven generations and thousands of miles, the narrative of their claim to freedom was alive today. Short-Colomb was the living recipient of that powerful legacy.[1]

Long before we met in New Orleans, I had told Short-Colomb, Karran Harper Royal, and Sandra Green Thomas about my ancestors in Prince George's County, their slaveholding, and what I knew about their role in the freedom suits. No one was surprised, and no one thought it was a coincidence. Short-Colomb was convinced that the connections among all of the various ancestors in this story, however distant, however faint, were being reawakened and that a profound historical event was taking place in the United States. Voices of the past were speaking, many for the first time. "Ancestors are calling our names. One by one," she announced. "Sandra, Karran, Mélisande . . . one by one, they're calling our names." After a deliberate pause she looked at me across the table, her head tilted, her eyes lit with sincerity, and declared, "They called your name."

I left our meeting that day with those words echoing in my head. How would I respond to the call of these ancestors? How would you? At one point Short-Colomb offered her own answer to that question. We had a shared responsibility, she said, to uncover "the layers of this American Family story . . . pulling together the bits and parts of how this travesty [slavery] came to be." When we peel back the layers of history, we are not always prepared for what we find. In these circumstances the nation has an obligation, she argued, to "deal with our history" and in so doing to bring forth "a better America." There was only one way forward: "The truth."

CHAPTER 4

A Public Scandal

Whereas kind providence has enabled me to purchase my daughter named Ann, who was born in a state of slavery.

—CHARLES MAHONEY, MAY 7, 1816

As Charles Mahoney's case reached its final and dramatic conclusion, Susanna Queen confronted an especially uncertain future. Whatever the nature of her relationship with the priest, she knew that her freedom, her children's freedom, and her marriage to an enslaved man depended in no small measure on John Ashton's approval, perhaps on his position as manager, on his standing within the Jesuit order, and even more precariously on his whim. Court records indicate that Susanna Queen won her freedom in April 1796 with the other descendants of Mary Queen, including Nanny Cooper's son Simon, Edward Queen's twin brothers, Gervais and Proteus, and his sisters Betty and Mary. By virtue of that decision Susanna's two children—Charles, age fifteen or sixteen in 1802, and Elizabeth, age seven or eight—would have been free as well. As a result, when Ashton arrived at the Jesuit trustees meeting with what appears to have been Charles Queen as his servant, everyone knew that the young mixed-race teenager was free. What they did not know for certain was whether Ashton was his father.

Nearly sixty years old, the Reverend Ashton in 1802 had spent the previous ten years warding off the freedom suits of the Queens and the

Mahoneys. As the manager at White Marsh, he had become not only the principal defendant in two of the most momentous petitions for freedom in Maryland but also the plaintiff in a curious land dispute case against Mareen Duvall, one of Prince George's most powerful and well-connected planters, whose massive plantation bordered White Marsh.

Although Susanna Queen and her children were free, her struggle to make their freedom real and lasting would take decades and span generations. In fact, the Queen family's freedom, secured in the courts, was entangled with the expectations and allegiances of all of the white slaveholders who both resisted and enabled it. When the August 1796 jury in Charles County accepted at face value the testimony of Benjamin Duvall about Mary Queen as an African slave, despite obvious flaws in his memory, a pivotal verdict against the Queen family temporarily shut down further freedom suits. In that case Nancy Queen was the lead plaintiff against the Reverend Charles Sewall, John Ashton's fellow Jesuit, former ally, and purported friend. Her branch of the family in Charles County did not gain their freedom. Other branches living far away from White Marsh on isolated plantations probably never received word of the Queen family's initial success in the courts. Slaveholders undoubtedly tried to keep them in the dark. The same was true for the Mahoneys.

So, in the aftermath of the freedom suits, the Queen and Mahoney families were divided in ways both visible and invisible, both obvious and obscure. One part was free, one part enslaved, but there were other divisions in the families. The free branches of the families experienced no magical unity conferred by their freedom, no uniform solidarity accompanying their separation from White Marsh. Many remained inextricably connected to the Jesuits, the Duvalls, and other Prince George's County slaveholders. For these people freedom did not sever ties as much as strain, twist, and bend them into new configurations. Not all free Queens had the resources to follow Edward Queen out of Prince George's County up to Baltimore. Not all could lodge suit after suit against their former enslavers, as Edward did.

Motivated by the desire to leave White Marsh and all it symbolized behind, a few, like Edward Queen and eventually Charles Mahoney, achieved a substantial degree of personal independence. They settled nearby at first and married newly emancipated men and women from the Snowden, Parker, and Hopkins plantations, where Quaker slaveholders had manumitted families for decades. The Jesuit plantation at White Marsh included land on the eastern side of the Patuxent, so it is possible that some of the Queens with enslaved husbands or wives became tenants on the Jesuit plantation, though no account book records indicate this. Gradually the Queens established a free black community closer to Baltimore that they came to call Queenstown. Others, like Susanna Queen and Simon Queen, were married to enslaved husbands or wives who continued to be held in bondage at White Marsh, and as a consequence they were not as free to move away from or to defy their former slaveholders. Some, like Simon and Proteus Queen, who gained their freedom in the courts, decided to remain on White Marsh plantation at first, negotiate work for wages, and secure their freedom by staying close to where whites knew them. For some of the men, including Charles Mahoney, their wives remained enslaved and therefore so did their children.

Susanna Queen's freedom proved decidedly constrained at first. She was married to an enslaved man at White Marsh, a man Ashton said "belonged" to him, so Ashton knew that Queen with her young children would not move far away from wherever he sent her husband. Like so many slaveholders, Ashton seemed perfectly willing to manipulate the power he wielded over a free woman's husband to control her and her children.

When Ashton was removed as the manager of White Marsh, and when the jury handed down its final verdict against Charles Mahoney, Susanna Queen and her children were pulled into the swirling, internecine battles of their former enslavers. Even under intense pressure, Susanna Queen refused to admit the paternity of her two eldest children, but the vortex of that controversy widened far beyond White Marsh. The storm over their relationship hit Charles County just as the rest of the Queen family—still enslaved—embarked on an alternative strategy to win their freedom. While the Jesuits were in crisis, Nancy Queen sued one of John Ashton's fiercest antagonists, the head Jesuit priest at St. Thomas Manor in Charles County. As the scandal over Susanna Queen and John Ashton circulated publicly, Nancy argued that she could not receive a fair trial in the county.

But she made another, more heartrending argument—that she was descended from a white woman. Native women like the Queen family's ancestor were increasingly treated under the law as white—that is, as not black. And if the fact of her native ancestry could be established, if it could be proven in a court of law, Nancy might then be considered free. It was the first and only time a member of the Queen family made such an assertion in court. And it was cruel irony. To win freedom, the family might have to use its native ancestry to become "white." In such a situation the ancestor's status as a *free* woman no longer counted as much as her color. The trial that followed in Charles County, the last of the freedom suits by the Queens in Maryland, laid bare the racist presumptions behind Maryland's slave law. It also brought the young lawyer Francis Scott Key into the highly charged political contest over the freedom suits.[1]

"An Important Falsehood and Barefaced Lie"

News of the verdict against Charles and Patrick Mahoney would have traveled west in October 1802 from Annapolis to Charles Carroll's plantation at Doughoregan Manor in Anne Arundel County, and across the Patuxent River to the Jesuit plantation at White Marsh, where the Reverend Germain Barnaby Bitouzey had replaced John Ashton as manager. The court ruling would have reached Ashton in Charles County near Port Tobacco, where he had taken up residence at the Hermitage, one of several properties he personally held. Ashton was still embroiled in a dispute with Bishop John Carroll and the members of the Jesuit corporation over his removal from the corporation's board of trustees. At a special meeting at Georgetown College in August 1802, Carroll was elected to the trustees even though he was a bishop and therefore barred by tradition from exercising authority over the church's temporal affairs. At the same time Ashton's three-year term on the board was not renewed. Carroll took his seat. Ashton and a few other priests protested that the meeting was "improper, if not illegal," "null and void," and "plainly surreptitious."[2]

After the Mahoney trials, Ashton lodged repeated requests that the Jesuit corporation owed him retirement pay, as well as principal and interest on various loans and reimbursement for all of the lawyers' fees he had incurred at White Marsh. Fed up with the failure of the corporation to respond, Ashton placed a runaway slave ad in the *Maryland Gazette* in January 1803 to recover Isaac, a fifty-seven-year-old carpenter, and Moses, "a lad about [fifteen] years old." The ad was little more than a brazen public announcement that he was taking White Marsh's enslaved property. Bitouzey responded with an ad placed in the same newspaper, alongside Ashton's, clarifying that Isaac and Moses were part of the "the estate commonly called White Marsh" and "actually the possession" of Bitouzey as its manager. He called Ashton's advertisement a "pretense," warning anyone against attempting to arrest or detain the alleged fugitives on the basis of Ashton's ad.

Within weeks, Ashton had his attorney, Allen Bowie Duckett, file a "replevin" suit naming Bitouzey as the defendant, essentially suing him to recover property, including the enslaved people whom he claimed Bitouzey had seized from him on behalf of the corporation. Ashton also sought reimbursement for the legal expenses he had paid to defend the Queen and Mahoney freedom suits. Those fees totaled more than $200. The young, well-connected lawyer Allen Bowie Duckett acted on behalf of a client—Ashton—who no longer served his master—the Jesuit corporation. Directed by Ashton to sue the Jesuits, Duckett may not have known the true source of his client's motivations or how the Queen and Mahoney families may have maneuvered the situation to their advantage.[3]

On May 23, 1803, Bishop John Carroll, Bishop Leonard Neale, and Bitouzey took control of the corporation in a special meeting at White Marsh. Clearly frustrated with Ashton's petulance, litigiousness, and secrecy, they required all managers of the estates to submit accounts and inventories within six months. Anxious that Jesuit managers, following Ashton, might sell slaves or manumit them without recording the transaction or accounting for the property, the corporation directors sought to "remove uncertainty and ambiguity" by issuing clear directions for selling, exchanging, or freeing slaves. The regulations were prospective and designed to shed light on all future transactions. Having laid down the rules, they then reprimanded Ashton by name for "having removed sundry slaves, stock, furniture, plantation utensils & materials for building, from the [White Marsh] Estate lately under his management." Among other offenses, Ashton employed "tradesmen" hired on White Marsh Estate funds "for considerable time" on projects for himself. In short, the trustees accused Ashton of embezzling from the corporation and said that he had never provided a full accounting "to justify his claim to the [enslaved] property so transported."[4]

Carroll hoped that the Reverend Francis Neale, the duly appointed agent of the corporation, would arrange a settlement with Ashton. So Neale sat down with Ashton to discuss terms. Poorly suited for such a role—an ineffectual manager, averse to conflict, and monkish—Neale was no match for the conniving, worldly Ashton. Neale discovered that Ashton's main concern was what would happen to "the Negroes he purchased while at the Marsh," if left to the corporation. Ashton apparently feared that they would be sold, and he claimed that the enslaved were his property, not the corporation's. Neale informed Carroll that Ashton's claim was nonsensical "when seriously examined." Neale, however, knew that Ashton was a formidable adversary, one who would "reach at everything to defend whatever he [had] in his power." Somehow, Neale speculated, Ashton had been allowed to hold White Marsh as if he were its tenant, not its manager or trustee, and therefore for years he had "acted as for himself." Finally, Ashton promised Neale that he would provide "a just & faithful account of all he took from the Marsh, & of the use of waggons, tradesmen, & c."[5]

We cannot know for certain whether Ashton sought to hold on to the enslaved people from White Marsh, including the Mahoneys and Susanna Queen's husband, because he knew that Bitouzey and the Jesuit corporation would sell them and break up their families. What we do know is that Ashton refused to pay the court costs for his many lawsuits and disregarded the corporation's claim that his accounts at White Marsh were overdrawn. Instead he settled into a prolonged dispute with his Jesuit superiors, issuing long-winded, often meandering dispatches from exile at Port Tobacco. Each missive contained venomous and pleading passages.

"I am not disposed to go over every particular of my administration of the Marsh during the period of [twenty-nine] years," he informed John Carroll in a characteristically defensive tone. He reminded Carroll that his judicious management of White Marsh more than anything else made the college at Georgetown possible. When the trustees pressed him to explain whether he had allowed some of the enslaved to "purchase their liberty" and, if so, to produce the contract for their freedom and explain how it had been secured, Ashton refused. The accusation that he had taken White Marsh's enslaved people from the Jesuit corporation was an "important falsehood and barefaced lie."[6]

But Ashton may have been doing exactly what he denied doing—selling the Mahoneys their freedom. An observer at the *Mahoney v. Ashton* trial a few years earlier, a Quaker who was active in antislavery circles, heard that the Mahoneys "were at liberty from the time a judgment was obtained in their favour, until the time it was reversed in the Court of Appeals." When the 1799 verdict freeing them was overturned and the final judgment against the Mahoneys handed down, he heard that "they were all immediately taken back into bondage."[7]

Nothing of the sort can be found in the historical record.

Charles and Patrick Mahoney had negotiated a separate arrangement with John Ashton. Neither appears to have been reenslaved, though they were not yet legally free men. While the Jesuit corporation paid the court costs and attorney's fees to keep them in bondage, the more the corporation alienated Ashton, the closer he came to negotiating with them. In December 1803 Ashton quietly signed a deed of manumission freeing Patrick Mahoney. In another twist, Ashton's fellow Jesuit and Queen family slaveholder, the Reverend Charles Sewall, witnessed this deed. Having promised Patrick Mahoney his freedom and having renounced all "right and all claim whatsoever" to him, John Ashton waited for an opportune moment to record the deed at the Charles County Courthouse.

The sequence of these events was significant. Nearly a year after the final verdict in *Mahoney v. Ashton,* Patrick Mahoney in late 1803 came to visit John Ashton at Port Tobacco and must have asked for his legal freedom. He was already living away from Ashton and away from White Marsh. In all likelihood so was his brother Charles.

For his part, Ashton complained bitterly to the Jesuits that he was owed money from the corporation for loans he had extended to White Marsh and for retirement benefits he was due. In March 1804 the sheriff of Prince George's County found Ashton in Charles County and demanded that he pay the court costs and fees for all of the various lawsuits of the previous year, including the Mahoney freedom suits. Ashton maintained that the bill was not his to pay, that the new manager of White Marsh, the Reverend Germain Bitouzey, should pay the court costs out of White Marsh's coffers. Hoping to reach a settlement on "friendly" terms, Ashton presented an official "memorial" to the trustees of the Jesuit corporation requesting reimbursement for the "extraordinary trouble" and expenses he incurred over fifteen years of "attending lawsuits" on their behalf. In April 1804 the trustees met at White Marsh and resolved to "settle, on the best terms . . . the respective claims of Mr. J. Ashton." The Reverend Francis Neale was appointed once again to negotiate a settlement.[8]

The dispute dragged on for months.

So, on May 4, 1804, Ashton took his deed manumitting Patrick Mahoney down to the Charles County Courthouse and had it recorded. Patrick was "absolutely free." On the same day, "at the request of Charles Mahoney," Ashton also recorded a deed that "forever set free Charles Mahoney." Charles was living in Anne Arundel County, where he presumably had been ever since the May 1799 jury verdict in his favor. Ashton swore to "relinquish and renounce all claim whatever which I have or ever had to him." A few days later Ashton manumitted Fanny Queen in Prince George's County. She was twenty-six years old, five feet five and a half inches, and within weeks she left Prince George's County for Baltimore, where she registered for a certificate of freedom.

Then, on August 13, 1805, Ashton signed another deed of manumission, this one for Daniel Mahoney. It is the only physical description we have of Daniel. He was six feet tall, about thirty-three years old, and "yellow" in complexion. Meanwhile, Daniel Mahoney negotiated with Charles Carroll of Carrolton for the freedom of his wife and children. On March 11, 1806, he persuaded Carroll to go to the Anne Arundel County Court to manumit his wife, Nancy, and their two children, Ann and Charles. Two years later

Charles Carroll agreed to another round of manumissions, for Prudence Mahoney, Thomas Mahoney, and their five children. In Prince George's County the Mahoneys extracted a string of manumissions from other slaveholders.[9]

Unsuccessful in the courts but alert to the full extent of Ashton's estrangement, the Mahoneys and the Queens may have purchased their own freedom in some cases. For decades as the lawsuits unfolded in the courts, the Jesuits had been paying some of the enslaved on the plantations for extra work. Such arrangements were common in the Chesapeake after the Revolution, as enslaved men and women negotiated for wages and any degree of independence they could extract. The slaveholders conceded nothing in making these payments, nor were the monies intended to ameliorate slavery or erode its legal and social foundations. Charity was paid £2 to make shirts for the farm manager. Henny, a midwife, received the same for attending two women in childbirth. Monica earned 5s. for supplying pullets to the priests' dinner table. Charles took cash on the side for ditching work. Others sold produce from their own gardens, dug for oysters, and harvested fish and wild game. A few raised livestock for market. Such hard-won earnings may have fueled the Queen and Mahoney freedom suits and certainly provided the resources when they were unsuccessful to negotiate for freedom.[10]

By selling freedom to the Queens and Mahoneys or manumitting them outright, John Ashton perversely proved his authority over them as property. The disgruntled Jesuit may have liberated the families to send a message to the corporation, demonstrating beyond a doubt that some of the enslaved of White Marsh were indeed his property to do with what he pleased, including manumit them under the law, even if Bishop Carroll and the other corporation leaders denied that Ashton had any right at all to the enslaved property.[11]

It had been nearly fifteen years since Charles Mahoney and his brothers filed their original petitions for freedom. Probably the youngest of the brothers, Daniel was eighteen at the beginning of the freedom suit and thirty-three when he finally gained his freedom. All three men had wives and children by the time *Mahoney v. Ashton* ended, and all three secured freedom for themselves and their immediate families even though the court ruled against their claim in October 1802. A few members of the extended Joice family also gained their freedom in these years, but many others remained enslaved, scattered across the Western Shore of Maryland and, like the Queen family, unable to gain a favorable hearing in a county court because of the final verdict in *Mahoney v. Ashton*.

Just a few years earlier, in the summer of 1800, a massive slave revolt shook Virginia and Maryland. Gabriel Prosser, a skilled blacksmith who lived a few miles outside of Richmond, Virginia, organized hundreds of artisans and skilled slaves. He recruited his followers on Saturdays and Sundays at church services, barbeques, and funerals. Prosser was convinced that the partisan division between Republicans and Federalists in the heated presidential election would give his followers an opportunity to seize their freedom. He made his appeal directly to black men, urging them to fight for their personal freedom and for the liberation of their families. Hundreds joined the clandestine plot. With scythes they converted into swords and pikes, Prosser and his lieutenants planned to invade Richmond, seize the armory, and take the governor hostage. On the day they planned to strike, torrential rains flooded central Virginia, and Prosser's army could not reach the city in time. Word spread of the revolt, and the Virginia militia arrested Prosser and dozens of others. A series of trials followed. Prosser and twenty-five other men were convicted of insurrection and publicly executed.[12]

The rebellion and another slave revolt in Norfolk in 1802 prompted a hollow debate about slavery among white leaders in both Virginia and Maryland. One young Virginia lawyer appealed to the state legislature to consider emancipation for reasons of public safety. He claimed that enslaved blacks "sought freedom . . . as a right," but his fanciful solution involved taxing slaveholders, buying all of the enslaved people with the revenue, and transporting all blacks out of the state. Instead of abolishing slavery, the Virginia legislature restricted slaves from attending worship at night without a slaveholder, beefed up the state's militia, and established a guard to patrol Richmond and defend the governor's mansion and the arsenal.[13]

In the years following what became known as Gabriel's Rebellion, legislators in Maryland and Virginia scrutinized free blacks and cracked down on black people's freedom generally. Free blacks had played almost no role in the rebellion, but white political leaders thought that their presence inspired enslaved people to seek their own freedom. The lesson slaveholders drew from the Haitian Revolution was similar: the demand for rights by free blacks unleashed a cataclysm. Both Maryland and Virginia eventually required every free black person to obtain a certificate of freedom signed by the clerk of the county court. Freedom papers, as they were called, were proof of freedom. The Butler, Queen, Mahoney, Shorter, and Thomas lawsuits liberated hundreds of men and women. Many others negotiated their manumission or escaped. All would need freedom papers.[14]

In the wake of the slave revolts and the controversial freedom suits, the Maryland legislature further restricted free blacks. Slaveholders eyed the rather lax 1796 manumission act. The law required only that a copy of the deed be deposited at the county court within six months of the manumission. Freedom papers could be written out and signed by any white person. There was no provision requiring free blacks to carry certificates of freedom. The legislature concluded that slaves obtained freedom papers with ease and "great mischiefs [had] arisen" as a result. To solve what they saw as a problem, beginning in 1806, only the clerk of the court could issue freedom certificates in Maryland. Second copies would no longer be granted unless a witness could vouch that the originals were lost. Manumission had to be proven.[15]

In 1806 Maryland's southern neighbor, Virginia, came within two votes of outlawing manumission entirely and then required that slaves freed by manumission leave the state within one year or be returned to slavery. All free blacks had to register at the county court and obtain a freedom certificate. Even as these draconian measures trickled out of the Virginia legislature, the distinguished lawyer and jurist George Wythe ruled in a freedom suit called *Hudgins v. Wright* that "freedom is the birthright of every human being" and that the burden of proof in such cases should fall on the slaveholder because slavery was unnatural and unjust. Wythe cited the first clause in the Virginia Declaration of Rights that "all men are equally free and independent, and have certain inherent rights."[16]

Although the Virginia case involved Native American descendants who were deemed to be "free" and therefore "white," Wythe's sweeping annunciation of the freedom principle in American law carried tremendous weight. He was chancellor of the state's chancery court, a distinguished law professor at the College of William and Mary, and revered by leading Virginia politicians. His personal commitment to revolutionary liberalism and the natural rights of freedom led him to emancipate the few enslaved people he inherited. Wythe's ruling in *Hudgins v. Wright* had the potential to open a Pandora's box of litigation against slaveholders. It was his last decision from the bench. He was murdered by a jealous relative in late May 1806.[17]

When the slaveholder appealed the case to the Virginia Supreme Court, Wythe's former student St. George Tucker snuffed out the idea that freedom was the birthright of everyone in Virginia. The Declaration of Rights, he argued, could not be used "to overturn the rights of property." The revolutionary promise of freedom in the Declaration of Rights was limited to "free citizens" only, and blacks had "no concern, agency, or interest" in the Revolution or its outcome. It was the beginning of a specious argument Roger B. Taney would reprise fifty years later in *Dred Scott*.[18]

Having written African Americans out of the Revolution, the rulings in the Maryland and Virginia freedom suits, both *Hudgins v. Wright* and *Mahoney v. Ashton,* introduced the significant presumption that blackness determined enslavement and that the burden of proof fell on the enslaved person, not the slaveholder. Enslaved persons seeking a petition had to prove their freedom and therefore their whiteness, their nonblackness. Virginia's St. George Tucker had declared that "all *white persons* are and ever have been FREE in this country." Again he rewrote history in stark racial terms to shut down freedom suits. In cases where the person suing for freedom was "*evidently white* . . . the proof [lay] on the party claiming to make the other his slave." In all other cases, the enslaved had the burden of proof. In the absence of documentary evidence about lineage, St. George Tucker encouraged judges to gaze upon the plaintiffs and examine their physical features to ascertain their race.

In such a situation the enslaved families of Prince George's County, many of them descended from Native American, African, *and* European ancestors, faced a profoundly disturbing set of choices. Judges and juries would observe their color, hair, and physical features. Testimony about the racial features of their ancestors would hold greater weight than what contemporaries said about their status as free persons. It could be advantageous in freedom suits to claim descent from a white ancestor, but such declarations in court proceedings could erase or distort generations of memory. And claiming to be free under these terms would do nothing to revive English antislavery precedents like *Somerset* in American courts.

A "Matter of Public Notoriety"

The manumission of the Mahoney brothers, along with Fanny Queen and Nancy Mahoney and her children, fifteen years after their original petitions, materialized only when John Ashton's alienation from the Jesuits reached a critical point. The enslaved families were well aware of the way these circumstances unfolded and the pressure their lawsuits brought on the Jesuits, especially on Ashton. They also knew that the embarrassment over his relationship with Susanna Queen could provide yet another opportunity for members of the family to gain their freedom.

**Manor House, Newtown plantation, St. Mary's County, June 2018
(courtesy of Letitia Clark).**

Some annual meetings of the Jesuit corporation were held at the manor house at
their Newtown plantation. The Reverend John Ashton informed the corporation
that he preferred to retire to Newtown, perhaps because he and Susanna Queen
had been refused confession at St. Thomas Manor.

The controversy exploded into the open when Ashton, Susanna Queen,
and her enslaved husband separately attempted to go to confession at
St. Thomas Manor in Charles County. We cannot know exactly what either
Ashton or Susanna Queen wished to say in the confessional, but judging
from the correspondence about all involved, it seems likely that each sought
regular confession only to find that they had been cast out of the confessional
on the grounds that neither had ever confessed the true nature of their relationship. Led by the Neales, none of the priests at St. Thomas Manor would
agree to hear their confessions, and Ashton grew increasingly incensed.[19]

Even at this juncture no one—not Ashton, not Carroll, not Neale, not
Sewall—had named Susanna Queen in writing. She was alternately "the
poor woman," "that Servant," or "the woman." Yet Susanna Queen and

her children were living with her enslaved husband at or near the Hermitage, Ashton's retirement residence in Port Tobacco, Charles County. According to Ashton, her presence at the Hermitage was temporary. He may have planned for her to return to White Marsh and to release her husband from enslavement. "She has a place to go with her children at the close of the year," he assured Carroll, but he doubted very much that her leaving would ever "satisfy the hotheaded tots who only wish evil to me." In late October 1804 Ashton asked Carroll to appoint someone to hear "my confession & that of the poor woman."[20]

In early December 1804 temperatures plunged below zero and driving snow fell in southern Maryland "with great fury." By February, the snow, gale-force northwest winds, and ice made the county roads impassable. The Potomac River was frozen solid seven miles across to Virginia. Susanna Queen and her husband and children remained stuck with Ashton at the Hermitage.[21]

By the summer of 1805 the situation had hardly changed. Every priest in the county "rejected" all three of them from the confessional—Ashton, Susanna Queen, and her enslaved husband. The priest at St. Thomas Manor was the Reverend Charles Neale, brother of Francis and Leonard Neale. Ashton complained bitterly to Carroll that Charles Neale refused to hear the confession of both Susanna Queen and her husband "after he discovered who they were." At this point Ashton continued to maintain a public face within the Jesuits, disavowing any relationship with Susanna Queen in his correspondence with his superior, John Carroll. He did not deign to use her name in his letters and reported with indignation to Carroll that the priests at St. Thomas planned "to break off all communication with me on acct. of a Servant which I employ from necessity in my family."

Carroll replied frankly that he thought the priests of St. Thomas had good reason to banish them from the confessional. Though he did not name her, Carroll explained that Susanna Queen had made "avowals and declarations to several persons of known integrity" and that these statements "render it exceedingly improper & unbecoming to keep that Serv[an]t near you." The whole affair had become a "matter of public notoriety to clergy and laity." Carroll instructed Ashton to submit, to do his duty as a priest, and to follow the Gospel precept "if your eye &c." The message was clear: remove Susanna Queen from his house.[22]

It took Ashton "some time" to reply because of the "indelicacy of the subject." Over a year earlier he had manumitted Charles Mahoney, Patrick Mahoney, Daniel Mahoney, and Fanny Queen, and he had secured an affi-

davit from an undisclosed person, probably Susanna Queen, that would exonerate him of the rumors about her children's paternity. "If this is not
sufficient proof," he proclaimed, "then no proof can be sufficient in cases of
fractio sigilli, stuprum & sollicitantes [the breaking of little figures, lust & agi-
tation]." Rather than file a defamation case against his accusers in the
county court and risk inciting further public prejudice against Catholicism,
Ashton told Carroll that he would accept the "loss of my reputation."[23]

In exchange, however, Ashton wanted something for Susanna Queen.
He pointed out to Carroll that one of the local priests had pressured her "to
tell him in confession who the father of her first child was." Susanna Queen
refused to comply. To keep the transgression out of the public eye, Ashton
asked Carroll to order his nemesis at White Marsh, the Reverend Bitouzey,
to give her "the poor cabin at the Marsh now empty, [and] which she formerly lived in [and] built at her own expenses." Ashton explained that when
she returned to White Marsh in June 1800, he let her and her husband live
there "during good behavior." He wanted the cabin "restored to her [and]
her husband now at the Marsh." If Carroll could make this happen, Ashton
promised, then "all is right." Ashton assured him that "she is willing to return to her friends [and] to her former occupations," but he said he was unwilling to turn her out on her own, because she had five children and was
expecting a sixth, and was "without a shelter from the weather or a morsel
of bread to eat."[24]

We do not know from the record what Susanna Queen thought of the
situation she faced. Or the nature of her relationship with Ashton—a man
who had in all likelihood assaulted and raped her nearly twenty years earlier.
But we can speculate based on the actions she took. Her husband had been
forced to go back to White Marsh. Whether Ashton ordered his return remains
unclear. But Queen and her children stayed behind at the Hermitage, on their
own with Ashton. Under intense pressure, she defied the priests at St. Thomas
who sought her confession. Those actions and her very presence pressured
Ashton to seek Bishop Carroll's intervention on her behalf—to restore her
"poor cabin" at White Marsh so that she could be reunited with her husband. Months later Queen and her children returned to White Marsh to live
with her husband. Presumably, Carroll had prevailed on Bitouzey to restore
her house. She secured Ashton's influence, even protection, but at what cost?

A few months later at St. Thomas, Ashton was told that he could not
even make "an ordinary priest's confession, not a word concerning any
woman whatever," unless he would make a "public penance." The Neales had
raised the stakes considerably. Ashton refused to make a public confession

unless his sins were "publicly proved." Susanna Queen, according to Ashton, was *"ready to make oath* that she had no conference with any priest whatsoever out of confession relating to any of her children." Ashton told Carroll that she had had a discussion with Francis Neale about her first child and reinforced what he had long maintained, that she had her first child "by Kelly," the white tenant and overseer at White Marsh in the 1780s. According to Ashton, the substance of Francis Neale's conversation with Susanna Queen was that he wanted her to hire the child out to Georgetown College, presumably because he considered the young man a potential source of public scandal and wished to remove him from Charles County.[25]

At this juncture we can assume that Ashton must have learned the details of this vital exchange from Susanna Queen, not Francis Neale. After all, she was a free woman, and she swore an affidavit detailing her responses to Neale's prying inquiries. Despite Vergnes's clever attempts to elicit a salacious confession, Susanna Queen held her silence. According to Ashton, she swore under oath that she *"never threatened a remedy by law* for the maintenance of any of her children." She said nothing "before him [Vergnes] or any other person." Queen was often asked "who the father of her children was," but according to Ashton, she "never discovered it." Ashton reported to Carroll that Susanna Queen stood ready to swear that no priest had ever had any children with her.[26]

As the controversy over the paternity of Susanna Queen's children intensified, Ashton doggedly maintained that the Jesuit corporation owed him reimbursement for legal expenses as well as a salary in his retirement. The former totaled more than $200, and he was considering filing a lawsuit to recover the expense from the corporation. Fearing another round of litigation, the Jesuits appointed the Reverend Francis Neale yet again as a mediator to settle the dispute, but Neale construed his authority in exceedingly narrow terms. He refused to discuss either of Ashton's complaints and stubbornly insisted that the corporation should be reimbursed for the property Ashton took with him from White Marsh when he left.

Stonewalled by Neale and the corporation, Ashton wrote to his replacement, Germain Bitouzey, in early 1806, ostensibly about his libel suit for damages that remained on the docket in Prince George's County, which had dragged on for three years. Offering to "settle it between ourselves" and to end "this disagreeable business," Ashton proposed to forgo all reimbursement for the legal expenses in the freedom suits if Bitouzey would send him an enslaved boy named Davy who had been with Ashton in Charles County before he was sent back to White Marsh. "I will take him in lieu of all de-

mands against the Marsh," Ashton said. If Bitouzey declined the offer, however, Ashton promised to revive his lawsuit, issue summonses, and get the
sheriff involved.[27]

Why would Ashton offer to drop all of his claims against the corporation if Bitouzey would send him just one enslaved boy? Part of the answer
lies in the fact that the Jesuits considered enslaved people to be property and
therefore subject to trade, sale, exchange, and collateral. Ashton knew that
his request would be, in that respect, unremarkable. The future value of Davy
came reasonably close to the sum of Ashton's claims, even as Davy's present,
much lower value made the offer an obvious bargain for the corporation.

Yet there may have been more intricate motivations. Davy's mother had
been enslaved, but his father may have been Simon Queen, the man who won
his freedom in court and then testified for Ashton in a major land dispute
case against Mareen Duvall, one of Prince George's largest planters. Ashton
had enlisted Proteus and Simon Queen, both now free, as witnesses in the
case against Duvall. Because Maryland law did not bar freeborn black men
from testifying in open court, even in cases between white men, the Prince
George's County Court issued a summons for Simon Queen to appear. Queen
came into court and testified before the grand jury on behalf of John Ashton
against Mareen Duvall. In response, Duvall filed a countersuit against Simon
Queen alleging that he was trespassing on a portion of Duvall's property that
bordered White Marsh. The area was called the Plaine, probably because the
tract lay along the river bottom. Apparently Simon Queen had taken up
farming on the Plaine with Ashton's encouragement because Ashton considered the property within the bounds of the White Marsh estate. The lawsuits
over the Plaine were one way of contesting who could live on this property
and who exactly owned it, but they were part of a larger struggle over how
Ashton handled the freedom cases, the property holdings at White Marsh,
and the families who gained their freedom in the courts.

Because of that testimony, Mareen Duvall in turn sued Simon Queen
for trespassing on his land, won the case, and had Simon evicted from the
property. Homeless, Simon Queen returned to White Marsh and lived in the
slave quarters there with his wife and their son, Davy. Within months she
died and left Davy, according to Ashton, "motherless." So despite his freedom, Simon Queen found himself back in the quarters and his son enslaved
for life. That being so, he may have asked Ashton to help him secure Davy's
eventual freedom.[28]

At some point in 1806 free Simon Queen left White Marsh and traveled up to Baltimore to find work. Two of his older sons, who were in their

early twenties, remained enslaved at White Marsh. One of them was also named Simon, the other Michael. Both men ran away in the summer.[29]

Neither Bitouzey nor the corporation responded to Ashton's proposal regarding Davy, and Francis Neale did little to settle Ashton's claims. Within the Jesuits, manners and civility broke down under the stress of financial and personal rivalries. When Ashton went to dine at the manor, the priests told him to leave because his presence was "unacceptable there." In response Ashton wrote a long letter to the Neales and the priests at St. Thomas Manor alleging that they violated their vows because they shunned him at every turn.[30]

In late 1808 the impasse suddenly escalated. At White Marsh, Bitouzey evicted Susanna Queen from her house, giving her little time to find other accommodations before year's end. Ashton complained bitterly to John Carroll about Bitouzey's "cruel conduct." After years of referring to her as "the poor woman" or "the woman," Ashton at long last used her full name in correspondence, writing that "poor Sucky Queen" had been turned out. He thought it "scandalous" that she would be "separated from her husband." Even more galling, Bitouzey gave Susanna Queen's house to Simon Queen, who "keeps a woman called Molly living near the place, to whom he cannot be married, his wife having been her aunt." Ashton considered the house Susanna Queen's property, and not subject to Bitouzey's control or direction. Still, on the last day of the year he offered Bitouzey rent for Susanna Queen to stay at White Marsh with her husband. "The inhuman creature refused it," Ashton recalled, referring to his fellow priest, "and ordered her to go off immediately or he would turn her & her children out of doors [the] next day."[31]

The abrupt eviction of Susanna Queen from White Marsh, Bitouzey surely realized, would send a blunt message to Ashton, the pariah priest, that his tenure and his authority at the plantation had come finally to an end. Bitouzey also likely suspected that Queen would return yet again to Ashton's residence in Charles County and that the rumors of their relationship would follow her there. For her part Susanna Queen "contrived" to stay temporarily with neighbors near White Marsh, but on New Year's Eve 1808, Bitouzey and Simon Queen nailed the door to her house shut so that she could not return.

In early 1809 Susanna Queen left White Marsh and went back to Ashton's plantation in Port Tobacco with her children. Ashton sent her to the slave quarters, where a family took her in. He reported that she was "greatly distressed at her separation from her husband & a burden to me."

He asked Carroll to "rectify matters & have Simon turned away as he ought to be," his own house restored, and "justice to be done to him," so that Susanna Queen could return to White Marsh and claim "her house."[32]

Months went by, but Bitouzey refused to allow Susanna Queen back at White Marsh. She and her children remained at the Hermitage with Ashton. Eventually, they settled on another of his properties nearby called Litchfield Enlarged. Still, neither could go to confession. One priest encouraged Ashton to "make use of violence to remove her." Ashton replied that it would create "a scandal tenfold" and that she had no other place to go, "being driven out of her old poor place by the malice of others." The same priest suggested bribery, recommending that Ashton simply give her money to go away, but Ashton could hardly believe the suggestion.

"To give her money!!! Where would be the end of it," he wondered. Ashton said that giving her money to leave would amount to "an acknowledgement of guilt on my side." Meanwhile, Charles Neale, the priest at St. Thomas Manor, went out of his way to remind both Ashton and Susanna Queen that a reckoning awaited them: "1. you must certainly know that if there ever has been any criminality between you for which I must take the word (in confession viz) a removal will be necessary, 2. If you come to me I shall insist on the removal of the subject of scandal whether real or supposed." For a third time, Ashton asked Carroll to intervene, but clearly the bishop had already made up his mind. Carroll's silence amplified his last written words to Ashton, urging him to admit his offenses ("if your eye &c."). Carroll thought that Ashton had something to confess and should do so, that if his eye sinned, he should, as the Gospel demands, pluck out his eye.[33]

But Ashton never confessed to the paternity of Queen's eldest children. Instead, a curious series of events led him to file yet another lawsuit. In the summer of 1809 the trustees of the Jesuit corporation, meeting again at White Marsh, resolved to apprehend a runaway from White Marsh they called Negro Tom. They authorized any of the priests and overseers on their plantations to seize Tom on sight and bring him back to White Marsh. They probably knew full well that Tom was living at the Hermitage with Ashton. In fact, he may have been Susanna Queen's husband. In any case, one day in late August the overseer at St. Thomas Manor and three other men attempted to take Tom by force from the Hermitage. Ashton promptly went to Port Tobacco, where he swore out an affidavit in the county court accusing "four nuns in men's clothes" of an "attack" on "Negro Tom." The suggestion that the men were "nuns" was vintage Ashton: a smear, a snide insult, and an alcohol-induced extravagance implying that they were weak, womanly cowards.[34]

The very attempt to seize Tom ironically provided Ashton with an opportunity to drum up a case in chancery court about the still unresolved settlement of his claims against the corporation, one that might drag into public all of the internal correspondence among the Jesuits about his relationship with Susanna Queen. Ashton threatened to bring into court the private letters from Carroll that would substantiate his claims that the corporation and the priests had acted with malice, propagated slander against him, and attempted to take his property. Because the so-called nuns came from St. Thomas Manor, where the Reverend Charles Neale managed the estate, and because Neale had refused his confession, Ashton sued him for slander along with the Reverend Joseph Fenwick, who allegedly had spread some of the rumors.

When Leonard and Francis Neale learned of Ashton's slander suit against their brother, they were outraged. Leonard Neale, now president of Georgetown College, wrote Carroll that Ashton intended to violate the confidentiality of their private correspondence and that Ashton thought that the letters would ultimately exonerate him. Horrified that Ashton would turn an ecclesiastical inquiry into a public airing of their dirty laundry, Neale warned Carroll that the "pretended slander" at the center of Ashton's lawsuit constituted "a glaring insult to [Carroll's] Episcopal Authority." Only Carroll had the legal and divine power to adjudicate the questions that surrounded Ashton's potential confession. "It appears to me," Leonard Neale informed Carroll in August 1809, "that the lenity hither shown him has plunged him into folly where he must finally perish." According to Neale, Ashton "declares that he will shortly root me out of C[harles] County—He is condemned + despised by all. He says that before long he will show us that he has a right to five or six more Negroes at the White Marsh."[35]

The last sentence of Neale's missive revealed what had remained bubbling below the surface of the dispute since at least 1789. Underneath the controversy between the priests surged the enslaved families of White Marsh and their quest for freedom, two decades of resistance that had roiled Maryland. The Neales had gradually emerged in those decades as the most strident and committed slaveholders in the Jesuit order. They bought and sold slaves routinely and defended their slaveholding as natural, lawful, and biblically sanctioned. One of their relatives was the principal slave dealer and trader for the Sisters of Visitation, routinely selling the enslaved people held in the dowries of the sisters entering the convent. Ashton's great offense, they implied, came from his softness on the question of slavery. After all, Ashton manumitted the Mahoneys and some of the Queens, intervened in the affairs of White Marsh in his retirement, and provided sanctuary for defiant enslaved men such as Tom. Moreover, he intervened on behalf of Susanna Queen for years, fueling the rumors that he was the father of her first two children. After Ashton appeared in the Charles County Courthouse in August 1809 to say that the Jesuits tried to take the alleged fugitive Tom from him unlawfully, Leonard Neale exploded. "For God's sake," he pleaded with Carroll, "do something to correct the monstrous evil which flows in on us from this unhappy man."[36]

The Neales maintained that public opinion in Port Tobacco had soured against Ashton and that his actions would endanger the Jesuits, their estates, and their slaveholding much more broadly. They thought that Ashton's behavior threatened to weaken, even undo, the political position of the Catholic Church in an overwhelmingly Protestant slaveholding society. "The Protestants are universally scandalized at his conduct," Leonard Neale concluded. For the Neales, the problem was not so much Ashton's drinking as his proclivity to upend the slaveholding order of the Jesuits and in turn to undermine the gentry class up and down the Western Shore of Maryland. Ashton's manumissions, combined with his willingness to let Susanna Queen and her children live openly and freely at Litchfield Enlarged on the hilltop overlooking St. Thomas Manor, betrayed every precept of the slaveholders. In this situation the Neales and their allies considered Ashton's motivations immaterial because his actions and his conduct sent a message they could not abide. The Neales reinforced to Ashton that neither he nor Susanna Queen would be allowed to come into the confessional and pretend to avoid the question of the nature of their relationship, indeed of Ashton's paternity. Ashton maintained that placing such conditions on a sacramental rite trespassed far outside the bounds of their authority. None of Ashton's references to canon law and none of his threatened suits in common law seemed to persuade either the Neales or their bishop, John Carroll. In the midst of the affair Charles Neale was elevated to superior of the Jesuit order.[37]

Finally, under pressure from Carroll, Ashton retracted his slander lawsuit in chancery court and withdrew his highly charged affidavit. Ashton, it appears, never intended to bring the lawsuit to trial. Instead, he filed the case because he wished to scare Neale and Fenwick (to put them "*in terrorum*"). As for Carroll's private correspondence, Ashton said that it was "never intended to be brought into evidence." To prove his loyalty to Carroll, Ashton went down to the Charles County Courthouse and filed another affidavit officially retracting his earlier statement about the attack on Tom. He swore that he had "no knowledge of the attack" except "from Negro Tom."

By admitting that his earlier testimony was based on hearsay, from statements Tom made to him, Ashton avoided responsibility for his earlier statement without actually saying it was untrue. In fact, Tom's account to Ashton remained plausible: that Charles Neale's overseer and some others came onto Ashton's property to seize him by force and that one of them had on Neale's "breeches."[38]

As 1809 drew to a close, Ashton and Carroll seemed to have reached a tenuous accord. Ashton asked Carroll to keep the decision to remove his faculties as a priest a secret. He was prohibited from saying Mass. The prohibition, if made public, could become the most damning evidence of his guilt, affirming at least within the Jesuits that Carroll did not believe his denials of paternity. If it became public, Ashton admitted, the Neales would see it as "a triumph." Even at this desperate hour, Ashton maintained his innocence to Carroll, claiming that the "infamous lie" about him and Susanna Queen was a "ridiculous story" that was used against him by the Neales and twisted "into a canonical fault requiring investigation for suspension." The longer he went without saying Mass, the more awkward the situation would become, and his fellow priests would expect some sort of explanation. The matter could not remain private for long. To Ashton's delight Carroll responded in early November with a letter expressing forgiveness, restoring his faculties, and indicating that he would not launch another internal investigation into the matter. Ashton considered himself vindicated, if not in the eyes of the denizens of Port Tobacco, then at least in the eyes of his superior.[39]

Meanwhile, enslaved families continued bring large-scale lawsuits against Maryland slaveholders. The Ogleton family claimed that they were descended from a free woman. The Queens still had cases on the docket. Dozens of witnesses in Prince George's County and Charles County were being called into court. Despite the outcome in *Mahoney v. Ashton,* the freedom suits were by no means finished.[40]

In early 1810, still without a pension from the Jesuit corporation and still excluded from the confessional at St. Thomas Manor, Ashton privately decided to rewrite his last will and testament. If he could not make a statement in public about Susanna Queen, he would do so in private, a statement that would send a clear message to the Jesuits and to the Queens, a statement that would send shockwaves through several generations. He directed most of his property to his fellow Jesuit the Reverend Notley Young, including seven tracts of land totaling more than a thousand acres. By tradition Jesuits in Maryland gave all of their property to another Jesuit in a chain of wills that concentrated and maintained their properties in the hands of the society. In the 1790s, when the corporation gained its Maryland charter, all priests including Ashton surrendered all of their property at that moment to the trust, but Ashton continued to acquire more property off the books through either purchase or inheritance. When he died, he possessed not only more than a thousand acres of land but also bank stocks, insurance policies, credit accounts, and to the very end a family of enslaved people he may have brought from White Marsh.

But unlike his fellow priests, Ashton did not give all of his property to the corporation or to Georgetown College. Instead he specifically named the eldest children of Susanna Queen in his revised will and gave them everything else he possessed. "To a youth called Charles Queen and his sister, Elizabeth Queen, the children of Susanna Queen," Ashton bequeathed the tract of land called Litchfield Enlarged, "whereon they now live." He specified that all horses, cattle, grain, tobacco, and utensils on the place were included in his bequest. Next, he named Charles as the inheritor of "a negro man called Butler" and all of the male children of "a Negro woman called Linny." Finally, he named Elizabeth the inheritor of "the negro woman Linny" along with all of her "other children."[41]

No other piece of evidence is as persuasive as Ashton's will that Ashton had coerced Queen in a sexual relationship when she was in her teens. She won her freedom suing him in court in 1796. She married a man he enslaved at White Marsh. She had her own house on the plantation, on a promise she extracted from Ashton. Susanna Queen's eviction from White Marsh set in motion events that she turned to her ultimate advantage. After her eviction she took her children to Charles County and bargained with Ashton to live on his property at Litchfield Enlarged. A year later Ashton revised his will to name two of her children as beneficiaries. They received a large piece of his property when he died in 1815, and in that same bequest her children became the owners of another enslaved family.[42]

By this time nearly all of the free Queen family members from White Marsh had left Prince George's County and moved across the Patuxent River into Anne Arundel County, where Quakers such as James and Gerard Hopkins had already manumitted numerous other families. Some, like Susanna Queen, were married to enslaved persons who still lived at White Marsh. Others in the family may have married enslaved men or women nearby. In 1807 Proteus Queen leased a piece of property from Richard Hopkins for 1,600 pounds of tobacco a year, striking the deal in partnership with James Parker, a free black man whose family the Quaker Hopkins manumitted.[43]

Proteus was head of his own household in 1810. Winifred, Phillis, Mary, Lewis, John, Charity, Rachel, Nancy, Sally, Jemima, and Thomas Queen each also headed free families in Anne Arundel County. By 1810 the free Queens of Maryland had grown in number to 143, but only 7 remained in Prince George's County. The settlement became the foothold for the Queen family's freedom. Ashton's bequest to Susanna Queen's children added landed property in Charles County, another base in the family's climb toward freedom.

Ashton went to his death determined to keep his property out of the hands of the Jesuit corporation. When he died and left the Queen children as his beneficiaries, the corporation discovered that he had also written Georgetown College out of his will entirely. At this stunning revelation the corporation's trustees pressured Ashton's executor, the Reverend Notley Young, to turn over Ashton's assets for the benefit of the college. They based their request on Ashton's earlier will and quite possibly on his misleading letter to Francis Neale. The trustees decided to pressure Young given "the tenor of the late Mr. Ashton's last instructions" and directed him "to transfer to the College (by sufficient deed and Instrument) all the property devised to him for the pious purposes expressed in those Instructions." But Young responded cautiously, agreeing only that if documents indicated that Ashton clearly intended to make such a bequest, then he would "yield up the property to the Corporation or to Geo Town College immediately." If on the other hand there were no such positive or even partial proofs about Ashton's intent, or if there were any doubt about Ashton's intentions, then the provisions in Ashton's will were to be enforced to the letter. Neither the Jesuit corporation nor Georgetown would receive anything in that case, unless and until Notley Young died and gave them whatever remained of Ashton's property in his will. Pressured to do just that, Notley Young provided for the college in his own will, passing on to the Corporation what Ashton bequeathed to him.[44]

Litchfield Enlarged went to the Queens. So did Butler and Linny and her children, putting them at least out of reach of the Jesuits and the corporation forever.

"An Impartial Trial"

In 1810, when the Reverend John Ashton changed his will, Susanna Queen and her children were already living at Litchfield Enlarged near Hill Top, the prominent high ground overlooking the Jesuit manor situated on the Potomac River. Ashton's surprising bequest to Charles and Elizabeth Queen held up under Maryland law because they were free persons, and under the common law of property they could inherit whether they were his children or not. No Maryland law barred them from inheriting either the land or the two enslaved people. Susanna Queen's children remained the owners of Litchfield Enlarged for decades after Ashton's death, and as late as 1830 they also continued to hold two of Butler and Linny's family enslaved.

Free blacks held enslaved people in bondage for reasons both benevolent and at times exploitative. Many did so to protect family members or because the age restrictions in manumission laws made people ineligible for freedom. Some free black slaveholders used their ownership to control a spouse or reap temporary financial gains. Charles and Elizabeth Queen appear to have liberated some of the Butler family, even as they continued to hold some of Butler and Linny's children as apprentices, perhaps intending to free them at the age of thirty-one.[45]

Susanna's position, reputation, and influence in Charles County and her manipulation of Ashton's relationship with his fellow Jesuits may have been part of a much wider campaign to win freedom for the branch of the family still enslaved there. Nancy Queen's 1796 suit against the Reverend Charles Sewall failed in the county court, but the family brought another freedom suit in 1808, this time against the Reverend Charles Neale, the priest in charge at St. Thomas Manor and the recently appointed Jesuit superior who had refused to hear confession from John Ashton, Susanna Queen, and her enslaved husband. Neale was also the agent of the Jesuit corporation. A successful verdict against him might lead to the liberation of all of the Queens held by the corporation.

The local counsel for the Queens in Charles County made two unexpected moves. First, he requested a change of venue, arguing that the Queens could not receive a fair trial in the county. While the reasons were unspecified, we can imagine the grounds for his request. Since 1793, when petitions for freedom were reassigned from the general court down to the local district courts, Charles County had proven especially unreceptive to freedom suits. More to the point, given the public notoriety of the Queen-Ashton affair in Charles County and the powerful influence of the Jesuit priests around Port Tobacco, finding an impartial jury to hear the case might have been impossible. The local judges dismissed the motion for a change of venue, and the case went to trial in March 1810.

Second, in an even more radical departure from earlier cases, the Queens' lawyer introduced an entirely novel claim that the Queens were descended from a white woman. He may not have consulted with the Queens on this matter. Perhaps he assumed that the jury would look more favorably on the assertion that Mary Queen, though a native of South America, was not African and therefore was "white." Perhaps the Virginia and Maryland rulings on Native American ancestry persuaded him to make the claim. Perhaps he expected to try the case with little of the specific evidence about Mary Queen and hope that a sympathetic jury rendered a positive verdict for the family. If so, the strategy backfired. The jury in Charles County decided that the Queens were not descended from a free white woman and were not entitled to their freedom.[46]

It was at this juncture in 1809–1810, with the cases in Maryland at a standstill, that families like the Queens began to open another round of freedom suits in the federal enclave of Washington, D.C. All of these cases went forward in parallel, the ones in D.C. just beginning, the ones in Maryland coming to a final resolution. In late 1809 other members of the Queen family had already retained Francis Scott Key as their lawyer to bring petitions on their behalf in the Circuit Court of the District of Columbia, a relatively new jurisdiction in which Maryland law and precedent applied. Key's first appearance for the Queens, however, took place not in Washington but in the county courthouse in Port Tobacco, where he argued the case against the Jesuit superior the Reverend Charles Neale at the jury trial in March 1810.

It is not known for certain how the Queen family retained Francis Scott Key's services as their lawyer, but in August 1809 he joined the team of attorneys representing Nancy Queen. His uncle Philip Barton Key had represented Edward Queen and won dozens of their freedom suits in Prince George's County. The younger Key started his apprenticeship in the law with his uncle in Annapolis when he was sixteen, a student at St. John's College, in 1794, the year of Edward Queen's freedom suit in the general court. The young Key was in Annapolis through 1796 and would have been present for the Shorter, Mahoney, and Thomas freedom suits.

In the late 1790s he met Roger B. Taney, who was reading law with Jeremiah Townley Chase, the Federalist jurist who succeeded his cousin Samuel Chase as chief judge of the General Court of the Western Shore. Together young Key and Taney struck up a friendship and set out for Frederick, Maryland, in 1800 to open a law office. Before Key left Annapolis, he fell in love with Mary Tayloe Lloyd, daughter of one of the largest slaveholders in Maryland. Edward Lloyd's Wye plantation encompassed thousands of acres on the Eastern Shore. He held 320 people in slavery when he died in 1796. Frederick Douglass wrote about Lloyd's reputation, "If a slave was convicted of any high misdemeanor, became unmanageable, or evinced a determination to run away, he was . . . severely whipped, put on board the sloop, and sold to Austin Woolfolk, or some other slave-trader, as a warning to the other slaves remaining."[47]

Frank Key and Mary "Polly" Lloyd were married in 1802 in Annapolis, and in 1806 Roger B. Taney married Key's sister, Ann Arnold Phoebe Charlton Key. The two young brothers-in-law practiced law together for a few years. Key counted himself a Federalist, like his uncle, and so did Taney. Key personally purchased and inherited enslaved people. Although he enslaved just five people in these years, it would be a mistake to think that his relationship to slavery was minimal. Instead, every time he visited Terra Rubra, the Key plantation in Frederick County, or his in-laws' Wye plantation on the Eastern Shore, it was plain to see that his family enslaved hundreds of men, women, and children.

For the elder Philip Barton Key, the Mahoney trial had been costly. He was voted out of office in 1800, so he abandoned Annapolis and moved his still lucrative practice to Georgetown in Washington, D.C. President John Adams appointed him to the Fourth U.S. Circuit Court in 1801, but a year later the Jefferson administration shuttered the court. Key built a massive, three-story brick mansion he called Woodley near Georgetown. In addition, Philip Barton had acquired hundreds of acres in Montgomery County on the outskirts of the District. He regained his political prominence defending Samuel Chase in the U.S. Senate against impeachment charges leveled by the Jeffersonian Republicans in the House of Representatives. Chase had been accused of excessive political partisanship in Baltimore, but with Key's skillful defense the Senate voted to acquit Chase. His name in the press once again, his Federalist allies supporting him, Philip Barton Key decided to run for Congress in 1806 and won the election.[48]

At this opportune moment, attracted by the booming legal business in the new city, Francis Scott Key joined his uncle in Georgetown. After Philip Barton Key won the congressional seat, his nephew took over their legal practice. Within a few years, thanks to his uncle's patronage, the young lawyer was busier than he ever dreamed. The "confounded courts" trapped him for months on end. With four children, he was "in a perpetual hurry." Key found his footing quickly and even rose to a degree of early fame because of his family connections, his marriage, his political allies and friends, and the influence of his uncle. Philip Barton Key discredited nearly every freedom suit brought against the slaveholders of Prince George's County, but he had won Edward Queen's case in 1794 and Phillis's case in 1796. When the Queen family looked for lawyers in Washington, D.C., they probably turned to Philip Barton Key, and he sent them to his enterprising nephew.[49]

The essence of the Queens' appeal in Maryland's High Court of Appeals was that the trial should have been moved out of Charles County in order to ensure "an impartial trial." The young Key hustled over to Annapolis to argue the appeal. The justices on the appellate court upheld the lower court and its verdict against the Queens. The grounds on which they did so indicated just how unsympathetic the Maryland courts had become to petitions for freedom and correspondingly how far the political wheel had turned since Edward Queen won his freedom in the general court sixteen years earlier.

The Maryland high court decided that the Queens could not even file an affidavit requesting a change of venue because as slaves they were not "competent" to do so. In the technical language of the court their cause was sub judice—that is, under consideration. "A negro, petitioning for his freedom," in the parlance of the judges, had no standing before the law other than to petition. Avoiding any assessment of whether the Queens had legitimate reason to seek another venue, the judges barely acknowledged the personhood of the enslaved petitioners. They had the means to petition the court, but that was all. With their appeal dismissed, the Queen family had exhausted all options in Maryland.[50]

It was a chilling moment, one that reversed the assumption behind decades of Maryland freedom suits. For the first time in Maryland, the high court appeared to restrict the scope of petitions and to treat enslaved persons as something other than persons before the court.

As human property.

Between 1789 and 1810 enslaved families in Maryland had won hundreds of freedom suits and used their hard-won emancipation to liberate other family members, acquire property, and use the law to document the history of freedom in their families. From the day he filed his freedom suit in October 1791, it took Charles Mahoney thirteen years to gain his own freedom. In 1807 he registered for a certificate of freedom. Fifty years old, he reported that he was "a free man" who resided in Anne Arundel County and had been raised in Prince George's County.

Nine years later, in 1816, Charles Mahoney was finally able to purchase and free his enslaved daughter Ann. She was sixteen years old; he was almost sixty. When he recorded the official deed for her emancipation and had it witnessed at the courthouse, Charles used the occasion to express the profound nature of what her freedom meant to him. Going well beyond the dry standard language of the legal instrument, he turned the justification for Ann's emancipation into a condemnation of slavery itself. Charles began, "Whereas kind providence has enabled me to purchase my daughter named Ann who was born in a state of slavery and I being willing in consideration of the natural love and affection that [I] have for her to free from obligations of a slave." Though every legal deed required consideration, a price or a value—in this instance, for granting freedom—Charles shunned the typical phrases of the slaveholders, who usually nodded to faithful service or inserted a small symbolic amount of money. He spoke instead of his "natural love and affection" for his daughter. Charles signed with an "X," yet his eloquence in these sparse phrases indicates the personal depth of his long quest to free his family.[51]

Charles's brother Patrick did the same. He managed to buy and free his seventeen-year-old son Gabriel Mahoney on April 5, 1815. Described as a "bright mulatto" in the Prince George's County manumission record, the young Gabriel had a small scar on his left leg where he had been bitten by a dog. A year later seventeen-year-old Eliza Mahoney, possibly Gabriel's sister, was also freed in Prince George's County.[52]

The Mahoneys, like the other families, had accumulated a substantial reservoir of legal experience and knowledge. Earlier, when Charles Mahoney needed to find witnesses who could testify about his great-great-grandmother's freedom, he went to Washington, interviewed knowledgeable whites, and returned to Prince George's County with more evidence for his case. He attended all of the depositions in person so that he could hear every word the slaveholders said about his family. Independent, determined, and acting on his own initiative, Charles built the case against the Jesuits and then forced some of the largest and most powerful slaveholders in Maryland to liberate his wife and children. Sometime in the 1810s, he moved his family into Washington. In addition to Ann, he and his wife had two younger daughters. All three were free by 1820. They also had three enslaved boys living in their household. Perhaps Charles planned to free them as well. Mahoney had established a legal foothold on freedom in Washington, and for the time being their freedom was secure.[53]

Around this time, in the spring and summer of 1810, five of the principal families in the White Marsh trials brought another round of freedom suits in Washington. Whether they coordinated with Charles Mahoney is uncertain, but the relatively new Circuit Court of the District of Columbia

offered a fresh venue for their old claims. The Queen family, the Joice/
Mahoney family, the Davis family, the Shorter family, and the Thomas family
all won cases in Maryland in the 1790s but suffered later reversals, culminating in the *Nancy Queen v. Charles Neale* decision in the High Court of
Appeals. These families had depositions and evidence stretching back centuries. Even though Maryland law governed the District, the jury pool and
judges were not the same, so their petitions could be heard again. Whether
the judges and the jurors would follow the Maryland precedents remained
unclear. Legal rules and procedures were changing. Freedom suits in the
D.C. court were literally untested.[54]

Looking into the murky future, the Queens, in particular, may have
realized that only their family was in a position to do in the Washington,
D.C., court what the Mahoneys attempted in Maryland—use their ancestor's
unusual history to raise the *Somerset* principle of freedom and open up a wider
debate about the legitimacy of slavery in the United States. To do so they
would have to prove that their ancestor, Mary Queen, set foot in England.

ABD

During the Reverend John Ashton's long battle with the Jesuit corporation, a young Prince George's County lawyer named Allen Bowie Duckett vaulted into the leading ranks of Democratic-Republicans. I knew little about this ancestor of mine other than that he was appointed to the D.C. Circuit Court by Thomas Jefferson and therefore stood among the more distinguished and notable figures in my family. Then I found out that one of his first clients was the Reverend John Ashton and that he defended the Jesuit corporation against the Queen family freedom suits. I did not know at first what to do or think about Allen Bowie Duckett in light of this new information, so I decided to find every scrap of evidence I could assemble about him. At the Maryland State Archives in Annapolis, I searched for days through the dusty old court dockets and judgment books, but I found almost no trace of him in these volumes. What little I could find eventually overshadowed the inoffensive sketch I had in hand from my family's narrative.[1]

After graduating from the College of New Jersey (now Princeton University) in 1791 and reading law, Duckett aligned himself with the ascendant party of Jefferson. He was elected to the House of Delegates in 1796 and again in 1798, then was selected by the new majority in the Democratic-Republican legislature to serve on the governor's executive council, presumably to keep the Federalist governor in check. In 1800 Duckett held four enslaved people in bondage. He neither personally manumitted an enslaved person nor professionally represented a person of color in court. Instead, he made his mark defending slaveholders in freedom suits. He represented the Reverend Ashton and the Jesuits in their cases against the Queen family in 1796. He appeared for Ashton in the land dispute with Mareen Duvall and in the suit against Germain Barnaby Bitouzey, his initials, "ABD," neatly positioned in the margin of the court docket, his presence noted and recorded.

In 1806 his father, Thomas Duckett, the judge in whose court Phillis Queen and more than twenty others had won their freedom, died, leaving an enormous estate to Allen Bowie. The thirty-one-year-old lawyer inherited 929 acres in Prince George's County valued at £4,649, forty-nine enslaved people, 97 ounces of silver plate, and other property valued at £6,235.71. Elevated in rank and position, Allen Bowie gained an appointment that year from President Thomas Jefferson as a federal judge on the Circuit Court of the District of Columbia.[2]

Allen Bowie Duckett left no letters or correspondence. Instead, a singular piece of his writing has survived, an advertisement he placed in the *National Intelligencer* for the capture of a runaway slave. Duckett offered a $100 reward for the return for a man "who calls himself Robert Thomas." Using the occasion to disparage freedom suits such as those filed by the Mahoneys, he warned his readers that Thomas could "read and write very well" and speculated that he would forge a certificate of freedom claiming to be "one of the Negroes, who, a few years ago, petitioned by the name of Thomas, and obtained their freedom in Maryland." Duckett was suggesting that he had no basis for freedom other than his claim to the surname "Thomas." The disparagement was a tactic of slaving, well honed and widely used. Slaveholders referred only to the name they gave the enslaved person. They denied the enslaved any legitimacy as a member of a separate family. They assumed the supremacy of the master's "family."

Duckett's physical description of Robert Thomas was even more revealing. Here, Allen Bowie traded in the racial language of enslavers like his political idol Thomas Jefferson. He told his readers that Thomas was about five feet ten, twenty-four or twenty-five years old, and had "large black eyebrows, large full eyes, not very dark, and is a stout, well made, handsome fellow." His hair was "thick, but not quite straight, and he wears it nicely trimmed, combed and ridged on the top." He was "fond of wearing boots, and pays great attention to his dress."

Then Duckett elaborated in characteristic fashion. "He speaks deliberately, and is more correct in conversation than persons of his color usually are." The diminishment was the signal, the way of thinking, the presumption of racial superiority that men like Allen Bowie Duckett inherited, repeated, and circulated. There can be no doubt that this arrogance was widely shared among the planter elite. Thomas Jefferson made similar statements in his *Notes on the State of Virginia*. The character of the conversion to slavery and its acceleration over the eighteenth century in the Chesapeake produced on the one hand presumptive racism like Allen Bowie's and on the other hand the specific conditions for Robert Thomas's resistance to that racism, including his appearance, his speech, his manners, and his literacy. We can add to those qualities his family's legal successes and his subsequent escape.[3]

Because Allen Bowie Duckett began his career representing the Jesuits against the freedom suits of the Queens in Prince George's County, he knew that the Thomas family in next-door Charles County tried simultaneously to gain their freedom in the general court. Led by Robert and Judy Thomas, the family enlisted Gabriel Duvall as their attorney in the 1790s and sued several Catholic priests and a number of the county's largest slaveholders. Philip Barton Key stepped in to defend the priests. Lawyers on both sides collected more than thirty depositions. The Thomases claimed that they were descended from a free white woman, but Key disparaged the testimony and succeeded in having some of it thrown out because the white women who testified for the family also "kept company with Negroes." The smear campaign against the character of these women worked, and the courts largely disregarded their testimony. The Thomas claims fell apart under this assault.[4]

The Thomases were met with another, even fiercer round of disparagement. When they threatened to sue slaveholder Alexander Scott, he responded by writing personally to every lawyer in the District to warn each them not to take the case. "Two of my negroes," he explained, ". . . have assumed the surname of Thomas and are about to apply to you to file petitions for their freedom . . . The fact is that these fellows of mine are two of the most worthless, drunken, & notorious scoundrels in the District." Eventually with the cases still pending, Philip Barton Key wrote Scott to inform him that the Thomases lost their cases in the Maryland courts. On this word from Key, Scott immediately sold Walter Thomas and Dennis Thomas out of the District before they could take their cases further.[5]

The enslaved people who did not escape, did not win their freedom in court, or were not able to bargain for their own manumission, faced a newly terrifying prospect after 1800: they might be sold south to the cotton fields of Georgia. The interstate slave trade began in these years, and the threat of sale hung over every lawsuit, every runaway advertisement, and every negotiation. When Allen Bowie Duckett's client John Ashton tried to strike an

out-of-court settlement with Germain Bitouzey, Ashton asked for the enslaved boy Davy in exchange for dropping all of his claims against the Jesuit corporation. Bitouzey refused the barter and kept Davy at White Marsh.
Over the years Davy must have burned with indignation. His father, Simon,
was free, his cousins were free, yet he remained enslaved. Years later, for "bad
conduct," the Jesuit successors at White Marsh sent Davy to the jail in Washington, D.C., where he was to remain "until sold." Later, Davy was sent to
Baltimore for sale, potentially into the Georgia market. Somehow, at least
temporarily, Davy averted this terrible fate and returned to White Marsh
with "promises of amendment."[6]

Whether the Jesuits intended to sell Davy or just to intimidate him,
everyone involved knew that he could be sold, that the interstate slave market ran through Baltimore and Washington, D.C.

It was always there, anticipating Davy and thousands and tens of thousands of others.

In the round of freedom suits that followed *Mahoney v. Ashton,* the
enslaved men and women of Prince George's—the Joices, Queens, Butlers,
Thomases, and Shorters—would challenge the racial assumptions of men
like Allen Bowie Duckett again. Like Davy, they were taken to Washington,
D.C. Like the Thomases, their claims would be subjected to intense scrutiny
and widespread derision from slaveholders. Every attempt to discredit them
would be made.

When the slaveholding families of Prince George's County, like mine,
moved into the District of Columbia and slowly colonized the federal enclave, slaveholders like Allen Bowie Duckett brought with them the inheritances of many generations. None was more insidious than their presumption
of racial superiority. None more was destructive than their bland willingness to sell anyone they deemed necessary.

PART II

The Inheritance

He had still one other, a beloved son; finally he sent him to them, saying, "They will respect my son." But those tenants said to one another, "This is the heir; come, let us kill him, and the inheritance will be ours." So they seized him, killed him, and threw him out of the vineyard. What then will the owner of the vineyard do?

—MARK 12:7–9 (RSV)

CHAPTER 5

Queen v. Hepburn—A Question of Freedom

I was born free and lived in Wyorkill in New Spain & was taken
from thence by Capt. Woods Rogers in Queen Ann's reign.

—MARY QUEEN, VIA FREDUS RYLAND,

FEBRUARY 26, 1796

Priscilla and Mina Queen arrived at the U.S. Capitol on June 20, 1810, for a
court hearing that would decide if they were free. The building they entered
was hardly a symbol of national permanence. It had been under almost constant repair, its original timbers rotten, its plaster cracked, its wooden staircases giving way. In the Senate wing, both the Supreme Court and the District
court met in the basement, where the din of brickwork and plastering rum-
bled ceaselessly through the lobby, entrance halls, and staircases. Dozens of
carpenters, plasterers, and tradesmen—enslaved as well as free—were fin-
ishing the vaulted ceilings outside the courtroom. Painters were at work on
the trim. The exterior entrances were equally chaotic. A ramshackle set of
wooden planks composed a precarious walkway between the two wings of
the Capitol, and a shallow brick platform greeted visitors to the court. The
grounds up on the hill were otherwise "seamed with numerous gullies."
Pennsylvania Avenue, one observer wrote, "was little better than a common
country road. On either side were two rows of Lombardy poplars, between

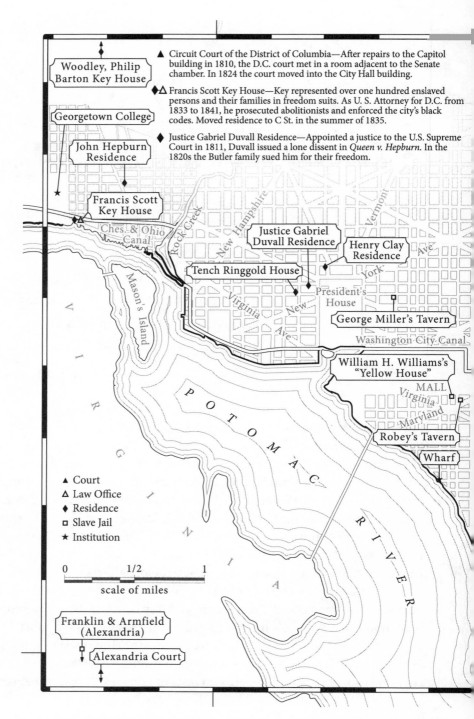

Woodley, Philip Barton Key House

▲ Circuit Court of the District of Columbia—After repairs to the Capitol building in 1810, the D.C. court met in a room adjacent to the Senate chamber. In 1824 the court moved into the City Hall building.

Georgetown College

◆△ Francis Scott Key House—Key represented over one hundred enslaved persons and their families in freedom suits. As U. S. Attorney for D.C. from 1833 to 1841, he prosecuted abolitionists and enforced the city's black codes. Moved residence to C St. in the summer of 1835.

John Hepburn Residence

◆ Justice Gabriel Duvall Residence—Appointed a justice to the U.S. Supreme Court in 1811, Duvall issued a lone dissent in *Queen v. Hepburn*. In the 1820s the Butler family sued him for their freedom.

Francis Scott Key House

Ches. & Ohio Canal

Rock Creek

New Hampshire

Vermont

Justice Gabriel Duvall Residence

Henry Clay Residence

Tench Ringgold House

York

Virginia

New

Ave

President's House

George Miller's Tavern

Washington City Canal

Mason's Island

V
I
R
G
I
N
I
A

P O T O M A C

R I V E R

William H. Williams's "Yellow House"

MALL

Virginia

Maryland

Robey's Tavern

Wharf

▲ Court
△ Law Office
◆ Residence
◻ Slave Jail
★ Institution

0   1/2   1

scale of miles

Franklin & Armfield (Alexandria)

Alexandria Court

A narrative map of the Washington, D.C., freedom suits, ca. 1815–1838
(M. Roy Cartography).

♦ Woodley, Philip Barton Key House—Key was retained by the Jesuits to stop the freedom suits. A staunch Federalist, he won a seat in Congress, serving from 1807 to 1813. His son Philip Barton Key Jr. bought a sugar plantation and moved to Louisiana in 1833.

❑ George Miller's Tavern—After Ann "Anna" Williams leapt from the third-floor window in 1815, the tavern became notorious as a "slave pen." When it caught fire in 1819, antislavery neighbors refused to help fight the blaze.

♦ Henry Clay Residence—Clay was Secretary of State during the presidency of John Quincy Adams from 1825 to 1829. Just before he left office and returned to Kentucky, Charlotte Dupee sued him for her freedom.

★ Washington Navy Yard—In the summer of 1835 white mechanics went on strike. Slave traders seized Daniel Bell from the blacksmith shop and hauled him in shackles to the notorious Yellow House. The strike turned into a race riot that swept the city.

❑ William H. Williams's "Yellow House"—Daniel Bell was confined here in 1835, James Ash in 1839, and Solomon Northrup in 1841, among others. In *Twelve Years a Slave,* Northup called the house "a slave pen within the very shadow of the Capitol!"

★ Georgetown College—In 1838 Rev. Thomas Mulledy negotiated the sale of 272 men, women, and children to sugar planters in Louisiana for $115,000. The enslaved families and their future offspring were mortgaged as collateral to secure the contract.

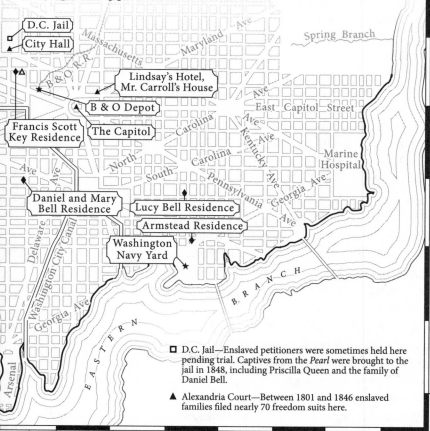

❑ D.C. Jail—Enslaved petitioners were sometimes held here pending trial. Captives from the *Pearl* were brought to the jail in 1848, including Priscilla Queen and the family of Daniel Bell.

▲ Alexandria Court—Between 1801 and 1846 enslaved families filed nearly 70 freedom suits here.

which was a ditch, often filled with stagnant water, . . . in dry weather the avenue was all dust; in wet weather, all mud."[1]

Surveying this scene, Priscilla and Mina Queen might have been confident that the scales of justice would tip in their favor. Fourteen years earlier their aunts and uncles had been freed in the Maryland courts using much of the same evidence they would present. One of them, Simon Queen, now a free man, would take the stand and testify for them in the Circuit Court of the District of Columbia.[2]

But almost nothing about their cases went as they expected.

The lawyer for the Queens was Francis Scott Key, an ambitious, articulate, and supremely confident thirty-year-old, who had already made a name for himself in a high-profile treason case and in several appearances before the U.S. Supreme Court. As Key knew well, the D.C. court offered Priscilla and Mina Queen an especially favorable venue not only because Maryland law applied there but also because juries in the District had already proven themselves mildly sympathetic to enslaved petitioners.[3]

Priscilla Queen's lawsuit singled out the Reverend Francis Neale, the nemesis of John Ashton, a Jesuit, a slaveholder, and the incoming president of Georgetown College. By all accounts Neale was a fine parish priest, but in every other role his lethargic inactivity and lack of imagination frustrated Bishop John Carroll no end. As vice president of the fledgling college he drove off students with his excessive piety and rules against drinking. According to Carroll, Neale was a "worthy" and "virtuous" man, but his administration was "too monastic" and the college had "sunk to the lowest degree of discredit." Neale had managed one of the Jesuit plantations in Charles County where Priscilla Queen was probably enslaved. Installed as the college's president in late 1809, he probably forced Queen to come with him to Georgetown. She undoubtedly realized that the minute she set foot in the city she had new legal grounds, and a new venue, to sue for her freedom.[4]

The defendant in Mina Queen's case, a thirty-five-year-old slaveholder named John Hepburn, was barely solvent. He came from a family of considerable wealth and position in Prince George's County, but he went bankrupt in 1800. To avoid debtors' prison, Hepburn had to place himself at the mercy of the state legislature. His creditors took everything except a handful of books, a bookcase, and his clothes. He left Prince George's County, moved just south to Charles County, relocated to Baltimore, and eventually made his way to Washington, D.C., the new capital city on the Potomac River. Scheming to reconstitute his lost wealth, Hepburn contrived within a few years to claim Mina Queen and her daughter Louisa as his property and forced them to go with him to Washington. The lawsuit could free both mother and daughter.

In fact, it seems plausible that some of the Queens may have contrived to get *themselves* into Washington, that they planned, plotted, and even arranged their presence in the city and orchestrated their lawsuits in the circuit court. Priscilla Queen may have seized the opportunity that the feckless Reverend Francis Neale gave her when he left Charles County in 1809 and returned to the presidency of Georgetown College. She would have been acutely aware of Nancy Queen's pending freedom suit against the Reverend Charles Neale, Francis's brother, the Jesuit superior, and the agent of the Jesuit corporation. The trial had been delayed throughout 1809 as the lawyers in Charles County collected depositions. In similar fashion Mina Queen knew that John Hepburn's move from Baltimore to Georgetown on the heels of his recent bankruptcy gave her an unprecedented opening. By happenstance she found herself just blocks from her cousin Priscilla and less than two miles from the estate of their family's erstwhile attorney, Philip Barton Key. Both were even closer to the law offices of Francis Scott Key, in Georgetown.

The younger Key took their cases, perhaps at his uncle's urging, perhaps because the Queens were the only freedom cases Philip Barton Key ever won, or perhaps because theirs was one of the only freedom claims that his uncle ever believed. At some point in mid-1809, when Francis Scott Key came to Charles County for a hearing in Nancy Queen's freedom suit, either Nancy or Priscilla may have met with Key, informed him of the Reverend Francis Neale's imminent departure for Georgetown, and persuaded him to bring Priscilla's freedom suit in Washington, D.C. The Queens in Charles County had already concluded that an impartial trial could not be heard there. They may have put him in contact with Mina Queen, as well as with Alexis Queen and Hester Queen, because all three had been taken to D.C.

From that moment on, Priscilla and Mina Queen's lawsuits opened a dramatic second phase in the freedom suits, just as the capital city was being built on the Potomac River and another war with Great Britain appeared on the horizon. Based on what had happened to the Mahoneys in Maryland, the Queens likely knew that their freedom suits had the potential to turn into a sprawling legal contest. If they could prove that their ancestor had set foot in England, especially if they could establish that she came into Maryland before 1715, then they might be able to use the English precedents that declared slavery unlawful. They could not have foreseen the perverse course their cases would take: how their legitimate claims to freedom would be twisted into a set of rules that would protect the property rights of American slaveholders for generations to come.

"Spoke the English Language Plain and Distinct as Any Body"

By 1810 approximately a thousand African Americans were already free in the District—nearly four out of every ten black people—and the number of free blacks had quadrupled in less than six years. Many of these free people, including Charles Mahoney, had won their freedom in Maryland either in court or through hard-won negotiations that led to their manumission. They moved to the federal capital, where skilled workers were in demand and slaveholders were outnumbered.[5]

It seems likely that Priscilla and Mina Queen knew that Charles Mahoney was living as a free man in Washington, D.C. And he may have helped them. A growing network of free black families could support more freedom suits. The freedom to travel through the city and back and forth from Virginia to Maryland made a crucial difference.

Such independence and initiative alarmed white slaveholders across the borders of the new capital, in Virginia and Maryland. One Virginia congressman tried to clamp down this kind of mobility, because he thought that it led inevitably to freedom suits and escape attempts. The enslaved, he complained, "now begin to think they are all to be free."[6] Slaveholders in and around the District pushed for curfews, vagrancy ordinances, and slave patrols to limit free black people's mobility. The mayor and the city aldermen enacted a series of the toughest black codes in the United States, imposing a ten o'clock curfew on all black residents. Only Richmond, Virginia, rocked by Gabriel's Rebellion, attempted to control free black citizens as closely as the District did.[7]

Still, the city hummed with construction. Bricklayers were everywhere. In the Senate Chamber they shored up the original rotten timbers. On Capitol Hill new houses and hotels were under way. Contractors scoured the countryside to find free and enslaved skilled laborers, tradesmen and artisans who would spend years constructing the federal government's numerous installations, including the Capitol and the White House. Slaveholders in nearby counties in Maryland and Virginia scrambled to compete for the relatively lucrative and reliable government contracts so that they could hire out slaves they no longer needed on their tobacco plantations. The District's largest single landowner, Daniel Carroll of Duddington, raced to complete a fifty-room hotel, three stories high, with one hundred feet of frontage on First Street directly across from the Capitol. The whole block on First between East Capitol and A Streets was known as Carroll's Row.[8]

Despite the construction boom, Washington looked and felt like a cluster of rural villages. Pierre L'Enfant's masterful layout of the federal capital featured grand avenues but had yet to be realized. Vast meadows and common spaces separated Capitol Hill from Georgetown three miles to the west, the largest residential area in the city. Another settlement was springing up to the southeast of the Capitol around the Washington Navy Yard, situated on the East Branch of the Potomac River. Five miles south of the Capitol and on the opposite bank stood the bustling town of Alexandria, a part of the District but distinct from the City of Washington. In Alexandria at least forty or fifty brick houses were laid out on a grid of cobblestone streets, facing numerous wharves along the river. Ships lined up bound for the West Indies or the European trade.[9]

One close observer of Washington's landscape at the time recalled, "The Capitol itself stood on a steep declivity, clothed with old oaks and seamed with numerous gullies. Between it and the navy-yard were few buildings, here and there, over an arid common. Following the amphitheater of hills from the southeast around to the heights of Georgetown, houses few and far between indicated the beginning [of the city]." The White House was a "conspicuous object" on the horizon, but otherwise, gazing down Pennsylvania Avenue, a visitor would see only a handful of scattered houses.[10]

The chief judge of the circuit court in Washington was William Cranch, a Massachusetts-born Federalist and a nephew of Abigail Adams. Cranch moved to Washington almost as soon as the federal city was established and earned a reputation as an expert in property contracts and land transactions. He was appointed to the D.C. court in 1801 by President John Adams, one of the so-called midnight appointments the Federalist Adams made as he left office. Despite his Federalism Cranch was elevated to chief judge in 1806 by Thomas Jefferson. Not yet forty years old when the Queen petitions were filed, Cranch had dedicated himself to turning the law into a profession. He published meticulous reports of cases in volume after volume, in a prodigious effort to define the legal rules to be followed, cited, learned, and studied. In each individual case Cranch looked for its distilled essence, its precedent-setting statement, to be applied in cases to come. He led a court that often gave the benefit of the doubt to slaves and petitioners and applied Maryland law to freedom suits. In Cranch's court black plaintiffs would gain a fair hearing.[11]

The defendant in Mina Queen's case, John Hepburn, was a recent arrival in the District, and he stood for all the contradictions and moral failures of the slaveholding class. Steeped in Enlightenment philosophy and the latest literary works, Hepburn kept a library that included *Cook's Voyages* (three volumes), *The Beauties of the English Drama* (four volumes), *Play House Companion* (two volumes), and *The Plays of Sophocles*. Perhaps he read law in his twenties, for he held on to his edition of Cesare Beccaria's *Essay on Crimes and Punishments* and William Hawkins's *Treatise on the Pleas of the Crown*. The volume of Hawkins delineated every aspect of English law, including the acts outlawing the slave trade. Had Hepburn consulted it, he would have read, "Dealing in slaves on the high seas to be declared piracy" and "carrying away a person as a slave, a felony."

Beccaria's 1767 *Essay on Crimes and Punishments* was one of the most revolutionary works influencing American legal thought. An Italian Enlightenment philosopher, Beccaria argued against tyranny in every form and opposed both torture and the death penalty as cruel and unwarranted. He opposed treating bankruptcy as a felony potentially punishable by death. He also opposed slavery, a condition of unfreedom acceptable only as a punishment for the most violent and heinous of crimes. Otherwise, slavery had no foundation in liberal ideas about the law. Its hereditary condition was offensive, its cruelty suspicious.

Prominent American jurists and lawyers routinely cited Beccaria, especially James Wilson, who was the leading antislavery voice at the Constitutional Convention and had been appointed in 1789 to the U.S. Supreme Court. Beccaria distinguished between tyrannical societies based on "the laws of families" and liberated ones based on the "fundamental laws of a state." The former inspired "submission and fear," the latter "courage and liberty." Beccaria promoted the widest individual autonomy. To those who adhered to the "vain idol called the good of the family" with its warped sense of private morality at the expense of public good, Beccaria asked, "How frequently are men, upon a retrospection of their actions, astonished to find themselves dishonest?"[12]

When Hepburn declared bankruptcy, he had to swear that the books were his only real or personal property and in effect admit that he had squandered the inheritance he had received in 1775. His grandfather had bequeathed him over a thousand acres, including Weymouth, 517 acres, and John and Mary's Chance, 553 acres, as well as several other plantations. Desperate for money to maintain his social rank in the 1790s, the young Hepburn sold off Weymouth and rented out John and Mary's Chance to a relative,

Samuel Hamilton. The lease included two enslaved families at John and Mary's Chance: Andrew and his wife, Henny, and their four children, as well as William, Monica, and her four children. Even with the rental income Hepburn's appetite for high living was undiminished, and he borrowed even more money by mortgaging John and Mary's Chance and the enslaved families of Henny and Monica. When creditors called in these loans, Hepburn could no longer finance his debts. At this desperate moment, Henny and Monica sued John Hepburn for their freedom in Prince George's County Court. Their suit may have been an attempt to avert a creditors' sale that would in all likelihood separate them from their children. Both suits were eventually dismissed because Hepburn was insolvent.[13]

After his bankruptcy John Hepburn left southern Maryland and struck out for Baltimore, where he probably hoped to regain his fortune and reclaim some part of his misspent inheritance. He sued a local slaveholder and tobacco merchant in Baltimore who had also gone bankrupt. Hepburn discovered that the man had hidden some of his remaining property from creditors, most of whom had exhausted their remedy in the courts. When he found out that the Jesuits were pursuing the same assets, Hepburn wrote the agent of the Jesuit corporation to collude. "The less you say about it the better," he advised. If they both kept quiet, others on the list of creditors might miss the opportunity. He knew that enslaved people were often hidden from creditors, sometimes placed with relatives or hired out, occasionally far away, off the books, never declared to the court during insolvency proceedings. Chafing at his loss of rank, grasping at any means to restore his former wealth and position, John Hepburn easily could have used this creditor's suit to claim an enslaved mother and daughter, such as Mina and Louisa Queen.[14]

We do not know precisely how John Hepburn brought Mina Queen and her daughter Louisa into Washington, D.C. Nor do we know exactly how and when the Reverend Francis Neale brought Priscilla Queen to Georgetown. However, we do know that both Mina and Priscilla came from Maryland and traced their ancestry to Mary Queen. They may have been related to Monica and Henny, who sued Hepburn first, or they may have been related to Nancy Queen in Charles County, who sued the Reverend Charles Neale in 1808, the last of the family to bring a freedom suit in the Maryland courts. In either case, there is strong evidence that both Hepburn and Neale spent considerable time in Charles County in this period and therefore that both Mina Queen and Priscilla Queen came from the Charles County branch of the enslaved Queen family.[15]

A singular peculiarity in the District's legal boundaries derived from its status as a federal territory. The city was divided within itself because Virginia law applied in Alexandria whereas Maryland law applied across the Potomac River, in what was called Washington County. No other city in the United States drew on two different bodies of law and negotiated a boundary between courts like the one in the District. Both Virginia in 1778 and Maryland in 1783 prohibited the importation of slaves within their borders. Both provided that anyone brought across their borders illegally was immediately free, but both also exempted slaveholders who intended to become bona fide residents of the state and who therefore would not be bringing enslaved people into the state to sell them into the slave trade. Enslavers had to wait three years before selling someone they brought with them into Maryland.[16]

The curious and unique outcome of the District's legal apparatus meant that a new but invisible boundary was at work. An enslaved person could be brought into the County of Alexandria from the Commonwealth of Virginia without violating the importation law because, effectively, she or he never left Virginia. Similarly, an enslaved person could be imported into the County of Washington from the State of Maryland, but enslaved people could not be carried into either from anywhere else without enslavers having to comply with the law.

Another, more nebulous boundary was created by these parallel legal regimes: enslaved people within the District could not be transported from the County of Alexandria across the river into the County of Washington, and vice versa, without meeting the requirements of the respective importation laws. In such cases, the enslaved persons were entitled to immediate freedom. Congress would close that loophole in 1812, but until then a violation of this sort could give enslaved persons an opening for freedom. Even after, the bar on importations remained. Enslavers ignored the law, sometimes quietly, sometimes brazenly, but the laws remained operative. Under the right circumstances, enslaved people carried across these boundaries could use the law's requirements to bring an airtight case for their freedom.[17]

Both the United States and Great Britain had abolished the international slave trade in 1808, yet in Washington, D.C., trading in slaves continued openly as an everyday affair. Former New York congressman John P. Van Ness advertised in the newspaper a year later that he had "A Negro Boy for Sale." The young man was "about 13 or 14 years old—healthy, able, honest, and strong." Meanwhile, in nearby Prince George's County, the property of Mary Meek Duckett was being auctioned at a public sale, including "the

PERSONAL PROPERTY of the deceased, consisting of Negroes, Beds, Furniture, Cattle, etc. etc." The administrator of this sale, Jacob Duckett, announced that he would be giving nine months of credit on all purchases to qualified buyers. Such sales threw enslaved people into a vast interstate market, as slave traders bought and sold people from Maryland and shipped them to the cotton and sugar plantations in Georgia, Tennessee, Louisiana, and Mississippi.[18]

Even as the transatlantic slave trade was being suppressed, another horrifying traffic was growing within the borders of the United States, equally unchecked, inhumane, destructive, and insidious. Tens of thousands of enslaved people were sold in the 1800s from Maryland and disappeared to the cotton frontier. Free black people too could be taken, sold, and separated from their families before they could get the courts to intervene.

In fact, slaveholders routinely tried to deceive enslaved people that they planned to bring to Washington, D.C., especially when they planned to sell them or send them even farther away from family. When the Reverend Francis Neale arrived in the District to take up his duties as president of Georgetown College in 1809, he was already well practiced in this art. A year earlier Neale used "the profoundest secrecy" to carry an enslaved man named George into an unexpected sale. Slaveholders hid their intentions from the enslaved at such crucial moments and always tried "to keep secret" their plans and financial dealings. A common tactic was to send enslaved people into the city bearing letters of introduction for their own hiring out, but not to tell them that those letters contained corollary instructions such as "sell . . . [the bearer] in any way you may judge best."[19]

Alert to these deceptions, Priscilla and Mina Queen must have moved quickly to file their cases in the first weeks of 1810. They recognized that they were at the greatest risk of being sold, hired away, or moved in late December 1809. Typical hiring contracts usually were up at the end of the year, and slaveholders often made snap decisions to sell. As such, each woman faced potentially distinct dangers. For Priscilla Queen, there was the fact that the Reverend Francis Neale's family included the principal slave trader for the Sisters of the Visitation Convent at Georgetown. As women from prominent Catholic families came into the nunnery and took their vows, they gave over their dowries to the convent. More often than not, these dowries were in the form of enslaved people, so the convent retained a full-time slave trader in Charles County, Maryland, named George W. Neale. Priscilla Queen knew that the Jesuits at Georgetown had ready access to slave traders in Washington and Maryland.[20]

For Mina Queen and her daughter, the situation was equally precarious. They were among John Hepburn's only enslaved property. Given Hepburn's shaky financial history and abrupt movements from Prince George's County to Charles County, to Baltimore, and then on to Washington, Mina Queen had every reason to suspect that she and her daughter might be separated. Her cousins Alexis and Hester were in a similarly treacherous situation. The men who enslaved them owned substantial interests in western lands in Kentucky, and they could be taken west at any moment without notice.

There may have been some urgency when Francis Scott Key filed the Queen petitions for freedom in the south wing of the Capitol, where the D.C. court had its chambers. Perhaps the Queens sensed an imminent sale. The petitioners, Key wrote, "are entitled to their freedom and are unjustly held in bondage." William Brent, the clerk of the court, recorded the petitions and wrote up the subpoenas that the U.S. marshal for the District of Columbia, William Boyd, would issue to the Reverend Francis Neale, John Hepburn, and each of the other slaveholders. "All excuses and delays [be] set aside," Boyd demanded; Neale and the others were to "appear before the Court here immediately, to answer the Petition for freedom."[21]

Priscilla and Mina Queen's claim was as straightforward as it was momentous: their ancestor Mary Queen was a free woman of color born in New Spain who came to the Maryland colony from London in 1715 and was sold as an indentured servant, only to be held in bondage as a slave. Then her children and her children's children were treated as slaves for life. The question before the court was not whether Priscilla or Mina was descended in the female line from Mary. All agreed that they were. Instead, Mary's status as slave or free woman would determine the outcome of the case. Sixteen years earlier, the Maryland courts had ruled unequivocally that "Mary Queen . . . was not a slave," but later rulings in Maryland reversed these decisions. The D.C. court would hear the evidence about Mary Queen all over again and ask, Was she ever free? Was she ever in London?

Even to begin to answer the central question of whether Mary Queen was free or a "slave for life," the Queens faced a deeper, more procedural conundrum. What evidence could be used in a court of law to prove Mary's status a century earlier? After all, many witnesses were long dead. Written records were few and far between. Would the court allow secondhand testimony, which was increasingly called hearsay?[22]

Maryland courts had done just that in the 1790s, and members of the Queen family, led by Edward Queen, had been freed as a consequence. Depositions from earlier cases were introduced in court even though the witnesses could no longer appear. Often they testified to direct knowledge about the status or condition of the ancestor in question. Such out-of-court statements were by definition hearsay, but Maryland judges allowed them into evidence on the understanding that exceptions should be allowed in cases of freedom. In several instances, judges had gone so far as to allow in their entirety secondhand statements about what the declarant heard others say about the status of the ancestor. Other judges tried to make a distinction in out-of-court statements between hearsay based on direct knowledge and what some called "hearsay of hearsay," a secondhand account of what someone heard another person say. Judges often allowed the former and barred the latter.

Francis Scott Key's strategy was to assemble an authoritative cast of witnesses and statements about Mary Queen's origins and status. Priscilla Queen's case against Francis Neale proceeded first. Mina's against John Hepburn followed on the docket a few days later. Key called Simon Queen as one of the first witnesses. Free since 1796 and living at White Marsh, Simon Queen probably testified that his family was descended from Mary Queen. Then Key called Gabriel Duvall, the sitting comptroller of the U.S. Treasury, a former congressman, and the former chief judge of the Maryland General Court. In the 1790s, Duvall represented twenty-two Queen family members in freedom suits, and he had done more than anyone in Maryland to make hearsay testimony admissible in these cases. Duvall's standing alone, as a leading figure in the Jefferson and Madison administrations, would impress the jury. Duvall could personally testify to the clarity of the finding by the Maryland jury in Edward Queen's trial that Mary Queen was not a slave.

Key also hoped to use a series of depositions that Gabriel Duvall had taken in earlier cases. These statements pinpointed crucial details of Mary Queen's life, indicating that Captain Thomas Larkin brought her into the colony in Annapolis and that James Carroll bought her as an indentured servant, not as a slave. As an indentured servant, she would have been contracted to work for Carroll likely for seven years, but her status as a free woman would have been established and recognized, if not ultimately honored. An indentured servant had rights that an African slave did not—even if Carroll bequeathed her in his will to the Jesuits priests.[23]

Most important, Key had unearthed the stunning deposition of Fredus Ryland taken in 1796. Ryland had met Mary Queen when he was in his twenties and heard her story firsthand. Gabriel Duvall took Ryland's deposition in Cecil County, across the Chesapeake Bay, where Mary spent the last years of her life on the Jesuits' Bohemia Manor plantation. Duvall did not identify Ryland until two years after Edward Queen won his freedom in Prince George's County. If Edward was freed on the basis of hearsay depositions about Mary from less reliable sources, then Key probably considered Ryland's nearly direct testimony about Mary Queen unimpeachable.

Ryland's statements about Mary's origins could not have been more astonishing. He reported that she said she was "born free" in Guayaquil (on the coast of present-day Ecuador) and that she had traveled across the Atlantic on the famous privateering voyage of Captain Woodes Rogers, lived in London for three years, and came to the Chesapeake from London. Ryland reported Mary Queen's words directly: "She related to the deponent many circumstances of her life and told him that she was born free and lived in Wyorkill in New Spain." Only in the Mahoney case had the words of an enslaved ancestor been so directly reported; in no other freedom suit had the ancestor in question made such unambiguous statements about her status.

Key knew that proving Mary's residence for three years in England and her origins in New Spain would potentially define her as a free woman, under the common law of England, the landmark *Somerset* decision, and some of the Maryland precedents set in the 1790s. He also knew that Woodes Rogers wrote one of the eighteenth century's best-sellers, *A Cruising Voyage Round the World: First to the South Seas, Thence to the East-Indies, and Homewards by the Cape of Good Hope.* Rogers had conducted a nearly flawless eighteen-month circumnavigation up the Pacific Coast of South America to the Indies and back to London, securing riches for himself, his crew, and his creditors while losing only a handful of men to disease. Most spectacular, Rogers had picked up a stranded sailor named Alexander Selkirk, whose story Daniel Defoe would turn into *Robinson Crusoe.* He also seized twenty Spanish ships and captured hundreds of people. In *A Cruising Voyage* he listed some as "negroes," some as "passengers," some as "prisoners," and others as "Indians."

Fredus Ryland, sixty-five years old when he gave his testimony, remembered Mary as "a sensible woman [who] spoke the english language plain and distinct as any body & had nothing of the Guinea or Negro Tongue in her speech." All the depositions, but especially Ryland's, pointed to the likely conclusion that Mary was not African but a South American who had spent enough time in England to speak the language fluently. As such, these accounts suggested that Mary Queen had to have been an indentured servant, not a "slave for life."

But Neale's attorneys were equally energetic. They brought into court the deposition of Benjamin Duvall, taken in 1794 in Phillis Queen's case and used with great effect against Nancy Queen in her failed suit in 1796. The elderly Duvall was the only witness other than Fredus Ryland to have met and spoken with Mary Queen personally. He described her as African in appearance and manner. Duvall's testimony invented a past for Mary Queen that would predetermine her status as a slave by calling her the "Poppaw Queen." He probably did not know that the Jesuit estates in Popayán, in the southwest highlands of present-day Colombia, modern-day Ecuador's northern neighbor, were some of the largest slave-based plantations in South America by 1700. Jury members would have had little familiarity with the region in New Spain. With this in mind, Benjamin Duvall's deposition created an alternative history for Mary Queen similar to the one Ashton's attorneys developed for Ann Joice as a "Guinea Negro."[24]

When the case went to trial in June 1810, Francis Scott Key did not object to Benjamin Duvall's deposition in court. After all, the deposition was heard in Phillis Queen's 1796 successful case in the Prince George's County Court, when more than twenty Queen descendants won their freedom. The judge in that trial, Thomas Duckett, allowed all of the hearsay evidence in front of the jury. Even a jury of slaveholders disregarded the testimony about Mary Queen as an African. So Francis Scott Key may have expected a similar result and perhaps, furthermore, expected to counter Duvall's hearsay testimony with Fredus Ryland's more compelling statements about Mary.

But when Key attempted to bring Ryland's deposition into evidence, Neale's attorney immediately objected on the grounds that it constituted hearsay and furthermore that Mary Queen's own words, the words of an enslaved person, should not be allowed in court. The judges agreed and announced that "the declarations of an ancestor, while held as a slave, cannot be given in evidence, to prove that the ancestor came from England." The ruling rendered Ryland's deposition a dead letter. In *Priscilla Queen v. Francis Neale* the court had effectively silenced Mary Queen and any other enslaved ancestor whose words might have been remembered.

Key was likely surprised. Surely both Mina and Priscilla Queen saw at that moment that their case had suddenly become precarious. The rule of evidence against hearsay had taken shape in American courts only in the 1780s, and in Maryland, judges such as Samuel Chase and Gabriel Duvall had allowed hearsay in dozens of freedom cases. However, over several decades, lawyers began to invoke the rule to exclude out-of-court statements, and judges began to apply it more strictly. There were exceptions to the rule,

The Capitol in 1800 (Glenn Brown, *History of the United States Capitol*
[Washington, D.C.: Government Printing Office, 1900], pl. 38).
In 1810, when the Queen freedom suits were heard, the court shared a room with
the U.S. Supreme Court. One observer described the courtroom under the Senate
chamber on the south side of the Capitol as "little better than a dungeon."

of course, such as allowing "dying declarations" and other testimony deemed
too important to exclude. Some out-of-court or secondhand statements were
allowable as long as the party introducing the statement was not asking the
jury to believe the statement—that is, to take it as proof of what attorneys
began to call "the truth of the matter asserted." To this point the D.C. court
had been relatively lenient, agreeing to allow the testimony of several deceased persons who had known or heard about Mary Queen. The judges
could have allowed the jury to hear all of the evidence, use its discretion,
and determine which account it deemed more credible, but the judges on
the D.C. bench, led by William Cranch, were at the vanguard of legal pro-
fessionalism. Applying new procedural rules to limit what juries might consider as "fact," the judges began fashioning a more uniform, regular, and
predictable set of outcomes.[25]

In *Priscilla Queen v. Francis Neale* statements from an ancestor
herself would not be heard. The crucial evidence in the Ryland deposition
was out.

A few days later, when Mina Queen's case against John Hepburn went
forward, Key introduced the will of James Carroll into the trial record.
Ashton's lawyers had offered the same piece of evidence in Edward Queen's
case in 1794. The will allegedly bequeathed a woman named Mary to Carroll's
seven-year-old nephew, Anthony Carroll, who subsequently went to London

to study for the priesthood. Neither attorney realized that the will contained a crucial error of transcription. Nor perhaps did the opposing counsel. But the will proved nothing. No other testimony corroborated it. Worse, it raised doubts about the validity of the Queen claim because it was obvious that Mary Queen arrived in the colony long before Anthony Carroll was born. At best it offered a theory that Mary at some point set foot in England.

Desperate, Key attempted for a second time to introduce Fredus Ryland's deposition, even though Hepburn's attorneys—who represented Neale also—had succeeded in keeping it out of Priscilla's trial. And again, all of Benjamin Duvall's deposition was admitted as evidence whereas almost none of Ryland's was. Mary's words as spoken to Ryland, the only ones ever recorded from her, would not be heard in court. The jury could hardly have reached a different verdict, given its instructions. It decided in favor of the slaveholder John Hepburn.

Mina and her daughter Louisa remained enslaved.[26]

"They Arrived in London in the Lifetime of Queen Anne"

The Queen family did not have access to the records that would have proved Mary Queen's origins and freedom, though some of those records existed then and are available today. Their attorney, Francis Scott Key, did not bother to double-check the copy of James Carroll's 1728 will introduced in Edward Queen's 1794 case. What's more, he likely did not know that the copy was inaccurate and that Carroll never referred to Mary Queen in his will. The mistake was costly; it led Key to rely on a line of argument with little evidence in hand and may have precluded him from looking for other evidence.[27]

At the center of Mina's case were competing stories about who Mary Queen was, where she came from, and what happened to her. Both James Carroll, who bought Mary Queen in 1715, and the Jesuit priests in Maryland who were alleged to have inherited her in 1729 kept detailed if irregular account books. The Jesuits managed five major plantations in Maryland, and some of their records traced Mary right up until her death on February 12, 1759.[28]

The voyage of Captain Woodes Rogers generated its own voluminous set of records, largely because Rogers's creditors sued him in chancery court in 1711 in the case of *Creagh v. Rogers*. Every transaction, every item of value on his ships during the voyage, was meticulously accounted for and entered into elaborate balance sheets by the special master in that case.[29]

No single piece of evidence conclusively states that Mary Queen was a free woman when she came to the colony of Maryland, but like finding the missing pieces of a puzzle, each piece aligning with others, the evidence could have been introduced in court to reveal a more accurate portrait of the Queen ancestor. When assembled, in fact, that portrait comes into surprisingly sharp focus.

The first piece of evidence we have about Mary Queen was taken on September 27, 1715, when James Carroll composed a list titled "an account of my negros." Carroll, like other gentry planters, was beginning to acquire enslaved people to work his tobacco fields. So new was his "account" that several of the people he listed had been bought "yesterday." There, second from the bottom, he wrote "Mary bought of Phillips & Larkin." Deponents Benjamin Duvall, Caleb Clarke, and Thomas Warfield all identified Captain Larkin as the man who sold Mary to James Carroll, and Carroll's account book confirms that Carroll had indeed bought a Mary from Phillips and Larkin.

The son of an innkeeper, "Captain" Thomas Larkin had risen in Maryland society through marriage and guile. He owned an 855-acre plantation in All Hallows Parish of Anne Arundel County. He served as a chief justice of the Anne Arundel County Court from 1716 to 1718, and he owned one of the few stone or brick houses in Annapolis. Larkin rose from councilman to alderman to mayor of Annapolis, probably because he had taken advantage of a title dispute to assume 232 acres of prime real estate in town. Mary Queen arrived in Maryland just as Larkin was securing his reputation, just as the colony was expanding beyond the primitive settlements along the rivers into the tobacco lands of the interior, and just as James Carroll was transitioning the labor system of his plantations from indentured servitude to enslavement.

Edward Phillips of London commanded the vessel *Chiswick,* and in April 1713 he signed a power of attorney that allowed Captain Thomas Larkin of South River, Maryland, to represent his interests. Phillips and Larkin, therefore, were associates, and Larkin was empowered to represent Phillips in Maryland. Larkin could sign any legal documents, sell goods, and hold credit for Phillips. A voyage from London in 1714 could easily arrive in Maryland in mid-1715. Whether on the *Chiswick* or another vessel, Phillips and Larkin brought a woman named Mary into Maryland and sold her to James Carroll that summer.[30]

Almost immediately after purchasing Mary Queen, James Carroll sent her with three other enslaved people to work at his Elk Ridge plantation, twenty miles west of his home farm, Fingaul. Elk Ridge was a 990-acre tract that Carroll called the Out Quarter. On May 9, 1716, Carroll recorded that Mary gave birth to a daughter, Suzy, who died in infancy sometime before September. Perhaps because of the child's death, Carroll brought Mary back to Fingaul on July 23, 1716. Then, in October 1717, Carroll purchased a white indentured servant as an overseer, a man named Thomas Barm.

A few months after Barm arrived at Fingaul, in April 1718, James Carroll noted that Mary Queen had a son with an enslaved African man whom Carroll called "Tomboy." Over the next several years, Mary had at least three children who survived into adulthood: Nan or Nanny, Phillis, and Ralph. Richard Disney, a witness in the Edward and Phillis Queen cases in the 1790s, described Nanny as "black as most negroes." Phillis and Ralph, on the other hand, were called "mulatto." Benjamin Duvall testified that Thomas Barm "kept her [Mary Queen] as a Mistress" and that Ralph was their son.

When James Carroll died in 1729, Mary Queen would have been approximately thirty to thirty-five years old, with at least three children. A devout Catholic with no heirs, Carroll took great care to provide direction about the disposition of his large and complex estate. Tomboy, Jack, Jerey, and Dick, all mentioned by name, all enslaved, were to receive, as he put it, "such of my apparel as may be fit for my slaves to wear." Furthermore, Carroll urged that these men be instructed "in the Christian Doctrine." He then gave the majority of his property to Father George Hunter, a Jesuit priest. Carroll's bequest to Hunter included Fingaul, 486 acres, and more than 2,000 acres in Prince George's County, encompassing "White Marsh," "Carrolsburgh," "Chenys Plantation," "Ridgely," and "Taylors Chance," and all of the chattel, enslaved people, and servants on these plantations. In the inventory of Carroll's estate taken in 1729, Mary was listed with a "Negroe Girl" named Nan who was about twelve years old. Her son Ralph was also listed, age five.[31]

Years later, in his deposition, Benjamin Duvall said that James Carroll "gave her [Mary] away or sold her a considerable distance off." Queen's daughters Nanny and Phillis remained at White Marsh in Prince George's County and appear in the records there, but neither Mary nor Ralph was at White Marsh after 1730.

Instead, they can be found in the ledgers for Bohemia Manor, one of the Jesuit plantations in Cecil County, across the Chesapeake Bay on Maryland's Eastern Shore. By the standards of eighteenth-century Maryland, they were indeed sent "a considerable distance off." The priest in charge at Bohemia listed "Old Mary" and "Negro Ralph" repeatedly in his account books. Mary would have been about sixty years old in 1755. She appeared to be living somewhat independently, sold "molasses" and "fowls" to the priests, and was hired out to a man named "Col. Baldwin."[32]

The Jesuit records elevate the overriding importance of Fredus Ryland's deposition. Had Francis Scott Key been able to review the Jesuit accounts and introduce them into evidence, he could have connected specific facts in them to Ryland's statement. He would have had an explanation, as well as a clear timeline, for when Mary Queen came to Maryland and what happened to her after she arrived. Her purchase was listed in James Carroll's "account of my negros" alongside both servants and slaves. Every deposition indicated that her complexion was light. And Ryland's deposition offered an explanation for how and why the Mary Queen described in the Jesuit records could have been a free person when she arrived in Maryland.

Ryland testified that he met Mary Queen in the mid-1740s, when she was living with "John Baldwin who was called Col. Baldwin." He said that before then she lived at Bohemia Manor with the priests. Ryland also knew Ralph, her son. With these details, Ryland established that he had met and spoken with Mary Queen firsthand. What he knew about her is worth quoting in its entirety, but here rearranged and edited from the original into a first-person account:

> She related . . . many circumstances of her life and told me, "I was born free and lived in Wyorkill in New Spain & was taken from thence by Capt. Woods Rogers in Queen Anns reign." After she was on board Capt. Rogers took a Spanish Aquapulco Ship & he also releived a Scotchman named Alexander Selkirk from an Island in the South Sea. She was carried in the ship to London & Capt. Rogers had taken so much money that when he got to england it was landed and carried away in waggons. They arrived in London in the lifetime of Queen Anne & she continued there untill after Queen Anne died. I heard my mother say that the Daughter of Col. Baldwin by a former wife told her that Mary was brought into this Country as a miss by a Captain of a Vessell whose name he does not recollect to have heard and that she had many fine clothes, particularly silk Gowns, but did not hear that she was sold by the said Captain. I knew the Daughter of Col. Baldwin.[33]

Practically every literate person in Washington, D.C., in 1810 knew of Woodes Rogers's voyage. In the hands of novelist Daniel Defoe, the castaway

Rogers rescued, Alexander Selkirk, became *Robinson Crusoe,* the most famous novel of the century. But the story Mary Queen related was too detailed to have been ripped from Defoe or invented out of whole cloth. Instead,
each piece was like a single link in a chain of evidence: each could potentially
be verified, and each might survive independently or be forged together in
the oral record over many generations. We can imagine Mary Queen telling
this series of facts over and over again, repeating the essential parts to connect
the chain of evidence she hoped to pass on.

Fredus Ryland's deposition raised questions that none of the Queen attorneys seemed to have tried to answer. Could Mary Queen really have
been taken from Guayaquil and brought to London by Captain Woodes Rogers? Did she or any passengers other than the soon-to-be-famous Scotsman
Alexander Selkirk arrive in England? Were any people sold as slaves in
England after the voyage?

In short, Rogers's voyage was not a slaving voyage, and some persons
of color were clearly considered free, but Rogers captured scores of people
he referred to as "Negroes" who were sold, given away, and accounted for at
the end of the voyage. In *A Cruising Voyage Round the World,* Rogers revealed little of his captives' fates, whether native or African. On the one hand,
he celebrated the exploits of a free black man who escaped the Spanish. On
the other hand, he gave one of the Spanish priests the object of his desire as
a gift, "the prettiest young female Negro we had in the prize."[34]

The special master appointed by the chancery court in *Creagh v. Rogers* had to provide more clarity about these matters than Rogers himself. He
tabulated an account listing each item bartered or sold on the Rogers voyage, including slaves. He also itemized and sold everything in the holds of
the three ships that returned to Bristol—the *Duke, Dutchess,* and *Batchelor.*
The sales took place at nine public auctions between February 1712 and
May 1713.

The Rogers raiding voyage, to its creditors' surprise, brought almost
no gold back to England. Instead, Rogers captured hundreds of chests of fine
silks, linens, damasks, woolens, ribbons, satins, chintz, serge, and cotton,
in every color and style imaginable—green, yellow, blue, white, calico, and
black. Broadsides and advertisements for the public sales lured buyers to see
these rare fabrics from China, Bengal, and the South Seas.

Several depositions in the 1790s described Mary Queen as a woman
who had "a great many fine Cloaths" and "silk Gowns." In fact, Mary's apparel, clearly an unusual sight in colonial Maryland, was her most distin-
guishing feature, and all the depositions taken in Maryland agreed that she

brought these possessions with her. The timing of the Rogers voyage and its public sales in England, furthermore, fit with all of the other statements on record about Mary Queen. She would have arrived in London in 1711, during the reign of Queen Anne, and she would have embarked for the Maryland colony in late 1714 or early 1715, arriving in summer 1715.[35]

Rogers captured hundreds of prisoners, passengers, and enslaved people. He took at least 183 "negroes" off fourteen Spanish ships between September 1708 and December 1709. Some died. Others ran away. Rogers and his officers enslaved some people for themselves and sold some of the enslaved captives on their way back to England.

Yet the final account books in *Creagh v. Rogers* indicate that thirteen black people "came home to the Owners hands." No corresponding entries in the ledgers indicated that any of the thirteen were ever sold in England. The line in the account book—"Money owing for several Negroes Sold in England"—appeared on the special master's balance sheet, but it was never filled with an amount. The entry remained blank.

What is clear is that thirteen "negroes" from New Spain landed in Bristol, England, and came ashore. They had with them various possessions or "goods" that needed to be transported. They stayed in a boardinghouse. And they had their clothes washed on the company's expense. But no other record of their enslavement or freedom could be found.

What happened to these thirteen "negroes" who arrived with Rogers is, thus, a mystery. Given the rising temper of reform, their public sale as slaves in England would have been highly unlikely, though not inconceivable. Lord Holt, chief justice of the King's Bench, had ruled recently that blacks could not be considered property in the recovery of debts because under English common law "no man can have property in another." The principal merchant behind Rogers's privateering voyage, Thomas Goldney, a Quaker, faced substantial criticism from the Society of Bristol men's monthly meeting for "a voyage carrying commission to fight and force." The society censured Goldney and the other Quaker investors for sponsoring such a violent enterprise, and the Bristol society's pressure may have ensured that the thirteen were not sold in England.

Who were the thirteen, and was Mary Queen among them?

In April 1709, just after Rogers found and rescued Alexander Selkirk in the Juan Fernández Islands, he captured his first prize with "negroes" and women on board. The *Ascension* was a 450-ton galleon out of Panama bound for Lima, commanded by Joseph Morel, with 72 black people (12 women, 50 men, and 10 old men and boys), 14 white sailors and servants, and 7 passengers. A few days later he captured the *Havre de Grace* (renamed the *Marquis*) with 74 black people, 29 white sailors and servants, and 29 passengers. The names of the passengers and mariners, now prisoners, were recorded. Then, a few weeks later, Rogers sailed into Guayaquil, raided the city, and took more prisoners, hostages, and slaves. He released or "turned ashore" some of the prisoners and by all accounts all of the Indians. Nearly six months later, after many of the black passengers had been sold, ransomed, or bartered, Rogers compiled a comprehensive list of the fifty-four left on board the *Ascension.* Thirteen women were on the list, seven of them "young women." One of these was named "Maria."

According to Ryland's statement, Mary Queen was on board before Rogers seized the "Aquapulco" ship, and this timeline was significant. Many of the men were sold at Gorgona Island, off the Pacific Coast of present-day Colombia, where Rogers resupplied before he headed north to hunt the great Acapulco ships he had heard were so heavily laden with booty. Unable to feed all of his prisoners and captives, he consolidated everything of value into the *Duke, Dutchess,* and *Marquis,* and left the rest on the island. Rogers wrote in his report to the investors: "We took what prize goods we could aboard our ships. 10% were mostly Europe course. Bale goods of all sorts, and a good quantity of Negroes."

The woman named "Maria" was one of the few who left Gorgona with Rogers in July 1709. A few months later, Rogers captured the Acapulco ship *Incarnation* (renamed the *Batchelor*). From there, he was bound for the Dutch East Indies, around the Cape of Good Hope to Holland, and finally to Bristol, England.

All of the elements of Mary Queen's statements to Fredus Ryland align with the records of the Rogers voyage. A young woman named Maria (Mary) was on board before Rogers took the Acapulco ship. A small number of black people stayed on the ships and later arrived in England. There was no record of their sale as slaves, and the timing of their arrival was entirely consistent with Mary Queen's account of her years as a free woman in London.

"Better Evidence Than This Cannot Be Expected"

As we have already seen, the circuit court judges in D.C. ruled that Fredus Ryland's deposition about Mary Queen was inadmissible because the words of an enslaved ancestor could not be used as evidence and because Ryland's secondhand account was hearsay. Their decision instructed the jury to disregard these statements and to toss out parts of several other depositions favorable to Mina Queen. Left without any evidence that Mary Queen was a free woman, the jury rendered its verdict in favor of John Hepburn. In the wake of this decision, none of the other Queen cases, including Priscilla's against the Reverend Francis Neale, could go forward unless the verdict in Mina's trial could be overturned.

Mina Queen appealed the decision to the Supreme Court, which heard the oral arguments in February 1813. By this time the largest slave revolt in American history had erupted on the German Coast, up the Mississippi River from New Orleans in Louisiana Territory. Led by the enslaved man Charles Deslondes, hundreds of enslaved people armed with cane knives and axes marched on New Orleans in a dramatic bid to free themselves amid the political instability on the frontier of clashing Spanish, British, and American empires. A U.S. Army cavalry detachment was dispatched to put down the rebellion, and a militia force organized by the slaveholders brutally executed Deslondes and dozens of others. Those captured and tried in New Orleans were also executed, their decapitated heads placed on pikes along public roads. In 1812 war broke out between Great Britain and the United States, this second conflict just as continental and imperial in scale as the Revolutionary War. Like the earlier struggle, the War of 1812 threatened to destabilize every facet of American life, including—indeed perhaps especially—slavery.[36]

The Queens had good reason to feel hopeful that the court might overturn the jury's verdict and allow a new trial to hear the crucial testimony that had been stricken from the record. It seemed plausible that the court might consider the Queen case an opportunity to dampen the allure of freedom from the British. A limited decision allowing hearsay evidence only in cases of personal freedom might serve multiple purposes while not greatly endangering fundamental property rights.

More encouraging, Gabriel Duvall, who was at one time the Queen family's lawyer, had since been appointed an associate justice on the U.S. Supreme Court. He filled the seat vacated by his mentor Samuel Chase. Duvall had been on the court for little more than a year, but he knew the facts of the case better than anyone. As a young lawyer in Prince George's County, he had represented the Queen family when the Maryland courts determined unequivocally that Mina Queen's ancestor "was not a slave." Before he was nominated to the Supreme Court, Duvall's loyalty to the family was such that he appeared as one of Mina Queen's three witnesses in her 1810 jury trial and testified to the validity of her claim to freedom. When Francis Scott Key stood to argue the appeal, Duvall did not recuse himself.[37]

**Portrait of Francis Scott Key by Joseph Wood, ca. 1816
(courtesy of the Walters Art Museum, Baltimore).**

Key represented more than a hundred enslaved families in freedom suits, but he also bought slaves and married into one of the largest slaveholding families in Maryland. Although he manumitted several people in the 1810s, Key never stopped being a slaveholder.

In his oral remarks before the Supreme Court, Key made a fundamental argument that hearsay testimony was necessary in freedom suits. "After a lapse of 100 years, better evidence than this cannot be expected," he said of the hearsay in the depositions. "The general reputation of the fact that the ancestor was free is sufficient to rebut the presumption arising from color, and throws the burden of proof on the other side." Furthermore, Key pointed out that hearsay was introduced to "prove that a certain ancestor came from England" and should be allowed as an exception to the rules of evidence in "cases in which the strength of the claim depends upon its antiquity." Hearsay evidence in these cases, Key maintained, "is always admitted in the Courts of Maryland, under whose laws this case was tried, and its use had been sanctioned by the authority of the highest Court of that state."[38]

It was a strong argument, but Chief Justice John Marshall was not persuaded. He brushed aside the fact that Maryland had allowed hearsay. The rules of evidence would not be broadened further, and the exceptions to allow hearsay would be strictly limited. Marshall would not extend them to petitions for freedom. Nor, according to Marshall, would the court consider "the feelings of the individual . . . on the part of a person claiming freedom." The "danger" of expanding the use of hearsay was simply too great. More to the point, the property at stake was much too valuable. "If the circumstance that the eye-witnesses of any fact be dead should justify the introduction of testimony to establish that fact, from hearsay, no man could feel safe in any property, a claim to which might be supported by proof so easily obtained."[39]

At this point Gabriel Duvall, an otherwise exceedingly reticent justice, issued a brief but strongly worded dissent, one of his only opinions in nearly twenty-five years on the court. Duvall had represented dozens of enslaved people in petitions for freedom, including the Queens, and did more than anyone to develop the exception in the Maryland courts for the admissibility of hearsay evidence in petitions for freedom in the 1790s. He may have wished to be consistent with his participation in the earlier Queen cases. He may also have distrusted the memory of his great-uncle Benjamin Duvall and considered his testimony far less reliable than the depositions the Queens produced. He may have thought that the D.C. Circuit Court justices were trampling on the precedents he had created in the courts in Maryland. Or this case may have hit so close to home because Duvall, a Jeffersonian Republican recently appointed to the court, saw the justices under Marshall nationalizing what had always been a state matter.

Queen v. Hepburn was always about more than the technical questions of evidence and procedure. At its core, the case turned on the question of individual freedom. A Maryland court of law had found that Mary Queen was a free woman. What about her descendants? The freedom suits implied that local conditions and circumstances mattered. They suggested that the power of slaveholders was not absolute but that there were limits on who might be considered a slave—that a person's color was not enough to presume a person's status, that blackness did not mean enslavement. A person's status, after all, was subject to change.

The leading Federalist in the nation, Chief Justice John Marshall personally held more than 150 people in bondage. He accumulated extensive landholdings in Virginia, and he bought and sold enslaved people regularly. Marshall acquired more human property than he inherited, and he sold and transferred dozens of enslaved people to his children, his siblings, and his other relatives. His two sons enslaved more than 250 people. Marshall invested in banks, turnpikes, canals, and other companies, yet human property accounted for his greatest wealth. Marshall's court heard fourteen freedom suits and decided nearly all of them for slaveholders. In the Queen case, Marshall could both uphold the lower court's decision and at the same time render a decision that treated enslaved people as a legitimate form of property.[40]

Duvall was a slaveholder, too, but his Jeffersonian Republicanism led him in a different direction. In the political rivalry of the 1790s, the Jeffersonian Republicans touted local and individual freedom. They championed the authority of elected bodies such as juries and the legislatures. And they depicted the Federalists as dismissive of the people, distrustful of elected bodies, and obsessed with national control. The Federalists, in their view, clung to a powerful judiciary and aristocratic ideas of inherited property.

Duvall may have viewed Marshall's opinion in the Queen case as a troubling sign of how Federalist judges were seizing power from juries in American courts. "The [hearsay] rule . . . is not of great antiquity," a leading treatise explained. "So late as the year 1790, it does not appear to have been settled with regard to depositions taken before magistrates, whether upon criminal charges or upon other occasions." In cases of pedigree—that is, proving a person's lineage—hearsay evidence, even from deceased witnesses, was allowed under the premise that it was necessary to establish facts of an "ancient date." As families in England tried to prove claims of inheritance or status, they introduced all sorts of evidence into court: monument inscriptions, family Bibles, tombstones, murals, coats of armor, shields, correspondence, engravings upon rings, and parish books. Friends, neighbors, relatives, and those with intimate knowledge of the family could give depositions, and these were all accepted into evidence.[41]

Now ironically the Federalists, otherwise so protective of inheritance, wanted to exclude evidence of ancestry in freedom suits. Allowing hearsay in English cases of pedigree was usually "founded on the principle of necessity," when there were no other ways to determine the facts. Such testimony was also a means of preserving and enhancing a jurisprudence of common sense, a more democratic approach to the law that allowed all evidence to be heard and that trusted the jury to determine the law and the facts of any given case. Rules like hearsay were dangerous precisely because they could be wielded by judges to tie a jury's hands. To a Democratic-Republican like Duvall, this was a recipe for subverting fundamental justice.[42]

It seemed obvious to Duvall that Mina Queen's enslavement had been predicated on a historic violation of her ancestor's right to freedom—namely, that her great-grandmother Mary Queen was a free woman who had been trapped in bondage because of her color. It also seemed obvious to Duvall that Queen was not freed in the lower court because the evidence she could produce about her ancestor, testimony allowed in dozens of earlier cases, had been arbitrarily excluded as no longer valid in a U.S. court of law. Duvall aimed his most withering fire at Chief Justice Marshall's callous disregard for individual freedom and pretentious defense of property rights. "It appears to me that the reason for admitting hearsay evidence upon a question of freedom is much stronger than in cases of pedigree, or in controversies relative to the boundaries of land. It will be universally admitted that the right to freedom is more important than the right of property."

Taking note of the stakes in the Queen case, Duvall went on to conclude that the decision would have immediate effects, set a powerful precedent, and subvert fundamental justice: "People of color from their helpless condition, under the uncontrolled authority of a master, are entitled to all reasonable protection. A decision that hearsay evidence in such cases shall not be admitted, cuts up by the roots all claims of the kind, and puts a final end to them, unless the claim should arise from a fact of recent date, and such a case will seldom, perhaps never, occur."

Marshall's opposition to freedom suits and what they implied about slavery became even more clearly stated in a subsequent case that reaffirmed the decision made in *Queen v. Hepburn*. It was also a petition for freedom, but this one was based on descent from a free white woman, the first such case to reach the Supreme Court. A Maryland court with Duvall presiding had allowed hearsay testimony and had ruled that the white woman's descendants were free. In Washington, D.C., the circuit court allowed the Maryland verdict as evidence in subsequent cases. The children of a woman declared free by a verdict in Maryland, under this logic, would without question be considered free in D.C. under the law. Once free, always free. The D.C. jury agreed, following the earlier Maryland verdict in favor of freedom, but when the slaveholder appealed to the Supreme Court, Marshall ruled that a verdict like the one in Maryland could not be used in evidence in a subsequent case to establish a person's freedom.[43]

When the case went back to the circuit court, the hearsay evidence was disallowed on the basis of the freshly minted ruling in *Queen v. Hepburn*. The family descended from a white ancestor remained enslaved. In a highly unusual interjection in open court, Gabriel Duvall interrupted the proceedings to clarify that the hearsay rule was now being applied to descendants of white women. He noted that in the Queen case the ancestor was "a yellow woman, a native of South America." Duvall probably expected the justices to reconsider the hearsay ruling that, if applied in this case, would effectively keep the descendants of white women enslaved. His brief comment is the only mention of Mary Queen's origins in the official record of the Supreme Court. It was ignored. Moreover, Marshall used the occasion to reaffirm his earlier ruling in *Queen v. Hepburn* that "evidence by hearsay and general reputation is admissible only as to pedigree, but not to establish the freedom of the petitioner's ancestor, and thence to deduce his or her own."[44]

Despite the doubts Duvall expressed at the time, Marshall's opinion in the Queen case has lived on in the rules of evidence as the definitive expression of the "frauds which might be practiced" by hearsay. The classic explanation for rejecting hearsay evidence warned against "the greatly increased expense and the vexation which the adverse party must incur in order to rebut or explain it, the vast consumption of public time thereby occasioned, the multiplication of collateral issues for decision by the jury, and the danger of losing sight of the main question and the justice of the case if this sort of proof were admitted."[45]

In hindsight, the hearsay rule's primary definition came in a case where its application was most specious, a case that would become a cornerstone in the perpetuation of slavery in the United States. The majority opinion in *Queen v. Hepburn* defined enslaved people as property, regardless of the nature of their claim to freedom. Chief Justice Marshall disregarded not only hearsay evidence but also the verdicts of earlier courts in Maryland, all because the property rights of slaveholders would be jeopardized if the freedom suits were not stopped. For Marshall the legal focus was no longer on the individual parties in this civil suit but on the thousands of enslavers in Maryland and elsewhere who held people as property. Marshall's court made a "question of freedom" for a single individual a question of property for slaveholders generally.[46]

We are left with a double irony too glaring to ignore in the tragic outcome of *Queen v. Hepburn.* Mary Queen's oral story of her origins survived long enough to make it intact into the documentary record through the deposition of Fredus Ryland. What's more, evidence in the chancery courts in London, even if circumstantial, substantiated nearly every detail in her account, enough to plausibly conjecture that a woman named Maria may have come into London with Captain Woodes Rogers. Yet when Mina Queen's lawyer, Francis Scott Key, introduced the will of James Carroll into the trial record, it contained a crucial error of transcription, one that proved self-defeating. Mary Queen was in London much earlier, with Captain Woodes Rogers, just as Fredus Ryland testified. The error in the copy of James Carroll's will went unexamined, and it led to a dead end. No evidence could be found that Anthony Carroll took Mary Queen to London.[47]

The hearsay evidence ruled inadmissible was likely the best evidence on record, while the documentary evidence the court considered legitimate was patently inaccurate.

Marshall also upheld the decision of the lower court striking several jurors who said that they detested slavery. Under this ruling, jurors could be removed if they were not perfectly "indifferent between the parties" or if they expressed any opinions against slavery as a public policy. Marshall admitted that the difficulty of finding jurors who were "entirely uninfluenced" in situations where a "private right depends on such a [public policy] question" would be "undoubtedly considerable." The incident indicated that D.C. jurors were willing to express antislavery opinions in court. A freedom suit was a private civil suit between two parties, and jurors should be indifferent to the two parties, but in this case the court introduced a different test: whether jurors were indifferent to slavery as a question of public policy. The highest court in the nation presumed that the unwritten priority of slavery must be protected even in private cases.

For the Jesuits, the cumulative weight of *Queen v. Hepburn, Queen v. Neale,* and the other freedom suits prompted a surprising reassessment. Immediately following the *Queen* decision in May 1813, the Jesuit trustees met at Georgetown College and debated whether they ought to begin freeing the enslaved people on their plantations. The plan they came up with was to sell "the whole or greatest part" of the enslaved persons on their plantations for a term of years "after which they should be entitled to their freedom." Such a sweeping resolution to extricate themselves from enslaving had never been proposed before. Nor had a plan for the eventual freedom of all of the enslaved people ever been considered. At their next meeting in September 1813 a majority of the members of the Jesuit corporation endorsed the proposal to sell nearly all of the enslaved persons with the provision that they would gain their freedom. Then, in June 1814, the Jesuits voted to approve the plan. The direction of the corporation was clear: sell all of the enslaved people on their plantations for limited terms that were to be followed by freedom. If carried out, it would be one of the largest manumissions in the nation, however indirect the means.[48]

Motivated by pragmatic concerns about the profitability of their estates and by paternalistic views of the enslaved people, most of the priests wanted to lease their lands to white tenant farmers. One explained to the president of Georgetown, "It is better to sell for a term, or to set your people free . . . Because *we have their souls to answer for.*" The thrust of his main argument was decidedly more practical: that the enslaved people were "more difficult to govern now," that leasing would be more productive, and that the tenants would be more tractable. Neither Christian charity nor revolutionary idealism seemed to inspire the Jesuits. It appears instead that nearly two decades of freedom suits had taken their toll on the corporation and had worn down the Jesuits' commitment to slaveholding.[49]

Then, a month later, in July 1814, British forces landed at the Jesuits' plantation near St. Mary's, Maryland, ransacked the church, seized the silver, confiscated everything from razors to kitchen furniture, and liberated numerous slaves, including several of the Queens and Mahoneys. HMS *Dragon,* a seventy-four-gun ship of the line, was anchored offshore in the Potomac River along with two frigates, several gunboats, and numerous tenders. "We can scarcely sleep in our beds," one of the priests wrote in fear of another raid. He ordered the enslaved families "to run off" so that they would not be taken, but more than seven hundred enslaved people in southern Maryland fled slavery and joined the British, most of them in the summer of 1814. Like other slaveholders, the priest in charge at St. Inigoes could not imagine the independence of the enslaved people or their possible disloyalty. He reported to his superiors, "Our people seem well disposed, much attached to the place, & to one another—behave well—I feel no apprehension on their account." Nevertheless, the threat of their potential freedom was real enough that he recommended abandoning St. Inigoes entirely and removing all of the enslaved families to White Marsh, well out of British reach. "We cannot work—constant alarms—always on the watch, we know not at what moment the enemy may appear in our rear + surprise our blacks."[50]

In August the British squadron moved up the Potomac to Washington, D.C., burned the Capitol and the White House, raided Prince George's

County, and took several prisoners, including a well-known physician named William Beanes. Friends of the doctor persuaded Francis Scott Key to rush to Baltimore, where the British fleet was anchored and Beanes was being held. Key's mission was distinctly lawyerly—to negotiate with the British forces for Beanes's release. Once aboard the British vessel with Beanes, Key was detained as the British bombarded the American forces at Ft. McHenry. Key wrote "The Star-Spangled Banner" in response to the opening salvos of the battle on the morning of September 13, 1814. He closed the poem disparaging the "foul footsteps" of the British and dismissing the decisions of the enslaved who seized the chance to flee slavery in the war:

> No refuge could save the hireling and slave
> From the terror of flight, or the gloom of the grave;
> And the Star-Spangled Banner in triumph doth wave
> O'er the land of the free and the home of the brave![51]

It is impossible to know fully what Key thought of the Queens, of their claim to freedom, or his role in their historic cases. His most famous lines of poetry betray him as condescending to those whose decisions did not accord with his own. In his correspondence he made no mention of the Queens or of the other enslaved families he represented. Judging by "The Star-Spangled Banner," he seems not to have considered them part of "the land of the free" or their cause part of the nation's cause.

Yet the Queen case may have gnawed at his self-image. Key maintained a voluminous library of legal treatises, reports, and opinions, much of it inherited from his uncle Philip Barton Key. These volumes contained hundreds of pages of American and British precedents. Nearly thirty years later, preparing one of his final freedom suits for a free black man who had been kidnapped, Key wrote in the margins of his copy of *Peters' Digest* to highlight a reference to a single case: *Mima Queen v. John Hepburn*. "See above," he advised, as if to remind himself of their claim to freedom and its unfortunate outcome.[52]

For their part, the Jesuits moved painfully slowly to implement their plan of emancipation. Worse, they initially disregarded the decision and sold some of the enslaved without any provision for manumission. When Bishop John Carroll discovered that the Reverend Francis Neale and other managers had blithely continued to sell enslaved men, women, and children "for life," he was "surprised and mortified." The sales were "in direct contradiction to the humane decision of the Corporation." Furthermore, Carroll wrote

Neale that he doubted the sales were valid, and he expected that "the persons sold may recover, by law, their absolute freedom." *Queen v. Hepburn* closed down one avenue of freedom for the enslaved, but the Jesuit resolution to sell and free the enslaved families opened up another entirely unexpected pathway. A suit on the grounds that these sales "for life" violated the corporation's decision and were invalid might force the corporation to give the buyers a partial refund *and* free the enslaved who were sold. So worried about this were the trustees that they attempted retroactively to rescind all sales that did not ensure eventual emancipation.[53]

John Hepburn appeared to entertain no such qualms. The Supreme Court decision in 1813 gave him definitive authority to hold Mina and Louisa Queen as slaves "for life." Mina was fifty-three years old. When Hepburn paid his property taxes five years later in the District, he listed the following:

Furniture	$500	
1 Girl	16	$350
1 Man	25	$400
1 ditto	21	$400
1 Girl	12	$300

One of the girls could have been Louisa, but her mother, Mina, disappeared from the historical record. Like the Mahoneys, she may have bargained for her freedom. More likely, she may have been sold and separated from her daughter.

From 1789 through the 1810s, the legitimacy of slavery as a matter of law remained in question. In no small degree this was because the Queens, the Mahoneys, the Butlers, and other families from the Western Shore of Maryland kept suing slaveholders. Their private civil suits relied on venerable precepts in the common law that favored freedom. At the same time, the moral impulse of antislavery sentiment had steadily widened in American legal circles throughout the 1790s. The freedom suits combined with an increasing number of private manumissions, a successful campaign to outlaw the African slave trade, and the passage of gradual abolition laws in New Jersey and New York together indicated that the legitimacy of slaveholding appeared on the defensive.

The freedom suits, including the Queen suits, were more than idiosyncratic and individual. They threatened to erode the legal foundations of slavery out from under the slaveholders. One abolitionist in Washington, D.C., wrote President James Madison in 1813 to condemn slavery as "inhuman," barbarous, unchristian, and immoral. "This malignant disease will not only distroy the morrals, manners, industry & religion of the inhabitance, but will ere long subvert your very Constitution, & throw the U. S. into anarchy, & give a death blow to the Tree of Liberty." Yet in *Queen v. Hepburn* the Supreme Court had moved decisively in the opposite direction, as it professionalized the bench and the bar through the hearsay rule. The decision had immediate ancillary effects. It did more than resolve a private matter. It validated the property rights of slaveholders at a pivotal political moment.[54]

After *Queen v. Hepburn* the battle against hereditary enslavement being fought out in the courts stalled, and a period of uncertainty followed. Without hearsay evidence no family could prove their free lineage, and the promise of civil suits using common-law principles of personal freedom collapsed. Based on ancestry, both the Queens and the Mahoneys attempted in an American court to raise the *Somerset* principle. Neither was successful. When the full impact of the cotton boom was felt in the years around 1815 and the interstate slave trade surged in response, the property rights recognized in *Queen v. Hepburn* gained a more insidious footing. For the enslaved families, the strategy to oppose slavery would have to account for these unforeseen developments and to adjust to judicial decisions following the Queen case that had given slavery a new footing of legitimacy in the law.[55]

Dead but Not Forgotten

In the summer of 1809, Judge Allen Bowie Duckett died at the age of thirty-five and was buried in the family cemetery at Melford plantation in Prince George's County. His ledger proudly touted his signal achievement, his appointment by Thomas Jefferson to the Circuit Court of the District of Columbia. In 2019 Duckett's grave lay abandoned, its huge stone cracked in half, covered in weeds and debris, nearly unrecognizable at the top of a small hill, in a dense stand of mature oaks and scrub hickory. An office park and retail storefronts were under development at Melford. Bulldozers had flattened the terrain, erasing all trace of the old plantation except for the abandoned brick mansion.

There were no markers for the people Duckett or his descendants enslaved there.

From the Duckett cemetery, I could see the high ground at White Marsh, no more than two miles away, to the north, on the bluff of the Patuxent. The proximity of the two plantations surprised me, though it should not have. When the Reverend John Ashton at White Marsh needed a lawyer, who better could he have chosen than the young slaveholder next door whose father was a local judge?

I knew then and there that Mina Queen and Priscilla Queen filed their historic freedom suits in the Circuit Court of the District of Columbia only when they knew that Allen Bowie Duckett was dead and buried. It was a sobering realization. For three years before his untimely death, Duckett had been absent from the D.C. court more than he had been present. The exact nature of his maladies was never publicly stated, but in the summer of 1809 he died, and the situation changed. With the Jesuits' former lawyer from Prince George's County no longer on the D.C. bench, members of the Thomas and Queen families rushed to file new lawsuits in the District's court. Undoubtedly, they viewed the young judge Duckett as an obstacle to their freedom. Their actions speak now louder than his words.[1]

The old cemetery at White Marsh lies just north of the Duckett plantation. To the east of the original basilica, there are dozens of headstones in neat rows, nearly all from the twentieth and twenty-first centuries. But to the north, a small section interrupts the lawn between the church and the woods and stands on the edge of the bluff that overlooks the road to Annapolis. A thick stand of oaks protects that part of the cemetery, hiding it from passersby below and shielding it from all sound other than the song of larks and chickadees. On a cold day in March when I visited the cemetery, the big oaks swayed, their branches bare and lean, shimmering gray-white in afternoon light. Abundant sunshine filled the woods, and I could see through the forest to the low hills on the other side of the Patuxent River valley.

No more than twenty yards away a small headstone caught my eye. As I walked over to look at the stone, I noticed a few unmarked stones nearby, scattered along the wood line. Each of these had the shape of a miniature dome: flattened on the bottom, rounded on the top. Cracked, broken, and folded in over itself, the marked stone's inscription read simply,

DEAD BUT
NOT FOR
GOTEN.[2]

Although the Jesuit priests conducted proper burials for the enslaved people on their farms, they made no mention of these ceremonies except for a few scattered lines in their account books. At Newtown six enslaved people died between 1750 and 1770, and another six died between 1782 and 1796. All were buried in unmarked graves. In 1765 the Reverend Joseph Moseley brought eight enslaved people from White Marsh with him when he took over as manager of the new Jesuit mission at St. Joseph's in Talbot County. He arrived with Nanny, a fifty-five-year-old woman born in Africa, Tom and his wife, Frank, both twenty-eight, and their five children. Frank gave birth on December 27, 1765, to her sixth child, Mary. Moseley recorded the birth as "the 1st born at St. Joseph's" and named Mary's twelve-year-old sister and nine-year-old brother as the godparents. A year later Moseley wrote in his journal about the death of their mother: "Frank died the 11th of Nov. 1766 about 20 minutes after . . . 8 o'clock in the morning." She was twenty-nine. Moseley left no other notes about Frank, other than the strikingly precise time and date of her death. Perhaps she died in childbirth. Six years later, however, without so much as a second thought, he broke up her family and sent the six-year-old Mary, motherless, with Nanny and her eighteen-year-old godmother sister off to a Jesuit farm in the next county.

Frank's grave was unmarked.

Slaveholders routinely disregarded the deaths of those they enslaved. James V. Deane, who was born in Charles County on May 20, 1850, recalled the plantation burials this way: "I have seen many colored funerals with no service. A graveyard on the place, only a wooden post to show where you were buried." Charles Coles, a former slave from Charles County, reported that on his plantation, the Catholic slaveholder held Mass regularly, required enslaved persons to learn the catechism, and brought priests from St. Thomas Manor to baptize the children. When a slave died on the plantation, a priest came to the farm and conducted last rites. "The only difference in the graves," Coles noted, was that the white family "had marble markers and the slaves had plain stones." Other former slaves from all over the South said that slaves were buried without ceremony. "Didn't have no funerals for de slaves," one recalled, "but jes' bury dem like a cow or a hoss, jes' dig a hole and roll 'em in it and cover 'em up."[3]

Today, one of the most vivid, if often overlooked, remnants of the violence of enslavement is the contrast between cemeteries for white persons, with their rows and rows of epigraphs, stones, and vaults, and the absence of any markers at all for the eleven generations of the enslaved dead.[4]

The indignities of enslavement did not end with death. The enslaved person faced going into the ground without any lasting commemoration. It is true that most people, whether enslaved or free, were buried without a marker, and at many churches, burial records for the time indicate that for each gravestone there were three unmarked graves. However, with no means to ritualize death and no one to remember where the dead were, enslaved persons experienced what one scholar of slavery and death has called a "spiritual cataclysm."[5]

Enslaved families created rituals of their own and wove them whenever possible into those of the churches, plantations, schools, and people that held them in bondage. In 1819 Suckey, a seventeen-year-old woman enslaved by Philip Barton Key's family in Georgetown, fell gravely ill. On her deathbed the Jesuit priest at the college "baptized her conditionally, heard her confession, and gave her Extreme Unction." She died the next day and was buried in an unmarked grave on the college grounds. For her funeral, four hundred African Americans gathered at the college. They were a collective, physical, and public demonstration of what she meant to her family, friends, and community. Nearly half of the black population of Georgetown witnessed her service.[6]

CHAPTER 6

The Turning

You can manumit the slave, but you cannot make him a white man.

—ROBERT GOODLOE HARPER, AUGUST 20, 1817

On a late November day in 1815 near Bladensburg, Maryland, Ann Williams was taken from her family and sold to a Georgia slave trader. She and her two young daughters were tied to a coffle along with more than a dozen other men, women, and children and marched seven miles to Washington, D.C. When they arrived in the capital, they were locked in the garret of a local tavern run by George Miller. Miller's Tavern on F Street doubled as a slave jail, sometimes called a "slave pen," with its third-floor attic fashioned into a secure holding cell that the slave traders bound for Georgia used as a way station before continuing their journey to the booming cotton frontier. It was a private prison, one of several within blocks of the White House.

That night Williams lay awake. Violently and suddenly separated from her husband, in danger of losing her daughters, and with the long march to Georgia about to commence, she pried open the window of the third-floor garret, climbed up on its wooden sill, and leapt into the half-light of a breaking dawn.

She fell thirty feet to the stone street below, broke her spine, and fractured both of her arms at the elbow. Hours later the Georgia slave trader sold Ann Williams to George Miller, took her two daughters, left her behind, and set off for South Carolina. Williams would never see her children again.[1]

Word of the incident raced across the city. The fact that slave coffles came down Pennsylvania Avenue and passed the U.S. Capitol shocked the sensibilities of some residents and visitors. They were unaware of the scale of the slave trade even as it was happening, much less of what the interstate slave trade had become in a very short time. Even though the United States closed the African slave trade after 1808, a novel and insidious traffic had arisen within and between the states: the domestic slave trade, which would eventually take more than a million people from Maryland and Virginia and transport them against their will to South Carolina, Georgia, Mississippi, Alabama, and Louisiana. Jesse Torrey, a physician and a burgeoning abolitionist, watched with dismay as coffles driven by slave traders shuffled past the Capitol. He had heard stories that free blacks were being kidnapped routinely and sold south. "The act of depriving a free man of his liberty," he mused, "being a violation of the constitution of the United States and an *overt attack* upon the public liberty, ought to be declared treason of some sort or another."[2]

With these thoughts running through his head, Torrey decided to follow one of the processions. The men, women, and children were "bound together in pairs, some with ropes, and some with *iron chains*." Torrey could hardly believe his eyes. The utter dehumanization created by the chains and the intensity of the scene so shocked his conscience that he could scarcely catch his breath. He nearly fainted on the spot.

At that moment a black hack driver paused as he passed Torrey, who was standing nearly in the middle of Pennsylvania Avenue. "See there!" he muttered. "Ain't that right down *murder?*" When Torrey replied that he did not know what to think, the man persisted with his question, asking it again until Torrey would acknowledge, "It is *murder.*" From encounters such as this one in the street, Torrey heard other stories about the horrors of the slave trade. In Prince George's County, several women attempted suicide, and one of them, he learned, might still be locked up in the third-floor garret at Miller's Tavern.

On December 19, 1815, Torrey decided to visit the F Street tavern to inquire about the woman's fate, and he found Ann Williams lying on a makeshift pallet on the floor, under a bloodstained, white woolen blanket. The tavern owner, George Miller, claimed self-righteously that he bought Ann Williams for humanitarian reasons and that he was nursing her back to health. His true motives seemed to lie elsewhere and would become crystal

A Rider del.

"— but I did not want to go, and
I jump'd out of the window.— "

Designed and Published by J. Torrey Junr Philad.^a 1817.

Alexander Rider, *"But I did not want to go . . ."* (from Jesse Torrey,
A Portraiture of Domestic Slavery [Philadelphia: John Boiken, 1817], 43).
Ann Williams brought immediate public attention to the slave trade in the capital.
She told Torrey, "I jumped out of the window;—but I am sorry now that I did it;—
they have carried my children off with 'em to Carolina."

clear years later. Miller purchased Williams from the Georgia slave trader for one reason and one reason only: the potential that she might have more children, that those children would be enslaved, and that they would therefore become his property. Legal documents at the time routinely referred to the potential children of an enslaved woman as her "future increase." Ann Williams knew from her harrowing experience that Miller would eventually try to sell any children she and her husband might conceive, raise, love, and parent. The implications added up to a terrifying prospect: her unborn already had a price on their heads.[3]

Having learned that free blacks were being kidnapped in Maryland, Delaware, and Pennsylvania, transported to the nation's capital, and sold into slavery, Torrey went to see Francis Scott Key and filed a writ of habeas corpus in the Circuit Court of the District of Columbia on behalf of several people being held in the garret with Ann Williams. The right of habeas corpus—of the citizen to know under what authority he or she was being detained—was a long-standing prerogative in American and English law. In theory the court could compel George Miller to bring the bodies of Ann Williams and the other petitioners before the bench and to present whatever proof he thought he had of his right to hold them in his private jail.

The court issued the writ, but when the D.C. marshal visited the tavern on F Street, he was refused entry and could not hand-deliver and formally "execute" the writ. The proprietor, presumably George Miller, defiantly barred the door and claimed that the court had no evidence of a crime other than "stories." Miller went on. He asserted that Ann Williams and the others he held in the slave pen were nothing more than property, and therefore that the writ of habeas corpus did not apply and could not be served. This assertion proved especially controversial. How, after all, could a body not be a body under the ancient precepts of Anglo-American law?

Freedom suits like the Queens' and the Mahoneys' that were based on descent from a free ancestor had collapsed in the D.C. courts. One after the other they were dismissed, dropped for lack of admissible evidence, each a quiet victim of the new hearsay rule. Evidence that an ancestor spent time in England did not lead to a decision affirming the *Somerset* principle in Maryland, nor did this evidence ultimately call into question slavery's legitimacy under the common law. Instead, the *Queen v. Hepburn* ruling removed from consideration all of the old depositions used in Maryland.

But twenty-five years of freedom suits had had a powerful effect on those who held slaves. The trials clearly pressured slaveholders, calling them into court successively over three generations, asserting claims of ancestral freedom that were difficult to deny and impossible to uproot. Some slave-holders, including the Jesuits, who won their cases in court were begin-ning to question the legitimacy of slavery and to make arrangements for manumission and emancipation. Enslaved families negotiated for their freedom against the backdrop of these legal proceedings, pooled their re-sources to buy their freedom, and stayed in the area to help free other family members.

Beginning in the 1810s the manumission rate in Maryland climbed to record levels. In hindsight, few individual slaveholders in Maryland manu-mitted for ideological or religious reasons. Many more did so either as a means to contain the freedom suits or as a tool to maintain control over those they kept in bondage. As the cotton trade boomed in the decades after 1800 and the price on their heads increased, the enslaved families of Maryland and D.C. faced a volatile situation. On the one hand, they might win con-cessions from slaveholders with every freedom suit they filed. On the other, they might be sold at any moment, as every high point in the market cre-ated an attractive bonus for slaveholders.[4]

After *Queen v. Hepburn*, though, the politics of the freedom suits changed profoundly. For the first time, in the 1820s, political leaders in the South began to formulate an especially aggressive line of argument defend-ing slavery as a national institution, a national right, and a property right. George Miller's outburst that the writ of habeas corpus did not apply to slaves because they were property was suddenly given credence. Slaveholders pro-claimed that precedents, laws, and the Constitution itself protected their "right" to hold human beings as property and therefore that Congress could not bar slaveholders from taking slaves into federal territories like Missouri.[5]

Such blatant assertions that slaves were not persons offended the sen-sibilities of slaveholders like Francis Scott Key who considered themselves reformers. These slaveholders continued, however disingenuously, to refer those they enslaved as "persons held to service." And they avoided referring to human beings as chattel property. The preferred solution of slaveholders like Key was breathtaking in its scope. Their plan was colonization. With the fervor and confidence of evangelists, they aimed to purify the Republic by liberating enslaved people and sending all free blacks from the United States back to Africa. The entire project promised to save whites from the debasement and corruption of holding slaves by removing slavery's petty tyr-anny and moral jeopardy and by removing blacks en masse from American society and politics. Some advocated for compulsory removal; others called for voluntary removal. In either case, removal.[6]

Colonization and removal raised a fundamental question: If the federal government or a state could remove free blacks by legislation, what rights exactly did black Americans possess under the Constitution?

To many observers in Maryland and Washington, D.C., the situation cried out for reform. The explosive rise of the domestic slave trade and the slave jails scattered throughout the capital brought the cruelty of slavery into public view. A congressional inquiry into the slave trade in Washington got under way in early 1816, led by Virginia congressman John Randolph. The testimony, all of it from whites, revealed scenes of terror that would "*shock* every spectator that has the least regard for mercy or for justice." Sold away from her family, one woman tried to cut her throat. Another chopped off one of her hands.[7]

Washington seemed to have become a sprawling Bastille, a prison fortress. The chained coffles, slave patrols, police constables, black laws, slave pens, auction blocks, slave jails, and prisons in the garret attics of local taverns made residents aware of the churning violence at the heart of the domestic slave trade. Ann Williams's dramatic act of resistance thrust the contest over slavery from the realm of private civil actions into the arena of public political movements.

Going forward, every freedom suit in the capital had the potential to become a political showdown over the future of slavery in the Republic, none more so than the daring lawsuit that Charlotte Dupee eventually launched in 1829 against Henry Clay, outgoing secretary of state, former Speaker of the House, founder of the American Colonization Society (ACS), and aspiring presidential candidate.[8]

"I Was Previously Deceived"

In December 1816 at Washington's Davis Hotel, Francis Scott Key joined Senator Henry Clay, Senator Daniel Webster, Congressman John Randolph, General Andrew Jackson, and President-Elect James Monroe at the founding meeting of the American Colonization Society. Robert Finley, a Presbyterian minister from New Jersey and director of Princeton Theological Seminary, called the first meeting and acted as its leading light. Finley and other Northern whites warmly embraced colonization as the best means of encouraging Southerners to end slavery. Clay agreed to chair the distinguished group.

At the outset Clay observed that free blacks confronted "unconquerable prejudices resulting from their color" and that they "never could amalgamate with the free whites of this country." The rationale for colonization, therefore, was paternalistic and racially motivated, couching removal as charity, as the best outcome for both blacks and whites. A Westerner from Kentucky, Clay judiciously assured the group that the society would never "deliberate on, or consider at all, any question of emancipation." Such assurances were necessary, he pointed out, to secure the cooperation of slaveholding planters in his part of the country, who would countenance no organization that talked openly about abolition of slavery.

Like Francis Scott Key, local attorney Elias B. Caldwell was present at the founding of the ACS. He too was convinced that slavery could be ended only by colonization and repatriation of blacks back to Africa. He had been especially concerned about kidnapping, because those who were captured were citizens "whose freedom and *moral* rights are guarenteed [sic] by our national and state constitutions." As a lawyer Caldwell might advocate for freedom in individual cases, but Ann Williams's leap from the window, the various incidents that took place in December 1815, and the congressional investigation that followed in 1816 raised policy questions beyond what the law might afford individuals. At thirty-nine, Caldwell was just four years older than Key, but he had served for fifteen years as the clerk of the U.S. Supreme Court and had fought in the War of 1812, commanding a troop of cavalry in Maryland at the Battle of Bladensburg. Like Key, he had gained a measure of national fame in the war; he had singlehandedly rescued the archives of the Supreme Court when British forces burned the Capitol on August 24, 1814. He was also the Reverend Robert Finley's brother-in-law.[9]

Caldwell served as the ACS secretary. Like Clay, Caldwell argued that prejudice in American society condemned free blacks to "a state of degradation." Their treatment and the lack of civil rights they were accorded in most states flew in the face of the Declaration of Independence's guarantee that "all men are created equal." So Caldwell implied that free blacks were noncitizens or resident aliens and could not fall under the Declaration's purview of equality. "How can you expect from them anything great or noble, without the motives to stimulate, or the rewards to crown, great and noble achievements?" Caldwell asked.

> The more you improve the condition of these people, the more you cultivate their minds, the more miserable you make them in their present state. You give them a higher relish for those privileges which they can never attain, and turn what we intend for a blessing into a curse. No, if they must remain in their present

situation, keep them in the lowest state of degradation and ignorance . . . Surely, Americans ought to be the last people on earth
to advocate such slavish doctrines; to cry peace and contentment
to those who are deprived of the privileges of civil liberty.[10]

The early colonizers' sheer exuberance can be jarring to modern ears.
Caldwell, who gave the most extensive speech at the opening meeting, believed that the whole enterprise was one of the "great movements . . . in the
moral and religious world." Colonization was nothing less than "some great
design of Providence," uniting Christians of different denominations from
New Jersey, New York, Virginia, and Tennessee. North and South. Baptist
and Episcopalian. The colonizers would save Africa, save the United States,
rescue blacks from perpetual degradation, and offer "a national atonement
for the wrongs and injuries which Africa had suffered."[11]

The contradictions in the colonization movement were plain to see.
How could manumission and colonization—programs to *free* the enslaved—
ever really protect slavery or give slaveholders greater security in their so-
called property? Wasn't colonization, even if based on humanitarianism and
opposition to the slave trade, inevitably a form of abolition? Why would free
blacks wish to leave their families and the land of their birth for Africa? One
Maryland delegate questioned the colonization plan on just these points, especially whether free blacks would participate at all. "I fear the gentlemen
are too sanguine in their expectations," he cautioned. He doubted that free
blacks "would be willing to abandon the land of their nativity." Such skepticism drew little comment, however. The men forming the colonization society thought they knew what was best for black Americans.[12]

None more so than Robert Goodloe Harper, the former attorney for
the Jesuits in *Mahoney v. Ashton,* who had been elected one of Maryland's
U.S. senators in 1814. A dyed-in-the-wool Federalist, Harper resigned his Senate seat to run for the vice presidency in 1816. After losing the election, he
devoted his energies to the ACS and took the time to write a thirty-two-page
printed letter to Elias B. Caldwell, the society's secretary. His argument was
directed at Northern whites who questioned the necessity of colonization.
Harper's argument was explicitly racial. Because free blacks would always
be associated with slavery, he said, they were "condemned to a state of hopeless inferiority and degradation, by their colour."

We cannot help considering them and treating them as our infe-
riors . . . Whatever property they may acquire, or whatever re-

spect we may feel for their characters, we never could consent, and they never could hope, to see the two races placed on a footing of perfect equality with each other: to see the free blacks or their descendants visit in our houses, form part of our circle of acquaintance, marry into our families, or participate in public honours and employments . . .

You may manumit the slave, but you cannot make him a white man.[13]

In short, the colonizers' fantasy was an America not so much free of slavery but free of free blacks. Colonizers denied that free blacks could remain in the United States because they never considered them to be citizens or persons under the meaning of the Constitution. By this logic blacks were being defined as an alien population to whom constitutional rights and liberties did not apply. Harper called blacks "a distinct nation, which can never become incorporated with us."

The racist overtones of the argument pushed by Caldwell, Clay, Harper, Key, and the other supporters of colonization were not lost on black Americans. By claiming American nationhood, and resisting colonization, free blacks also claimed a form of personhood and citizenship under the Constitution. The struggle of black Americans to remain in their birthplace was nothing less than existential—a political act and a claim of national belonging and citizenship. Black Marylanders greeted the American Colonization Society with cold skepticism. In Georgetown, Washington, D.C., and Richmond, Virginia, in December 1816 and January 1817, free blacks held meetings to consider the ACS proposal. They saw African colonization as exile from "the land of our nativity." The idea of leaving the United States for a black-led republic such as Haiti proved attractive to some, who calculated that white slaveholders, indeed white Americans, would never give black Americans the rights of citizenship. They had good reasons to be unconvinced. Colonization gave whites cover to oppose the international slave trade and profess a sentimental humanitarianism without threatening to disturb racialized hereditary enslavement. In fact, white reformers could satisfy their desire to be seen as humanitarian even as they strengthened and secured slavery under the law.

As colonization ideas circulated, a large group of free blacks and enslaved men and women in St. Mary's County, Maryland, staged an uprising against slavery. On the Monday after Easter in April 1817, as many as two hundred people gathered at a "dram shop" in St. Inigoes, the little hamlet where the Jesuits maintained one of their largest plantations. It had been two and a half years since the Jesuits voted to begin selling and freeing all of the enslaved persons on their plantations, including St. Inigoes, yet there had been no progress, no change. Instead, most of the families with roots in the county—the Shorters, the Thomases, the Mahoneys, the Queens—had seen their freedom suits wither in the face of slaveholder opposition and judicial adherence to the new hearsay rule. The unruly crowd "turned upon the whites, and drove them off the lot, with outrageous violence," beating them with sticks and threatening to burn houses down, according to a disparaging report in a New York newspaper. Whites later blamed the uprising on "spirituous liquors" and did everything they could to discredit the "turbulence," but the men and women who revolted said that "they meant to be free" and that it "was their time."[14]

Faced with white prejudice and deep resistance to black freedom, some free blacks and enslaved people saw emigration as an attractive alternative. Even before the War of 1812 Paul Cuffee, an African American shipowner from Philadelphia, established ties to the British colony of Sierra Leone. Cuffee advocated for colonization as a means to oppose slavery and affirm the human rights of blacks. And in 1815 he led a group of thirty-eight free black emigrants from the United States to Sierra Leone. But two years later, at a meeting in Philadelphia attended by thousands of black men, none volunteered to join Cuffee. James Forten, a free black sailmaker in Philadelphia and one of the wealthiest men in the city, wrote, "The plan of colonizing . . . is not asked for by us . . . We renounce and disclaim every connection with it."[15]

Thomas Smallwood, who was born in Prince George's County and gained his freedom in 1831, advocated for African colonization for a few years because, like Cuffee, he thought that the ACS's aim was the abolition of slavery and that colonization was a step toward slavery's "final extinction." Smallwood realized later that the society would do nothing to end slavery. "I was previously deceived," he recalled. "The object and policy of that Society proved to be, under the mask of philanthropy, the draining of the free colored population from among the slave population by inducing them to emigrate to Africa." Those who advocated for colonization perpetrated nothing less than a grotesque ruse that "if we can get rid of the free negro population, we can put a stop to any further emancipations, and thus have perpetual slavery without danger." Smallwood began to see how the ACS conspired to eliminate free black employment on government works in Washington, D.C., with federal rules to hire whites only. Facing unemployment and reduced prospects, free blacks would be "easy prey" for the "designs" of the society, for colonization and emigration. Smallwood watched with disgust as the ACS induced some free black civic leaders to promote colonization. They became "willing tools" of the society and part of what he disparaged as the "African colonization trap."[16]

For decades, black abolitionist Frederick Douglass opposed colonization. He consistently disparaged colonization as a "gross and barbarous villainy." The ACS, he concluded, was "diabolical," "an offender and slanderer of the colored people." Douglass considered all talk of colonization absurd and the idea that blacks would consent to removal nothing less than a satanic illusion, a "sophistry," and a lie. "The whole plan would be *utterly defective* without the contemplation of force." Douglass decried the "mean, hypocritical, and monstrous" claims of white slaveholders like Clay, Key, and Caldwell that no one would be colonized without their consent. Douglass could foresee that denying the legal standing of free blacks under the Constitution could certainly lay the foundation for the forced deportation of the entire population. And when Clay and others asked in racist pejorative terms about free blacks, "What is to be done with them?" Douglass knew that the answer depended in large part on what the law could be made to allow.[17]

Indeed, the founding of the American Colonization Society in 1816 and 1817 by such white lawyers as Caldwell and Key who represented black plaintiffs in the freedom suits was part of their response, as slaveholders, to the legal challenge posed by those suits. The logic of every freedom suit was that enslaved blacks had a claim as persons under the meaning of the law and the Constitution. And the logic of colonization was that they did not.

But the colonizers' paternalism was boundless. They could not believe that blacks would be "unwilling to be colonized." Black reluctance was an affront to their vision of a white republic. "Are they not men?" Caldwell responded. "Will they prefer remaining in a hopeless state of degradation for themselves and their children, to the prospect of the full enjoyment of their civil rights and a state of equality?" In a fatuous comparison that revised colonial history, Caldwell venerated white Europeans who had voluntarily indentured themselves, crossed the ocean, and battled "the savages" because of their "desire of liberty, of standing upon an equality with his fellow-men." He suggested that blacks could do the same, if they acted like whites.[18]

Roger B. Taney, too, was part of this circle of paternalistic Marylanders. In June 1818 Taney manumitted seven people, and by 1822 he had manumitted all of the people he held with his brother and other family members. He never purchased another slave. In 1819 Taney defended a Methodist minister in Frederick, Maryland, who spoke out against slavery, calling it a "national sin." Taney argued, "Slavery is a blot on our national character, and every real lover of freedom confidently hopes that it will be effectually, though it must be gradually, wiped away; and earnestly looks for the means by which this necessary object may best obtained." Like Key, Taney was an early proponent of the American Colonization Society and active in its Maryland chapter.[19]

For decades, white politicians from Maryland and Virginia, including Jefferson, Randolph, Caldwell, and Key, burnished a veneer of respectable antislavery humanitarianism, but beneath the surface they maintained that the racial superiority of whites would make black freedom impossible. Randolph railed against the African slave trade and introduced numerous bills in Congress to make the penalties for slave trafficking on the high seas tougher and their enforcement more effective. Influenced by his stepfather, St. George Tucker, a prominent jurist who wrote one of the most widely circulated criticisms of slavery in the United States, and by his brother Richard, who freed all the enslaved he inherited and provided them land, Randolph rewrote his will in 1818. "Heartily regretting that I have ever been the owner of one . . . my conscience tells me they are justly entitled [to freedom]." He allocated funds to purchase land to resettle all of those he enslaved in a free state. A heavy drinker and habitual opium user who fell into deep bouts of depression, Randolph took contradictory positions as a so-called Old Republican—vigorously critical of slavery and the slave trade yet equally skeptical of any federal, religious, or political interference in the affairs of slaveholders in the slaveholding states. These struck some of his contemporaries as incoherent "madness." He believed that thousands of slaveholders would free their slaves if they could be colonized, yet it became increasingly obvious that the patronizing solution of his fellow colonizers rested on the idea that they considered free black Americans "a great evil" and unfit to be citizens alongside whites. Disgusted with its duplicity, Randolph abandoned colonization. "A spirit of morbid sensibility, religious fanaticism, vanity, and the love of display, were the chief moving causes of that society," he concluded.[20]

Their statements on behalf of freedom in the abstract, while extravagant, may have been genuine, but when the political crisis over Missouri's admission as a slave state erupted in February 1819, Jefferson, Randolph, Key, and Taney showed their true colors. Missouri's aggressive, indeed blatant, embrace of slavery dispensed with the idea that slavery was in any way inconsistent with American principles of freedom. Missourians premised their state constitution explicitly on slavery. For the first time, an American state's constitution proposed to bar the legislature from abolishing slavery without the consent of slaveholders. Freedom suits were already under way in Missouri, under an 1807 Louisiana territorial law allowing suits for freedom. But the debate over Missouri's statehood fractured the political parties and laid bare the hypocrisy of the slaveholders in Virginia and Maryland.[21]

"It Is the Freedom of Man"

In February 1819 New York congressman James Tallmadge introduced an amendment to Missouri's bill for statehood that would bar slavery in Missouri as a condition of Missouri's admission as a state. For decades the leading Maryland and Virginia politicians considered themselves faithful Republicans dedicated to liberty despite their slaveholding, but they could not avoid the candor demanded by the Missouri question: Would they restrict slavery as illegitimate or embrace it as legitimate? Would they tolerate slavery as a local institution or sanction it as a national one? Would they agree with the view that enslaved people were merchandise or hold that they were human beings?

Tallmadge was a freshman congressman and a staunch Jeffersonian Republican who considered slavery unchristian, sinful, and immoral. Like Jefferson, he blamed England for "the original sin of bringing slaves into our country," so he proposed "that the further introduction of slavery or involuntary servitude be prohibited [in Missouri] . . . ; and that all children of slave[s], born within the said state, after the admission thereof into the Union, shall be free at the age of twenty-five years." Tallmadge's motives were surprisingly elementary. His Republican convictions led him to the conclusion that slavery could not be reconciled with the nation's founding or with the Enlightenment principles of natural law. Tallmadge wanted to remove the "foul stain" of slavery from the American experiment in republican government. The language of uncleanliness, with its racist overtones, echoed that of Jefferson, Caldwell, and all of the colonizers who wished to remove free blacks from the Republic at the same time as they would end slavery.[22]

Tallmadge's proposal set off a furious debate in the House. Henry Clay immediately leapt to the defense of slaveholders and, in an artless, spur-of-the-moment response, asserted "the inviolability of this species of property [slaves]." Clay's comments surprised Northerners who had long taken Southerners at their word that at least they agreed with the bedrock principle that the enslavement of human beings was wrong; that slaves were persons, not

A Slave-Coffle passing the Capitol.

A Slave-Coffle Passing the Capitol, ca. 1815, published 1876–1881
(**Library of Congress, Prints and Photographs Division, Washington, D.C.**).
Virginia congressman John Randolph called for a congressional hearing on the
kidnapping of free blacks and the interstate slave trade. Opposed to any interference in the affairs of slaveholders, Randolph called the slave trade a "crying sin
before God and man." The capital, he said, had become "an assemblage of prisons"
in a nation "which prided itself on freedom."

property; and that slavery was contrary to the spirit of the nation's founding. However, Clay set the tone for Southern congressmen of both parties to
jettison their rhetoric of antislavery humanitarianism and speak in forth-
right terms defending slavery as a legitimate form of property. Those like
Clay who were prominent colonization men now seemed to deny that there
was any incongruity between slavery and the national ideal of liberty, between slavery and the Declaration of Independence, between slavery and the
tenets of the Constitution.[23]

Northern congressmen could hardly believe what they were hearing. New Hampshire's representative cautioned, "Let us no longer tell idle tales about the gradual abolition of slavery." For Northerners the Missouri debates suddenly recalibrated all of their assumptions about Southern political leadership. The South's long-standing opposition to the slave trade appeared disingenuous in the bright light of Missouri, a calculated move to "prevent the glutting of a prodigious market for the flesh and blood of man." Northerners were incensed that the "national character" was at stake and thought that the entire question was whether the Constitution "was made to impose slavery, and not to establish liberty." James Tallmadge considered constitutional arguments supporting slavery absurd and dangerous. "You boast of the freedom of your Constitution and your laws . . . If you allow slavery to pass into Territories where you have the lawful power to exclude it, you will justly take upon yourself all the charges of inconsistency; but, confine it to the original slaveholding States, where you found it at the formation of your Government, and you stand acquitted of all imputation."[24]

When some Southern congressmen made thinly veiled threats that the Union would be dissolved in "seas of blood," Tallmadge responded: "Sir, if a dissolution of the Union must take place, let it be so! . . . My purpose is fixed, it is interwoven with my existence, . . . it is a great and glorious cause, setting bounds to a slavery most cruel and debasing the world ever witnessed; it is the freedom of man; it is the cause of unredeemed and unregenerated human beings."[25]

The issue fractured the political parties along deep sectional lines. Northern and Southern Democratic-Republicans split. Southern Federalists ditched their Northern counterparts. They voted with the Republicans against the Tallmadge amendment and for Missouri's admission as a slave state. Every single member of the Maryland congressional delegation, whether Federalist or Republican, voted against the Tallmadge amendment. In the flurry of resolutions and counterresolutions that followed, only one Marylander in the House voted for a gradual emancipation provision. The controversy emboldened slaveholders to dispense with antislavery humanitarian doubts and embrace a full-throated defense of slaveholding on the basis of racial superiority and property rights. The proposed Missouri state constitution drove a wedge through Congress because it featured two unprecedented provisions: one clause barred the legislature from ever terminating slavery without a referendum of slaveholders approving abolition, a near impossibility, and another barred all free blacks from emigrating into the state. The Missouri constitution represented the most distilled version of an American slaveholders' republic yet proposed, a society where all blacks were slaves, all slaves were property, and all whites supported slavery.[26]

Yet for the first time an open challenge on the floor of Congress to slavery's legitimacy was not summarily dismissed. Southern congressmen led by John Randolph violently objected to broaching the subject and retreated into a constitutional defense of "states' rights" to avoid talking about the fundamental illegitimacy of slavery. Repeatedly, Tallmadge and other Northern congressmen assured Southerners like Randolph that they were well aware of "the delicacy of the subject," using the very phrase Southerners preferred when referring to slavery's unpleasant aspects. Henry Clay asked in astonishment "what the people of South had done" to be treated with such disrespect by Northerners, to be "proscribed" from taking slaves, as property, wherever they wanted. Clay suggested that Northern "negrophobia" was at the root of Tallmadge's proposal to restrict slavery from Missouri. It was a stunning accusation from a slaveholder, a masterful if sickening attempt at deflection, suggesting that the real issue on the floor of Congress was Northern fear and racism in contrast to benevolent Southern paternalism. Tallmadge stressed at the outset that his amendment would not free a single slave and that he intended to ensure "the safety of the white population" and avoid "the dangers of free blacks intermingling with the slaves." At one moment Southern congressmen wanted to halt the floor debate because "a black face" appeared in the public gallery, and Tallmadge lost his patience with Southern notions of propriety. "A delicate subject!" he scoffed, "in which is involved the security and happiness of unborn millions; a subject too delicate for discussion!— because our debate may be overheard by a negro in the gallery."[27]

The rights of free blacks, whether to sit in the gallery and hear the debate or to sue and be sued in an American court of law, became the driving question at the heart of the Missouri debate. If free blacks were U.S. citizens with some basic rights, if not always the right to vote, then Missouri's constitution barring them from the state conflicted with the U.S. Constitution's protection under article IV, section 2, which stated that "the citizens of each state shall be entitled to all privileges and immunities of citizens in the several states." If free blacks were something less than citizens, perhaps aliens or nonpermanent residents, then their rights might be restricted through black laws. Other more severe measures, such as forced deportation and colonization, might be constitutionally permissible. To be sure, some Northern states barred blacks from voting, and a few passed laws limiting the right of free blacks to travel or reside in the states. However, even in the South free blacks used the courts and acted like citizens. In Maryland free blacks voted until 1802. But the Missouri state constitution took a decisive and draconian position on the matter: "to prevent free negroes and mulattoes from coming to and settling in the State, under any pretext whatsoever."[28]

In April 1820, with the Missouri debate over free blacks in the Sixteenth Congress in full swing, the trustees of the Jesuit corporation backed away from their earlier plans to free the enslaved people they held in bondage on their Maryland plantations. Meeting at St. Thomas Manor in Charles County, they repealed the momentous 1814 resolution. "On mature reflection," they explained, the idea of freedom for enslaved people was "prejudicial." The Jesuits offered no other reason and no other explanation for their actions. For the enslaved families at White Marsh, Newtown, Bohemia Manor, St. Inigoes, and St. Thomas Manor, as well as at Georgetown College and other Jesuit holdings, the decision marked a decisive turning point in their three-generation pursuit of freedom. It seems undeniable that the clarifying, sectionalizing debate in Congress over slavery and free black rights influenced the Jesuits. Even Jesuits who advocated freeing enslaved persons and who considered slavery an "erroneous system" were resigned to slaveholding, their antislavery humanitarianism a spent force. One Jesuit explained, "I sincerely regret that slaves were ever introduced into the United States, but as we have them we know not how to get rid of them."[29]

Such fatalism echoed William Pinkney's public speeches and Jefferson's private letters throughout the Missouri crisis. Pinkney, once an ardent antislavery Maryland delegate, now one of Maryland's U.S. senators, denied that Congress had any authority to restrict the practice of slavery as a condition of a state's admission to the Union. Moreover, slavery was already "established among us," he pointed out with resigned indifference. Whatever its original "fraud or violence," whatever racial ideas it harbored, citizens could take action to "mitigate its evils" only within the states themselves. Congress, he argued, could not overstep its authority and trample the individual rights of slaveholders under the Constitution.[30]

Observing the congressional firestorm from his home at Monticello, Jefferson for his part blamed the Northern Federalists for wasting their energies on "the miseries of slavery, as if we [slaveholders] were advocates for it [slavery]." And he opined that Northerners should "unite their counsels with ours in devising some reasonable and practicable plan of getting rid of it [slavery]."[31]

The plan Jefferson advocated was the diffusion of slavery into the West. Spread out across the territories, slavery would become less concentrated, and the states would resemble the North, where there were fewer enslaved people in proportion to the total population. In a series of private letters Jefferson argued that "diffusion over a greater surface would make them individually happier and proportionally facilitate the accomplishment of their emancipation; by dividing the burthen on a greater number of coadjutors." John Randolph agreed. "Dispersion is to them a bettering of their present condition, and of their chance for emancipation," he wrote. "It is only when this can be done without danger and without ruinous individual loss that it will be done at all." Unlike the ACS's plan for emancipation and colonization, this alternative required no congressional intervention or federal power. Diffusion relied only on the passage of time, presumably on the ticking of the Revolution's clock of republican liberty.[32]

Even the Jesuits tried their hand at diffusion. In 1823 they took three married couples from White Marsh and sent them to Missouri, where the corporation was expanding its mission. Among them were Thomas and Mary Brown, Moses and Nancy Queen, and Isaac Hawkins and Susanna Queen. All were relatives of those who had won their freedom but were still enslaved because their mothers remained enslaved. All three pairs were separated from their families in Maryland. Moses Queen made repeated attempts to convince the priests that he should be permitted to visit his family in Maryland to no avail. In 1829 the Jesuits sent sixteen more people from White Marsh to work at the new mission in St. Louis, where the Jesuits planned to start another college.[33]

Thomas Brown wrote the provincial superior of Maryland that the president of the Jesuit-run university in Missouri treated them so "poorly" that they were afraid they would die from hypothermia. After years of "faithful" service, he and his wife "have not a place to lay our heads in our old age . . . We live at present in rotten logg house so old & decayed that at every blast of wind we are afraid of our lives." The president had decided that they could live in a loft above the outhouse. No heat. No fireplace. Brown offered to buy their own freedom from the corporation for $100. He could pay $50 in cash immediately. "Have pity on us," he pleaded. "Let us go free for one hundred dollars or else we will Surely perish with the Cold."[34]

No reply came.

The political controversy over Missouri left almost no room for Southern slaveholders to continue the fiction that they opposed slavery as immoral or that they favored black freedom in certain circumstances. The Jesuits, like Jefferson, William Pinkney, John Randolph, and Francis Scott Key, were faced with the prospect of choosing between openly admitting that slavery was unconstitutional and immoral and asserting that holding human beings as property was both lawful and justified on the basis of white racial superiority and black inferiority. William Pinkney's and John Randolph's hair-trigger defense of slavery as constitutional under the theory of states' rights obscured a deeper shared resolve to avoid talking about slavery in the vain hope that individual slaveholders would come to their senses and end the practice themselves—as Randolph eventually would in his last will and testament—or that diffusion would work its magic and revolutionary ideals would be fulfilled in due time. Each in his own way resolved the paradox by convincing himself that slavery could not be ended through the law or government action and simultaneously that blacks were not meant to be free in the United States because whites would not allow them either to succeed or to become citizens.

For the enslaved families involved in freedom suits, therefore, the legal and political terrain became decidedly steeper and more unforgiving in the aftermath of the Missouri debates. Northern Federalists such as Rufus King openly questioned the constitutionality of slavery and argued that "all laws upholding slavery are absolute nullities" and "that man cannot enslave his fellow man." Southerners such as William Pinkney let go of their previous antislavery views and responded, "The actual Constitution recognizes the legal existence of slavery." A newly strident determination to oppose and discredit black freedom, whether privately or publicly obtained, gripped the slaveholding class in Maryland, Virginia, and the District of Columbia. When the Jesuits privately scuttled their plan of emancipation in 1820, the families on their plantations felt the retrenchment firsthand. They could see that the passage of time would not bring freedom, nor would diffusion, nor colonization.[35]

"Have Her Imprisoned"

In the wake of *Queen v. Hepburn* and the Missouri debates, enslaved families abandoned the legal strategy of claiming descent from a free woman and embarked on a more public, political course: high-profile lawsuits against well-known slaveholders based on technicalities in the law of slavery.

A series of trials in 1822 for the Shorter family revealed how the slaveholding class would react. Like the Queens, the Shorter family won their freedom beginning in 1794 in Maryland's General Court of the Western Shore. They won more cases more quickly than nearly any other enslaved family except the Butlers. They, too, relied on the lawyering of Gabriel

Duvall, by the 1820s a prominent figure in Washington, D.C., and a sitting justice on the Supreme Court bench. Their cases in the 1790s featured free black witnesses and were among those that prompted the Maryland legislature to pass statutes barring black testimony in freedom suits. But white slaveholders never let go of their suspicion that the Shorters' claim was, in the caustic words of Archbishop Leonard Neale, "perfectly groundless."[36]

In July 1822 a branch of the Shorters in Washington filed lawsuits against two of the most prominent residents in the city: the District's second mayor, Daniel Rapine, and a well-connected widow named Ann Casanave. Rapine owned a renowned bookstore on the southwest corner of New Jersey Avenue and B Street near the Capitol. In addition to the latest political tracts, histories, legal treatises, translations, and medical volumes, he sold romances, biographies, travelogues, and novels. Rapine's shop also featured anything anyone would need for correspondence, such as writing paper, sealing wax, pencils, and ink. He was a prolific printer who published Judge William Cranch's court reports. He accumulated property throughout the city, and he had enslaved Kitty Shorter since at least 1808, when she first sued for her freedom. By the 1820s he served as the postmaster of the House of Representatives.[37]

Ann Casanave was just as visible in D.C. society. She was the daughter of one of Prince George's County's largest planters, Notley Young Sr., who held 295 people in slavery in 1790. Her brother was the Catholic priest Notley Young Jr., who inherited John Ashton's estate on behalf of Georgetown College, at least the part that did not go to the children of Susanna "Sucky" Queen. Her sister Eleanor married Robert Brent, Washington's first mayor. In the social circles of early Washington, Ann Young may have surprised her peers when she married Pedro Casanave, a Spanish-born merchant who emigrated from Navarre to the United States in 1785 and rapidly accumulated a small fortune in Georgetown as a real estate agent. Skilled at making friends and not lacking for confidence, Pedro Casanave asked Notley Young Sr. for his daughter's hand in marriage just six years after emigrating, and he subsequently became, for a short time, the mayor of Georgetown. Together the couple built a brick mansion on the corner of Fourteenth and C Streets, within a block of the White House and with commanding views of the Potomac. Pedro Casanave died in 1796, just five years after their marriage, leaving his widow and their two children the mansion and whatever property he possessed. Ann Young Casanave held five slaves in 1800, but a few years later she inherited a considerable estate from her father, including in all likelihood the enslaved persons Rachel Shorter, Mary

Shorter, Sarah Smith, and William Shorter, who each filed freedom petitions twenty years later.[38]

Perhaps because Philip Barton Key may have disparaged the Shorters
as he did the Thomases or perhaps because Ann Young Casanave was part
of a close circle of Maryland slaveholding families, Francis Scott Key took
up her case and defended her against the Shorter freedom suits. After he spent
ten years working on behalf of particular enslaved plaintiffs such as Mina
and Priscilla Queen, defending free blacks against kidnapping, promoting
his plans for wholesale colonization, and all the while regarding himself as
an antislavery humanitarian, Francis Scott Key's views on black freedom
may also have begun to harden. Although he continued to represent a handful of black plaintiffs in freedom suits, later he would claim that "no northern
man began the world with more enthusiasm against slavery" than he did and
that his zeal for freedom suits cooled when he concluded that "the freedom I
so earnestly sought for them was their ruin."[39]

When Rachel Shorter sued Ann Casanave, she also asserted an entirely
novel claim, that she and the other Shorters were descended from a white
woman named Ann Wells in Prince George's County. Eventually, as members of the Shorter family came forward to file other lawsuits, the cases were
consolidated, and the D.C. court appointed a commission to look into the
matter in Prince George's County, to find any testimony about Ann Wells,
including "knowledge or remembrance," and to take depositions "without
partiality." Every witness they could find was to be summoned and deposed.

The commission gathered evidence throughout 1823 and into 1824.
They spoke with an eighty-two-year-old former overseer of Notley Young's
estate, the Forest. The overseer had worked for Young for twenty-eight years
and said that he knew a mulatto woman named Rachel Shorter but had never
heard of Ann Wells. He dismissed the idea of a free white ancestor as a myth,
stating in matter-of-fact terms that he considered Rachel "a Breeding
woman." The term, shocking as it is, was a raw reminder of the reproductive value of enslaved women; the former overseer used it to indicate in a
circular argument that the hereditary enslavement of the Shorters had to be
undeniable because their ancestor Rachel Shorter's children were enslaved.[40]

But considerable evidence suggested that Ann Wells had been an indentured white woman who had children with an enslaved black man. One
of the white witnesses was the son of a local midwife, and as a young boy he
met Ann Wells at a cockfight. His mother pointed her out because she had
attended the birth of Wells's children. Other white witnesses confirmed that
Ann Wells had mixed-race children, but they indicated nothing about her

status. Meanwhile, in Alexandria, Virginia (then part of the District of Columbia), the attorney for Daniel Wells, whose suit became one of the companion Shorter cases, signed an affidavit attesting to the validity of the claim. He wrote, "I am of the opinion that the petitioner Daniel [Wells] is the son of Monica, that Monica is the daughter of Rachael, that Rachael was the daughter of Kitty, that Kitty was the daughter of Ann Wells, and that the said Ann Wells was a white woman." He also weighed the expert opinion of "some eminent physiologists" that the children's hair "resemble[d] the father" and as a result he concluded that the reports of the Shorter women as "mulatto" with "short woolly hair" confirmed their claim that they were descended from a white woman rather than disproved it. "On the whole," he decided, "after considering the facts and circumstances argued on each side of the petition, . . . I am of the opinion that the petitioner claims his freedom on probable grounds." Daniel Wells's suit was folded in with the Shorters and would be decided by the outcome in *Rachel Shorter et al. v. Ann Casanave.*[41]

In late May 1824 the commission wrapped up its investigation and forwarded its inconclusive depositions to the D.C. court. Rachel Shorter's case went to trial in early June. The proceedings took less than a day, in part because the deputy marshal of Prince George's County never summoned several of the witnesses. He also mistook the date of the trial and "did not think it worth while to make" further attempts to find the witnesses. Rachel Shorter and her lawyers later maintained that the trial was a farce and that the family had "discovered new testimony" since the trial "to support their cause which they did not know of before or during the trial."

The jury quickly returned a verdict for Ann Casanave.

The rest of the Shorter freedom suits were summarily dismissed.

When the Shorters lost these cases, it became clear to the enslaved families that freedom suits based on hereditary descent from a free ancestor, whether black or white or Native, would no longer have any real chance of success. In these cases, judges, lawyers, and juries began acting on racial characteristics, on appearance, focusing on the black plaintiff's hair type, color, and facial features. If the Shorters, who had won dozens of cases in Maryland, could not prevail, then the prospects for others were dim. If the persuasive, indeed unassailable, testimony of the Queens about Mary's origins in New Spain could be rendered inadmissible as hearsay, then the odds for other similar depositions were no better. Slaveholders like Ann Casanave and their attorneys could stonewall claims of white ancestry, sow confusion, enlist friendly sheriffs, lose witnesses, and raise skepticism about the validity of any ancestral claims. Even sympathetic juries in the District of Columbia found the suits based on ancestry difficult to judge. As a result, *Rachel Shorter et al. v. Ann Casanave* marked the final chapter for these types of freedom claims.[42]

After Ann Williams leapt out of the third-floor window of the slave pen at Miller's Tavern, a movement grew to petition Congress to abolish slavery gradually in the capital. Though Congress's authority to prevent slaveholders from taking slaves into the federal territories like Missouri was debated, Congress had explicit authority to enact law in the District of Columbia. Presumably, if slavery required positive law to exist anywhere, and if Congress had the power to decide that the capital city would be governed by the laws of Maryland, including those regulating slavery, then Congress also had the power to remove those laws and abolish slavery in the District.

White residents offended by the grotesque spectacle of slave coffles, slave jails, and slave dealers gathered signatures and presented a memorial to Congress in March 1828. The memorial stated in unambiguous fashion a catalog of reasons for abolishing slavery. The "evil" of slavery diminished

F Street, between Thirteenth and Fourteenth Streets (General Photograph Collection, Historical Society of Washington, D.C., Kiplinger Library).
George Miller's Tavern on F Street in this block was notorious as a slave prison. In April 1819 Miller's Tavern caught fire, and some local whites refused to help extinguish the blaze.

prosperity and harmed the principles of freedom for everyone. The domestic slave trade was no better than the foreign slave trade; indeed, it was "disgraceful" and "even more demoralizing in its influence." Men, women, and children were "without their consent, torn from their homes"; husband and wife were "frequently separated and sold into distant parts"; children were "taken from their parents." Furthermore, "some who [were] entitled to their freedom" and many with contracts to serve a term of years were being "sold into unconditional slavery." The loopholes in the law, indeed the "defectiveness of our laws," meant that people entitled to freedom were often taken out of Washington before anyone could intervene. The practice of "man stealing" had become so routine that authorities looked the other way whenever violations of the law occurred. The city jailors, the local slave dealers, the slave traders at Franklin and Armfield's Alexandria slave pen, and the buyers in New Orleans and in Natchez, Mississippi, counted more than anything else on speed and casual indifference to the law.

The abolition of slavery memorial called for Congress to declare all children born after July 4, 1828, to be free at the age of twenty-five. A year earlier on the same date New York's final emancipation and abolition of slavery took effect and was widely celebrated. The memorial also directed Congress to pass a series of laws to prevent the enslaved from being sold in the intervening time before their ultimate freedom. It was the first time the residents of Washington, D.C., had the opportunity to give an opinion on the matter of slavery in public. Notably, Francis Scott Key did not sign the memorial, nor did Henry Clay, nor any of the founders and members of the American Colonization Society. Nor did any of the Jesuit priests at Georgetown. Nor did Gabriel Duvall.

Still, more than a thousand men signed their names to the memorial, out of approximately thirteen thousand white residents in the city. The number of signatories was surprisingly high. Among the first signers of the memorial were all three judges of the D.C. Circuit Court—William Cranch, James S. Morsell, and Buckner Thruston. This was not so perplexing. Cranch and Morsell, both slaveholders, had difficulty reconciling the inhumanity of slavery with the principles of the common law, even if they regularly applied procedural rules in favor of slaveholders. Thruston, as we will see, had become gradually more irascible and unpredictable, his Kentucky slaveholding roots notwithstanding. John P. Van Ness, a former New York congressman and the commanding general in the D.C. militia, now active in antislavery circles, signed the memorial. William P. Gardner, who refused to help put out a fire at George Miller's slave pen and rallied the neighborhood against Miller, signed as well. He later served as a witness for Ann Williams when she sued Miller for her freedom.

What was more surprising was that slaveholders who were defendants in freedom suits signed the memorial, too, perhaps because they had come to believe the claims of the enslaved families they held in bondage or perhaps because they wanted to maintain slavery for themselves even as they took a stand against it as a grotesque perversion of republican ideas of liberty. John Hepburn died in 1825, but his cousins and the administrator of his estate signed in favor of abolition.[43]

The 1828 memorial to abolish slavery in D.C. revealed a broad cross section of white residents with abolition leanings. Some opposed human bondage on principled grounds. Many more may have signed the memorial because they thought that slavery depressed white workers and they wanted to remove blacks. To counter the vaunted property rights of the slaveholders, enslaved families would have to find new ways of exposing the illegalities and illegitimacies of slavery. After the Missouri debates the families bringing these freedom suits needed to discredit the slaveholders; to weaken, if they could, the resurgence in white public support for slavery; and to use their legal actions to articulate the principle that freedom was national and slavery was local as a matter of law and constitutionalism.

On June 2, 1828, Thomas Butler and his family in Prince George's County filed the first and only freedom suit ever directed at a sitting Supreme Court justice: Gabriel Duvall. He was one of the best-known residents in the city of Washington and had pioneered the use of hearsay in the Maryland courts to win freedom suits for the selfsame Butler family in the 1790s. Now, the judge was a defendant in his own freedom suit, against the family he had once represented. The suit involved not only Thomas Butler but also his wife, Sarah, four of their children, and two of their grandchildren. At first, Duvall represented himself, appearing at trial as his own attorney, perhaps overly confident that his presence would lead the judges to dismiss the case. The Butlers asked Francis Scott Key to take their case, while a worried Duvall finally enlisted Walter Jones, the so-called dean of the Washington bar.[44]

This freedom suit threatened Gabriel Duvall in a direct way. At Marietta, in Prince George's County, he held thirty-nine enslaved people in bondage, the largest proportion of whom were children under the age of fourteen. The three generations of the Butlers who sued Duvall may have been the largest enslaved family at Marietta. Their freedom would jeopardize his entire plantation; the economic loss would be substantial. Moreover, one of the enslaved men at Marietta had absconded to Washington, D.C., in the summer of 1828 and was attempting to convince a local lawyer to purchase him from Duvall and then to allow him to purchase his own freedom. One of Gabriel Duvall's cousins had bumped into the man and reported to Duvall that "your boy John" was "about Washington" and "up to something." Duvall obviously did not want to permit John, an alleged fugitive with a reward price on his

Associate Justice Gabriel Duvall, ca. 1828
(Collection of the Supreme Court of the United States).

Duvall was the attorney for numerous enslaved petitioners, including Edward Queen and Charles Mahoney. He personally testified as a witness for Mina Queen at her freedom trial in 1810 and wrote in favor of freedom in *Queen v. Hepburn*. A lifelong slaveholder, he was sued by the Butler family in 1828.

head, to arrange the purchase of himself because it would set an example that others might try to follow, but Duvall's cousin pointed out that there was "a chance of losing him altogether." He counseled Duvall that it was "better to satisfy him [John] by selling him home, than to run the risque of his escape which would have a still more pernicious effect."[45]

Duvall went on the offensive in the freedom suit immediately. He maintained that he was an official resident of Prince George's County, Maryland, and therefore that the Butlers sued in the wrong jurisdiction and that the case in the D.C. court should be dismissed. "Negroes under the control & held in bondage by a white man, must be esteemed slaves until the contrary is established in the manner directed by law," he responded to their petition. The argument in his own defense was the exact opposite of the argument he had upheld in *Queen v. Hepburn*.

Duvall knew, given his reputation and prominence, that the local judges and juries in Prince George's County would favor him and that they would regard the Butlers with considerable skepticism. "In short, a petition for freedom is a local action," Duvall concluded. The idea was critical to his defense. If freedom suits should be tried only in the most local courts, then there was nothing universal about freedom. Duvall, in effect, had reversed the underlying premise of his bold dissent in *Queen v. Hepburn*. He now maintained, at least when his own property was threatened, that freedom was not universal, but instead that freedom had to be locally proven and sanctioned, that enslaved persons had no right to petition for freedom outside of their local jurisdictions. Freedom was local. Slavery was national.

But in May 1829 the D.C. judges denied Gabriel Duvall's motion to dismiss the case on these grounds. They affirmed the right to petition for freedom as a fundamental one. It was not restricted in any way to local circumstances. "Wherever the master exercises his power over the supposed slave, there the right of action exists [to petition for freedom]. It is, in its nature, strictly personal . . . Personal rights, acquired by the laws of Maryland, follow the person everywhere." The ruling was powerfully significant. The petition for freedom was a "right" that existed "long before" the Maryland statutes regulated it, and its existence came from "daily use." In sum, the court noted, "A petition for freedom is not a local action. The right is personal, and accompanies the person wherever he goes."[46]

Butler v. Duvall sustained an important idea, the premise that every person held a potential right to freedom wherever he or she went. Local slave law could neither take that preexisting right away nor remove the potentiality for freedom. By this logic, Duvall was wrong: slavery was entirely *local;* freedom was *national.* The long line of freedom suits in Maryland proved that such rights had always existed.

Although held in bondage on Duvall's plantation at Marietta for more than twenty years, the Butlers had filed their freedom suit in the D.C. court because Duvall obviously spent so much time at his Washington residence. What's more, they filed there because they had been bought and sold in Washington, D.C., twenty years earlier in violation of the law. In fact, the Butler family's decision to use the D.C. venue to sue Duvall indicates that they knew a great deal about the courts and the mechanisms that made for potentially successful freedom suits. Why did they wait until 1828 to file their suit? We can only speculate. But New York's total emancipation took effect July 4, 1827, an inspiration and a rallying moment for enslaved men and women across the United States, and the memorial to abolish slavery in D.C. had been circulating for months. They would have known that Duvall did not sign it.

Once the case went to trial, the evidence pointed to a violation of Maryland's law against the importation of slaves. Duvall's motion for a new trial was overruled. The jury ruled in favor of the Butler family's freedom, and Thomas and Sarah Butler, their four children, and two grandchildren were free.[47]

Within months, a black abolitionist in Boston named David Walker penned one of the most revolutionary antislavery arguments ever written. Walker's *Appeal . . . to the Coloured Citizens of the World* condemned "the inhuman system of slavery" and urged black Americans to "rise up" against the slaveholders he called "tyrants" and "oppressors." Walker took particular aim at the duplicity of the slaveholders. Those who claimed that the Bible sanctioned slavery were instead "pretenders to Christianity." Those who invoked the Declaration of Independence yet continued to hold slaves contorted its very meaning beyond recognition. Slaveholders routinely violated the Declaration's ideals with "cruelties and murders." Those who promoted colonization were the most duplicitous of all. Walker excoriated the founders of the American Colonization Society, including Henry Clay and Elias B. Caldwell by name:

> Do you believe that Mr. Henry Clay, late Secretary of State, and now in Kentucky, is a friend to the blacks, further than his personal interest extends? Is it not his greatest object and glory upon earth, to sink us into miseries and wretchedness by making slaves of us, to work his plantation to enrich him and his family? Does

he care a pinch of snuff about Africa—whether it remains a land of Pagans and of blood, or of Christians, so long as he gets enough of her sons and daughters to dig up gold and silver for him?[48]

David Walker's appeal rang like a clanging fire bell in the night. He would not accept the lies that slaveholders told about colonization. To Henry Clay's claim that slaveholders were "innocent" victims of slavery, Walker responded:

> Are Mr. Clay and the rest of the Americans, innocent of the blood and groans of our fathers and us, their children?—Every individual may plead innocence, if he pleases, but God will, before long, separate the innocent from the guilty, unless something is speedily done—which I suppose will hardly be, so that their destruction may be sure. Oh Americans! let me tell you, in the name of the Lord, it will be good for you, if you listen to the voice of the Holy Ghost, but if you do not, you are ruined!!! Some of you are good men; but the will of my God must be done. Those avaricious and ungodly tyrants among you, I am awfully afraid will drag down the vengeance of God upon you. When God Almighty commences his battle on the continent of America, for the oppression of his people, tyrants will wish they never were born.[49]

No freedom suit in Washington, D.C., perhaps in American history, held more political significance than Charlotte Dupee's lawsuit against Henry Clay, the outgoing secretary of state, in February 1829. Over the previous six months the D.C. judges had affirmed the right of enslaved persons to petition for freedom in *Butler v. Duvall*. The memorial to abolish slavery had circulated widely. New York had celebrated its first year of emancipation. Like the Butlers, Charlotte Dupee had waited for the right moment. Clay's term as secretary of state was drifting to a close. On February 11, 1829, Congress unsealed and counted the electoral votes officially certifying Andrew Jackson's election. Two days later, on February 13, Charlotte Dupee sued Clay. The inauguration of President Jackson would take place within weeks. Henry Clay was about to leave Washington and return to Kentucky, and he expected to take Charlotte Dupee with him.

Born on the Eastern Shore of Maryland, Dupee came from a family with a long history of freedom. Her father, George Standley, was counted in the first U.S. census as a free black man. Her mother, Rachel, however, was enslaved when Charlotte was born around 1787. Charlotte's father was able to purchase Rachel and their two older children and free all of them with a deed of manumission. But Charlotte, five years old, remained enslaved. In 1796, when she was nine, a local tailor in Cambridge, Maryland, named James Condon bought her for $100. Condon held one slave: Charlotte. In 1805, when she was eighteen, he took her to Kentucky, where he hoped to elevate his status and start anew with his growing family.

Ripped away from her free relatives, Charlotte was Condon's principal and perhaps only real asset, an enslaved woman with potential "increase" who would fetch a high price: enough for Condon to buy a new building in downtown Lexington for his shop. Once in Kentucky, Charlotte met Aaron Dupee, a man Henry Clay had enslaved as his personal attendant and driver. Their courtship lasted a year. Condon sold "Lotty," as he called Charlotte, to Henry Clay for "a very high price"—$450. Charlotte and Aaron were married soon after.

Clay brought both of them to Washington, D.C., in 1815, when he was Speaker of the House. They stayed in the city for more than a year. He brought them with him again in 1825, for four years during his term as secretary of state. They had two children, Charles and Mary Ann, and lived at Decatur House on Lafayette Square with Clay, in the shadow of the White House. Charlotte and Aaron Dupee became widely known among the city's political class and within its circle of free black residents. As a result, they would have known about the sensation Ann Williams caused when she jumped from Miller's Tavern. They would have known about the congressional inquiry into the slave trade that followed. And they would have known about the Supreme Court's ruling in *Queen v. Hepburn* and the long line of freedom suits by the families from Maryland.[50]

During her stints in Washington, Charlotte visited her free family in Maryland. Her father had been a free man since 1790, her mother and siblings since 1792. Perhaps aware that the documentary record might be turned to her advantage, Charlotte argued that when she was born, her mother was a free woman and therefore that her removal to Kentucky and her sale as a slave to Clay had been illegal. She also knew that all sorts of other arguments might be introduced at a trial. Most of all, she knew that her suit on behalf her two children would tie Clay up in court, keep them all in Washington, D.C., and delay their imminent return to the plantation in Kentucky.

When Charlotte Dupee sued Clay for her freedom, she publicly questioned the character of one of the most powerful politicians in the nation.

He reacted with astonishment, defensiveness, and intense concern for his reputation. Clay dashed off an immediate, formal, and elaborate answer to the court. Arrogant and prickly, like most slaveholders who were sued, he could hardly believe that his reputation was being called into question. He maintained that he did not have "the remotest suspicion that Charlotte had any title whatever to her freedom, nor does he yet believe she has any." In fact, Dupee's freedom suit seemed to take him by complete surprise. He repeated for emphasis that he did not have "the least idea of her having any just pretension to her freedom." Acting as if Dupee should have informed him of her claim to freedom before suing him, Clay deflected blame for the suit on her. Then he patronizingly suggested that something else must be behind her actions. He alleged that her freedom suit had been "instigated by motives distinct from the desire of liberating the petitioners." He worried that the lawsuit was trumped up "for the purposes of injuring and embarrassing" his political reputation.[51]

Clay's answer to Dupee's petition is one of the most remarkable documents of its kind in American history because it is one of the few direct responses we have from a defendant slaveholder being sued. Most slaveholders had their attorneys issue pro forma replies to the court. Clay's response was personal. He discredited Dupee and searched for someone else to blame for the embarrassment.[52]

Even before his response to the court, Clay made an immediate inquiry to James Condon requesting specific information about Dupee's family and any claim to freedom she might have. Writing several days before the legal papers were filed, Clay already had an idea what she would say: that Condon had taken her from Maryland and sold her illegally. Condon was mortified. His response is equally remarkable, for it tells us precisely how slaveholders reacted to being sued.

Condon thought the suit amounted to an accusation of "moral turpitude" on his part and complained that it was one of the most "exceedingly painful" events he had ever experienced. He claimed to have never before been called before a court to answer for any crime, and he was shocked to be asked to answer Clay's questions. Condon maintained that, although Dupee's mother was in fact a free woman, Dupee herself "was born" a slave. He assured Clay that the bill of sale was legal. "I must confess that I was truely astonished at the contents of your letter," he replied, "[a]nd cannot account for the origin of this business in any other way, than that of some evil disposed person opperating upon the mind of Lotty improperly."

Then, in a stunning admission, Condon told Clay that "upon reflection" there was "another circumstance that may have had some influence upon her mind." He divulged, "I did once promise Lotty freedom."

Reading that sentence, Clay's eyes must have narrowed.

Of course, Condon tried to explain why this promise had gone unfulfilled. He said that her potential freedom was conditional, predicated on "long and faithful service." Because she chose to marry Aaron Dupee and asked to be sold to Clay, she had "voluntarily relinquished" her long and faithful service to Condon and therefore her freedom.

The explanation made matters worse for Clay. What jury would believe it? Condon's overt promise of Dupee's freedom could become the entire basis for her lawsuit. Downplaying the signal importance of what he had just revealed, Condon reassured Clay that he should not "for a moment entertain the belief that any serious attempt will be made to bring you or myself into a difficulty about this matter." If the freedom suit did become serious, though, Condon worried that many of the white witnesses in Maryland who could testify on their behalf had long since died. Figuratively, Condon was sweating with trepidation.[53]

Charlotte Dupee had launched a very public affair, an assault on Clay's sense of his own integrity and his public reputation. Clay went back to Kentucky, and he took Aaron Dupee and the children with him as punishment. But Charlotte remained in D.C. because her freedom suit was pending and she therefore could not be removed from the District. He told her to hire herself out until the trial. She was left at Decatur House, his orders meant as another punishment, a withdrawal of the care and benefit of his paternalism. Yet Dupee managed quickly to find employment. She hired herself out to Clay's principal political enemy, the new vice president, Martin Van Buren, leader and organizer of the insurgent Democratic Party and the incoming occupant of Decatur House. Dupee lived for more than a year in the cramped slave quarters there while she waited for her trial to begin. Meanwhile, Clay wrote his friends that he anticipated "with some anxiety" the news from the court. Dupee's lawyer requested that the court appoint a commission to take depositions from witnesses in Maryland and Tennessee, where James Condon then resided. Because Dupee was working for the Van Burens, Clay imagined that his enemies in the Andrew Jackson administration had sponsored her petition for freedom, but he failed to recognize what was right in front of him: the long history of freedom suits in Maryland, the rising antislavery sentiments in the District, and the deep experience with freedom in Charlotte Dupee's family.

Her freedom suit went to trial in May 1830. A jury heard all of the evidence and concluded that Charlotte Dupee was born "a slave for life." In his deposition James Condon said nothing about his promise to free her, perpetrating a lie designed to keep her enslaved and at the same time to save his own reputation among slaveholders. Even if the jury wanted to free Charlotte Dupee, there appeared to be no basis in the law for it.

After the court's verdict in his favor, Henry Clay asked his attorney to locate Dupee at Martin Van Buren's house (Decatur House) and tell her to return to Kentucky immediately. Because she had been hiring herself out for eighteen months, Clay thought that she should have the means—that is, the money—to "bring herself home." He instructed his attorney, however, "If she shews any perverse or refractory disposition, be pleased to have her imprisoned."[54]

But Charlotte Dupee refused to return to Kentucky. Clay was furious. From Kentucky he wrote his attorney in D.C. with growing indignation. His letter is worth quoting at some length:

> I approve entirely of your order to the Marshall to imprison Lotty. Her husband and children are here. Her refusal therefore to return home, when requested by me to do so through you, was unnatural towards them as it was disobedient to me. She has been her own mistress, upwards of 18 months, since I left her at Washington, in consequence of the groundless writ which she was prompted to bring against me for her freedom; and as that writ has been decided against her, and as her conduct has created insubordination among her relatives here, I think it is high time to put a stop to it.[55]

Dupee's freedom suit threatened every precept of the slaveholder in Clay. He interpreted her actions as "unnatural," her independence as "prompted" by others, his enemies. He simply could not imagine her refusal, and he could not countenance the "insubordination" it sparked at Ashland.

At Clay's request, Dupee was seized and taken to the D.C. City Jail while he considered various options to have her transported to Kentucky. He sent her to his daughter in New Orleans instead. This was also meant as punishment. Dupee would not see her husband, Aaron, or her children for more than two years. After Dupee arrived in New Orleans in December 1830, Clay's daughter wrote in patronizing tones that Charlotte was "now very penitent" and felt relieved that the "unpleasant affair" was finished.

But it was not. Dupee continued to press for her freedom. Ten years later Henry Clay signed a deed of emancipation in Kentucky, freeing Charlotte, fifty-three years old, and Mary Anne, one of her adult daughters. To justify the emancipation, Clay noted that she "nursed most of my children and most of my grandchildren." But he specifically excluded all of Charlotte's and Mary Anne's children born into slavery before the deed was executed. All of those children, he wrote, were "subject to me."

Henry Clay fought Charlotte Dupee's freedom suit to the bitter end, imprisoned her in the D.C. City Jail for "insubordination," and separated her for years from her husband and children. His grudging manumission enslaved more people than it freed.[56]

No newspapers reported Charlotte Dupee's freedom suit, and it has gone largely unnoticed ever since. Her husband, Aaron Dupee, was much more widely known. Fawning obituaries in the mid-nineteenth century written by white editors praised his association with Clay, lauded his faithful service, and remarked on his skill as a footman and driver. Clay himself dismissed Charlotte's freedom suit as trumped up by his political opponents. Later his biographers overlooked her.[57]

But Charlotte Dupee's freedom suit was unmistakably her own, an act that defied and challenged one of the foremost slaveholders in the nation. Others would follow in her footsteps. Delay, disruption, negotiation, and tactical lawsuits—these were the components of a strategy to undermine the legal power of the slaveholders.

Freedom suits had always been private acts with public consequences, but after Nat Turner's 1831 slave insurrection in Southampton County, Virginia, they took on newfound significance. The public nature of the freedom suits intensified and the politics of the freedom suits turned. Slaveholders throughout Virginia and Maryland greeted almost any bid for freedom with a bilious mixture of fear and suspicion. One from Fauquier County, Virginia, seethed that "astute and cunning lawyers" in the capital made it "their business to pry into every man's title to his negroes." The leading Whig newspaper the *National Intelligencer* defended the law of Maryland by pointing out that "all colored persons are held to be slaves until proven free, as all horses are presumed to be somebody's property."[58]

Two major political parties—the Whigs and the Democrats—were beginning to take shape in the early 1830s. Each party offered a competing vision of the nation's future. Each attracted slaveholders in the South. Neither party opposed slavery in any serious way. The Whigs, led by Henry Clay, emphasized a program of national economic growth through transportation and communication, a central bank, and protective tariffs, what Clay called the American system. With some of the wealthiest lawyers, planters, and businessmen in their ranks, Whigs defended slavery as a natural feature of the social order. Self-proclaimed conservatives, they believed in the rule of law and the protection of property. A loose coalition, the Whigs organized themselves to oppose Andrew Jackson after his reelection in 1832 to the presidency. The Democrats, led by Jackson, saw themselves as the true successors to Jeffersonian Republicanism. Jacksonians believed in the sovereignty of the people expressed in popular elections, championed majority rule, and celebrated individual freedom for white men uninhibited by government. They attracted the small farmers and working white men in the urban centers. Jackson himself promoted westward expansion, white supremacy, and Indian removal. Jacksonian Democrats, therefore, defended slavery as an expression of white freedom and opposed abolition as an unconstitutional interference in the states and a threat to majority rule.[59]

But Turner's revolt and a major slave rebellion in Jamaica the same year led even some slaveholders to conclude that something had to be done. Parliament subsequently abolished slavery in the British colonies in 1833, emancipating more than eight hundred thousand enslaved people and compensating slaveholders in the process. American slaveholders were startled by the dramatic change in British public opinion that drove the move to abolish slavery. A petition campaign in Britain led tens of thousands of citizens to question the imperial and constitutional arrangement that tolerated British slaveholding. The lesson was not lost on American abolitionists, who organized the American Anti-Slavery Society in 1833 and began petitioning Congress to end the slave trade and abolish slavery in the United States. Because Congress had direct authority over the District of Columbia, the antislavery petition campaign took aim at the incongruity of slavery in the nation's capital. In Maryland, slaveholders undertook the largest state-financed program in American history to colonize free blacks in Africa, appropriating $20,000 a year and requiring in 1831 that all blacks manumitted in the future be required to leave the state, unless a court allowed them to stay for "extraordinary good conduct and character." Legislators considered even more drastic proposals, including a bill to forcibly remove all blacks from the state.[60]

More proposals to restrict free blacks gained a hearing in the Maryland State House. A joint committee recommended barring free blacks from moving into the state and limiting free blacks visiting the state to stay for no more than ten days; if a free black resident left Maryland for more than thirty days, he or she would be considered an "alien" and unable to return. The committee's report condemned free blacks in the bluntest terms, calling their presence an "evil" ruining the state.[61]

Meanwhile, in the Jackson administration, Attorney General Roger B. Taney was asked for an internal opinion on the constitutional rights of free blacks. His response was unambiguous: free blacks in Southern states had no legal rights under the Constitution. "The African race in the United States even when free, are everywhere a degraded class, and exercise no political influence. The privileges they are allowed to enjoy, are accorded to them as a matter of kindness and benevolence rather than of right. They are the only class of persons who can be held as mere property, as slaves." Taney denied that the Declaration of Independence applied to blacks in the United States, who, he maintained, "have never been regarded as a portion of the people of this country & have never been considered as members of the body politic." What rights blacks held they did so at the "mercy" of whites. They were "not looked upon as citizens by the contracting parties who formed the Constitution." Nor were they "supposed to be included by the term citizens."[62]

These assertions were patently inaccurate. Taney knew that blacks voted in Maryland before 1802, sued in court, made contracts, and bought and sold property. He knew that Philip Barton Key lost his seat in the Maryland House of Delegates because he represented the slaveholders in freedom suits and black men voted against him. Taney's opinion was never published, but it guided the Jackson administration's thinking and foreshadowed what Taney would say twenty-five years later in *Dred Scott*. The opinion circulated and undoubtedly found its way into the hands of Taney's brother-in-law Francis Scott Key, whose own views of black freedom had become similarly cramped.[63]

In Washington, slavery and the slave trade continued uninterrupted. "The District [is] the grand slave mart of the nation," the abolitionist minister and organizer Amos Phelps concluded after his visit to Washington. He found the capital overrun with "private prisons," "travelling traders," and "government prisons built with the people's money." Slavery had become "entailed, i.e. . . . it has come to be sanctioned by law." What Phelps witnessed in D.C. led him to muse that slavery's "great end was the subversion of the Constitution and the government itself."[64]

But the freedom suits by Rachel Shorter, Thomas and Sarah Butler, and Charlotte Dupee challenged the legality of slavery and attempted at least to restrict it to particular places, conditions, and circumstances. Small victories in these suits had large consequences. Increasingly, the possibility of a favorable verdict in any given freedom suit in Washington seemed more than plausible. In fact, in the early 1830s the enslaved families had their greatest successes in the District. Black plaintiffs secured a string of verdicts, winning nearly as many lawsuits as they filed in 1831 and 1832, a record that would never be repeated. Perhaps most prominently, on July 2, 1832, a D.C. court rendered a verdict in favor of Ann Williams and her children.

It had been seventeen years since Ann Williams leapt from the garret at Miller's Tavern. The reasons for the decision were not recorded, but the jury may have determined that Williams was brought to the District of Columbia in November 1815 in violation of the Maryland act of 1796. Alternatively, the jury may have been persuaded that Williams had been living independently as a free woman for more than ten years and had to be considered free on that basis alone, or the jury may have simply sympathized with Ann Williams and despised and distrusted George Miller.[65]

Another round of upcoming cases was making its way through the courts.

Chloe Ann Johnson, for instance, was forty-four years old. She had scars on her eyebrow, the corner of her mouth, and her upper lip; her forefinger had been broken at one time; and she had suffered a third-degree burn on her right arm. Imprisoned by the slave traders Isaac Franklin and John Armfield in Alexandria, Virginia, she sued for her freedom. Keziah Crawford was twenty-nine years old, and she, too, had scars all over her body. She sued on July 12, 1834. Meanwhile, Rebecca Hobbs sued the slave traders Thomas Magruder and Washington Robey for attempting to subvert the last will and testament that freed her, to "defraud" her of her freedom, and to sell her to "strange parts where she would not from her situation have it in her power to make good and available her rights." Magruder planned to take her to Mississippi.[66]

The chorus of black petitioners reached its height in 1834 and 1835, becoming a visible, vocal, and increasingly powerful movement. The major slave traders in the city were being sued for the first time by multiple plaintiffs. A small band of abolitionist lawyers, far more determined to end slavery than Francis Scott Key ever was, began to help the families. At the Washington Navy Yard and other federal installations, enslaved men such as Thomas Smallwood worked to buy their freedom. Led by Smallwood, whose initial views of colonization had soured, a growing network of free blacks raised funds to purchase freedom, hire lawyers, and aid individual escape attempts. More than a dozen freedom cases were pending in the summer of 1835.[67]

Juneteenth

I t was Juneteenth, and Dr. Letitia Clark had not slept much. Neither had her cousin Guilford Queen. Nor had I, for that matter. Clark is a medical doctor at the Georgetown University Hospital and a descendant of the Queens. Guilford Queen, a retired official in the Office of Inspector General for the Department of State, had spent years tracing his family's lineage and thinking about the legacies his ancestors passed down from one generation to the next. We met for the first time at the Georgetown liturgy, and our friendship had deepened in the intervening year. For months, we three had been planning an informal road trip. We were going to tour the plantations of southern Maryland together, follow the Potomac River on its course down to the open water of the Chesapeake Bay, and talk through the meaning of what we were learning about our families and our interlaced histories.

A few days before our excursion, in anticipation of the history we would encounter, Letitia Clark realized the source of her sleeplessness. "I just wish our parents were alive to know this," she explained as we drove south on Route 210 toward southern Maryland. "To find out that our family intersects with parts of history that we've known about all our lives, like Francis Scott Key . . . and to think that our ancestors intersected with that period even though they were never mentioned or never thought of, but they were there and they were known."

The source of my insomnia was different. I had been reading the proceedings of the first slaveholders' convention ever held in the United States. One hundred and fifty of Maryland's leading slaveholders had gathered in

Annapolis in January 1842 to turn back the tide of abolitionism, and one of my distant relatives, Thomas S. Duckett, had taken a leading role. He was a Whig Party man, forty-five years old, and a delegate in the Maryland legislature. He considered himself a moderate, but like Francis Scott Key and Roger B. Taney, he disparaged black freedom. Duckett announced that he "viewed the free negroes in this State as a great evil." He came out "decidedly opposed to emancipation" and pronounced himself in favor of the removal and colonization of all free blacks to a location outside the United States. "You can never amalgamate[,] and separation or annihilation must ensue," Duckett concluded. The slaveholders blamed free blacks for "infecting the slaves with bad doctrines." Because the 1831 law requiring free black persons to leave Maryland had never been enforced, the slaveholders proposed to outlaw private manumissions. They disagreed on whether to ban this practice, because some of them, including Duckett, perversely saw it as an infringement on their own rights of property. That did not stop them from proposing that no free black person could leave the state and return. Nor did it stop them from passing a series of resolutions urging the legislature to clamp down on the rights of free black people, preventing them from immigrating into the state, traveling on railroads, owning guns, selling alcohol, meeting after sunset, or ever owning and bequeathing real estate.[1]

It was a shameful list of proposals, conferring the most degrading caste status on all free black citizens, a tableau designed and arranged to humiliate. In truth, the legislature was unlikely to pass such draconian measures, but Duckett and his fellow slaveholders had taken the opportunity to speak with grotesque disdain for black freedom. His words haunted me. They were a rebuke, a constant reminder of how his generation had seduced themselves and justified themselves and extricated themselves from responsibility for the moral problem of slavery.

His grandfather Thomas Duckett, the county judge, had allowed hearsay to be entered into evidence against the Jesuits, and more than twenty Queen family members won their freedom as a consequence. Perhaps he allowed their evidence out of generosity, but he may have done so simply because he was not a professional lawyer and did not know anything about such new procedural rules as hearsay. The Queen family's freedom hung in the balance, but it would be presumptuous to guess at his motivations in that moment. I could not ascribe to his actions some wisdom or generosity he would not have possessed. Neither could I dismiss his actions as entirely self-serving or trivial.

Reading the proceedings of the slaveholders' convention was a lesson in the pretense and artifice of the slaveholders, a tutorial in the backfilling and mythmaking they practiced to convince themselves of their moral uprightness, and an appraisal of the blunt force of racism. At one point Duckett had chased an abolitionist editor and organizer, Charles T. Torrey, out of the convention. The image of this "bare-headed" relative, however distant, hunting Torrey down so that he could challenge the abolitionist to a physical confrontation burned like a hot ember lodged in my windpipe.[2]

We arrived at Chapel Point at midmorning, the temperature and humidity climbing rapidly. Together we walked through the historic cemetery and stood for a long time in front of the grave of the Reverend Francis Neale, the slaveholding president of Georgetown College whom Priscilla Queen had

Queen descendants Letitia Clark and Guilford Queen at St. Thomas Manor, Port Tobacco, Charles County, June 2018 (courtesy of the author).
The Queen family won a series of freedom suits in Prince George's County in the 1790s. Letitia Clark and Guilford Queen are among their descendants. "I still have not been able to put into words all the poignancy I feel," Queen told me.

sued in 1810. This was the site near Port Tobacco, Maryland, where the Jesuits managed a large plantation with dozens of enslaved men, women, and children. High on a ridge overlooking the Potomac River, St. Thomas Manor House, the cemetery, and the church are still prominently visible for miles in every direction.

Neale's headstone is among the oldest in the cemetery, positioned in a section for priests bordered by ancient boxwoods under sweeping oaks near the manor house. His fellow Jesuits form a line of memorials beside him. The Reverend Sylvester Boarman died in 1811. Like Neale he, too, was sued by the Queen family. The Reverend Charles Neale died in 1815. He was also sued by the Queens. And he refused to hear Susanna Queen's confession.

We looked out over Francis Neale's headstone and could see Litchfield Enlarged, the hundred-acre plantation that the children of Susanna "Sucky" Queen inherited in Hill Top, Maryland, from their onetime adversary at law, the Jesuit priest John Ashton. The past seemed so close to us that it was disorienting. Today Hill Top is little more than an obscure crossroads where there was once a post office, but for a branch of the Queen family it was the beginning place of freedom. From its heights they could look down on St. Thomas Manor, where they had once been enslaved, on Francis Neale, whom they had once sued, and on the other Jesuits whose corporation had once tried to sell them all.

"I was thinking about the trip before we came," Letitia Clark reflected as we talked later, under the locust trees next to the old manor house. "And . . . I hope that coming here and trying to sort it out was a way of honoring the people who were here before me, who worked so hard and lived and died here." She wanted them to know that what they did "counted for something."

Recalling the verse from Jeremiah 29:11, Clark recited it from memory: "'For I know the plans I have for you,' declares the Lord, . . . 'plans to give you hope and a future.'" Thinking about her ancestors, Edward Queen, Priscilla Queen, Sucky Queen, and all the others, Clark speculated, "We're their hope and future. I don't know if they heard that [verse] from Francis Neale, or John Ashton. Who knows, right? Who knows. I don't know. Maybe they did."

Dozens of little Confederate flags left over from Memorial Day fluttered in the breeze in front of polished granite headstones, stanchions marking the past-present, reminders of the long history of slavery and a war to perpetuate enslavement. "It's not like there's not something here," Letitia Clark quipped about the Confederate mementos and the region's racial history. Her arched eyebrows were raised over the rim of her sunglasses.

Neither Clark nor Queen had heard about the slaveholders' convention, the racist proposals by Duckett and others to reverse black freedom in Maryland, or the potential ramifications of the convention on the Queen family's enslaved and free ancestors. "A lot of people really decided at the individual level, and [even] at the Catholic Church level, how are we going to stand when it comes to the rights and liberties of a person or a group of people," Guilford Queen explained in response. People in these situations, he pointed out, lied to themselves, dissembled, and allowed themselves to be enticed into ugly postures. Yet we have to hold them accountable. The slaveholders at the convention could not stop the force of history. The stories of the freedom suits were "not part of our popular imagination of history," but to Guilford Queen, "all the little vignettes [of freedom] are just amazing, they are like small nuggets of truth that are precious gems."

Both Clark and Queen told me that learning about their Louisiana cousins was a shock. They met Mélisande Short-Colomb, Sandra Green Thomas, and the descendants of the other families sold to Louisiana for the first time at the Georgetown liturgy in 2017. Both described feeling "guilty" because it had been "so hard for the cousins that went to Louisiana." Clark thought that there was nothing she could say to them to explain this bitter realization. She was profoundly troubled by the disparity she saw between the Maryland and Louisiana branches of her family, one side freed in the courts, the other enslaved until the Civil War. Two branches: hers owning property, free, though not without struggle; the other enslaved, then forced into sharecropping, lynching, violence, displacement, poverty, natural disaster. Turning the history over and over in her mind, Clark decided that because her ancestors won their freedom, they were able to hold their families together and create "a sort of wealth you can't buy." This was a wealth that she now realized came not solely from individual hard work but from collective, familial endeavor made secure through freedom. Her ancestors, she said, had a fifty-year "head start" on freedom. "I want to say, recently, that it's made me appreciate my ancestors even more," she explained. "I almost felt guilty in a way. Why should you feel guilty for getting free before somebody else?"

"These are the things that have been haunting me and making me wake up at night," Clark said. It was the tearing apart of her family and the other families and the consequences that flowed from that historical trauma that did. "Once you're free, you can stay together as a family . . . A family is the strongest unit there is, right?"

CHAPTER 7

Mob Law

The "great moral and political evil" of which I speak, is supposed to be slavery, but is it not plainly the whole colored race?

—FRANCIS SCOTT KEY,
IN *U.S. V. REUBEN CRANDALL*, APRIL 1836

The black men who worked at the Washington Navy Yard, both enslaved and free, experienced an unusual degree of independence from slaveholders, an oasis of freedom in a city organized around enslavement. One of the enslaved men, Charles Ball, recalled his days as a cook on the USS *Congress* as mildly liberating. He met various officers and "gentlemen who came on board" and soon discovered that the situation afforded him considerable benefits compared with the tobacco plantations in Prince George's County. "One gave me a half-worn coat, another an old shirt, and a third, a cast-off waistcoat and pantaloons," he explained. "Some presented me with small sums of money, and in this way I soon found myself well clothed, and with more than a dollar in my pocket." He spent Sunday afternoons walking the city, often "as far as Georgetown." He took in "the new and splendid buildings" and made "many new acquaintances amongst the slaves." Although he saw coffles "chained together in long trains, and driven off toward the south," at the Navy Yard he met free black men from the North and began to plan his own escape with one of them.

As Charles Ball discovered, the Washington Navy Yard offered an unlikely harbor in the storm, a distinctive refuge where he could at least nur-
ture ideas of freedom. Since 1799, when the Navy Yard was established, the
federal installation had employed more African Americans than any other
site in the city, and as a consequence hundreds of black men, free and enslaved, interacted with its military officers, civilian foremen, clerks, sailors,
and laborers. The close working conditions in the Navy Yard, combined with
the facility's federal purpose and proximity to Congress, made for a distinct
situation within the twenty-eight-acre compound.

An imposing gate marked the entrance. Designed by Benjamin Latrobe
in the Greek Revival style, the gate featured two Doric columns. Atop its par-
apet was a huge sculpture of an eagle grasping a massive anchor. Meant to
symbolize the democratic ideals of the Greek state as worthy of the American republic, the Latrobe gate was a landmark for the Navy Yard's black
workers who passed through it every day. The yard, enclosed by a high brick
wall, gave the men a measure of protection and even solidarity.[1]

The men on the Navy Yard's payroll worked as employees of the national government, and they lived in a city that was a federal district of that
selfsame government. They came and went through the gate every day together. They sang at work to keep pace together. Frederick Douglass worked
as a caulker in a similar installation in Baltimore in the 1830s. He described
the effect on his thinking in this way:

> It was new, hard, and dirty work, even for a calker, but I went at it
> with a glad heart and a willing hand. I was now my own master—a
> tremendous fact—and the rapturous excitement with which I
> seized the job, may not easily be understood, except by someone
> with an experience something like mine. The thoughts—"I can
> work! I can work for a living; I am not afraid of work; I have no
> Master Hugh to rob me of my earnings"—placed me in a state of
> independence, beyond seeking friendship or support of any man.[2]

But no enslaved man was ever entirely safe, even at the Navy Yard. One
day, before he realized what was happening, Charles Ball was sold and sent
to rural Calvert County, Maryland, where white slaveholders took each other
to court over who owned him. For two years the case dragged on, and when
it was over, he was sold again to slave traders, chained in a coffle, and marched
to South Carolina. His taste of freedom at the Navy Yard became a distant
memory, replaced by a "sad reversal of fortune" and "dreadful suffering."[3]

Ball's fate was not unusual. In the 1820s and 1830s, the interstate slave trade took off. The price of enslaved men, women, and children soared to unheard-of heights. Slave dealers fetched $350, $400, as much as $450 for a healthy "hand" in South Carolina, Georgia, and Louisiana, often triple the prices of only a decade earlier. The enslaved men hired to work in the Washington Navy Yard lived with the precarious possibility that their hiring might be terminated and that they might be sold or rented out elsewhere with little or no foreknowledge. Their families were caught in a similar web, because spouses were often enslaved by different people, often in different places. Their children had a price on their heads and were subject to the harrowing potentiality of the slave market. Written agreements and even notarized legal documents promising freedom did little to assuage their fears. Verbal assurances could be broken, written contracts might be subverted, and wills might be contested by an heir who stood to inherit an enslaved person.

Then in the summer of 1835 the nation's cities erupted in racial violence and political tension. There were more urban riots that year than in any other year before the American Civil War.[4]

Amid this political turmoil, forty-year-old Daniel Bell, an enslaved blacksmith at the Washington Navy Yard, launched a delicate and potentially dangerous bid to free his wife, Mary, and their six children. Described by his allies as "robust, worthy, and industrious," he was born in Prince George's County, Maryland, and like Charles Ball saw his family broken up, sold, and separated over several generations through a succession of wills. Bell had been taken to Washington by the slaveholding Greenfields and hired out to the Navy Yard. As early as 1810 an initial freedom suit against the Greenfields stalled in the courts, and for the next twenty-five years the Bell family lived and worked in the city under the long shadow of the possibility of another sale and another breakup.[5]

As the politics of slavery and antislavery exploded in the nation's capital during the summer of 1835, Daniel Bell's battle to free his family was just beginning. The legal contest over black freedom in Washington, D.C., entered an unpredictable and devastating phase. Faced with the dynamism of the domestic slave trade and the moral blindness of the slaveholders, enslaved families searched for new tactics. They turned to Ann Williams's leap from Miller's Tavern and her eventual freedom. They drew on Charlotte Dupee's challenge to Henry Clay. They would interrupt the slave trade, sow confusion and obfuscate if necessary, disrupt the pace of transactions, and, wherever possible, use the procedures of the law against the slaveholders.

"Snatcht Away from Me and Sold"

In late July 1835 the white mechanics, carpenters, blacksmiths, painters, and laborers at the Navy Yard seethed with frustration over long hours, petty rules, and rigid hierarchies. Working twelve hours a day, six days a week, they toiled at breakneck pace to finish the refitting of a frigate-class warship, the USS *Columbia*. Thirteen slaves and three free black men worked in the Navy Yard, but a force of black caulkers, some enslaved and some free, had been brought down from Baltimore in the rush to finish out the *Columbia*. White mechanics greeted the appearance of the black caulkers with suspicion and skepticism. They knew from experience how quickly employers might turn to slave labor, and they could see how hard enslaved labor might be driven in an industrial setting. Opponents of slavery in their workplace, but simultaneously opposed to black freedom and abolition, the white workers at the Navy Yard felt the pinch of industrial slavery and wage capitalism, the squeeze of its daily humiliations and indignities.

A minor incident inspired a walkout that turned into a strike. Given the nature of the grievances, the work stoppage had the potential to spark a riot. One day authorities in the yard discovered that a large number of compression pins had been stolen from the blacksmith shop while most of the men were eating their midday meals. The thief made another attempt to steal more pins. Chased through the yard, he managed to escape on foot. Commodore Isaac Hull issued orders that the men could no longer eat their lunches on the shop floors where there were "public property tools." The men were also forbidden to bring their lunches into the yard "either in baskets, bags, or otherwise." The rash of thefts had made everyone a suspect. Already disgruntled, the men were incensed by the orders, outraged by the insinuation that one of them was a thief, and offended by the pettiness bordering on disrespect.[6]

"Every one of them struck," an enslaved blacksmith recalled. The white mechanics moved quickly to intimidate the black caulkers who had been brought in from Baltimore. They told the black men to "knock off" and tried to force them out of the shops. The next day the white mechanics on strike stood outside the Navy Yard gate. As the daily roll call was being taken, they shouted at their fellow workers, "Don't answer! Don't answer!" Still, more than a hundred men remained on the job, including the black workers. Over the next week, a committee of strikers met with the commodore, and while neither side conceded any points, Hull allowed the men to come back to their jobs without penalties. Most of the white mechanics returned to work at the Navy Yard. An uneasy truce had been reached.[7]

CITY OF WASHINGTON
Viewed beyond the Navy Yard

**W. J. Bennett, *City of Washington from Beyond the Navy Yard*,
after painting by G. Cooke, 1834 (Library of Congress,
Prints and Photographs Division, Washington, D.C.).**
The Navy Yard was the single largest complex in Washington, D.C., in the 1820s.
Three enslaved men who worked at the Navy Yard sued for freedom.

One of the enslaved workers there was an astute, well-informed, and literate carpenter named Michael Shiner. He kept a faithful account of everything he witnessed over fifty years at the Washington Navy Yard. Born in Prince George's County, Shiner in the summer of 1835 was twenty-nine years old, married, and had three young children. His diary is perhaps the most remarkable on-the-ground perspective there is from an enslaved person in Washington, D.C. When the white mechanics in the Navy Yard went out on strike, Shiner had just one year remaining on the term of his enslavement. He knew that at any moment, his prospective freedom might be revoked. For years Shiner had relied on the force of his personality to get him through sticky situations. A raucous drinker in his youth, he admitted that he often went out on the town "to have fun," caroused late into the night, and more than once got into a brawl. Shiner's quick wit and larger-than-life enthusiasm attracted his fellow workers, white and black, and ingratiated him with senior officers and civilians at the yard. He wrote in his diary that he bore no "ill feeling against any man white or black." Shiner cultivated friendships around the city, but a chaotic strike, a race riot, or a change in political circumstances could upend his plans for his own freedom, endanger his children, and break up his family.[8]

Other events in the summer of 1835 shook the nation and the capital. After months battling a progressive illness, Chief Justice John Marshall died in Philadelphia on July 6. A conservative, old-line Federalist, Marshall had long feared social chaos, political disorder, and disregard for the rule of law and the Constitution. He worried that the American Constitution "cannot last" under the pressure of raucous democratic political parties, but his nationalist stance was an awkward one. On the one hand, Marshall distrusted Southern constitutional ideas, loosely called "states' rights." On the other, he personally bought, inherited, and sold hundreds of enslaved people. Since *Queen v. Hepburn,* his decisions had protected slaveholders and sanctioned the concept of human property. The Liberty Bell in Philadelphia, so-called by abolitionists, who asked when the bell would ring for the enslaved, tolled Marshall's death, an ironic symbol to some Americans of Marshall's legacy of conservatism on the matter of slavery. A few years earlier President Andrew Jackson had nominated Roger B. Taney to fill Gabriel Duvall's seat after his retirement, but Taney's nomination proved so controversial that the Senate ignored it. Who would succeed Marshall? Jackson planned to nominate Taney again, this time for chief justice.[9]

At the same time, an eighteen-year-old enslaved man named Arthur Bowen was arrested for the attempted murder of a prominent white woman in the city, and a furious crowd assembled at the city jail. Some of the white carpenters at the Navy Yard, still out on strike and nursing their grievances, joined the crowd. "The mob raged with great vigor," Michael Shiner observed that August night. The arrest and imprisonment of Bowen did little to appease the white men outside the city jail. They wanted to "pull the jail down" and to hang Arthur Bowen "without judge or juror." As the rioters grew steadily more clamorous, the U.S. district attorney Francis Scott Key arrived at the jail and implored the mob to disperse. "Every effort was made . . . to preserve peace and harmony," Shiner noted, but Key's pleading "appeared in vain." Someone, perhaps Key himself, alerted the secretary of the navy, and a detachment of marines from the Navy Yard soon surrounded the city jail to keep order. The mob grudgingly retreated into the night when the marines fixed bayonets and loaded their blunderbusses. Shiner noted approvingly that the marines had "done their duty without faction or favor."[10]

Key had been U.S. attorney for two years, appointed by President Jackson in 1833, probably because Jackson admired Key's commitment to colonization, saw it as a sign of his even deeper commitment to slavery, and knew that Key might hold back the tide of Northern antislavery advocates in the capital. In two years, Key made a name for himself as a law-and-order prosecutor, indicting gamblers, arresting public drunks, and shutting down bawdy houses. He enforced the black codes with a vengeance and cracked down on any public expression of antislavery opinion. So, in August 1835 Francis Scott Key was predisposed to blame the public disorder in Washington on a handful of local abolitionists distributing pamphlets that he thought encouraged slave insurrections and whom he considered responsible for instigating the attempted murder. Within days of interviewing Arthur Bowen, Key arrested a Yale-trained professor of botany, Reuben Crandall, for circulating abolitionist pamphlets and newspapers.[11]

One of the enslaved men at the Navy Yard, Joe Thompson, had already won his family's freedom in court. He worked as a blacksmith at the yard for nearly a decade. He and his wife, Nelly, were promised their freedom after ten years. Just when they reached their moment of liberation, though, they faced the terrifying prospect that the will freeing them would be contested, their manumission rescinded, and their young daughter sold as a slave for life. Thompson brought a freedom suit and won the case in 1817. His lawyers were Francis Scott Key and Key's brother-in-law Roger B. Taney, both of whom were manumitting slaves they personally held and advocating colonization through the ACS. Whatever antislavery convictions Key and Taney may have held then were at their apogee. Their appearance together on behalf of Joe Thompson came long before the skepticism toward black freedom they displayed in the 1830s, when each turned to the Democratic Party and took appointments in the Jackson administration. Word of Thompson's success in court would have spread through the Navy Yard among his fellow black workers. A decade after his freedom suit, Joe Thompson was still working at the Washington Navy Yard as a free blacksmith earning 90 cents a day, working twelve hours a day, six days a week. As a free man he earned more than $20 a month.[12]

Thompson's success stood out at the time and would have made a significant impression at the Navy Yard, including on his fellow workers Michael Shiner and Daniel Bell. Perhaps in response to Thompson's suit and the concerns of white laborers that might be displaced, the Board of Naval Commissioners had already issued circular orders specifically barring the use of enslaved labor at the Navy Yard without its express permission. Benjamin King, the yard's master blacksmith, was notorious for whipping the slaves he employed in the anchor shop. Some of the foremen in the yard, like King, preferred enslaved labor for obvious reasons; as one foreman candidly explained, slaves were "less capable" of leaving the yard for better wages elsewhere, and enslaved workers could be severely disciplined. Officers and civilian foremen at the yard both resisted the Board of Naval Commissioners' orders and sought exceptions to employ slave labor. Even so, there were fewer enslaved men in the shops; those who remained came to know one another exceptionally well.[13]

A decade after his freedom suit, Joe Thompson was one of just three free black men on the Navy Yard payroll. Among the thirteen enslaved men there were Daniel Bell and Michael Shiner. Bell worked side by side with Thompson in the blacksmith shop, and Shiner labored nearby in the paint shop. Every day, the men entered the prominent Navy Yard gate at Eighth and M Streets. Every month they filed into the purser's office, signed the payroll with an "X," and drew their pay.

The workingmen of the Navy Yard lived near one another, clustered in residences to the north around a tight, four-block section of the city. In this neighborhood, the whitest ward in the city, there were no banks, less than a handful of congressmen, and no government buildings not associated with the military. Compared with the neighborhood around the U.S. Treasury, City Hall, or White House, with dense blocks of public buildings, banks, hotels, schools, and congressional residences, the Navy Yard was characterized mostly by two types of public buildings: taverns and churches. One of the most important of these was Ebenezer Methodist Church on Fourth and G Streets, where both Joe Thompson and Michael Shiner heard the white pastor deliver sermons on the triumph of grace and the gift of God's love for every person, black or white. At Ebenezer all men were equal in the sight of God because, according to Shiner, "it made no difference what kind of man he was." However, some of the white parishioners thought that the pews should be segregated, and in 1827 the black members left to form their own Ebenezer African Methodist Church at the Navy Yard.[14]

The Washington Navy Yard emerged in the 1820s as a powerful counterpoise to the city's slave pens and jails. More than eighty white employees at the Navy Yard signed the citywide petition in 1828 asking Congress to abolish slavery in the District. As a group, the largest number of signatories came from the Navy Yard. Thomas Howard, the clerk of the Navy Yard, who enslaved Michael Shiner, signed, as did John Rodgers, commodore and president of the Board of Naval Commissioners. So did Thomas Carbery, a surveyor and inspector at the yard who was elected mayor of Washington, D.C., a few years earlier. Caulker Robert Armstead, boatbuilder William Easby, master joiner Thomas Lyndall, shipwright James Owner, navy construction supervisor William Doughty, and clerk of the commandant Mordecai Booth also signed. Most of these men were slaveholders. Many men may have signed the memorial because they thought that slavery degraded their own labor. They despised black competition and wished to see black laborers removed from the Navy Yard—indeed, from American society.[15]

Just as the memorial was published and sent to Congress in 1828, Michael and Phillis Shiner were married. They were enslaved by two brothers, William and James Pumphrey, respectively. James Pumphrey purchased Phillis when she was just nine years old and brought her from Virginia to his house in Washington. Michael Shiner may have met her when he began attending Ebenezer Methodist Church, where the Pumphreys were members in the 1820s. In 1827 William Pumphrey died and directed that his slaves, including Michael Shiner, were to be sold for a term of years, then manumitted. Michael was twenty-two and was to be sold for a term of fifteen years. Thomas Howard, the clerk of the Navy Yard, purchased Shiner in 1828 from the Pumphrey estate for $250. Four years later, in 1832, Thomas Howard died and in his will mandated that Shiner should be freed in 1836 "if he conducted himself worthy of such a privilege."[16]

Shiner's freedom was precarious, but he lived together with his young wife for four years in relative quiet, somewhere near the Navy Yard. Their first daughter, Ann, was born in 1829, their second, Harriet, in 1830, and their third, Mary Ann, in 1833. Then, in May 1833, James Pumphrey fell sick and died with significant debts owed to various creditors. The family needed cash, and suddenly Phillis and the children were subject to sale. James Pumphrey's oldest son, Levi, bought Phillis and the children from his father's estate, expecting quickly to turn around and sell them to slave dealers.

Phillis, Ann, Harriet, and Mary Ann were captured in the west alley between Seventh and Eighth Streets, just a few blocks from the Navy Yard. Phillis was twenty-five years old, Ann was four years old, Harriet three years old, and Mary Ann four months old. Heartsick, Michael Shiner wrote in his diary that his wife and children were "snatcht away from me and sold."[17]

At first, Shiner did not know where they had been taken. Phillis and the children simply disappeared. He must have checked the D.C. City Jail and the various slave pens, such as William H. Williams's Yellow House and Washington Robey's. Days later, Shiner discovered that they were taken to Franklin and Armfield, the slave traders in Alexandria, Virginia, who would send them to the Cotton South and resell them there for Levi Pumphrey on commission. Washington Robey may have helped broker the deal and spirit Phillis and the children across the Potomac to Franklin and Armfield's. There was not a moment to lose.

Shiner raced across the Long Bridge to Alexandria to find Phillis. "I was in great distress," he recalled. Within days of her sale, Phillis managed

FRANKLIN & ARMFIELD'S SLAVE PRISON.

American Anti-Slavery Society, *Slave Market of America,*
Franklin & Armfield's Slave Prison, **1836 (Library of Congress,**
Rare Book and Special Collections Division, Washington, D.C.).
Isaac Franklin and John Armfield operated one of largest slave trading businesses in the United States. The volume of slave sales was so high that Franklin and Armfield opened their own packet line to ship captives to New Orleans and Natchez.

to file a freedom suit in Alexandria against Levi Pumphrey. Her local attorney was "satisfied that she is entitled to her freedom," but the exact grounds for her suit were unclear. Perhaps they planned to argue that Pumphrey bought her with the intent to sell her out of the state, a possible violation of Maryland's nonimportation law. More than anything, her freedom suit would delay another sale and give Michael time to enlist supporters and allies to intervene. The court under Virginia law assigned counsel in freedom suits, but Shiner appears to have arranged for Francis Scott Key to come to Alexandria as her counsel. The court assigned Key to the case on June 1, 1833. On Friday, June 7, Michael walked back and forth to Alexandria three times in a desperate race to prevent his family's sale.[18]

Shiner turned to the Navy Yard and the connections he had cultivated over decades of service. Somehow, he was able to get a ranking officer to issue a writ of attachment in Alexandria against Franklin and Armfield, a maneuver that at least kept the company from removing his family from the city until the legal issues were resolved. Phillis and the children were taken from Franklin and Armfield to the county jail for holding. Calling on his allies, Shiner secured the help of Navy Yard commodore Isaac Hull and at least a dozen of its employees, including officers, clerks, boatswains, and storekeepers. "I shall never forget them," Shiner wrote in his diary. He felt he owed them "ten thousand obligations" for their "kindness." Meanwhile, he made new friends in Alexandria who became "acquainted with the affair" and helped bring food to his wife and children in the county jail. By Tuesday, June 11, Michael Shiner's race to secure the freedom of Phillis and the children came to a dramatic close. Levi Pumphrey, known as "a perfect savage" for beating his slaves, had been either cajoled or compensated to free Phillis and the children with a deed of manumission. The next day, Phillis and the children, all freed, returned home.[19]

Michael Shiner remained enslaved because three years were left on his term under Thomas Howard's estate, and he still faced many of the dangers that had befallen his wife and children. Another estate sale. Another liquidity crisis in a white family. He could be taken off the streets, too, or seized outside the gates of the Navy Yard. Michael's harrowing days in June 1833 seared his memory. The hours he spent trying to free his wife and children revealed that the law afforded few victories on its own, but its technicalities might be used to disrupt the slave trade long enough to make a difference.[20]

When the white mechanics went on strike at the Washington Navy Yard in August 1835, the sentiment for gradual abolition so widely shared there faced a severe test. Riotous mobs gathered on August 12 outside the city jail, demanding that Arthur Bowen be handed over for summary punishment. Reuben Crandall's arrest enraged the mob further, but it was not the only match thrown into the fire. The white mechanics and carpenters on strike at the Navy Yard caught wind of a vicious rumor that further inflamed their anger and resentment. They heard that a free black restaurateur named Beverly Snow had said something disrespectful about their wives and daughters. "God knows whether he said those or not," Michael Shiner noted. The mechanics rushed to Beverly Snow's Epicurean Eating House on the corner of Sixth and C Streets, a block away from City Hall, and, according to Michael Shiner, "broke him up Root and Branch." Although Snow himself escaped, the crowd outside his restaurant searched for him and for any other free blacks in the homes along his street. Within minutes they seized a free black man who had some abolitionist newspapers in his possession and took him to the magistrate. "Bring him out! Bring him out!" they chanted. Then the mob turned its ire on Snow's Epicurean Eating House, where, in addition to destroying the property, they drank all the spirits in the place. For two days the mob ransacked black businesses, schools, homes, and churches. White mechanics hunted down any blacks they deemed "obnoxious," like Beverly Snow. Young white boys took to the streets, eager to get in the middle of the action. Newspapers called the public disorder an "outrage" and considered it "mortifying" and "disreputable."[21]

The whole city seemed to be in disarray. The mayor and the city council organized a force of roughly fifty citizens under posse comitatus who were armed with "muskets and fixed bayonets" to protect City Hall, while a mob of three hundred to four hundred rioters led by the mechanics milled about at Snow's restaurant two hundred yards away. Both stood their ground late into the night, but the violence could not be contained or stopped. Squads of twenty or thirty white men rampaged around the city, targeting places associated with black independence. They broke windows in a black church, burned down the home of a black woman who was a "conjurer," and destroyed a black school. After the Navy Yard mechanics attacked the Epicurean Eating House, according to Michael Shiner, they even threatened to come "after Commodore Hull" at the yard.[22]

Rumor drove the mob in every direction. Word leaked out that Arthur Bowen, the enslaved man accused of attempted murder, had planned a full-scale slave insurrection with sympathetic whites. Fears of another Nat Turner's Rebellion ran through white residents in the city. Bowen, after all, had been arrested because he allegedly sneaked into the bedroom of slaveholder Anna Thornton in an attempt to kill her with an ax as she slept. Bowen was determined to fight the charges, and his defiance in the face of his arrest likely took the magistrates by surprise. Bowen had blurted out that "he would be free." He told one of the magistrates that "he had a right to be free, and until they were free there would be so much confusion and bloodshed as would astonish the whole earth."[23]

It is difficult to say when Daniel Bell set his plan to free his wife and six children in motion, but in the aftermath of the August rioting he may have felt a higher degree of urgency. If Arthur Bowen could be railroaded into jail without evidence on charges of attempted murder, and if Michael Shiner's wife and children could be taken off the streets without a trace, then no black person was safe in private or in public. The man who enslaved Bell's wife and children was a carpenter and caulker at the Navy Yard named Robert Armstead. In point of fact, Armstead was one of the men who had signed the memorial to abolish slavery in the District of Columbia. Although the memorial was submitted to Congress in 1828, the names of its signatories were not published until February 1835, when a New Hampshire congressman ordered the memorial printed with the names of signatories affixed, presumably so that Southern slaveholders might see just how many of its prominent residents were in favor of gradual abolition in the District. In February 1835 Daniel Bell would have known, if he did not already, that Robert Armstead harbored abolitionist views. Armstead enslaved Mary and their six children. Mary and the three youngest children lived with Daniel somewhere near the Navy Yard, while the three older children lived and worked at the Armsteads' home or had been rented out to work elsewhere. Six, eight, and eleven, the older children may have seen their parents once a week or even less.

At some point in the summer of 1835, Robert Armstead's health took a dramatic turn for the worse. Unable to work, he had left his job at the Navy Yard. Leaving his wife at home, Armstead moved into the city almshouse, where he grew weaker and frailer. His attending physician at the almshouse, Dr. Edward W. Clarke, had also signed the memorial to abolish slavery, affixing his name just a few lines above Armstead's. Later witnesses would say that in his final days Armstead could barely speak, that what he said was unintelligible, that his "manners" decayed beyond recognition, and that he was subject to "flights of fancy." By late August 1835 his illness was well advanced.[24]

For their part, Daniel and Mary Bell must have worried that Armstead's death would jeopardize their precarious situation. The poverty of his wife, Susan, was obvious, and the only assets she might inherit were Mary and the six children. So Daniel Bell went to the almshouse and visited with Robert Armstead numerous times in August and September. Finally, at death's door, Armstead signed a deed of manumission emancipating Mary Bell immediately upon his death and freeing their children gradually when each reached a specific age. Daniel Bell and Robert Armstead must have discussed the matter extensively. They made sure that a justice of the peace appeared at the Washington Asylum to serve as an official witness and to notarize the deed. The intendant of the asylum was also present and signed as a witness. Armstead swore on September 14, 1835, "I do hereby release and from slavery liberate, manumit, and set free my negro woman named Mary Bell, at my death, and her six children."[25]

Two days later, Robert Armstead was dead.

Within a week, Mary Bell went to the clerk at City Hall with the notarized deed and received an official certificate of freedom from the court. But when Daniel arrived at the Navy Yard one day soon thereafter, word of his private deal with Armstead had spread. As punishment, or perhaps as reprisal, the Greenfields summarily and secretly sold Daniel Bell to slave traders. Susan Armstead's family connections to the Greenfields were deep, and she obviously planned to contest the deed of manumission for Mary and the children. If Daniel Bell were sold and quickly sent south to the cotton fields, Susan Armstead would be able to take legal action without him to contend with. Enlisting Bell's slaveholders to sell him was her opening stroke. That she would so swiftly undertake this deception indicates the extraordinary measures slaveholders took to try to prevent lawsuits and legal proceedings that threatened their wealth and position. It also indicates the legal acumen enslaved people such as Daniel Bell accumulated and wielded. Obviously Susan Armstead would not have attempted to arrange Bell's sale if she did not believe that he posed a threat. Within days, the traders infiltrated the Navy Yard, assaulted an unsuspecting Bell, knocked him to the floor, and dragged him in chains to the slave pen at the infamous Yellow House. Desperate to avoid the breakup of his family, Daniel Bell sued for his freedom.

Imprisoned days after his wife's certificate of freedom, Daniel Bell had little basis on which to bring his own freedom suit. His petition said only that he was "unjustly held in bondage." There seemed to be no violation of the importation law. He made no apparent claim to a free ancestor, nor did he claim that a will or contract to free him after a term of years was breached. Crucially, though, Daniel Bell's lawsuit bought him time. Like Phillis Shiner's freedom suit two years earlier, Bell's would at least prevent him from being summarily sold and sent to New Orleans or Natchez. Edward Clarke, the abolitionist-leaning physician who treated Robert Armstead, provided the funds to cover the court costs for his lawsuit.

Bell moved quickly to alert his friends and associates at the Navy Yard. Within a few weeks, he managed to arrange for a marine colonel to buy him from the Greenfields with the understanding that Bell would pay the colonel back and buy his own freedom over time. The sale was executed, the Greenfields were paid off, and for the moment, Daniel Bell had managed to escape the slave trade and keep his family together. Mary had her certificate of freedom, and the deed freeing the children had been recorded.

Susan Armstead, however, had no intention of honoring their emancipation. She retained a lawyer and prepared to contest her husband's dying act of manumission for the Bells. She was going to argue that Robert was not of "sound mind" in his last days and that Daniel Bell had taken advantage of his illness, but none of her intentions was immediately apparent in the fall of 1835. We cannot know for certain when Daniel and Mary caught wind of what Susan was plotting.

The ordeal of the Bell family was far from over.

After the August 1835 riot, Michael Shiner had his own brush with the legal authorities. In September, after spending several weeks in confinement, Shiner was finally released. He and some of his friends went out drinking on the town. "I got so wild on Capitol Hill," he wrote in his diary. A group of local whites "jumped" him, and he had to fight his way down to the Navy Yard gates. Pelted with stones and brickbats, Shiner gave as good as he got. Eventually shots were fired, some of the marines were called out, and Shiner was thrown in the guardhouse lockup. The D.C. police and a magistrate arrived at the Navy Yard to arrest Shiner on various charges, including disorderly conduct, but Dr. Edward Clarke, who played a role in arranging the Bell family's freedom, came to Shiner's defense and dissuaded the magistrates from seeking prosecution. Shiner was given over to the commodore, and the incident blew over.[26]

Protected to a degree by the Navy Yard, Michael Shiner may have realized that his scrape with the authorities could have turned out very differently, that what happened to Arthur Bowen might also happen to him. He may also have witnessed the moment when slave traders seized Daniel Bell inside the yard and hauled him out of the smithy in chains. Shiner knew firsthand that he, too, might be sold at a moment's notice and taken south. Based on what happened to Phillis and their children, he had considerable

reason to fear that the white family who enslaved him would somehow re-
nege on the terms of his prospective freedom.

So, in March 1836, after the Navy Yard completed the USS *Columbia,*
Shiner preemptively launched his own freedom suit against the executors
of Thomas Howard's estate. With his term of slavery about to expire, Shiner
may have heard that the Howards planned to dispute his manumission. He
sought out a twenty-eight-year-old attorney named James Hoban Jr., the son
of James Hoban, the well-known architect of the White House and other
prominent public buildings in Washington, D.C. The young attorney had
represented an enslaved woman imprisoned by Isaac Franklin and John
Armfield in 1834. An astute, well-connected lawyer, Hoban was also a descendant of the Sewall family of Catholic priests and planters from St. Mary's
County. One of his brothers became a Jesuit priest. His father had signed
the memorial to abolish slavery in Washington, died in 1831, and stipulated
in his will that his slaves not be sold out of the city. It was a modest measure, a nod to the humanity of the enslaved, but without any definitive commitment to emancipation. James Hoban Jr. may have inherited some of his
father's modest antislavery convictions. Like Francis Scott Key and many
other white slaveholders, he was also a vehement antiabolitionist in 1835. Regardless, Michael Shiner knew that he needed to put pressure on the Howards, the family who enslaved him. Who better to enlist than an attorney
with a pedigree like James Hoban Jr.'s?[27]

Michael Shiner secured his freedom as promised without a legal contest
from the Howards. His case papers were filed away in the D.C. court and forgotten. Shiner made no entry in his diary about these legal actions, nor did he
mention his final emancipation. Intensely proud of his service in the Navy
Yard, Shiner was now a free man with a wide array of associates and friends
he had cultivated over the years. Indeed, as an enslaved man Michael Shiner
acted very much like a rights-bearing citizen. Neither the law nor the prevailing antiblack views prevented him from securing his freedom through the
courts. Despite the deceptiveness of slaveholders and slave dealers, Shiner
was able to outmaneuver them and free his wife and children, too.[28]

"The Freedom I So Earnestly Sought
for Them Was Their Ruin"

Imprisoned for nearly eight months in the D.C. jail, Reuben Crandall suffered
failing health. Awaiting trial, the botanist accused of libelous sedition and slave
insurrection lost weight, steadily grew weaker, and eventually contracted

tuberculosis. For months, the U.S. attorney, Francis Scott Key, did not bother to charge him. Though Crandall languished in prison, he had retained two prominent local attorneys: Richard Coxe, forty-three years old, experienced at the D.C. bar, son of a New Jersey congressman; and Joseph H. Bradley, a thirty-three-year-old whose cousin William A. Bradley had just been elected the mayor of Washington. Coxe possessed little flair for the dramatic and instead relied on dogged persistence to win cases. Bradley, on the other hand, would display a rapier-quick wit and a knack for exposing the weaknesses of his opponent's arguments. A brilliant orator with a "commanding presence," Bradley earned a reputation for winning acquittals for criminal defendants. Late in life, when he was a widower, he would marry one of his clients, a woman charged with murdering her husband. He was unafraid of causing a sensation. In 1835 Bradley, though a slaveholder, had his reasons for opposing Key's prosecution of Reuben Crandall. Bradley nursed the grievance that President Andrew Jackson, in one of his first official acts, had removed his father, an old Federalist, who had served as first assistant postmaster general since the Washington administration. The young Bradley became an inveterate Whig Party man, an admirer of Henry Clay, and a leading partisan in the city. Given to causes, lenient with his fees, Bradley was known for chewing tobacco relentlessly.[29]

Throughout the fall of 1835, angry white Southern congressmen denounced Crandall as a fanatical abolitionist and fulminated over the antislavery pamphlets and newspapers that abolitionists were circulating in the South through the mail. In November 1835 President Andrew Jackson nominated Roger B. Taney to replace John Marshall as chief justice of the Supreme Court. Then in December Jackson gave his annual message to Congress and called for a law to prohibit the circulation through the mail of "incendiary publications intended to instigate the slaves to insurrection." The Maryland legislature wasted no time outlawing the circulation of any "pictorial representation, or any pamphlet, newspaper, handbill, or other paper, printed or written, of any inflammatory character, having a tendency to create discontent among, and stir up to insurrection, the people of color of this State." A felony in Maryland, the offense carried a minimum sentence of ten years in prison.[30]

When Congress reconvened in December 1835, antislavery petitions poured into the House and the Senate, calling for an end to the slave trade and for gradual abolition in D.C. Southern legislators exploded in outrage and launched a campaign to prevent the petitions not only from being heard, or even tabled, but from ever crossing "the threshold" into Congress. The proposal to "gag" antislavery petitions, not even to receive them, stunned Northern congressmen. They initially rose to defend the petitioners as men of "pure hearts" and noble motives, who looked "to the letter of the Constitution." Even some of the Southern congressmen thought that the petitions should be at least referred to a committee, where they might be tabled. Such reasonable responses quickly gave way, though, and threats of violence and insults flew across the aisles. Given the intensity of the debates, Crandall's lawyers thought it best to delay his trial, sure to be controversial, until public passion cooled.[31]

Finally, Key brought formal charges against Crandall in January 1836. The five-count indictment was an exhaustive condemnation of both Crandall and abolitionism. Key accused him of

> unlawfully, maliciously, and seditiously, contriving and intending to traduce, vilify, and bring into hatred and contempt, among the citizens of the United States, laws and government of the United States . . . to inflame and excite the people of the United States to resist and oppose and disregard the laws and Government aforesaid, and the rights of the proprietors of slaves in the said county, and to inflame and excite to violence, against the said proprietors of the said slaves, not only the ignorant and ill-disposed among the free people of the United States and free persons of color in the said county, but also the slaves; and to produce among the said slaves and free persons of color, insubordination, violence, and rebellion, and to stir up war and insurrection between the said slaves and their said masters.[32]

Key recited for the grand jury numerous passages from the newspapers and pamphlets in Crandall's possession, asserting that Crandall had in effect "published" them. With rhetorical flourish, Key hoped to drive his point home that all abolitionist words were patently dangerous and irresponsible. Such words encouraged enslaved men like Arthur Bowen to pick up axes and consider murdering slaveholders in their beds. They led free blacks like Joseph Thompson and Michael Shiner to the "obnoxious" delusion that they could be citizens with rights. They were spread by men like Crandall in the fanatical conviction that slavery should be ended even if it meant bloodshed. Such words were "peculiarly dangerous and atrocious," Key told the jury.[33]

Furthermore, Key charged, the publications that Crandall possessed and "published" contained "disgusting prints and pictures of white men in the act of inflicting, with whips, cruel and inhuman beatings." The images were "calculated . . . to excite the good people of the United States in said county to violence against the holder of slaves."

Key asked the court for an astounding sum of $15,000 as bond for Crandall's release on bail. Justice Cranch reduced it to $5,000, itself a shockingly high figure. Neither Reuben Crandall nor his family could come up with that much money, and he remained in his eight-foot-by-eight-foot cell in the D.C. jail until his trial three months later.

U.S. v. Reuben Crandall began on Friday, April 15, 1836. It took nearly the whole day to impanel a jury because so many prospective jurors were struck. Nearly every one seemed to have already formed an opinion about Crandall's guilt or innocence. On Saturday, the trial began in earnest. Crowds flocked into City Hall for the spectacle. Several congressmen attended. Key's prosecution of Crandall for "libelous sedition" offered a sensational showdown between a renowned prosecutor and a mysterious abolitionist whose sister Prudence Crandall opened a black school for girls in Connecticut, drew the wrath of angry whites, and was prosecuted for violating the state's black laws.

The nature of Key's five-count indictment exposed an Achilles' heel in his prosecution. As the first case of common-law libel tried in the United States, the whole charade appeared to revive long-discredited Federalist concepts about the legal limits of the freedom of the press and of speech. Key's zealous arrest and prosecution attempted to turn the clock back to the 1790s and appeared to sidestep the First Amendment. In effect, Key had trampled all over Crandall's rights of speech, assembly, and publication. To do this, he planned to rely on Maryland's constitutional common-law doctrine, ironically the very same legal principles drawn from English sources that did not sanction in any fundamental way the practice of slavery. "In point of law," Key blustered, the words "read and circulate" on the pamphlets in Crandall's handwriting were enough to constitute a libelous act "of a most dangerous and inflammatory tendency."

By the time Crandall was brought out of his cell to stand trial, he had lost considerable weight. A pale visage, he seemed determined to stand firm in his convictions. Asked how he would plead, Crandall quietly replied, "Not guilty." Newspapers reported him as a young man of "respectable appearance," who listened to the arguments being made with patience. Dressed in

a black suit, Crandall betrayed "no appearance of fear." In fact, his calm de-
meanor and purposeful steadfastness won over the crowd.[34]

Crandall's defense attorneys took the position that he may have possessed abolitionist literature, but he did not "publish" anything. The material was seized in his shop. No witnesses could assert that he published or
distributed any newspapers or pamphlets. Possession, they argued, did not
constitute publication. Defense attorney Coxe interrupted Key's examination of the prosecution witnesses right away by objecting that the pamphlets
and newspapers could not be introduced to the jury as evidence without first
proving that they had been published or distributed by Crandall. As was
standard practice, Key had handed out copies of the pamphlets to the attorneys and the judges as exhibits, and just as he was about to introduce them
officially into the record as evidence, Coxe raised his objection. Even Judge
Cranch was taken aback at the line of argument Coxe was making. In jest,
Coxe then pointed out that if placing a single paper in the hands of a well-
known respectable individual met the standard for publication, then the district attorney had just violated the law and himself might be prosecuted.

The whole exchange flustered Key, who appeared unprepared. "You
must wait for the evidence," he fulminated. "Does any one suppose that if I
had taken advantage of this assemblage, to distribute to the court such papers with the intent to excite commotion, insurrection, and rebellion, I
should not have been liable to indictment?" Without showing a hint of sarcasm
Coxe replied, "The learned Attorney has misapprehended my point."

Within minutes Coxe had unspooled a promising line of defense.
"Every man has a right to put his thoughts on paper, if he does not exhibit
them to others." When a written libel is in the possession of another person, the prosecutor has the obligation to show how he "came by it." Key had
not shown how Crandall had published anything, and he had offered no effective counterargument to Coxe's objection. Newspapers reported that the
lawyers spent hours on the points of law about the admissibility of evidence.
Far from dramatic, Key's prosecution became mired in minutiae. The judges,
evidently frustrated with his argument, began questioning Key's witnesses
themselves.

Judge Buckner Thruston took an especially dim view of the whole pro-
ceeding. Thruston said that he "concluded that before the prosecutor could
give evidence of other bad publications he must first show the actual publication, . . . of the libels charged in the indictment. If you show that he published them, and that they have been in actual circulation, then you bring

the proof up to the rule of law." Thruston thought that Crandall's arrest was unnecessarily provocative and possibly unconstitutional. Key's overzealous prosecution had "led to a very alarming mob" in the District, a citywide riot, and a breakdown in the rule of law and order.[35]

The other two judges on the bench, Cranch and James Morsell, were more lenient and voted to allow Key to introduce the pamphlets as evidence without first proving that Crandall published them. He could only introduce the specific papers found in Crandall's office. "He will not be permitted to give in evidence to the jury the contents of any of the papers other than those charged as libels in the indictment," they decided.

The crowd in the gallery grew bored with the dry legal arguments and soon disappeared. Blotting out Key's argument even further, Judge Thruston delivered a long dissent against the ruling by his fellow judges. It turned into an hours-long soliloquy. Thruston ruminated on one of the most famous cases in English legal history, known to every schoolboy in early-nineteenth-century America, about the prosecution of two men in Scotland for possessing a copy of Thomas Paine's *Rights of Man,* a book printed in the United States and deemed by authorities in Britain as a libelous provocation. The men were sentenced to long prison terms at Botany Bay. "It is very long since I read the case," Thruston proclaimed, "but I have never heard the judgment of the court on their cases spoken of but with reprobation."[36]

Key probably sank further into his chair as Thruston continued:

> I think I may boldly assert then, that the *merely* having in [one's] possession a libel printed and published in a foreign country only, is not an indictable offence here, and no publication of the same libel here . . . This in my view, amounts to nothing more than that he appropriated to himself and adopted the thoughts of others . . . Every man has an unquestionable right to his own moral or religious sentiments; there is no crime in this; it would be criminal to restrain any man in this country in his own, or in adopting the moral or religious opinions of others, if he please.

Thruston went on to reveal the coolness he felt for the entire case. "It is very clear, it seems to me, that if there were no other evidence of any other publication of any of the pamphlets in question, than the inscription on the cover, of 'read this and circulate,' that the indictment could not be sustained, because such inscriptions of the pamphlets are never shown to any other person, is, in the eye of the law, harmless."

Thruston's long-winded but devastatingly effective remarks loomed over the proceedings. Witnesses were called and questioned, and the trial veered into the farcical. Cranch noted that he had received two copies of the *Emancipator* in the mail even though he was not a subscriber. Was he a criminal? Key seemed to say so. Attempting to portray Crandall as a fanatical abolitionist, Key questioned one of the magistrates about exactly what he said to Crandall when he arrested him. The magistrate told the jury, "I remarked that [emancipation] would be attended with direful consequences. We should all be murdered and have our throats cut . . . [and] the next thing they would be for, would be amalgamation."

Thruston drolly interjected from the bench, "Would the amalgamation occur after our throats are cut?"

The sarcasm was obvious.

Thruston could not restrain his annoyance with the overblown reaction of the magistrate to the quietly professional botanist.[37]

At this Key rested his case and sat down, probably not at all confident that he had persuaded the jury. Thruston's diatribe certainly hurt. At least one juror had signed the memorial to abolish slavery in the District eight years earlier. Others may have been impressed by Crandall's quiet courage in the face of Key's onslaught. Even Key's own magistrates testified that Crandall was a careful man, not given to lying or obfuscation. When directly asked, Crandall "didn't deny that he was an anti-slavery man."

To open the defendant's case, Coxe's brash, young co-counsel Joseph H. Bradley began reading, verbatim and without introduction, a speech from a printed pamphlet excoriating the slave trade and lamenting the sin of American slavery. "If we believe in the existence of a great moral and political evil amongst us, and that duty, honor and interest call upon us to prepare the way for its removal, we must act . . ."[38]

Perplexed, Judge Cranch interrupted Bradley, asking for its relevance, and where he was going with his remarks. Bradley answered that the speech was Francis Scott Key's, an address given at a meeting of the American Colonization Society in Washington, D.C., in 1828. Cranch and Thruston snorted with laughter. Everyone thought that Bradley was reading "from some of the libels that had been given in evidence." This was precisely Bradley's point, of course. It was a clever maneuver at Key's expense. Everyone in the room knew that Bradley's uncle had been a founder of the ACS alongside Key.

Clearly rattled, Key demanded an opportunity to reply to this "most unusual course" of an opening argument. He objected that the ACS was nothing like the abolitionist libel he accused Crandall of perpetrating because it did not endorse immediate emancipation, nor did it encourage insurrection and rebellion. Bradley pulled the stunt, Key said, because it was "calculated to prejudice the case before the jury." But no amount of protestation could put Key's own words back in a bottle. Bradley quoted other speeches before the society, printed and circulated in the *African Repository,* that the success of colonization would be "the triumph of freedom over slavery—of liberality over prejudice—and of humanity over the vice and wretchedness which ever wait on ignorance and servitude." There seemed to be little difference between Key's language and the abolitionists'.

Bradley and Coxe turned Key's prosecution of Crandall upside down. They asked the jury if possessing a copy of the *Emancipator* was libelous sedition, then was not the same true for possessing a copy of Thomas Jefferson's *Notes on the State of Virginia?* "Are these libels?" they asked in disbelief. They reminded the jury that the ACS's journal, the *African Repository,* "contains language . . . far transcending any thing set out in this indictment." They compared the language in the abolitionist pamphlets with "analogous passages" written by Key, Patrick Henry, William Pinkney, Thomas Jefferson, and others.

In his summation, Coxe told the jury that "during the whole course" of his professional career, he had never had more "feelings of intense anxiety." The case involved bedrock principles of American freedom—the enumerated rights in the Constitution against illegal searches and seizures, for the protection of speech and the press—that affect "each member of this community, and upon our children's children." Coxe concluded that the entire trial was "tyrannical, oppressive, illegal, and unconstitutional." The idea of trying citizens for libelous sedition was "preposterous . . . It is monstrous. It has no foundation in any principle of law—it can find no support in any dictate of reason. It is a reproach to our community—it is a slander upon our institutions."[39]

His case in disarray, Francis Scott Key decided to stoke the embers of racism and ask the jury to defend not just themselves but something larger: the entire white South. He appealed to the jury as white men. At issue, he bellowed, was the South's right to fight for "our property and our homes, under the sanction of the Constitution," against relentless, misguided, and dangerous fiends, intent on sowing the seeds of slave insurrection. The abolitionists, Key sensationalized for the jury, would allow free blacks "full and equal participation in all civil and social privileges." They were friends of "amalgamation."[40]

What men like Reuben Crandall did not understand, Key strained to point out, was that Patrick Henry, Thomas Jefferson, and William Pinkney openly discussed ending slavery only when it was "safe and fit to discuss such a subject." The difference in the temper of the times, he argued, was obvious: Arthur Bowen awaited execution in the D.C. jail, but Nat Turner killed more than fifty slaveholders in Southampton County, Virginia, in a matter of hours.

Race, the precepts of white supremacy, became Key's final argument. To make that argument he recast the meaning of the antislavery rhetoric he used years earlier in the *African Repository*. "The 'great moral and political evil' of which I speak, is supposed to be slavery," he told the jury, "but is it not plainly the whole colored race?"[41]

The rhetorical question hung in the courtroom air. Ugly and distorting, Key's views at this point took their shape from Thomas Roderick Dew, the eminent historian and legal scholar at the College of William and Mary whose compilation of the 1832 Virginia legislative debates over slavery sketched the proslavery position in the mid-1830s. Slavery, Key agreed, was a "necessary evil, not to be removed (except gradually, and on the condition of colonization) without being followed by far greater evils."[42]

Shedding his reputation as the lawyer for the families who brought freedom suits, Key disparaged the idea of black freedom and cited his "own experience" trying their cases. He told the jury that he began his career in the law with great "earnestness" to advocate for the oppressed. For years, no other trials were as "exulting" as those when he won an enslaved person's freedom. But most of those who won their freedom, according to Key, "had been far from finding in the result the happiness he had expected." Key decided that freedom "produced for them nothing but evil."[43]

Key's disavowal of his role in the freedom suits was a stance he had been considering for some time. Over thirty-five years, he said, "much of his ardour" for the freedom suits had "abated." *U.S. v. Reuben Crandall* allowed him to voice what he had been thinking. He told the jury that he "could not rejoice, as he once did," in the role he had played in the lawsuits of enslaved black families. Freedom, he said, was a "most perilous gift" when it was granted to blacks, because, he argued, they fell into ruin and made a "dangerous mockery" of the nation's ideals. Key claimed that his many petition-for-freedom cases "greatly changed his opinions and feelings."[44]

In fact, in *U.S. v. Reuben Crandall*, Key made an argument against black freedom that he would repeat in various forms for the rest of his life. His accounting of black freedom was premised on a myth that freedom led to black failure, degradation, and vice. Key's apologetic formulation of these reprehensible ideas took this form three years later: "No Northern man began the world with more enthusiasm against slavery than I did. For forty years and upwards, I have felt the greatest desire to see Maryland become a free State . . . The laws of Maryland contain provisions of various kinds, under which slaves, in certain circumstances, are entitled to petition for their freedom. As a lawyer, I always undertook these cases with peculiar zeal and have been thus instrumental in liberating several large families and many individuals. I cannot remember more than two instances, out of this large number, in which it did not appear that the freedom I so earnestly sought for them was their ruin."[45]

Unconvinced by Key's summation against black freedom, perhaps offended by his flagrant disregard for the First Amendment throughout the trial, the jury in *U.S. v. Reuben Crandall* deliberated for one hour and returned a verdict of not guilty on all counts. For the first time in over eight months, Reuben Crandall was free to leave the city jail.

Weakened from his imprisonment in squalid conditions, Crandall returned to his parents' home in Connecticut having contracted tuberculosis, a fatal lung infection that gradually brought on fevers, further weight loss, and fatigue. Afflicted with what at the time was called "consumption" and hoping that a milder climate would alleviate his pain, he sailed for Kingston, Jamaica, in late 1836. Reuben Crandall died there two years later at the age of thirty-two.[46]

Meanwhile, the verdict incensed Southern congressmen, already vexed by the flood of petitions to abolish slavery in the District of Columbia. The most extreme of these proslavery voices called for the House of Representatives to prevent the petitions from being received at all. Just as Key attempted to silence Reuben Crandall, so Congress threatened to silence the petitioners. Tabling the petitions was not enough; it implied that antislavery petitions were ultimately worthy of Congress's consideration. "Non-reception," these zealous Southerners argued, would send a clear signal that the antislavery petitions should be deemed nothing less than dangerous provocations and that they were therefore inherently anticonstitutional. Divided by party and section, the House could not agree on such a restrictive measure, but it did pass a nonetheless profoundly anti–free speech gag rule in May 1836 that "all petitions, memorials, resolutions, propositions, or papers relating in any way or to any extent whatever to the subject of slavery shall, without being printed or referred, be laid upon the table and that no further action whatever be taken thereon."[47]

Within a year, Southern congressmen took another dramatic step to protect slavery—they reorganized the Supreme Court. They expanded the number of justices from seven to nine, giving President Andrew Jackson two more appointments. He made them on his last day in office. Overall Jackson had appointed seven of the nine justices, five in the last two years of his presidency. With Roger B. Taney as chief justice and the appointment of a majority of slaveholders, the Supreme Court was poised to turn back any challenge to the constitutionality of slavery and predisposed to view black freedom with skepticism and hostility.[48]

At this point, worried Maryland slaveholders tried to place slavery on a permanent legal and constitutional footing. Convinced that slavery was a public necessity and alarmed by the momentum of antislavery petitioning and freedom suits, the legislature meanwhile passed a law in 1836 amending the state constitution so that "the relation of master and slave, in this State, shall not be abolished" unless by a unanimous vote of the General Assembly and with full compensation to slaveholders. A year later, that constitutional amendment was ratified.

There was an additional reason for the amendment. Because slavery's existence in Maryland was questionable as a matter of law, some judges in free states saw no reason to send fugitives back to Maryland under the 1793 Fugitive Slave Act, even under principles of comity. The courts in free states considering the status of fugitive slaves were beginning to require proof that "slavery exists" in the law of Maryland. The Maryland General Assembly tried to fix the legality of slavery in the state once and for all by passing "An Act Declaring Domestic Slavery to Be Lawful in This State," officially defining slavery as legitimate "from [the colony's] earliest settlement."[49]

Slaveholders perceived a grave threat in the raucousness of the August 1835 rioting, the exuberance of the antislavery petitioning, and the daring persistence of the freedom suits. Each freedom case struck a blow at the "pretended rights of the slave-owner." The commotion in the 1830s exposed the "baselessness" of the property claims of slaveholders. Key's assertion that black freedom was an impossibility flew in the face of daily reality in Washington, D.C., and Maryland, where Joe Thompson, Michael Shiner, Ann Bell, James Ash, and Daniel Bell bought property, worked for wages, made contracts, married, and raised their families.[50]

Later, abolitionists referred to these watershed years in Maryland as a period of mob law, a reign of terror, a despotism of slaveholders. "Maryland has a constitution and laws, and pretends to be a free republic," one group of antislavery lawyers scoffed. "But dare to question the slave system, its rightfulness, its lawfulness and results and you find yourselves at the mercy of an irresponsible power more terrible and more ruthless than the Russian police." Even sympathetic judges like William Cranch were setting exorbitant bail amounts for minor offenses perceived as a threat to slavery, while prosecutors like Key were bringing specious charges "got up for the purpose of enabling infuriated despotism to glut its malice under the forms of law." Cranch had once worried about the dangers of "public feeling" in times of crisis reaching "the seat of justice." The worst precedents, he warned, "may be established from the best of motives." Famously he observed that "the constitution was made for times of commotion."[51]

But Maryland law now gave the slaveholders indisputable legal title over the enslaved. Susan Armstead intended to wield that authority to thwart her husband's dying deed of manumission freeing Mary Bell and her six children.

After Reuben Crandall's sensational acquittal, the Bell family enlisted his dynamic, well-connected lawyer Joseph H. Bradley to file a new round of freedom suits for them against the Greenfields.

For nearly a year, Daniel Bell had been working to buy his freedom, month by month, using his wages at the Navy Yard to pay off the marine colonel who purchased him in September 1835, only to discover that the colonel had mortgaged him to his sister-in-law for $1,000. She demanded to be paid in full, so Bell had to start all over. Mary and the children were ostensibly free under the terms of Robert Armstead's deed of manumission. Although Daniel's mother, Lucy Bell, and his sisters Ann and Caroline Bell had been living as free black women in Washington, D.C., the Greenfields had been quietly bequeathing them as property from one generation to the next. Ann Bell had been passed down, on paper, to Gerard T. Greenfield, who held more than fifty people in bondage on a cotton plantation in Maury, Tennessee. The precariousness of Ann's situation meant she could be seized like her brother, Daniel, and sold to slave dealers. So could her children. In fact, her children were even more vulnerable. In December 1836 Ann Bell sued Gerard T. Greenfield for her and her children's freedom. From Tennessee he refused to answer the summons.[52]

The Jesuits at Georgetown College, meanwhile, maneuvered to secure title to all of the enslaved people on their plantations. Their college's finances were in disarray, accusations of drunkenness among the students ran rampant, and charges of malfeasance had been raised against the board. Instead of emancipating those they enslaved, instead of attempting to colonize the families in Liberia, the Jesuits decided to sell 272 enslaved men, women, and children for $115,000 to sugar planters in Louisiana, one of the largest private slave sales in American history. Facilitated by the Key family, the sale was neither the only such transaction nor the end of the freedom trials.

Return to Pleasant Prospect

I had lived with the ghosts of this history for so long—my head buried in the archives of the court cases and my attention focused on what the descendants had to say—that I was unaware of a quiet controversy erupting on Duckett ground. The old Duckett plantation at Pleasant Prospect had been turned into a high-end housing development called Waterford Estates in 2006. The developer, Stanley Martin Homes, saw the archaeological report the county required as an opportunity to promote home sales. A four-color brochure was handed out to prospective buyers, depicting "What Lies Beneath: The History of Waterford Estates." The promotional materials told the story of the site's excavation as the unfolding of a mystery culminating with the discovery of Richard Duckett Jr.'s original plantation house, Sprigg's Request.[1]

At the entry into the gated community off Woodmore Road, Stanley Martin Homes installed a historical exhibit about the plantation. It stood in prominent view, no doubt intended to lend an air of sophistication, permanence, and drama to the property: all the better to boost home values and sale prices in 2007. Two large placards showcased some of 15,417 artifacts uncovered on the site. A short narrative summarized "What Lies Beneath," and close-up images of the artifacts were displayed with maps showing where they came out of the ground.

Both the brochure and the exhibit conveyed a particular story, one dominated by the aspiration of Richard Duckett to "a Georgian lifestyle." That story was told through the physical items he bought and used: wine bottles, porcelain, silver, linen, and luxury cloth. He purchased firearms, too, and gunpowder and musket balls. "What Lies Beneath" positioned Duckett as the sole, leading figure in the drama of the site and therefore in its entire history. Slavery and slaveholding were taken for granted, simply part of the "Georgian lifestyle," unworthy of further commentary or explanation. The brochure concluded with an evasive disclaimer: "We do not know whether Richard Duckett was part of a broader group of aspiring elite in Maryland, although it is likely."

The story that was being sold bore little resemblance to the historical record. Duckett was undoubtedly part of an aspiring elite. Enslaving people was the driving force behind everything uncovered on the site. The white-washed account of Sprigg's Request, now Pleasant Prospect, tried to hide the history of African Americans in Prince George's County and the memories of the descendants of the people the Ducketts enslaved.

When I visited the area in 2015, the exhibit seemed incongruous with the history of the site I had unearthed in the written record. Installed by a developer in one of the wealthiest majority-black counties in the United States, the display barely acknowledged African Americans. A homeowners association with significant African American membership managed all of the common property, including the entrance with its historical interpretation. Black residents, it seemed, were stuck with the signage, however offensive. I knew that no responsible historian would have presented the past in such a lopsided fashion, but only later would I admit to myself that I had not fully discerned the one-sided nature of the story about my ancestors being promulgated at Waterford Estates, much less how painful that history was each day for the people who lived there now, people whose ancestors had been enslaved at places like Pleasant Prospect.

When would the reckoning come?

I felt a renewed sense of urgency. My inquiry into the freedom suits had led me back into my own family history even as historical injustices in American society were under scrutiny and reassessment—from the participation of universities, colleges, and churches in the perpetuation of slavery to the memorialization of Confederate and white supremacist figures by towns, cities, and institutions across the South.

Then, in August 2017, white supremacists organized a violent rally in Charlottesville, Virginia, ostensibly to protest the removal of Confederate monuments. White nationalists brandished firearms, clubs, and torches, threatened counterprotesters, and chanted racist slogans. One drove his vehicle into the crowd, killed one woman, and injured dozens of people. Two state troopers lost their lives in a helicopter crash. Within weeks the governor of Maryland ordered the removal of a statue of Roger B. Taney from the grounds of the State House in Annapolis. In Baltimore, memorials to Taney, Robert E. Lee, and Stonewall Jackson were quietly taken away. The memorial to Francis Scott Key in Baltimore remained, but in September protesters spray-painted it with the words "Racist Anthem."[2]

At some point in 2017 the Waterford Preserve homeowners association decided to move the Richard Duckett exhibit into an even more prominent location directly along the entrance road into the subdivision. No passerby could avoid or ignore its celebration of the Georgian lifestyle, its failure to acknowledge slavery, and its incomplete history.

The exhibit said nothing about what the enslaved persons may have experienced at Sprigg's Request and Pleasant Prospect. There was nothing about the nine ninety-nine or the many other forms of violence that transpired there. Nothing about the families who toiled and lived there, and who taught, loved, and nurtured one another for more than five generations. Nothing about the African American Duckett family of Prince George's County, who traced its roots to these plantations. Nothing about how the Ducketts gained their freedom. Nothing about how, once free, they bought property and formed a settlement a few miles away they called Duckettsville.

When Cecilia Queen and I arrived at Waterford Estates in May 2019, we noticed immediately that the exhibit placards at the entrance were missing. Empty postholes, loose dirt, and a few lonely shrubs marked the spot where the archaeological exhibit once stood. Queen worked for thirty-one years in human resources with the Maryland state government, most of that time with the state highway administration. Recently retired, she was tracing her family roots when we met a few years earlier at Queenstown Day. The annual celebration in Queenstown, one of the largest African American family reunions in Maryland, features a political parade, marching bands, hot rods, semi-trucks, historical exhibits, and family picnics. Every candidate running for local office worked the crowd and solicited hundreds of Queen descendants for votes. As a part of the celebration, we had organized a booth displaying an exhibit about the history of the families that sued for their freedom, including the Queens, Mahoneys, Butlers, Shorters, Thomases, and Bells.

Now Cecilia Queen and I were visiting as many of the sites in Prince George's County as we could and sharing what we knew about our family histories. At the Woodyard we scrambled through scrub oak and periwinkle but found no trace of the old brick mansion, not even its foundation. Looking for Weymouth, John Hepburn's plantation, we followed the Piscataway Creek for a stretch to no effect. We headed north and resolved to go to Pleasant Prospect, the site of my Duckett ancestors and their slaveholding. At the entrance we stood in front of the empty postholes. As I fumbled for an explanation, Queen discerned instantly what had happened to the exhibit.

"It was damaged on purpose," she murmured as she caught my eye. "It was a memorialization of a slaveholder," Queen pointed out. Driving by the exhibit every day, many times a day, would be a constant reminder to everyone who lived there that the property was still in some sense Richard Duckett Jr.'s.[3]

Vandalism is not the right word for what happened to the Richard Duckett Jr. exhibit at Waterford Estates. It was a reclaiming, an action reaching back even to the freedom suits. The incident never appeared in the news or the public record, but it challenged those in the neighborhood to consider how they know what they know about the past. It tells us that history is real and contested, fiercely so. How history gets represented is not solely the province of experts, academics, and politicians. Queen told me that she could see how residents in the Waterford subdivision would be "annoyed" with a display commemorating the Duckett plantation. She speculated what would have happened if the exhibit had been placed in a more contemplative position. If it were less visible, less prominent. If the exhibit told a different story, she said. If it showed the history of African American progress, if it portrayed the families who actually lived at Pleasant Prospect, if it described their experience and led its audience on the path of their story through to emancipation. Then, it might give a more complete account. That story might be reconciling. That story might repair the one-sided narrative so many have inherited. That story, though it touches on one small corner of a county in Maryland, might redeem part of American history.[4]

CHAPTER 8

The Sale

Louisa (a woman of colour) . . . makes oath and say that she
believes the foregoing petition and the matter as therein stated
are true.

—LOUISA MAHONEY, MARCH 15, 1854,

ST. LOUIS, MISSOURI

When the Jesuit leaders at Georgetown decided to sell 272 enslaved people,
the families in Maryland had been expecting the betrayal for decades. They
had taken the Jesuits to court for most of the 1790s and 1800s. They had staged
a public revolt for their freedom in 1817 on a Jesuit plantation in southern
Maryland, and in the 1820s, when the Jesuits reneged on their promise to
emancipate the families, a period of bitter watchfulness followed.

The Georgetown sale was one of thousands, small and large, that forcibly migrated more than a million men, women, and children from Maryland, Virginia, and Washington, D.C., into the cotton and sugar plantations
of the Deep South. Throughout the first half of the nineteenth century, enslaved people disappeared from their families with numbing regularity. Sold
to "Georgia traders" operating in the region, they were marched and shipped
hundreds of miles south. In fewer than fifty years the interstate slave trade
in the United States assembled, sold, and transported more than twice as

many people as the Atlantic trade had done over two hundred years from Africa to North America. In some Maryland counties, 20 percent of the enslaved were taken every decade between 1800 and 1840. In the 1830s alone, slave traders sold more than 285,000 people in the interstate trade, most of them from Maryland and Virginia. Far from exceptional, the Georgetown sale in 1838 is disturbing because it was so horrifically common.[1]

Like other slave sales, this one was neither a single event nor an isolated moment in time, but many events and a cascade of financial arrangements, transfers, voyages, exchanges, losses, escapes, separations, conveyances, mortgages, and abstractions, unfolding over more than twenty years and across dozens of family groups. The Jesuit sale was, in fact, many sales. Some of the enslaved in Maryland who lived on nearby plantations were similarly entangled in the centripetal force of these sales, as they were "exchanged" for husbands or wives to meet one of the contract's most ironic and self-serving terms: the promise to keep families together that broke families apart. People neither sold by the Jesuits nor related in any way to the families from Maryland were pulled into its financing later, in the 1840s, their flesh and blood serving as collateral on highly leveraged mortgages to prevent the deals from collapsing. With each subsequent adjustment in financing, the renegotiated terms postponed any clear end to the sales. The Jesuit sales were still operating with legal force up to and through the American Civil War. Only the Thirteenth Amendment in 1865 ended their authority both in Maryland and in the parishes of Louisiana—Iberville, Ascension, Lafourche, and Terrebonne—where the enslaved from Maryland were sent. As late as the 1890s the heirs of Louisiana sugar planter Jesse Batey were still fighting among themselves over the value of the mortgages in the sales. Today the effects of these sales are still felt among thousands of descendants.

All of the slave sales and their financing in this antebellum period were premised on a widespread and troubling legal concept, what buyers, sellers, lawyers, and financiers called "the lot." The term referred to the buying and selling of enslaved people as chattel. Individuals were treated in every contract as part of a "lot" (that is, a group) in part because enslaved people in every group were always divisible by a factor of one. One body. One person. One soul. As a result, individuals could be rearranged, mixed, and grouped into different *lots* so that their ages, colors, genders, skills, histories, and bodies could be combined into particular configurations attached to different buyers, even different plantations, all through the instrument of the legal deed or contract.[2]

Here is a telling example. When the Jesuit priest Nicholas Sewall died in 1802, the inventory of his property listed six enslaved children all under fifteen months old, without any parents. How could Sewall own six infants and no parents? By what law or moral authority? Slaveholders mortgaged and leveraged each lot paying little or no attention to the families of the enslaved. These sales were premised instead on dividing people into groups that matched the number of dollars necessary to secure them as property and the collateral available to do so. Children were routinely separated from their parents in the lot. Infants were separated from mothers to suit the finances. Slaveholders minimized their role in creating orphans, in obliterating families, by referring not to individuals but to the lot, as if the concept were universal simply because it was invoked in a legal instrument.[3]

The Supreme Court sanctioned this practice in the 1820s. In the *Antelope* case of 1825, it ordered lots to be drawn to decide which of the African captives on board a captured slave ship would be freed under American law (and then sent to Liberia) and which would be sold as slaves for life to U.S. slaveholders. The proceeds were to be distributed to the Spanish and Portuguese owners of the vessel, since the laws of those nations allowed the slave trade. The court did not inquire into the legal statuses of the individual survivors on board the *Antelope*—that is, which individuals were lawfully enslaved and which were not. "The court must not yield to feelings," John Marshall warned, in the same vein as his opinion in *Queen v. Hepburn*. Property rights eclipsed human rights, even when they were "contrary to the law of nature." Marshall considered the Africans all cargo, an undifferentiated lot, chattel to be separated by the roll of the dice into those free and those enslaved, no matter their point of origin or their rightful claim to freedom. The legal notion of the lot perpetuated a horrifying logic. The enslaved would always be divided, and sometimes they would be forced to choose for themselves between who would be separated and who would remain, who would be sold and who would be freed.[4]

Nearly every clause in the Jesuit sale of 1838 would change. The financing of the sale would be renegotiated multiple times. The initial buyers would falter and sell out. The plantations would change hands. Families would be separated. Eventually the widow of a notorious slave dealer from Baltimore would purchase the plantations along with dozens of enslaved families and their descendants.

The Jesuit sales, and hundreds of others like them, ripped every legal claim of freedom up by the roots. Such sales were possible because procedural rulings in earlier cases, especially *Queen v. Hepburn,* deflected freedom based on ancestry. Sales tore the families apart and made their coordinated action nearly impossible. Each individual sale was premised on a presumption that slaveholders had the right to own, buy, and sell human beings under Maryland law, that they possessed what they called "legal title." By these means, tens of thousands of people were transported to the sugar and cotton plantations every year, separated from families that had been rooted in Maryland for generations.[5]

"Moral Burden Enough"

In the early 1820s the Jesuit corporation found itself at a crossroads. The Jesuits had abandoned their 1814 resolution to sell and free all of the enslaved people on their plantations, deeming freedom "prejudicial" and voting instead to maintain the plantations and keep all enslaved families in bondage. The farms, however, did not produce enough cash to fund all of their obligations, especially the expenses piling up around Georgetown College. By some estimates the Jesuit corporation's debts exceeded $30,000, a staggering sum at the time. The first sign of the looming disaster was that the Jesuits decided to mortgage the White Marsh plantation and all of the enslaved families on it, using the funds immediately to cover the debts of the college, the general fund, and the other farms. A month later they scrapped that plan. The Jesuits decided to sell another plantation in northern Maryland and simultaneously to "sell & dispose" of up to thirty enslaved people on the White Marsh plantation. Then, in a clear misunderstanding of how the Maryland Jesuits operated, the pope gave White Marsh, including all of the plantation's two thousand acres and enslaved families, to the newly appointed archbishop of Baltimore. The Maryland Jesuits, led by Francis and Charles Neale, were alarmed. White Marsh, they explained to Rome, was equal in value to one-third of all the assets that the Jesuit corporation in Maryland possessed. Rome backed off, but the Neales and their Jesuit associates were clearly in financial trouble.[6]

In point of fact, within a year of revoking their plan of emancipation, the Jesuits started selling children. They sold two children from White Marsh, taking $500 for a boy and a girl together. A few years later they sold two more children to a buyer in Washington, D.C. The boys and girls were offered from "any one of the farms, from which they can be spared with the least possible inconvenience." In each case the transaction treated boys and girls as chattel, a lot, to be divided and sold, grouped and separated, as the finances and convenience of the corporation demanded. At one point Francis

Neale complained to his fellow Jesuits that he was going to lose one of the best workers at St. Thomas Manor because the man's wife and children were enslaved on another plantation whose owner had decided to sell them. Neale said, "I cannot buy her." Her three children were "*all girls* of which we have 10 or 12 already." Ostensibly in the name of keeping the family together, Neale rationalized that he was "obliged" to sell the man to the neighboring slaveholder. The sale was a gain in the end for the corporation, Neale's paternalism intact. Meanwhile, the corporation's agent was authorized in another instance to "sell three children" of a woman named Maria who lived at the St. Joseph's plantation on the Eastern Shore. The children would either be reunited with their mother after more than four years of separation or separated from her permanently. Either way, their sale was part of a long pattern of Jesuit slave sales and exemplary of how all slaveholders categorized the enslaved without regard for their families.[7]

For more than a decade, the Jesuits squabbled within their society over what to do with the plantations and enslaved families in Maryland. As with other slaveholders, one line of Jesuit thinking disparaged slavery as ruinous and corrupting and the enslaved themselves as slothful, immoral, and untrustworthy. Slavery in their view was at best a necessary evil and at worst a millstone around the neck of the Society of Jesus. A priest of this latter persuasion wrote voluminous reports criticizing every aspect of the plantations. When an outbreak of cholera swept through St. Inigoes and killed young and old, he complained that the enslaved inhabitants lived too long into old age and prayed that more would die off sooner. He and a growing number of other Jesuits viewed those they enslaved as a financial drain and a moral burden. "Corn & tobacco ruin our land, but as long as we hold slaves, we must make these crops," he lamented in a typical entry in his diary. He also complained that since slaves had been "introduced" into the United States, "we know not how to get rid of them. It seems they become more corrupt every year & more discontented in their state of subjection. They are a great tax and a constant aggravation." Jesuit managers routinely complained about the expense of clothing the enslaved families. In addition, some wanted to sell all of the slaves because they feared a growing danger, a mass rebellion, such as had happened at St. Inigoes' store in 1817. The majority of Jesuits, however, took a different view. The plantations and the enslaved families, however badly mismanaged, offered the only source of possible revenue, the only collateral for the college, and the only assets the Jesuits could use to maintain their independence within the Church.[8]

In the early 1830s the debate society at Georgetown College considered the question: "Should slaves be liberated?" After two speakers on each side defended their positions, the society voted. The majority took the position that slaves should not be liberated.[9]

As early as 1832 the enslaved families on the Jesuit plantations in Maryland heard rumors of a big sale. Some heard that they had already been sold. Others said that they were about to be sold and "carried out of the state." A Louisiana planter came to visit the plantation a year after Nat Turner's revolt, presumably to buy slaves, and then, as if he had made up his mind, rushed through a furious rainstorm back to Washington, D.C. For months the enslaved families at St. Thomas Manor lived in "suspense," unsure what exactly the visit portended. The aging and increasingly infirm priest in charge, Francis Neale, grumbled that he wanted to retire because he was "tired of blacks and business."[10]

Some of the Jesuits seem to have redoubled their efforts to maintain the plantations and make slavery workable, if not entirely profitable. The truth was that some of the priests enjoyed the trappings of slaveholding. They touted their country estates as blissful retreats and referred to those they enslaved with paternalist affection as their "family" and as their "servants." John Carroll once described St. Inigoes as "a beautiful farm belonging to the clergy, on Potowmack river, possessing the usual advantages of chapel, servants &c." In 1832 Fidele de Grivel, one of the past presidents of Georgetown, described White Marsh to a fellow Jesuit in England as fetching an annual income of $5,000 under new management and supporting "a community of 25 [novices], the farms, & our 100 blacks, even with clothes." Writing from St. Inigoes, he rejoiced, "We have every comfort of life."[11]

In 1833, however, William McSherry, one of the first American-born Jesuits who had trained in Rome and had become the provincial superior of Maryland that year, took a decidedly less sanguine view of the plantations. He had little patience for those like Grivel and the Neales whose paternalistic vision left the Jesuits to sink under the weight of crushing debt and unpaid taxes. In the wake of the Nat Turner insurrection in Virginia and the subsequent debates in the Virginia legislature repudiating any form of gradual emancipation, the American Jesuits led by McSherry began laying the groundwork for a large sale of the enslaved families. This would extract them from slaveholding and redirect their mission away from the plantations toward the Catholic Irish immigrants increasingly coming into Northern cities, as well as toward Catholic German immigrants in Missouri and

Native Americans throughout the West. McSherry toured the plantations and wrote extensive reports aimed at convincing the Jesuits to sell all of the enslaved people and to lease the land to white tenant farmers. The plantations, he maintained, earned "nothing." McSherry estimated what would happen "were the servants sold." At St. Thomas Manor, 4,700 acres, the sale of the enslaved families would bring $16,000, and that sum would generate $1,000 in interest every year. At Newtown, "if the servants were sold," the Jesuits would fetch $25,000 and annual interest of at least $1,100. At St. Inigoes there were ninety enslaved people, McSherry pointed out, but he calculated that just forty-three could work: twenty-four men and nineteen women. McSherry built his case for selling all of the enslaved persons on the idea that fewer than half could work, yet "all must be supported, clothed, their doctor's fees paid." Slavery, he argued, was a losing proposition. But if the servants were sold, he repeated in a refrain in each report, if the servants were sold . . . [12]

A few years later, most of the Jesuit plantations failed to produce enough revenue to pay the county taxes on land and slaves. White Marsh was "in debt and unable to pay any tax." Perhaps to pay the taxes William McSherry sold four women from St. Thomas Manor in July 1835 for $1,300. Another sale of another lot, undifferentiated and unnamed in the record.[13]

At this decisive moment the Jesuits absorbed the dramatic events that began in the summer of 1835 and unfolded through 1836: the race riot in Washington, the trial of Arthur Bowen, the prosecution of Reuben Crandall, the antislavery petition campaign, and the unbridled rancor in the halls of Congress. The public uproar gave McSherry what he needed. He was the most vocal proponent of selling the slaves and wished to take advantage of high prices. He prompted a thorough examination within the Jesuit society in Maryland of whether to sell the slaves on their plantations. At his urging they held a private airing of the arguments for and against, debating whether it was "expedient to sell these 300 slaves." The reasons the Jesuits gave for not selling the slaves were mostly self-serving: selling would do nothing to assuage the spiritual evil within the Jesuit society; the greatest source of spiritual evil in American society was not slavery but the nation's radical spirit of independence leading Catholics away from the faith; the plantations provided a useful way to employ elderly priests; the slaves were a safer investment than holding "a great sum of money" because banks went bankrupt; and selling the slaves would give their enemies ammunition to second-guess and vilify the Jesuits either for not emancipating the slaves or for speculating on them like common slave traders. Only one Jesuit who spoke against the sale appeared to acknowledge that it would be "cruel" and that slave sales "ripped [families] away" from their homes.

McSherry and others in favor of the sale were unaffected by these arguments. Their position was just as self-serving. They responded that slavery posed a great danger to the spiritual calling of the priests because they "take on the habits, manner, and tastes of masters, of farmers, of businessmen, rather than those of humble missionaries." The riots and violence of the preceding years, moreover, meant that slaveholders would have to take "weapons in hand, to prevent or suppress uprisings." The situation already posed a grave moral risk: "It is moral burden enough for them [priests] to be forced to sometimes punish defiant slaves with the whip." All the same, they ruled out freeing the slaves after the riots in the summer of 1835. "Many of the scenes of disorder that occurred last year were popular riots on the part of whites against these unhappy free blacks in States where slavery is not tolerated," the Jesuits reasoned. They concluded that black freedom jeopardized white labor in Northern cities, especially where Irish Catholic immigrants competed for menial jobs. What's more, they had little faith in black independence and initiative. All of these observations pointed to a self-serving rationale that it was better to keep blacks enslaved than to free them. "To throw them into the masses now, free but without money and without means, would evidently be to expose them to a thousand miseries and dangers."[14]

At the end of the debate five priests voted for selling the slaves while four were opposed and wanted to continue to hold the enslaved on their plantations. Among those voting to sell was Thomas F. Mulledy, the president of Georgetown College. Under Mulledy's leadership the college had expanded its enrollment and embarked on a major building campaign, but like McSherry, he viewed the plantations as a drain on Jesuit finances. In the waning days of 1836, McSherry, Mulledy, and the Maryland Jesuits wrote their superior general in Rome, Jan Roothaan, and informed him of the corporation's plans to sell nearly all of the enslaved people on the Maryland plantations. There were two "rich and distinguished individuals," according to the Jesuits, who were interested in a large purchase. One was Catholic, the other Protestant. Both planned to take the enslaved families to Louisiana. Roothaan placed some conditions on the sales but replied that the slaves "can be sold and should be sold, whenever the opportunity presents itself."[15]

The rich and distinguished men the Jesuits had in mind were likely Henry Johnson and Philip Barton Key Jr.

Henry Johnson was a Louisiana congressman who had come to Washington, D.C., in the early 1820s as a one-term senator; while there, he met and married Philip Barton Key's daughter Elizabeth. Her brother Philip Barton Key Jr. studied law under his famous cousin Francis Scott Key. He married Mary Sewall, the youngest daughter of Robert Sewall, who had inherited Poplar Hill, the Darnall plantation near the Woodyard in Prince George's County. She died in 1831, and two years later Key married her cousin Maria Sewall from St. Mary's County. He converted to Catholicism. In 1835 they set out for Louisiana, a move no doubt facilitated by Key's brother-in-law, Henry Johnson. Johnson's relationship to the Key family was such that he and his wife named their Louisiana plantation Woodley after Philip Barton Key's Washington residence. Johnson was a large slaveholder and an Episcopalian. He counted himself an advocate of Henry Clay's national system of transportation projects, and he opposed the anti-bank Jacksonian Democrats. Like Henry Clay, he eventually found his political home in the Whig Party.[16]

Johnson had returned to Washington, D.C., in 1834 because he was elected to the U.S. House of Representatives. He probably helped guide his brother-in-law Philip Barton Key Jr. into the tight circle of Louisiana sugar planters and facilitated the young Key's move from D.C. to Louisiana in 1835. Johnson was present in the capital city throughout the tumultuous events of 1835 and 1836. For more than a year thousands of petitions to end slavery in D.C. deluged Congress, and the House adopted the notorious gag rule to table every petition touching on slavery without hearing it or sending it to a committee. But in early 1837 Rep. John Quincy Adams rose on the floor of Congress and, dramatically waving a piece of paper in his hand, announced that he had in his possession "a petition from slaves." Immediately, Southern congressmen exploded with rage at the very idea that Adams would attempt to introduce a petition from slaves. For two days they debated whether to censure Adams personally for having "given color to the idea that slaves have the right to petition." Then Adams revealed that the petition in his hands from slaves was actually that they wanted to remain in slavery. Amused Northerners on the floor and in the gallery guffawed at the rich irony of Adams's gesture. Would Southern congressmen bar slaves from petitioning to remain enslaved?

The mockery was too much for some Southern congressmen. Furious that Adams appeared to trifle with the slave system, South Carolina's Waddy Thompson said Adams was "guilty of a gross disrespect" and that despite Adams's stature as a former president "there [was] a point at which forbearance ceases to be proper." The whole contretemps exploded into such a distraction that Southern congressmen eventually proposed a resolution declaring that "any member who shall hereafter present any petition from the slaves of this Union, ought to be considered as regardless of the feelings of this House, the rights of the Southern States, and unfriendly to the Union."[17]

Amendment after amendment to the resolution followed, but in the heated exchange the overzealous members of Congress missed the larger point. In what appeared to be a condemnation of Adams, Congress had debated and voted on a resolution whose wording seemed to imply a congressional acknowledgment that slaves had a fundamental constitutional right to petition the government. The resolution did not pass, but the vote on it appeared to sanction the idea and amounted to a tacit admission that enslaved people were persons under the Constitution. After all, congressmen had debated on the floor the constitutional meaning of the right to petition and who could and could not exercise the right.

Realizing the full import of their blunder, Southern congressmen scrambled to plug the hole they had opened. The trouble was that even some Southern slaveholders argued that the House was "bound to receive petitions under the constitution." A full-blown legal and constitutional argument erupted over freedom of speech and the right to petition. Alert to the nuance of every phrase in the resolution, slaveholders tried to stave off any suggestion of constitutional rights for enslaved persons. "The history of the colonies may be examined, and no case can be found where the right of petition, for any purpose, was claimed for, or attempted to be exercised by, slaves," one Kentucky congressman maintained. Adams responded, "[The resolution] is a declaration, a menace, a threat, that any member who shall hereafter present a petition from persons held in slavery, . . . shall be amenable to punishment; it is a threat, a menace, a terrifying limitation to the freedom of speech and action in this House."[18]

Finally, the Southern leaders in the House proposed an additional, clarifying amendment to the resolution: "That slaves do not possess the right of petition secured to the citizens of the United States by the constitution." Their Northern colleagues would not allow an amendment on a motion already defeated on the floor, so Southern congressmen found themselves in a parliamentary bind. They put another motion on the floor: "Will the House reconsider the vote by which the resolution was rejected?" They mustered the necessary votes to pass this motion and to reconsider the wording of the resolution in its entirety. The now anodyne language of the revised resolution read: "That this House cannot receive the said petition without disregarding its own dignity, the rights of a large class of citizens of the South and West, and the Constitution of the United States."

At this point in the debate Henry Johnson, the Louisiana congressman, addressed his colleagues. In a brief speech, Johnson maintained that he could not believe that Congress, in rejecting the original resolution, had "intended to express the opinion that slaves had the right to petition." Johnson made it clear that he "did not believe that slaves had the right to petition." Calling the whole discussion "unfortunate," he urged Congress to disavow the idea of slave petitions "in the strongest terms."

Furthermore, Johnson was among the first to predict disunion "if the House should decide that petitions from slaves could be received." He proposed an amendment to add "and endangering this Union" as the capstone phrase in the reworded resolution. The motion was ruled out of order on technical grounds, and Johnson sat down in his seat while the less dramatic version of the amended resolution was debated. When the vote was called, Johnson was among the 160 ayes handily passing the resolution, a measure that had been intended solely to remove from the earlier resolution any implication that slaves had a right to petition. Just thirty-five congressmen voted against this dogmatic proslavery maneuver. John Quincy Adams, of course, led the bloc of Northern congressmen against the narrow interpretation of the right to petition. He was joined on this roll-call vote by a one-term Whig congressman from Illinois named Abraham Lincoln.[19]

The battle over the resolution unfolded as a loyalty test within each party. Southern slaveholders in both parties wanted assurances that slavery was constitutional and protected. What better way to assure this than to force members to take a stand either for or against the idea that slaves could petition Congress. By extension, the vote would have an impact on whether enslaved people were persons, not property, under the Constitution. Congress denied that enslaved people had any standing to petition the nation's governing body. Presumably Congress would also deny enslaved people any legal standing to petition local courts and governments.

The long history of the freedom suits in Maryland and the District suggested otherwise, but in the mid-1830s, forced by slaveholders in both parties, a majority in Congress began drawing a bright line treating enslaved people not as persons under the meaning of the Constitution but as nonpersons (or property) without any fundamental rights. On the eve of the Jesuit sale of 272 people from the Maryland plantations, Henry Johnson was one of the leading political voices for the most extreme line of argument in the Whig Party—that slaves had no right to petition and any suggestion otherwise was reason to dissolve the Union. Given his pending purchase, Henry Johnson needed this to be true.[20]

Just as the Jesuits began to organize their sale, a financial crisis plunged the United States into a major depression. The Panic of 1837 hit the country like a tornado, appearing suddenly, without obvious causes, and wrecking everything its path. Banks failed, thousands of workers lost their jobs, prices for cotton and sugar collapsed, and credit tightened.

The origins of the panic were clear in retrospect. Borrowing to finance the purchase of land and enslaved people, planters like Henry Johnson, Jesse Batey, and the young Philip Barton Key Jr. took out highly leveraged mortgages to expand their plantations in Louisiana and Mississippi. Prices skyrocketed for cotton, sugar, land, and slaves. These states issued millions of dollars in government-backed bonds to build railroads, canals, and turnpikes, borrowing the capital from British investors. Then the states chartered banks that were similarly overleveraged, borrowing to issue paper money backed by bonds. Every venture ran on a precarious sense of confidence; each debt was a potentially calamitous overdose of an irresistible drug. Everyone thought the risks were lower than they really were. And that they were guaranteed to induce untold riches.

In Louisiana a planter and merchant named Edmond J. Forstall emerged as one of the leading speculative bankers in the 1830s, and an archetype of the financier slaveholder. His family was party to at least eighty-seven slave sales over forty years. Given his banking connections to Henry Johnson, Forstall became embroiled in the financing behind the Jesuit sale of 1838. Forstall had pioneered a form of finance called "property banking" or "consolidated banking." The Union Bank of Louisiana, one of his early ventures, sold bonds that were secured by a pool of stockholder mortgages put up in exchange for stock in the bank. Slaveholding planters like Henry Johnson and Jesse Batey obtained stock in the Union Bank of Louisiana by mortgaging their land and slaves to the bank, and the bank sold bonds based on its "mortgage pool" to raise capital for further lending. Baring Brothers and other British and European investors bought the bonds, and the cycle of lending in Louisiana fueled more speculation in land and slaves.[21]

The technical term lawyers used for this form of financing was "hypothecation." In the language of the law of contracts, enslaved people were "hypothecated and mortgaged," their market value serving as the collateral for the loans that planters took out to buy them. Families were routinely divided up in these instruments even if they remained together for a period of time on any given plantation. Edmond J. Forstall, along with his business partner, his brothers, and their wives, hypothecated more than ninety-five enslaved people in 1832 alone, nearly all of them men in their teens and twenties. Financial instruments were signed, copied, and notarized, each with lists of enslaved people whose names, ages, and genders were recorded. The violence of hypothecation was quiet, if not subtle. On paper each enslaved person was rearranged into a grouping that utterly disregarded his or her family, kin, and history. The enslaved persons might never know they had been hypothecated, and thousands of enslaved people brought to the sugar fields of Louisiana and Mississippi were hypothecated in the feverish rush of the 1830s.[22]

Enslaved families did what they could to resist these deceptions. Bob and Milly, husband and wife in Adams County, Mississippi, upriver from New Orleans, had been promised their freedom when their youngest child turned ten. When the planter who enslaved them died, his will provided for their freedom on these terms or if they were sold out of the state before that emancipatory moment. The will instructed the executors to give the family $300 and, if necessary, to take them to Ohio if Mississippi law disallowed manumission by will. Because Bob and Milly had seven children and the youngest was not yet ten, they remained temporarily enslaved, so the executor of the estate decided to use them to enrich himself. He hypothecated all of them to buy land and slaves from John Thompson, one of the largest planters on the Mississippi River, and he took them out of Mississippi to his new plantations in Iberville, Louisiana. Subsequently, he hypothecated them again to the Union Bank of Louisiana, a third time to a merchant in New Orleans, and a fourth and a fifth time to various other creditors. When the planter finally went broke, his creditors sued him. Bob, Milly, and the children were subject to different terms in the train of mortgages and hypothecations. All would be sold and could be separated. Bob and Milly sued for their freedom in Iberville District Court, arguing that the executor had subverted the will of their previous slaveholder in Mississippi, promising them their freedom when the youngest of the children reached ten years old or if they were sold out of the state. In fact, they argued that he had acted as if they were "his own absolute property." Bob and Milly said that they had been "fraudulently deprived of their liberty and their rights."[23]

The jury in Iberville agreed and ruled in favor of Bob and Milly and their children, granting their freedom and awarding them $300. The case was just one of a handful of freedom suits that went to trial in the parish. All of the creditors immediately appealed the decision, and they took the most extreme position possible. They argued that under Louisiana law all "Negroes of black color" were "presumed to be slaves." An award of freedom based on a will with in futuro provisions was impossible, because all slaves freed by will were required to leave the state. Therefore, any blacks in the state not already free were presumed to be slaves for life. The circular logic may have been unconvincing, but the appeal emphasized the broad police power under the state constitution to regulate slavery. Even if Bob and Milly were right about the terms of the will, in other words, the will was invalid because those terms contradicted state policy. With so many creditors in line, the appeals stretched into 1837 just as the financial panic unnerved more creditors. Two years later the creditors were still filing appeals, a testament to just how overextended the hypothecation of enslaved people had become. Hoping to reverse the jury's verdict, one creditor put up a surety bond valuing Bob, Milly, and the children at $6,000.[24]

The financial house of cards in Louisiana simply could not stand. In the spring of 1837 the panic began when a few banks did not have enough gold, or specie, on hand to cover their loans and extensions of credit. The Louisiana property banks had issued bonds backed by mortgaged land and enslaved people and sold those bonds to foreign investors. As soon as the prices of sugar, cotton, land, or slaves slipped even a little, the momentum would quickly build, loans would be called in, and confidence in the bonds would be shaken. Nearly every plantation was financed by the hypothecation of enslaved people, young and old, men, women, and children, and the Louisiana planters seduced themselves into imagining that their debts were assets. They also pretended, even fantasized, that human beings could be interchanged and rearranged into forms of property that would suit any financial instrument and survive any liquidity crisis. When the Jesuits at Georgetown started looking to sell hundreds of enslaved people from the Maryland plantations, Henry Johnson, Philip Barton Key Jr., and Louisiana bankers like Edmond J. Forstall were well practiced in the art of hypothecation and ready to meet them.

"I Do Warrant the Said Negroes to Be Slaves for Life"

On May 29, 1838, sugar planter Jesse Batey placed a short advertisement in the *Washington Globe* newspaper seeking to sell or barter his 2,800-acre plantation on Bayou Maringouin, Louisiana, in exchange for slaves. Batey had come to Washington, D.C., that spring to buy slaves, and he planned to stay in the city for several weeks at Brown's Hotel. He promised any potential sellers that his terms were highly negotiable. He was willing to take one-fourth in cash for the land and would extend two or three years of credit for the remainder. He would be willing to trade the land for slaves in a one-time exchange or form a partnership with planters who had slaves but were looking for "suitable lands." Batey's advertisement came at an opportune moment for the Jesuits, who were determined to sell as many enslaved people as possible to pay off their mounting debts on the farms and at the college in Georgetown. Unwilling to sell during the financial panic, the Jesuits had been waiting for two years for a partner with the financial wherewithal to complement Henry Johnson.[25]

Two weeks after Batey advertised his Louisiana plantation, he and Henry Johnson signed an agreement with the provincial superior of the Jesuits, the Reverend Thomas F. Mulledy, to purchase 272 people for $115,000. The contract listed each person by name, beginning with sixty-five-year-old Isaac Hawkins, his sons, and their families. Each person was reduced to an age, a gender, a mental or physical disability. Here is one page:

> Joseph a man forty, Nell a girl sixteen, Kitty a woman twenty-two, Mary a girl six, Sam a boy four, Elizabeth a child one, Polly a woman sixty, Sally a woman fifty, William a man twenty-one, Mary Anne a woman eighteen, Robert an idiot twelve, Henry eight, Harriett forty-three, Elizabeth twenty-three, Isaiah a man twenty-one, Mary Ellen seventeen, Nancy fifteen, Martha ten, Jemmy one, Betsy a woman thirty-two, Austin her son thirteen, Adolph ten, Henrietta seven, Harriett Anne four, Richard thirty six, Nancy [Margy—crossed out] a woman thirty-four, Margery sixty, Len sickly a man thirty-eight, Minty a woman thirty-six, Nancy five, Mary eighteen months, Charles sixty, James fifty, Tom forty-five, Eliza twenty-six, Reverdy seven, Noble five, Edward three, William one, Bill an idiot forty-two, Maria twenty-six, Mary her daughter five, William six months, Charles seventy-five, Benedict sixty-five, Len Queen fifty, Susan thirty, John Butler thirty-five, John Coyle twenty-one, George sixty-five, Len Enston fifty, Daniel eighty, Nace fifty-five, Bernard thirty-five, William eighteen, Tom sixteen, Jim twelve, Henry ten, Francis eight, Stephen lame sixty, Anne Ned Queen's wife, two sons and a daughter, Betsy of Sam, and her two daughters, Matilda and her three daughters, Kitty wife of George, her son + daughter

Margaret + her daughter, Ginny wife of Charles, and her daughter, Crissy, her two sons + two daughters, Celestia, Henry (not married) Louisa, Teresa, Mary,—all the women except Ginny, Kitty and the last three of last mentioned are under fifty, and over twenty years of age, the children attended to are from one to seven years of age, Harry sixty-five, Dina his wife sixty.[26]

The list of names was written out in longhand and filled four manuscript pages from margin to margin. Despite the appearance of precision, the agreement was almost entirely speculative and provisional, an approximation of a future series of events. Each individual was imagined as picking cotton, planting cane, bearing children. The ages and valuations associated with each person offered an abbreviated summary of potentiality—something to be realized, something neither final nor fixed. Something entirely in the future. The sale was a prediction about the bodies of the enslaved, about their longevity and about the reproduction of their flesh and blood.

The people listed, however, were not necessarily the people who would be sold. One chilling admission of this was spelled out for the parties: "If there be any children on either of the places where the said slaves now reside, belonging to any of the women herein named, that they are to be included in this sale." Fifty-one were to be sold and transported to Louisiana "as soon as practicable" and the remaining 221 people were to be delivered to Batey and Johnson within the year by November. The two planters were obligated to pay $25,000 for the first shipment of 51 people. Mulledy agreed to give them ten years to pay the remaining $90,000 at 6 percent interest. Batey and Johnson were supposed to make five payments of $18,000 each. Mulledy promised to deliver the 272 people to Batey and Johnson, as if he, not the Jesuit corporation, were the sole slaveholder.

None of the initial terms would be met.

Batey, Johnson, and Mulledy, as fellow slaveholders, shared a fundamental presumption that the individual enslaved people named in their agreement were utterly interchangeable. A man age forty might be replaced by another. A woman of eighteen might be similarly swapped for someone on a different Jesuit farm. A child or an infant could be switched. The question hanging in the air, therefore, was whether one slaveholder might deceive the other about the age, skill, health, or ability of the individual people who made up the lot. Even as Johnson was negotiating in Washington, he was selling slaves in Louisiana. In September he sold four men for $5,000 in

Louisiana, and in November he sold a mother and her two daughters and, separately, a pair of twelve-year-old and a pair of ten-year-old girls. For $1,000 he sold another mother and her five-year-old daughter.[27]

The specificity of the June 19 agreement was meant to assuage the underlying uncertainty at the heart of every slave sale. Batey, Johnson, and Mulledy agreed that the individuals in the lot might be traded for others before the final sale and delivery. If any of the enslaved on the final list were different ages, if their value was "thereby impaired," or if they were "unhealthy, or in any manner unsound," then Batey, Johnson, and Mulledy assured one another that "a fair deduction [should] be made for such difference in age, or for such defects as shall lessen their value."[28]

From Georgetown Mulledy set out on horseback for the plantations at White Marsh, St. Thomas Manor, Newtown, and St. Inigoes to make the final decisions about who would be sold and sent to Louisiana and who would not. At this point Mulledy had become a quiet alcoholic. As provincial superior he treated the Maryland plantations as a baron would his manorial holdings. Reports circulated that under Mulledy's mismanagement the rules of sacred silence went unenforced, drinking was rampant, and women visited the Jesuit rooms. To preserve the element of surprise, Mulledy arrived unannounced at the plantations with the sheriff in tow to execute the sale and seize the enslaved families.[29]

At least twenty-five men and women named in the original agreement were married to enslaved people on other plantations. Mulledy planned to "exchange" them for other men and women who would then be sold to Louisiana in their place. Alternatively, he might arrange to have them "married off" and sold to a local slaveholder, with the value of the sale deducted from Batey and Johnson's total cost. However, at least five men and women were married to free persons of color. Mulledy had no definitive plans to exchange them. The sales threatened to rip each of them away from a spouse and children.

As rumors about Mulledy's plans began spreading through the plantations, some people decided to run away immediately. Given the determination of the Jesuits to execute such a large sale involving whole families, the choice to run away was agonizing. Isaac Hawkins's forty-year-old son, Charles Hawkins, escaped from White Marsh. His brother Isaac, age twenty-six, also fled the plantation, but he went without his wife, Kitty, or their three children. Perhaps he expected to negotiate for their freedom, perhaps he planned to help them avoid the sale. Regardless of his intention, all four were sold and transported to Louisiana without him.[30]

Forty-five-year-old Charles Queen escaped from White Marsh, too, perhaps expecting, like Isaac Hawkins, to stay in Maryland and somehow keep his wife and seven children from being sold to Louisiana. Described as brown in color, Queen stood an impressive five feet ten and three-quarters inches, well above the average height of the time. He and his family, however, were among the first fifty-four people sold to Jesse Batey. His wife, Sally, and all but one of his children were sent to Louisiana in late June on board a slave ship that arrived in Terrebonne Parish at the end of July. Charles, meanwhile, remained in Maryland, as did his daughter Eliza, who had been hired out to a local white woman. Perhaps unwilling to live apart from Sally and the rest of his family, he came back to White Marsh and went to Louisiana, or perhaps he was captured and imprisoned. In any case Charles Queen arrived in New Orleans in late December in the hold of a slave ship. He had been sent from the Jesuit plantations with the final group, including several others who attempted to run away. Eliza Queen, twelve years old, remained back in Maryland.[31]

At St. Inigoes twenty-year-old Nace Butler Jr. ran away. So did Louisa Mahoney. She recalled that she and her mother "ran off into the woods and hid there until the brig had sailed away." Decades later she was still furious at the breakup of the families, so much so that she could "scarce utter [Mulledy's] name." For years Isaac Hawkins had avoided capture. In 1838 he had been sold by Mulledy and Johnson to the man who enslaved his wife, but he ran away in Maryland when the rest of the Hawkins family was taken to Louisiana. In August 1843 Isaac Hawkins was captured and imprisoned in the Baltimore city jail. The bailiff contacted the Jesuit superior to ask whether he should be returned to the Jesuits or sold by the court. The Jesuit superior requested to speak with Isaac and asked the bailiff to "assure him that no violence at all, although the most legal, [would] be used in his regard."[32]

What must Isaac Hawkins have thought? The violence of the sale was fresh in his memory. The not-so-ancient violence at the Woodyard and the public execution that followed in 1770 may have come to mind. The law was the purveyor of violence—mortgages, sales, imprisonment, and the slave trade. The false promise that not even "the most legal" violence would be taken might have prompted a wry response or a bitter reply. A month later, perhaps after their conversation, the Jesuit superior curtly concluded the matter by notifying the bailiff, "You may sell Isaac."[33]

At least five people Mulledy planned to sell were married to free black persons. Each in different ways contrived to keep the family together, but all were up against the relentless schedule of transactions set forth in Mulledy's sale. Harriet Queen at White Marsh, forty-three years old, was married to James Queen, a free black man, and she was listed in the initial sale to Jesse Batey. Her daughters, Nancy, age fifteen, and Martha, age ten, promptly ran away, perhaps to their father. Her son, twenty-one-year-old Iasias Queen, ran away, too. Nevertheless, Mulledy included all three of her children in the first sale to Jesse Batey. None of them was on board the first slave ship sent to Terrebonne Parish. Harriet and James Queen refused to go easily to Louisiana and tried to drag out the negotiation long enough to wear down Mulledy and Johnson. In fact, James "secreted" three of his children away from White Marsh and moved them up to Baltimore out of Mulledy's reach for the time being.[34]

A priest visiting the plantation as these events were happening disparaged such resistance and, in a vast misapprehension typical of slaveholders, reassured his fellow Jesuits that all of the other families "are willing to go" to Louisiana. Every story of an enslaved person resisting the sale or claiming freedom was turned into a wild "tale" and deemed patently "false." The Jesuits discredited James Queen as a womanizer and a "rascal," using a term whites reserved almost exclusively for black men. Harriet's widowed sister, a mother of four young children, had escaped with James Queen, and Mulledy had sent her children to Louisiana without her. When she finally decided to return to White Marsh and go to Louisiana, the Jesuits, like many slaveholders, drew a convenient if inaccurate and patronizing lesson: that they were right about James Queen and when she discovered his true character she came to her senses, "refused to remain" at White Marsh, and "chose to go [to Louisiana] with her children."[35]

That the families "chose to go" was a monstrous distortion, a lie so bold it seemed true to the slaveholders. Twenty-five people listed in the original contract were married to other enslaved people in Maryland. Directed by his Roman superiors to keep husbands and wives together, Mulledy attempted to exchange or sell many of them to local planters, but he had few compunctions about sending any of them to Louisiana immediately if these deals could not be struck. Nelly Hawkins was married to an enslaved man named Peter. As the families were being rounded up and sent to the ships, Nelly fell "sick." Whether she feigned illness or not, she was left behind at White Marsh, where she was still close to her husband. A few months later Mulledy negotiated to buy Peter, and then sold both of them and their three children, ages thirteen, eight, and six, to Henry Johnson. They were all sent to Louisiana later the next year.[36]

Any veneer of a genteel, private arrangement between Mulledy, Johnson, and Batey was laid bare by slave ships waiting off the docks at Alexandria, Virginia. Mulledy commissioned three vessels, each associated with the notorious slave dealers Isaac Franklin and John Armfield. These men had ships trafficking slaves to New Orleans year-round. Their vessels, built in Connecticut, had been designed specifically for the slave trade, and their holds were similar to those in the ships that plied the transatlantic slave trade. Each captive had only about 36 cubic feet of space, sometimes less, when more than 180 people were jammed into the tightly packed holds belowdecks. Mulledy contracted first for the *Uncas,* a two-masted brig of 155 tons, approximately 80 feet long and 33 feet wide. Built for Franklin and Armfield's in 1833, the *Uncas* carried thousands to New Orleans in the booming interstate slave trade. In each of the holds there were two long platforms 5 or 6

Watercolor of the Katherine Jackson *of Baltimore,* 1844
(**Chesapeake Bay Maritime Museum Collection**).
The *Katherine Jackson* of Baltimore made voyages out of Washington, D.C., to New Orleans and carried hundreds of enslaved captives in the holds belowdecks.

feet deep onto which the enslaved were to lie down in what was referred to as "the tight pack," side by side, head to foot. Franklin and Armfield typically separated the men and boys from the women and girls on the voyage and heavily fortified the section of the ship holding the men. Nothing prevented the captain or the officers from entering the women's hold and seizing any of them for sex. On any given voyage, Isaac Franklin typically picked out his own "fancy," a young woman he took for his own sexual pleasure. The *Uncas* carried approximately 50 people Mulledy sold to Jesse Batey and sent to Louisiana in June 1838.[37]

The second ship was bigger and faster. The *Katherine Jackson,* built in 1833 in Baltimore, was used routinely by slave traders, merchants, and passengers for the voyage from Alexandria to New Orleans. At 456 tons and 133 feet, the ship was among the largest and fastest in the Atlantic. As on the *Uncas,* the holds belowdecks on the *Katherine Jackson* were fitted for the slave trade. In late October 1838 its captain placed advertisements in the Washington newspapers: "For New Orleans—The superior Ship KATHERINE JACKSON, expected to sail about the 20th October. Has excellent accommodations for passengers." Under full sail the *Katherine Jackson* could make the passage to New Orleans in two weeks. She left Alexandria on November 13 with 130 men, women, and children bound for Batey and Johnson's plantations and arrived on December 6.[38]

A few weeks later Mulledy contracted through Franklin and Armfield for a third ship to transport some of the remaining people sold to Batey and Johnson from the Jesuit plantations, including Charles Queen. The firm used its newest vessel, the *Isaac Franklin,* named for its slave-dealing principal. Built to impress his competitors in 1835, the *Isaac Franklin* weighed 189 tons and was designed for speed, but that did not stop it from packing more than 250 people into its slave hold on one voyage. The *Isaac Franklin* arrived in New Orleans on December 22, 1838, with 83 slaves in its hold, many of them not part of the Jesuit sales.[39]

Nearly two hundred people had been taken from their homes in Maryland, forced into the holds, and sent to Louisiana. Mulledy wrote a fellow priest, "Thank God I have succeeded in getting on board ship all the negroes except those who are married off the farm." Another brig was sent in February 1839. Mulledy's final contract with Jesse Batey sold 64 people for $27,057. His two contracts with Henry Johnson, signed on November 10 and November 29, sold respectively 56 people for $27,057 and 84 people for $29,163—totaling 140 people for $56,220. Together Batey and Johnson initially purchased 204 men, women, and children from Thomas Mulledy for $83,277. Johnson financed his entire purchase by mortgaging his land in Point Coupee and Iberville Parishes and by hypothecating the slaves he was buying and "their natural increase."[40]

Mulledy gave them a sweeping assurance standard in the slave trade business: "I do warrant the said negroes to be slaves for life, and the right & title . . . free from the claim or claims of all persons whomsoever." It was a claim he could make only because the Jesuits had fought the Queen and Mahoney freedom suits to a standstill decades earlier in *Queen v. Hepburn*. Jesse Batey complained that two of the men he bought were sick and one of the girls was too weak for the price he paid. Batey wanted a deduction. Johnson had sold "back" a twenty-year-old healthy woman to the Jesuits for $648. Johnson and Batey had agreed to pay annually the interest of 6 percent on five promissory notes for each contract. The principal on the first notes would not be due for seven years, not until March 1845.[41]

But on March 31, 1843, Henry Johnson failed to pay the interest on the loans. He mortgaged some of the slaves he had exchanged to banks in Louisiana for other loans. Worse, he had hypothecated enslaved people who were never transported to Louisiana. Then the Jesuits' lawyer and banker in New Orleans Edmond J. Forstall found out about the discrepancy.

Henry Johnson was about to go under in 1843. Drowning in debt, he and Philip Barton Key Jr. had borrowed thousands of dollars to purchase a new plantation, erect a brick sugar house, and outfit a state-of-the-art sugar mill with the latest steam engines and kettles. All of it was leveraged by the enslaved people he brought from Maryland to Louisiana. Then sugar prices dropped and creditors called in loans, and "owing to the difficulties of [the] times," he was unable to collect the debts others owed him. Johnson and Key tried to find a buyer for the sugar mill, but the market was soft.

Learning of Johnson's difficulties, the Jesuits and Forstall commissioned New Orleans attorney Louis Alexander Janin to review the enforceability of the Johnson and Batey contracts and to investigate the men's creditworthiness. Janin's painstakingly thorough review revealed troubling irregularities. Under Louisiana law, widows had "tacit" rights to their husband's land and slaves and stood ahead of creditors such as Georgetown College. Janin recommended that Elizabeth Key Johnson ought to be asked to renounce any claim in the refinanced mortgage. He also pointed out that the Reverend Thomas F. Mulledy "was not the real owner of the slaves." Instead, he acted "in a representative capacity" and "Georgetown College was the real proprietor."[42]

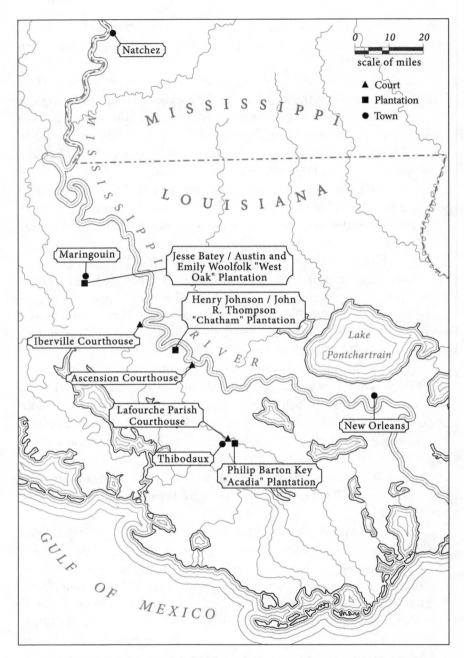

Iberville and Ascension Parishes, Louisiana, ca. 1838 (M. Roy Cartography).

But Janin's specific legal advice centered on the way Louisiana law required the filing of mortgages in every parish where slaves were dispersed. The requirement made for a cumbersome process if creditors wanted to file suit. "Suppose the case that the slaves embraced in one mortgage were dispersed in 5 or 6 parishes," Janin speculated, "[a]nd that simultaneous suit in each parish were advisable. In each of them the original mortgage would have to be produced, an inconvenience which might create additional delays." As a result, Janin recommended that Georgetown College stipulate "that none of the slaves shall be sold separately from the plantation to which they are attached, either in the lifetime or after the death of Messrs. Johnson & Batey, as long as the debt is unpaid."[43]

Keeping the enslaved families from Maryland together on single plantations, therefore, had nothing to do with charity and everything to do with how easily a creditor like Georgetown College might pursue and recover them as assets.

Johnson proposed to refinance the mortgages along precisely these lines. He planned to consolidate all of the enslaved people from Maryland, who for years had been working on his cotton plantations near Maringouin, and move them to his home plantation, Chatham, near Donaldsonville, where they would be mortgaged with Chatham, "the whole together" to Georgetown College. Parts of Chatham and its enslaved people were already mortgaged: $12,000 to Citizens Bank and $5,000 to Union Bank. Other enslaved people named on these mortgages would be divided up and remortgaged to the Jesuits as additional security.[44]

Mulledy and Johnson struck a new deal, but it suddenly became clear that Johnson had brought only fifteen people to Louisiana out of the "[eighty-four] slaves lot" that he had purchased and hypothecated. In other words, four years after the contract for eighty-four slaves was signed, and just as the interest and principal for the loans were coming due, Johnson declared that only fifteen of those eighty-four were "truly imported" and in Louisiana. He claimed that the others were "left" in Maryland. He had mortgaged some of the fifteen twice, once as security to the Jesuits and again as security for other loans from the Bank of Louisiana.[45]

Edmond J. Forstall could not believe what these figures meant. All of the mortgages Johnson had registered in the parish courts of Louisiana showed that eighty-four enslaved people "had been actually transported to Louisiana" and were therefore legitimate collateral for Johnson's many bank loans. Now it appeared that the loans were dangerously insecure—or that Mulledy, Forstall, and Johnson had engaged in fraud and were liable for any claims the banks might make. Johnson seemed to be suggesting that he was owed more slaves or that the renegotiated mortgage amount should be reduced proportionately. He admitted that he and Mulledy had exchanged or swapped some of the married people listed as slaves in the original contracts for other enslaved people who then took their places and were sent to Louisiana. In other cases, they sold or purchased a spouse. Johnson said he "disposed" of some of them in Maryland, selling to other slaveholders or into the slave trade. He made a list of the nine people who he said were exchanged and brought to Louisiana, which meant that approximately twenty-five out of eighty-four people were accounted for.[46]

What was also clear was that Johnson had mortgaged some of the exchanged husbands to one bank and had hypothecated their wives and children to Mulledy and Georgetown College. The Jesuit promises to keep husbands and wives together were as inconsistent as they were insincere. Even if couples were physically together, they were separated on paper, which could have long-term effects should a loan come under scrutiny.

Desperate to renegotiate the loans, Henry Johnson agreed to mortgage practically everything he owned. He would owe more than $94,000 spread out over fifteen promissory notes. These notes would be secured by the hypothecation of: fifty-six enslaved people he bought on November 10, 1838, and three children who had been born since then; nine enslaved people, "being the only slaves transported into Louisiana out of the eighty-four sold," on November 29, 1838; the nine enslaved people who had been exchanged; eight tracts of land; his plantation Chatham in Ascension Parish; and another fifty enslaved people, all at Chatham. Finally, Elizabeth R. Key Johnson renounced her dower rights.[47]

A year later Johnson sold half of his Chatham plantation, including all of the enslaved people on it, to his brother-in-law Philip Barton Key Jr., and in 1845 Johnson and Key sold an interest in both of their plantations—Chatham in Ascension Parish and Acadia in Lafourche Parish, respectively—to John R. Thompson as a joint and equal owner. Even with the co-ownership, within a few years Johnson and Key could not keep up with the interest payments on their part of the Jesuit mortgage. By the end of the decade one of Key's in-laws had sued them to recover more than $5,000. Through all of these conveyances the enslaved families from Maryland were yet again listed and enumerated. On paper they had been sold two or three times over, divided and recombined again into the collateralized groups necessary to secure the Johnson and Key loans and to meet the payments to Georgetown College.[48]

For the 64 people sold to Jesse Batey in 1838 and taken to a plantation near Maringouin in Iberville Parish, the story was similar. When Batey died in 1851, they were inventoried and appraised. Nace Butler, now sixty-five years old, was listed first, as he had been in the original sale. He was clearly the head of one of the largest Maryland families. He was valued at $300, Bibby, his wife of several decades, separately the same. Then Martha, their twenty-two-year-old daughter, was combined with her eight-year-old and two-year-old children and appraised "together at twelve hundred dollars." In this fashion the appraisal divided the families into saleable lots. Patrick Hawkins, now fifty-five, was listed as $500. His wife, Letty, and "her child" Isaac, age nine, together were listed at $900. Len Queen, now sixty-two, was listed separately from his wife, Ann Queen. Their eighteen-year-old daughter with her two-year-old daughter were appraised together at $1,000. Two years later the heirs of Jesse Batey sold the plantation and 112 enslaved people to Washington Barrow and his son John Barrow for $112,500. The Barrows mortgaged the land and the people to the Bank of Louisiana, named the

West Oak Cemetery, near Maringouin, Iberville Parish, Louisiana, April 2017 (courtesy of the author).

The families from Maryland, sold by the Jesuits, were taken in 1838 to New Orleans and transported up the Mississippi River by steamboat to Iberville Parish. Descendants of the families today maintain the aboveground tombs of their ancestors.

plantation West Oak, and three years later sold it to William Patrick and Joseph B. Woolfolk, son of the Baltimore slave trader Austin Woolfolk. In July 1859 West Oak and 138 people were sold again, this time to Austin Woolfolk's widow, Emily.[49]

In each of these transactions the men, women, and children taken from the Maryland plantations were divided in the financial instruments, and then divided again. Mortgaged and mortgaged again, hypothecated twice over. This happened so frequently that by 1859 Emily Woolfolk's deed dispensed entirely with any attempt to maintain a sense of lineage or family connections. All of the 138 enslaved were jammed into five distinct categories: Men, Boys, Women, Girls, and Children under ten years of age. Family groups had been obliterated. Infants were recorded without parents. The 138th person on the inventory was listed all by herself, "Annlitta an infant."[50]

At that moment the families from Maryland had spent twenty-one years in Louisiana on the West Oak and Chatham sugar plantations. Nace Butler was still there in 1859 at seventy-five years old. His wife of more than three decades, Bibby, had died. Three of their sons born at St. Inigoes, Henry Butler, Tom Butler, and John Butler, headed their own families at West Oak, but two other sons—Basil, who should have been thirty-four years old, and Gabe, who should have been twenty-nine—were either dead or sold away.

The sales had separated all of the families in profound and lasting ways: the enslaved branches of the families in Maryland were cut off from their relatives in Louisiana, the enslaved in Louisiana were cut off from their free cousins in Maryland, and the enslaved in Louisiana were sent to at least three plantations in as many parishes. Others in the families had been sent to Missouri. In Louisiana, the shattered remnants of these families had almost no access to lawyers, courts, or witnesses. No one, whites or free blacks, could testify about their family histories. Courts were willing to dispatch commissions to collect depositions, but Louisiana, unlike Maryland, had codified its slave law from the start. Slavery was woven systematically into the fabric of Louisiana law. Suddenly cut off from the free branches of their families in Maryland, those sent to Louisiana were unable to mount the freedom suits they had long pursued. Isolated from one another, miles away from the nearest courthouses and unable to rely on free relatives for support, it is no wonder that the families did not file freedom suits in Louisiana.

Initially, Louisiana code allowed suits for freedom, and judges, lawyers, and juries proved highly sympathetic. One historian has located more than two hundred freedom suits or actions in Louisiana. Juries often returned verdicts in favor of freedom. Manumissions were relatively common and nearly always approved by local "police juries." The overwhelming majority of those freed were not compelled to leave the state, as required by Louisiana law. Instead, freed people were exempted and allowed to remain in Louisiana in case after case. In the 1830s and 1840s, moreover, judges began ruling on the basis of ancient Spanish and Roman precedent for all sorts of interstitial categories of freedom not explicitly mentioned in the Louisiana code. Its grip only tightened, though, as the nineteenth century wore on. As a result, in the 1840s the Louisiana legislature passed statutes to close these legal loopholes. Louisiana prohibited the importation of term slaves, anyone who was "entitled to freedom at a future period." Beginning in 1852 all those who were to be emancipated had to be deported to Liberia at the slaveholder's expense, and in 1857 Louisiana totally prohibited manumission.[51]

Freedom suits required coordination and an extraordinary array of legal knowledge, experience, and resources. What made freedom suits not only possible but successful for the families in Maryland could not be readily reproduced either in Missouri or in Louisiana. Even in St. Louis, where courts and lawyers abounded, and hundreds of freedom suits were filed, the enslaved families sent from White Marsh found little opportunity to sue for their freedom. Instead, they tried to purchase their freedom or bargain with slaveholders to manumit them. Moses Queen pleaded to return to Maryland, but he had no apparent grounds on which to file a freedom suit in St. Louis. Only one of the White Marsh families took a case to the St. Louis Circuit Court. In 1837 Louisa Mahoney had been sold by the Jesuit corporation to a slaveholder in Maryland on the condition that she be freed in five years. He took her to St. Louis, disregarded the contract, and kept her enslaved.

Among all of the families sent to Missouri and Louisiana, only Louisa Mahoney managed to bring a freedom suit in a court outside of Maryland or Washington, D.C. She sued in 1854, but the case never came to trial, in part because the Jesuits claimed that they had no copies of the contract in their records. Cut off from her family and from the documents that would prove her claim, Mahoney was stonewalled.[52]

The last freedom trial for the families from Prince George's County, Maryland, unfolded neither in Missouri nor in Louisiana but in Washington, D.C., when the Bell family sued everyone who enslaved them and launched one of the largest escape attempts in American history.

Duckettsville

U ntil quite recently, I was unaware that people enslaved by my ancestors founded a free black community in Prince George's
County, Maryland, called Duckettsville. Today the place is no
longer on official road maps. Duckettsville is defined by the memory of the descendants of those who founded the neighborhood. I had no
family lore, no genealogy, and no stories at all about even the existence of a
black family with the Duckett name. A whole history was missing from what
I thought I knew. The same amnesia applies to tens of thousands of white
families across the American South and millions of their descendants today.
How did this come to pass, this deep historical forgetting, this profound,
unspoken, unacknowledged separation of American families? The answers
are painful. The end of slavery was not the end of racial subjugation and
discrimination in either Prince George's County or the United States. More
than 150 years later, we are only beginning to reckon with the legacies of
slavery and racism within families and communities.

For years as I researched the history of the Prince George's County
freedom suits, I could find little record of the black Ducketts and had no obvious way to locate their descendants. There were a few scattered references
to the family in William Still's monumental account of the Underground
Railroad published in the early 1870s. He recounted the escape of Benjamin
Ducket on the Underground Railroad in the fall of 1856. Twenty-three years
old, Ducket said that he fled from one of "the baddest men" in the county, a
slaveholder named Sicke Perry, who would "fight" his slaves and "kill up."

Ducket said that the unremitting violence was the "sole cause" for his escape. He left his father, his mother, two brothers, and three sisters who were enslaved by a different man. William Still described Ben Ducket as "chestnut color, medium size, and wide awake."[1]

Another Prince George's man, Thomas Ducket, helped organize the escape on the schooner *Pearl,* and he was sold away from his family to Louisiana as punishment for filing a freedom suit. The last name alone suggested he was from one of the Duckett plantations. I wondered if one of my Duckett ancestors was his cruel antagonist, his vindictive master. It seemed more than likely.

Then, in June 2019, Susan Pearl, the local historian for the Prince George's County Historical Society, called me to say that she had attended the annual gathering of the African American family in Duckettsville and asked if I would be interested in meeting with them to share family history? I readily agreed. Within weeks Cecilia Queen wrote me to say that her DNA matches connected her with members of the black Duckett family from Prince George's County. She, too, would come to the meeting. "I will be meeting my cousins," she enthused. "The plot thickens!"[2]

As the day of our gathering neared, despite Queen's warm encouragement, I became racked with anxiety. I had spoken with dozens of descendants of the families who sued for their freedom, but I had yet to meet a single descendant of the principal family enslaved by my ancestors. Sensing my profound angst, Cecilia Queen later told me, "One thing we descendants seem to have in common is the belief that the families of former slaveholders do not want the story told from our (or even a neutral) perspective . . . However, what the Word says is being manifested before our eyes: 'what is done in the dark will come to the light.'"[3]

We met in Bowie, Maryland, at a local museum. Marlene Colbert, Wanda Belt, Felicia Thomas, Clyde Bernett, Sherman Bernett, Thelma Bernett, and Roger Barnes were all descendants of Francis "Frank" Duckett and his son, Trueman Duckett. It was Francis Duckett, I learned, who founded the Duckettsville community on the eve of the American Civil War and shortly after the war began buying small pieces of property around Pleasant Grove. According to court records, Francis Duckett gained his freedom on March 3, 1859, through the will of Anne Duckett Hall.

I immediately recognized the name. She was the daughter of Richard Duckett Jr. of Sprigg's Request.

Our family histories were directly, inextricably connected. That realization dawned on all of us in the room. We agreed to find out what exactly

Anne Duckett Hall had stipulated in her will and to see if we could trace Francis Duckett's freedom and his family's genealogy back in time. I had to acknowledge that the white Duckett slaveholders, men like Thomas Duckett who took the hardest line against black freedom at the Annapolis Slaveholders Convention, were unlikely to have liberated Francis Duckett in the 1850s willingly.

We already knew from archival sources that Anne Duckett Hall died in 1815, but we still had questions. Why had it taken until 1859 for Francis Duckett to gain his freedom?

Her last will and testament was revealing. Anne Duckett Hall set out in 1815 to liberate all of the enslaved people over whom she had legal authority. Her will freed twelve people in all. Two of the men, Tony and Peter, were free "immediately." For the others, manumission would take place over a period of years on terms. The Jesuits made a similar decision in 1814, failed to carry it through, and six years later retracted their plan. But Hall followed through. The women would be free at the age of thirty-one, the men at thirty-five. Some would have to wait seven years. Others, who were younger, would have to wait much longer. The terms were similar in length to those in other emancipation bequests in Maryland. Both New York in 1799 and New Jersey in 1804 enacted gradual abolition laws that adopted lengthy terms before emancipation. Anne Duckett Hall made her intentions crystal clear: after their terms, each "shall be set at liberty & no longer bound to serve any person or persons whatsoever." None of her fourteen children inherited a "slave for life." Within a generation Anne Duckett Hall intended to extinguish slaveholding in her branch of the Duckett family. She repeated the word "liberty" over and over like a refrain. In both broad and specific terms her will was unmistakable—she set every enslaved person she held at Pleasant Grove on a legal pathway toward ultimate liberty. In this light her will appeared to be an implicit statement of conscience.[4]

The provisions stated in her will took more than forty-five years to unfold. It was still enslaving people when the Civil War broke out. Her will separated all of the enslaved Ducketts from one another and bequeathed each of them singularly to her children or grandchildren. Milton, age thirteen, was sent to her son Richard. Trueman, age eight, was sent to her son Baruch. Frank, age fourteen, was sent to her son Edward, and so on. Each of them would be free at age thirty-five, but in the meantime, all were separated from one another and their parents.

Six women were to be freed at age thirty-one, but their children would be enslaved until they turned either thirty-one or thirty-five. Slavery would terminate in a generation, but it could take decades. Meanwhile, Anne Hall's children would benefit from slaveholding for years to come. One of the women, named Nance (or Nancy), was twenty-three years old, so she had only eight years until she turned thirty-one. At the very end of her term of enslavement in 1823, she gave birth to a son named Francis Duckett. Under the terms of Anne Duckett Hall's will, strictly enforced, Francis remained enslaved until 1859. Hall's sons Grafton and William did not liberate Francis Duckett a moment before they were required to do so. Instead, they extracted all they could from their inheritance. Finally, in 1859, they freed Nance's son perhaps only because the terms of Anne Duckett Hall's will were indisputable and because Francis Duckett possessed the knowledge, experience, and fortitude to sue them for his freedom if he had to. He could draw on the long history of successful freedom petitions in Maryland and Washington, D.C., and the deep experience his family and others had in the courts.

The founding of Duckettsville, I learned from his living descendants, is a story of the burning pursuit of liberty by Francis Duckett and his family. His vision, his hard work, and his slow accumulation of land propelled the rise and success of a free black community. His descendant Clyde Bernett, a lawyer with Johns Hopkins University, told me, "Most of what we learned in school was that freedom came from white masters who manumitted or freed slaves. But this story is different. Our family used the law. And that's amazing and shouldn't be forgotten."

The will of Anne Duckett Hall is a microcosm of a much larger story about the failure of slaveholders to end slavery in the postrevolutionary United States. Hall attempted to extricate herself from the moral problem of slavery, and to a degree she succeeded. All the people she named, and their children, gained their freedom, but despite the clarity of her intentions in favor of liberty, Anne Duckett Hall's heirs continued to enslave, buy, sell, and inherit hundreds of people. Between 1815, when she died, and 1865, when slavery finally ended legally in the United States, Hall's heirs enslaved more people, not fewer.

With few exceptions, slaveholders like most of the Ducketts convinced themselves that slavery was justified, that the law was the unique inheritance of white people, their property alone. The law, controlled by whites, had upheld the legitimacy of enslavement, granting formal authority to a fragile dominion repeatedly challenged by those they enslaved. But not all believed what the slaveholders did about the law. Deployed for a higher purpose and in the right hands, those of enslaved people, the law testified to an inheritance of freedom. Would they be heard?

CHAPTER 9

The Last Freedom Trial

I long to hear from my family . . . For God's sake let me hear from
you all. My wife and children are not out of my mind day nor night.

—THOMAS DUCKET, FEBRUARY 18, 1850,

BAYOU GOULA, LOUISIANA

Word of Ann Bell's freedom suit against Gerard T. Greenfield, the Tennessee slaveholder who had inherited her from his aunt, would have spread
quickly through Washington, D.C., in December 1836. Bell sued on the
grounds that she had been living independently in the city for more than a
decade. She was the sister of Daniel Bell, the Navy Yard blacksmith determined to free his own family. Daniel was not yet free, paying the mortgage
on himself down month by month. Freedom eventually cost Daniel Bell a
staggering $1,630, nearly two years' wages, a sum that would take him five
years to pay off.

Within a month of Ann Bell's petition, Susan Armstead, a Greenfield
relation, began maneuvering in private to overturn the deed of emancipation that her husband, Robert, had signed a year earlier, freeing Mary Bell
and her six children. Desperate to thwart their emancipation, she asked her
lawyers to begin collecting affidavits at the Washington Asylum to show that
her husband had been incompetent to execute a deed two days before he died.
Some witnesses said that Robert Armstead was incoherent and given to

"flighty imagination" in his final weeks and days. When his estate was inventoried in 1838, Susan had Bell's children appraised for their value as "slaves for life."[1]

Thirteen-year-old Andrew was valued at $375.

Caroline, now nine years old, was priced at $250.

Eleven-year-old Mary Ellen and seven-year-old George were valued at $200 each.

Five-year-old Daniel and his three-year-old sister Harriet were priced at $100 each.

Mary Bell did not appear on the inventory, probably because she had her certificate of freedom. Ominously, Susan Armstead made sure to list Mary on the inventory as "not produced," indicating that she considered Mary's manumission invalid. The only other property Robert Armstead owned was some beds and miscellaneous furniture. The total amount of the estate that Susan stood to inherit was $1,299, but $1,225 of that consisted of the six children of Mary and Daniel Bell.

Eleanora Bell—Daniel and Mary's youngest daughter—did not appear on the inventory either. She had been born *after* the inventory was taken, *after* the estate had been appraised, and *long after* her mother's emancipation by Robert Armstead. When she was born, her mother possessed a freedom certificate. Her father was free. But Susan Armstead claimed that young Eleanora was a slave for life. In fact, Armstead made a point of holding on to Eleanora *because* she had been born after her mother's emancipation. It was another way to deny the legitimacy of the manumission.

Susan Armstead bided her time waiting for the right opportunity to seize Mary and the children as her property. She dragged out the probate for Robert's will. As long as the administration of Robert's estate, however paltry, was unfinished, Susan could claim income from hiring out Mary's children. Mary probably tried to negotiate with Susan. Years went by, Armstead's probate languished in the Orphans' Court, and Susan hired out the children and took their earnings.[2]

Eventually, on the verge of the children's sale and separation, of being "plunged into the abyss," as Harriet Beecher Stowe described the situation the Bells faced, the Bells raced once more to use the law to stop the sales and keep their family together.[3]

Eleanora Bell became the lead plaintiff in one of the last freedom trials in American history. Not yet born when the lawsuits were set in motion, she was nine and a half years old when her petition was filed, twelve and a half when her case went to trial.[4]

"There Is Nothing to Alien"

Gerard T. Greenfield enslaved more than fifty people at his plantation in Maury, Tennessee, but he had inherited even more people from his aunt Maria Anne T. Greenfield in 1824. Ann Bell and presumably her children. Her brother-in-law James Ash. And fifteen others. But Maria stipulated in her will that none of the enslaved persons could either be sold or removed from Maryland. If they were, they were automatically freed. The proviso stated: "He shall not carry them out of the state of Maryland, or sell them to anyone; in either of which events I will and devise the said negroes to be free for life." Daniel Bell was not listed in the will, but he too may have been enslaved by Gerard Greenfield. For more than a decade Greenfield complied with the terms of his aunt's will. He hired out Ann Bell, James Ash, and the other men and women to slaveholders in Maryland and Washington, D.C.

Perhaps prompted by his relative Susan Armstead, Greenfield decided in early 1839 that he would try to break the terms of his aunt Maria's will, terms that had kept him from selling the slaves he inherited or bringing them out of Maryland. Armstead was already trying to break the deed of manumission her husband had signed, freeing Mary Bell and her six children. Between Susan Armstead and Gerard Greenfield, the pressure on the Bell family was immense. One was contesting the deed, the other the will, and together they intended to enslave three families: Mary Bell and her children, Ann Bell and her two sons, and James Ash and his son.

Greenfield made the first move. He arranged to sell James Ash for $700 to the slave trader William H. Williams, who imprisoned Ash in his notorious slave pen at the Yellow House and presumably planned to sell him south. Ash sued Williams immediately, arguing that he was free because the terms of the will "took effect" the moment he was sold. Williams replied to the court that Greenfield had proposed the sale because the will was "repugnant [*sic*] to the nature of the estate" and therefore "void." According to Williams, Greenfield wished "to obtain a Judicial decision" and "informed" Ash of his intentions, giving Ash the "oppertunity [*sic*]" to "commence a suit for his freedom." Williams said that if he lost the freedom suit, Greenfield would pay him back and cover the costs.[5]

Williams and Greenfield's collusion was couched as a reasonable, even complicit, arrangement between the parties, including James Ash, but their story hid the real consequences of the power struggle at the heart of the freedom suit. If Ash lost, he would be sold. If Williams lost, he might be prosecuted for kidnapping a person "entitled to freedom," a criminal offense in

Maryland since 1809, with a minimum sentence of two years in the state penitentiary. Judging from the record of hundreds of freedom suits, arranged suits were rare, if not unheard of. Judging more specifically from the desperate measures Susan Armstead and the Greenfields had undertaken to hold on to the Bells, we should not be fooled into thinking that Ash's lawsuit was a test case.[6]

Instead, James Ash and Ann Bell used their freedom suits to shield their children from the grasp of the Greenfields. All of their children were in one way or another vulnerable. They secured the help of attorney Joseph H. Bradley, who had so ably defended Reuben Crandall. Though Bradley was a slaveholder and a colonization advocate, he defended a free black slave rescuer named Leonard Grimes who was arrested in Washington for attempting to transport a Virginia family to freedom. Grimes would serve two years' hard labor in Virginia. Bradley tried to delay his extradition. Although he defended slaveholders just as regularly, even in freedom suits, Bradley appeared to relish the underdogs, people with few resources fighting the legal system, and he waived or adjusted his fees on such occasions. After his celebrated acquittal of Crandall and his albeit unsuccessful defense of Grimes, Bradley had strong enough ties to the small circle of abolitionists in the city that he once risked harboring a man for weeks from the authorities.[7]

At Ash's trial in March 1840, Joseph H. Bradley took the position that "this is a will" and that the overriding consideration in the law of wills was the intent of the testator or testatrix—in this case, Maria Anne T. Greenfield. Bradley argued that she "meant to give the slaves a higher and nobler bequest," and she expressed her will with "clear intent." And she had the "right to bequeath the freedom, conditionally, or in a certain event." Her intent should be followed.

Williams's attorneys argued that the will infringed on the property right of the heirs, that slaves were property and could not receive a bequest of freedom, and that such a bequest amounted to a third-party transaction outside of the will. The court swept aside these arguments. Slaveholders in Maryland could attach whatever conditions they wanted to a last will and testament, including a bequest of freedom. The jury rendered a verdict for Ash, and Judge William Cranch ordered his immediate release from Williams's jail. Williams appealed the decision to the U.S. Supreme Court, saying the case raised "a question of law, important to the slave states."[8]

Meanwhile, Ann Bell's freedom suit against Gerard T. Greenfield went to trial in April 1840. Joseph H. Bradley argued her case as well. Bell persuaded the jury that she had lived independently since at least 1824, that she was in fact free, and therefore that her children were free too. Bradley pointed out that she had purchased property in the city, built a house, made contracts, and even hired a servant from the Greenfields. These were acts "inconsistent with the condition of slavery," the judges ruled. The Greenfields had known about them and did nothing in response. Given these facts, the jury was instructed that it could "infer" that Ann Bell had been manumitted.[9]

Remarkably, one of the jurors in her case was a notorious proslavery enforcer named John H. Goddard, who captained Washington's police force, called the Auxiliary Guard, a unit that doubled as the city's slave patrol. A Rhode Islander who had moved south, Goddard wore a cockade in his hat, a jaunty flourish and a reminder of his obsequious devotion to slaveholders. One writer compared his cloying insincerity to Uriah Heep's in Charles Dickens's *David Copperfield*. Ann Bell's witnesses included not only Dr. Edward Clarke, Daniel Bell's ally, but also the former mayor of Washington, D.C., William A. Bradley. The overwhelming evidence that she not only owned property but also acted as a free person for years may have convinced a skeptic like Goddard that he had no option but to render a verdict in favor of her freedom. In any case, Ann Bell and her two young boys were free, the second branch of the Bell family to break the Greenfields' fierce grip on her immediate family.[10]

If Gerard Greenfield merely wished to break the terms of his aunt's restrictive bequest, he had opened a potential Pandora's box. In the arguments before the U.S. Supreme Court James Ash's freedom suit now posed a much more fundamental question: whether slaves were property or human beings under the law. The slave trader's lawyers took the unambiguous position that "Negroes, by the laws of Maryland, are property precisely as money in the funds, or household effects." In fact, they cited *Queen v. Hepburn* and argued that the implications of the bequest of freedom in Maria Greenfield's will led to a "repugnant conclusion" that enslaved people were something more than property. Such a bequest could not "take effect" without at the same time denying the slaveholder "control over the negroes which he is by law entitled to exercise over them, and which he might exercise over any other property in like circumstances, without subjecting himself to forfeiture."[11]

Joseph H. Bradley countered with a bold argument for human rights, one of the few that would reach the U.S. Supreme Court in this period. He reprised Gabriel Duvall's powerful dissent in *Queen v. Hepburn* that "a question of freedom is superior to any question of property" and that the "laws of personal property" were not applicable. Instead, under the laws of Maryland, Bradley maintained that enslaved people were "regarded as responsible and intellectual beings, as 'persons' capable of contracting." In this respect, the law treated enslaved people as "human beings." James Ash's lawsuit presented the Supreme Court with the fundamental contradiction of slavery: "Can property take property? Can property be entitled to a trial by jury, or commit a crime, or acquire a right? Yet all this may be done by a negro; and they all imply a reasoning faculty, a conscience, an immortal spirit, in which there can be no property."[12]

Chief Justice Roger B. Taney considered slaves property, as his *Dred Scott* decision would eventually demonstrate, but his decision in *Williams v. Ash* attempted to sidestep the contradiction. According to Taney, in the case of James Ash, whatever legal rights of property inhered in his body, those property rights disappeared the moment the will's conditions were effected by his sale. "The bequest of freedom to a slave is a specific legacy," Taney concluded, and the restriction imposed in the will "was not a restraint or alienation inconsistent with the right to the property." As if by magic, the moment the will granted James Ash his freedom, there were no property rights to claim. "There is nothing to alien," Taney concluded, meaning in effect "There is no property to divide." He upheld the circuit court's verdict in favor of Ash's freedom.[13]

It seemed that not even Chief Justice Taney could deny the force of a legal argument in favor of freedom if it were properly couched; Ash's freedom, Taney pointed out without a hint of irony, "took effect the moment he was sold." Taney was unwilling to treat enslaved people as human beings in the law, but he had been forced to notice the moment Ash became a person with rights. Ash had taken on the Yellow House's William H. Williams and won his freedom. Like Charles Mahoney's, his was a significant political achievement. He had orchestrated a stunning victory in the law, one of the only freedom suits ever affirmed by the Supreme Court.[14]

But James Ash's unexpected success, following on the heels of Ann Bell's court victory, must have prompted Susan Armstead to tighten her hold on Mary Bell and her children. Susan's daughter, in fact, had testified as a witness for Gerard T. Greenfield against Ann Bell. In 1843 Armstead made a decisive move to seize Mary Bell and the children as her property. She requested the Orphans' Court administering Robert's estate to appraise Mary Bell and the children, including Eleanora, so that they could be deeded as slaves and given to her own children. She produced the affidavits from the Washington Asylum testifying to Robert's incapacity to execute a deed of manumission, and the Orphans' Court ordered the valuation and distribution of the Bells to go forward. Mary Bell responded with her own freedom suit.

For eight years, Mary and Daniel Bell had lived "as free" near the Washington Navy Yard. Ann Bell's verdict for freedom notwithstanding, Susan Armstead had suddenly convinced a court to treat Mary and the children as human property. The crisis they faced was severe. As with Michael and Phillis Shiner, as with Joe and Nelly Thompson, the threat of the sale of their children was immediate. Mary Bell rushed to the Register of the City of Washington to obtain another official certificate of freedom. Then she filed a countersuit against Susan Armstead in chancery court to stop the Orphans' Court proceedings. Bell asked for an immediate injunction because Susan had "the avowed intention of selling them."[15]

Eastman Johnson, *Negro Life at the South*, 1859
(Photography © New-York Historical Society, The Robert L. Stuart
Collection, the gift of his widow Mrs. Mary Stuart).

Eastman Johnson lived at 266 F Street between Thirteenth and Fourteenth Streets, next door to this house. He painted a series of realistic scenes and people, free black and enslaved, aiming to show their interior lives and implicitly question slavery.

When Mary Bell's suit against Armstead finally went to trial in December 1847, it had been more than twelve years since Robert Armstead signed the deed of manumission, liberating Mary and the children. The jury wasted little time in agreeing with Susan Armstead that her late husband's deed was not legally valid because he was unfit to take such action, his mental state deranged. Mary Bell filed a motion for a new trial, claiming that she had new evidence that Susan had long treated Robert "with great neglect and cruelty" and that for years before his illness they "did not live together as man and wife." She found new witnesses during the trial and said she "could prove" these facts. Joseph H. Bradley, the Bells' attorney, swore before the court that he had made "active exertions" to track down "living witnesses" who would offer new and important testimony.[16]

With the motion for a new trial pending, Daniel Bell was running out of money to pay for the long and protracted litigation. Bradley told them they had a very good case, but Susan Armstead's stubborn "pertinacity" did not appear to be wavering. The delays took their financial toll. Frustrated and concerned that Armstead would sell Mary and their children at the first opportunity, Daniel Bell hatched a daring plan to smuggle them out of Washington. He hoped to enlist an abolitionist merchant from Philadelphia named Daniel Drayton, who sailed up and down the coast and had successfully piloted a family of seven out of Washington to freedom in New Jersey the previous summer. In early 1848 Bell went to see an abolitionist lawyer in Washington who passed his request on to Drayton. Several weeks later Drayton visited Washington, likely met with Bell, and agreed to return as soon as possible with "a vessel fit for the enterprise."[17]

Word spread of the plans, and Bell probably turned to others with pending freedom suits to help him organize the escape. One of them, Thomas Ducket, was also trying to free his wife and children to prevent them from being sold away from him. The Duckets were from Prince George's County, enslaved for generations by the planters, lawyers, and judges of that name. According to Harriet Beecher Stowe, Thomas Ducket was "a poor, honest, hard-working slave man." He was also literate, industrious, and well connected. Ducket knew the leading white abolitionists in the city: lawyer William L. Chaplin, newspaper editor Gamaliel Bailey, and lawyer and reporter Jacob Bigelow. On April 10, 1848, a woman named Letha Duckett sued for her freedom and for the freedom of her five children. She may have been Thomas Ducket's wife. Her lawyer was a young abolitionist named David A. Hall, active in the Underground Railroad in the city.[18]

When the Duckets filed their freedom suit, Daniel Bell's plan for a large escape was moving forward. Drayton chartered Captain Edward Sayres and his fifty-two-ton schooner, the *Pearl*. They arrived in Washington on Thursday, April 13. The city was in a raucous state of excitement. A torchlit procession was under way to honor the revolution in France that had toppled the Napoleonic regime and inaugurated a new republic. Bonfires lit up the public squares. Crowds gathered in front of newspaper offices to hear the latest reports and listen to speeches proclaiming the advent of a new era of liberty in the world. Quietly, indeed surreptitiously, Daniel Bell and others spread the word among the families that the *Pearl* had arrived and was waiting at an isolated wharf near Seventh Street below a high bank in the river.

"Shortly after dark the expected passengers began to arrive, coming stealthily across the fields, and gliding silently aboard the vessel," Drayton recalled. At midnight on Saturday, April 15, the *Pearl* sailed out of Washington and headed down the Potomac bound for the open waters of the Chesapeake Bay and, if successful, to Frenchtown, New Jersey. Mary Bell, eight of her children, and two of her grandchildren were secreted belowdecks in the hold. Among them was eight-year-old Eleanora. Sixty-six other people joined the Bells to make their escape on the *Pearl*. They came from all over the city, seventy-seven in all. Priscilla Queen and two of her daughters, Harriet, age fifteen, and Priscilla, age nine, took refuge in the *Pearl*. They were fleeing William H. Upperman, a wealthy grocer in Georgetown. There were other people on board enslaved by well-known figures in Washington. Mary Ellen Steward had been enslaved by Dolley Madison, the former first lady, who had been selling slaves one at a time to maintain her station late in life. John Calvert was enslaved by the Reverend O. B. Brown, pastor of a local Baptist church, and Alfred Pope by South Carolina congressman John Carter.[19]

Within days of its departure, the *Pearl* was captured. An armed posse of thirty volunteers commandeered a steamship and two field cannons to intercept the *Pearl* on the Potomac one hundred miles downriver from Washington, near the Chesapeake Bay. The militia boarded the vessel, locked the enslaved families in the dank hold, and towed them back to Washington, where outraged slaveholders awaited their return and anticipated the prosecution of Drayton and Sayres. The Bells, the Queens, and all of the other men, women, and children were marched through the streets and imprisoned in the D.C. jail until they were claimed by their respective slaveholders. A few managed to escape en route, but they were found and seized within hours. To keep track of the fugitives, the court printed forms that reduced each person to nothing more than a monetary value and a slaveholder. No name. Each was described as part of the *Pearl*'s lot—"one Negro slave." The Bells made up the largest single family who attempted to escape, and all were still claimed by Susan Armstead as slaves for life. She placed their value at $5,000. Harriet Beecher Stowe later despaired over the fate of "poor Daniel Bell's family," whose "contested claim to freedom was the beginning of the whole trouble." Nine-year-old Eleanora Bell was valued by the court at $400.[20]

Slaveholders reacted to the attempted escape with muted fury. While the U.S. district attorney brought charges of larceny against Drayton and the crew, slaveholders sought to make an example of the fugitives. They would sell as many of the enslaved as quickly as possible to slave traders in Baltimore, who would send them to New Orleans. They would split the families up by keeping some members and selling others. Some of the slaveholders were willing to accept below-market prices, a markdown on account of the rebellious characteristics now evident in each of the enslaved escapees, but the immediate and terrifying consequences of the sales, they reasoned, would be a lesson for the enslaved people that remained.[21]

On Friday, April 21, the sales began. Mary Bell and some of her children were marched along with fifty others to the depot of the Baltimore and Ohio Railroad on Pennsylvania Avenue. They were destined for John B. Campbell's slave market in Baltimore. Harriet Queen had also been separated from her mother and sister, and she was probably in the coffle with the Bells headed for the railcars. At the station Daniel Bell faced the sickening prospect of losing Mary for good. From the platform he called out to her and the children. He decided to approach the railcars and appeal directly to the slave trader that his wife and their children were free. She had freedom papers! he cried. But no one paid him any attention. Desperately, he reached for Mary's outstretched hand, but the slave trader's guard clubbed him to the ground with swift, merciless blows.

At that moment, the train about to leave the station, a sympathetic bystander agreed on the spot to help Daniel Bell make an offer to purchase Mary. He had purchased his own freedom at great cost, and he had already paid for more than a decade of litigation against Susan Armstead. He knew that any arrangement would have to be a loan. He also knew immediately that the amount offered, $400, was not enough. Daniel and Mary would have to choose which of their children they would purchase and which would be taken to Baltimore, shipped to New Orleans, and sold there to the highest bidder.[22]

Bell accepted the offer to buy Mary. Together, husband and wife decided to buy the youngest two of their children: three-year-old Thomas and
his thirteen-year-old sister Harriet. The slave traders took four of their
children to Baltimore that day, sold them on commission for Susan Armstead, and sent them on slave ships to Louisiana and Mississippi.

Like Daniel Bell, Thomas Ducket faced his own agonizing choice. He
was not on board the *Pearl,* but his wife and possibly his children were. In
fact, he was suspected of helping organize the escape. In the swirling confusion of its aftermath, Ducket tried to sell himself to the slaveholder who
enslaved his wife and children. Nothing of the sort happened. He was taken
to Washington under a cloud of suspicion and sold to Louisiana within days,
swiftly and irrevocably separated from his family. No one knew where he
went. From Iberville Parish near Plaquemine, Louisiana, Ducket wrote his
abolitionist friends in D.C., lawyers Jacob Bigelow and William Chaplin. "I
have seen more trouble here in one day than I have in all my life," he said of
Samuel T. Harrison's sugar plantation at Bayou Goula. Ducket reported that
because of his alleged role in the *Pearl* escape, he had not been allowed to
leave Harrison's plantation since he had arrived more than two years before.
Imprisoned in effect, confined to the plantation, Ducket had no access to attorneys or the courts. For anyone sent to Louisiana, the situation was similar. Filing a freedom suit was almost impossible. It was "hard times here,"
he explained. Ducket hoped that the attorneys would not forget him or his
family, that they would "help me out of it." He longed for news of his family.
"For God's sake let me here [*sic*] from you all. My wife and children are not
out of my mind day nor night."[23]

The situation for the Bell family was similarly desperate as the new year
began in 1849. Slavery and the slave trade were still perfectly legal in Washington, D.C., the threat of a sale ever present. Susan Armstead continued to
enslave ten-year-old Eleanora Bell, and the *Pearl* indictments seemed to
validate further her legal title to the girl. Eleanora had been born after her
mother's manumission, but after several trials the manumission itself had
been effectively nullified. Daniel and Mary Bell exhausted their financial resources in the litigation. They may have turned to a "next friend" to bring
Eleanora's freedom suit because they could no longer afford the attorneys'
fees. On March 26, 1849, Eleanora Bell filed a petition for freedom arguing
that her mother had been "at large and free" ever since 1828, was officially
manumitted by deed in September 1835, and was certified by the court as a
free person in 1843.[24]

For months Susan Armstead ignored the summons. Finally, in October 1851 the court issued a warrant for her to appear, alleging that she had absconded and hidden herself to avoid the lawsuit. Threatened with contempt charges, Susan Armstead finally answered the court, and a trial was set for late October 1851. Eleanora had just turned twelve.

Eleanora Bell v. Susan Armstead went on for days and appeared to take on the character of a marathon for its participants. Twenty-four witnesses

Eastman Johnson, *Hannah Amidst the Vines*, 1859
(courtesy of Georgetown University Art Collection, Booth Family Center
for Special Collections, Washington, D.C., Gift of George Bliss).
Hannah, a mixed-race young girl of the same age as Eleanora Bell, was likely from F Street or the neighborhood nearby.

were called to testify, more than in any other freedom suit in the preceding fifty years. Eleanora probably attended the trial and would have sat behind the bar with her attorneys Duff Green, Benjamin E. Green, and Charles Wallach. Duff Green was a curious addition to the legal team, a onetime Jacksonian Democrat turned Whig railroad builder. He lent an unmistakable, if peculiar, political dimension to the proceedings. Wallach had represented Mary Bell, and furthermore, he was involved in a string of freedom suits for fugitives on the *Pearl*. No attorney appeared on the record for Susan Armstead.

Daniel and Mary Bell probably attended the trial, hoping that a jury would finally rule Robert Armstead's 1835 manumission legal. Eleanora's attorneys questioned fourteen witnesses on the stand, clearly in an effort to influence the jury's sensibilities. Ann Goddard, the wife of the slave patroller John H. Goddard, took the stand for Eleanora. Eleven years earlier, her husband had served on the jury that freed Eleanora's aunt Ann Bell. James Tucker, an English-born master anchorsmith at the Navy Yard, also testified for Eleanora. Seven women and five men followed, each of them connected to the Navy Yard, including the wife of Washington Duvall, one of the Navy Yard men who signed the memorial to abolish slavery in the District. All were representatives of the class of workingmen and women—skilled and unskilled—who probably knew Robert Armstead from the Navy Yard.

Susan Armstead called ten witnesses of her own, most of them relatives who would attest to her late husband's state of mind in the summer of 1835. As with Mary Bell's freedom suit, Armstead considered the deed of manumission invalid because her husband was mentally unfit when he signed it.

The jury ruled in favor of Susan Armstead yet again, and Eleanora Bell remained enslaved in Armstead's house.

"Never Was Lawful, and Never Can Be Made So"

By the 1840s the free branches of the Queen, Mahoney, Duckett, and Bell families had begun accumulating property and family networks necessary both to protect their own freedom and to assist others. Michael Queen settled north of Baltimore with his wife, Mary. In 1843 he began working for the Philadelphia, Wilmington, and Baltimore Railroad. It was a corridor associated with the Underground Railroad. Three years later Queen began buying ten-acre parcels from white neighbors near Middle Station near Baltimore. He became a founding member of St. Joseph's Catholic Church in Fullerton, Maryland. Michael and Mary Queen named several of their nine

children for relatives who had played significant roles in the family's freedom suits—Simon, Louisa, and Mima.[25]

Once free black families had obtained property, keeping it required
constant vigilance and no small measure of legal insight on their part. In
Charles County the children of Susanna "Sucky" Queen expanded Litchfield
Enlarged. Charles Queen, the heir of the Reverend John Ashton, managed
to buy several other parcels adjoining Litchfield Enlarged, including one he
named Small Profit. He amassed an estate of 186 acres worth at least $1,000
before his death in August 1848. But Charles Queen died without a written
will, and the property was subject to division or sale by any of his heirs, even
without the permission of the others. His daughter Susanna wanted the
property to be sold and the proceeds divided among her siblings. She may
have wanted the right to divide and sell off a piece of the property, whereas
her brothers and sisters did not want to sell Litchfield Enlarged in pieces. In
the summer of 1850 Susanna sued her siblings in equity court arguing that
her father verbally gave the land to all of his children to be held jointly and
that the property could not be divided or sold without the permission of
each. Susanna Queen asked the court to ensure that she "may receive what
she is entitled." The Charles County equity court agreed and ordered an immediate sale of the entire property with the proceeds to be divided equally
among the heirs. The court appointed a trustee to carry it out, and advertisements were taken out for four weeks in the Port Tobacco newspaper announcing the sale of Litchfield Enlarged. With a court-ordered sale, anyone
could buy what the Queens had inherited.[26]

The public auction took place in October 1850. The terms required at
least $50 cash up front, but none of the Queens could afford the down pay-
ment. So two of Charles's sons, Charles H. Queen and John E. Queen, arranged for a straw-man intermediary. One of the wealthiest white slaveholders
in the county, who lived next to Litchfield Enlarged, stepped forward and
bought the property for $481, then turned around and surrendered all of the
land back for $500. Susanna Queen and her siblings each received approxi-
mately $75 in distribution from the sale. She used some of the cash to buy a
twenty-five-acre parcel of land nearby. Charles and John paid off the purchase price for Litchfield Enlarged over several years and eventually held the
title free and clear. Then the Panic of 1857 hit. Whether they were under financial pressure or decided simply to leave Charles County for Washington, D.C., or Baltimore, the Queen brothers sold Litchfield Enlarged to a local
white taverner for $400, much less than they had paid for the property only
a few years earlier.[27]

The sudden loss of Litchfield Enlarged in 1857 should not obscure the larger point. The property the Reverend Ashton gave to the children of Susanna Queen was now in the hands of a white local with little tie to the family. But the Queen siblings had the legal acumen to navigate their inheritance and property transfer through the equity court. They had a powerful white neighbor who would act as their straw man. One of them had moved to Washington, D.C., where she and her husband had the legal papers witnessed and notarized. Further, the equity court in Charles County treated them like any other property holder, executing the responsibilities of the trust with swift and equitable results.

In the wake of the freedom suits and manumissions, thousands of African Americans were free in the Chesapeake. The free black population in Maryland had exploded, more than doubling over the 1790s to nearly twenty thousand in 1800, when one in every ten African Americans in Maryland was free. Forty years later, the number of free blacks had more than tripled to sixty-two thousand, and four in every ten African Americans were free. There were more free blacks in Maryland than in Pennsylvania, New Jersey, or even New York in this period. Nearly as many people gained their freedom in the Chesapeake as in all the Northern states combined after the Revolution. In hindsight, their emancipation was one of the largest in American history until the Civil War.[28]

Eleanora Bell v. Susan Armstead marked the end of the freedom suits for the families from Prince George's County, Maryland. For more than seventy years, they had challenged slavery in the courts, first in Maryland and then in the national capital. The Bell family brought a few more freedom suits in the 1850s, but the slaveholders ignored the court summons and refused to answer the charges. Their attorney Joseph H. Bradley kept the cases on the docket until the war broke out. In 1850 Congress had outlawed the slave trade in the District of Columbia, where it had exclusive authority to define local law. Paradoxically the end of the slave trade reduced the opportunity for freedom suits based on importation violations, one of the most reliable pathways in the law to win freedom. Of course, slavery persisted in D.C., and in the 1850s the constitutionality of slavery remained entirely unresolved. Freedom suits like Eleanora Bell's, by their very nature, suggested that slavery was locally defined and adjudicated, a creature of local law, neither sustained nor sanctioned by national legislation.

But the freedom suits had also sustained for generations an even more sweeping constitutional argument *against* slavery: that slavery was utterly incompatible with natural law and the U.S. Constitution. Legal theorists in the 1840s pointed to the constitutional guarantees of habeas corpus and a "republican form of government," and to the Fifth Amendment's language that no person could "be deprived of life, liberty, or property without due process of law." Under this constitutional theory, Congress had the power, and the obligation, to abolish slavery everywhere, including in the states.

The enslaved families from Maryland and Washington, D.C., had used the freedom suits to disrupt the legal operations of the slaveholders. They delayed the breakup of their families, sought legal assistance and funding, negotiated for freedom, and planned and coordinated escapes. A group of abolitionist lawyers in the 1840s and 1850s supported these tactics, including William Chaplin, Jacob Bigelow, David A. Hall, and to a lesser degree Joseph H. Bradley. In 1850 Chaplin was caught assisting the escape of two people enslaved by Southern congressmen. He was arrested and charged with stealing slaves in Maryland. Bradley joined his defense. By this time Chaplin and his associates had formulated a constitutional argument that slavery in Maryland had "no legal foundation." Maryland's colonial slave laws were "repugnant" to English common law as well as a violation of the king's charter. Those laws were "null and void." By extension, in Washington, D.C., the law inherited from Maryland "did not allow of or admit the holding of negroes in the perpetual hereditary bondage of slavery." They maintained that when the District of Columbia was created, "there was no *legal* slavery existing there." And Congress had no power to create it. The argument reached back to *Mahoney v. Ashton* but would never be made in court.[29]

With the passage of the Fugitive Slave Act in 1850, the constitutional ambiguities deepened. The new act followed the neutral language of the Constitution by referring not to slaves but to "persons held to service or labor." Even the enslaved, it could be argued, were persons within the United States with basic constitutional human rights, but the 1850 legislation also treated fugitives in ways otherwise unacceptable, denying them access to the writ of habeas corpus in a plain violation of both the Constitution and legal precedent. The act allowed the seizure of fugitives without a warrant, among other infringements of the Bill of Rights. In short, the act raised a set of fundamental questions that the freedom suits had kept alive for decades: Did enslaved persons have any rights under the Constitution? Was slavery a local condition without fundamental legitimacy in the law and therefore restricted to certain, specific restraints? Or did enslaved persons lack any rights at all, and was slavery national in scope and legal authority under the Constitution?

The controversy over the Fugitive Slave Act prompted Frederick Douglass to reframe his political resistance to slavery and to change his ideas about the relationship of slavery to the Constitution. Under the new act, Douglass realized that his own freedom might not withstand legal challenge. As a runaway, he could be seized. His freedom papers, issued locally, could be dismissed or ignored. His fellow abolitionists William Lloyd Garrison and his idealistic followers were so principled in their view of the Constitution as irredeemably proslavery—as a "covenant with evil"—that they chose not to interfere with the law's operation. Moral suasion would not change the facts on the ground. Unwilling to use the law or the Constitution, and to be complicit in the moral evil of slavery, the Garrisonians would not act in the face of the grave danger that the Fugitive Slave Act posed to black Americans. Their idealism was such that they would not participate in purchasing the freedom of a single enslaved person who fled bondage. Douglass realized that the Garrisonians might not come to his aid if he were captured, and he concluded that they could not mount an effective form of resistance to the political and legal power of the slaveholders.[30]

Douglass broke with the Garrisonians and began to argue that slavery was such a moral outrage that it could not be accorded legal status. The U.S. Constitution was not inherently proslavery. It contained the principles of freedom and liberty even if in practice the Constitution had been interpreted to protect slaveholders. Douglass now believed "that the Constitution, construed in the light of well-established rules of legal interpretation, might be made consistent in its details with the noble purposes avowed in its preamble; and that thereafter we should insist upon the application of such rules to that instrument, and demand that it be wielded in behalf of emancipation." Announcing his change of opinion, Douglass argued there was not "a single pro-slavery clause" in the Constitution if it were given "its plain reading." Douglass reached a dramatic conclusion: slavery "never was lawful, and never can be made so."[31]

The freedom suits proved Douglass's point, over and over again, but they had run their course. The lawsuits would not liberate Thomas Ducket in Iberville, Louisiana. Nor would they unshackle Isaac Butler in Maringouin, Louisiana, Samuel Queen enslaved in Prince George's County, or Eleanora Bell in Washington, D.C.

Total emancipation came only with war.

When the war started, the Butlers, Queens, and Mahoneys had become some of the largest free black families in Maryland. Laborers and farmers, waiters and brickmakers, they held on to hard-won jobs in Baltimore, Annapolis, and Washington. When the call for volunteers went out, they stood aside at first, perhaps seeing little gain in joining the army, with its unequal pay and terrifying danger. Eventually, many of these men were drafted in late 1863 and mustered into service in the spring of 1864. John Queen was "born free" in Anne Arundel County, had moved to Baltimore, and was married to Sarah, who was also free before the war. "We had no owners," she later said. But he had good reasons for avoiding service. Their marriage, performed by a Jesuit priest at St. Joseph's, was never recorded in the court. If he were at the front, there was no telling what could happen to Sarah and their two daughters. They could be seized and sold away or worse at any moment. Drafted into Company H of the Twenty-Ninth Regiment Infantry, U.S. Colored Troops, he served out the war. The Virginia campaign in the fall of 1864 left him permanently disabled from "exposure." His lungs were never the same. A fellow soldier later said that John had been rendered "weak as a kitten." Four Queen men died in the service. Twenty-one Butler men from Maryland did also. And at least one of the Mahoneys.[32]

For enslaved persons, whether in Maryland or Louisiana, the war created immediate but perilous avenues to freedom. Among the first of the Butler, Queen, and Mahoney men to volunteer for the Union Army were those enslaved. George Queen, born in Charles County, his parents living in Prince George's, made his way early in the war to Washington, D.C., where he enlisted at the first opportunity for black men—on June 17, 1863, in the First Regiment of the U.S. Colored Troops. A handful of enslaved Butler men also joined the First USCT. All hailed from the Western Shore of Maryland. In Louisiana Gabriel Mahoney, born in Prince George's County and probably sold to Louisiana in the 1830s, reached the Union lines and enlisted in Natchez, Mississippi, on December 8, 1863. He fought with Company I, Sixth Heavy Artillery, USCT. Daniel Mahoney, also born in Maryland, joined the First USCT in New Orleans. Twenty years old, he fled slavery and joined the Union Army. James Mahoney, born in St. Mary's County, Maryland, enlisted in Plaquemine, Iberville Parish, Louisiana. All three were likely descendants of the families who sued for their freedom in Maryland.[33]

Most of the Maryland-born men from these families fought in the war in Virginia, and by the summer of 1864 their regiments were with General Ulysses S. Grant in front of Petersburg. Daniel Queen, thirty-eight years old, was a free man living in Baltimore when he was drafted into the Nineteenth USCT. Married since 1851, father of four children, he went missing in action on July 30, 1864, at the "explosion of the mine" in the Battle of the Crater at Petersburg. His body was never found. He "never returned home." Noah Queen, likely Daniel's brother, served in the same unit. At the Crater "while in the actual line of battle," he was wounded in the right hip from an artillery shell. Years later, he was still "hardly able to walk." Andrew Queen from Anne Arundel County also fought at the Crater, sustaining a gunshot wound to the shoulder. Charles H. Butler, twenty-four, was wounded at the Crater, too—shot through both thighs. He survived. William Butler, thirty, from Anne Arundel, died of wounds he sustained at the Crater. Eighteen-year-old John Mahoney, enslaved in Maryland, enlisted in the Union Army in March 1864. Four months later he, too, fought at Petersburg in the Crater. George Mahoney, from Baltimore, fought alongside him. Promoted to sergeant, lauded for his "excellent character," he was killed at Petersburg.[34]

While these soldiers desperately fought to destroy slavery in the United States, slaveholders insisted on its legal force in Maryland to the bitter end. So much so that Ned Queen, Daniel Brown, Susan Bordley, Elizabeth Bordley, and Minty Chew, all descendants of the families who sued and won their freedom in the 1790s, were convicted in May 1864 for "enticing slaves to run away." As punishment they were each sentenced to be "sold as slaves" by the Anne Arundel County court—Ned Queen for two years. Slavery did not end in Maryland until November 1, 1864, when white voters barely approved a referendum for a new constitution that amended the state's Declaration of Rights. "All persons held to service or labor as slaves are hereby declared free." In Prince George's County only 149 white men voted for the abolition of slavery; 1,293 voted against. Statewide, absentee ballots cast by federal troops were decisive in passing the new constitution. But even Maryland's emancipation amendment permitted slavery for those convicted "in punishment of crime." Ned Queen's particular enslavement would continue to the end of the war.[35]

Early in the war, however, Republicans in Congress passed the Compensated Emancipation Act to abolish slavery in Washington, D.C. The measure was modeled on British emancipation, with the national government compensating slaveholders for the human property they agreed to relinquish. The plan satisfied conservatives who worried that emancipation amounted to a massive taking of property. Compensation, it bears repeating, went to the slaveholders, not to the people they enslaved. Eleven years after her unsuccessful bid for freedom, Eleanora Bell was nineteen years old and had a daughter named Caroline. They received nothing.

Instead, in April 1862 the government compensated the Armsteads.

Susan Armstead had bequeathed the Bells to her daughter, Sarah Jane O'Brien. She was as determined to hold on to them as her mother. O'Brien had testified as a witness for her mother against Ann Bell in her 1840 trial, and she testified again for her mother against twelve-year-old Eleanora in her 1851 freedom trial. The Bells' freedom had quite literally been stolen from them, and yet under the Emancipation Act, the U.S. government paid O'Brien $394.20 for Eleanor and $43.80 for Caroline.

Throughout the long struggle for freedom, Daniel's mother, Lucy Bell, a free woman since the 1820s, helped her children and grandchildren fight the harrowing legal and personal battles against their enslavement and separation. She was there when Daniel bought his freedom in 1835. She was there when her daughter Ann won her freedom in court in 1840. There when four of her grandchildren were sold and taken away to Louisiana. There when her youngest daughter, Caroline, lost her freedom suit in 1850. And undoubtedly she was there when her granddaughter Eleanora did not prevail in the last freedom trial.

But Lucy Bell lived to witness Eleanora's emancipation in April 1862. Ninety-nine years old, she died in the summer of that year. The sweep of her life encompassed the entire period from before the American Revolution to the American Civil War. Her family's history was the nation's. Over her lifetime tens of thousands of African Americans in Maryland gained their freedom, and yet countless men, women, and children had been taken away in the slave trade. Slavery in Maryland had continued unabated, its violence, duplicity, and degradation plain to see.

In the early summer of 1862, the Union Army was poised to attack Richmond, but the fate of slavery in the United States was still far from clear. The war might end with slavery intact in the states that had seceded, as well as in states like Maryland that had not. Or slavery might be ended entirely. The revolutionary promise of freedom might be fulfilled and human bondage declared illegal and unconstitutional once and for all. Daniel Bell, Ann Bell, Harriet Ash, and Caroline Bell pooled their resources to commemorate and honor their mother. Each of her children had sued for freedom. Each contended with the lies of the slaveholding class and the violence and theft of enslavement. Together they paid for a simple but eloquent headstone and purchased a burial plot at Washington's Congressional Cemetery, a marker of permanence, belonging, rootedness, and lineage symbolizing the family's birthright claim on the nation's history.

In Memory of Our Mother
Lucy Bell
Who died June 8th, 1862
Aged 99 years
Unseat thy bosom faithful tomb
Take this new treasure to thy trust
And give these sacred relics room
To slumber in the silent dust.

Appendix

The following diagrams are derived from the court records of the freedom suits and other published sources. They represent only the relationships of the main protagonists in this book and are not intended to be complete family trees or networks. Each diagram is a guide to the relationships at the heart of the freedom suits.

THE QUEEN FAMILY

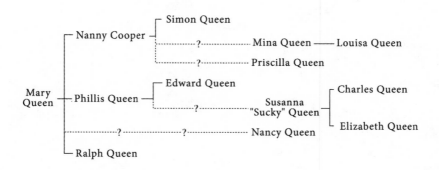

······ Possible relationship to ancestor

THE JESUITS OF MARYLAND

c. 1730s–1815	c. 1750s–1830s		c. 1790s–1860s
	Leonard Neale		
John Carroll	Francis Neale	Notley Young	William McSherry
John Ashton	Charles Neale	Joseph Mobberly	Thomas F. Mulledy
	Charles Sewall		

THE KEY FAMILY

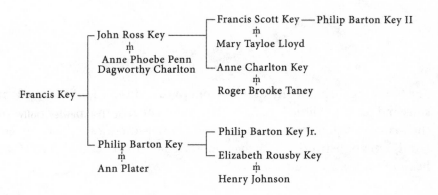

Francis Key —

- John Ross Key —
  ṁ
  Anne Phoebe Penn
  Dagworthy Charlton

  - Francis Scott Key — Philip Barton Key II
    ṁ
    Mary Tayloe Lloyd
  - Anne Charlton Key
    ṁ
    Roger Brooke Taney

- Philip Barton Key —
  ṁ
  Ann Plater

  - Philip Barton Key Jr.
  - Elizabeth Rousby Key
    ṁ
    Henry Johnson

ṁ Married

THE JOICE/MAHONEY FAMILY

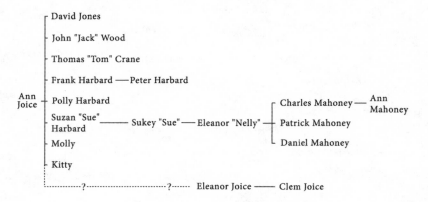

Ann
Joice

- David Jones
- John "Jack" Wood
- Thomas "Tom" Crane
- Frank Harbard — Peter Harbard
- Polly Harbard
- Suzan "Sue" Harbard — Sukey "Sue" — Eleanor "Nelly" —
  - Charles Mahoney — Ann Mahoney
  - Patrick Mahoney
  - Daniel Mahoney
- Molly
- Kitty
- ⸺?⸺?⸺ Eleanor Joice — Clem Joice

⸺ Possible relationship to ancestor

THE BELL FAMILY

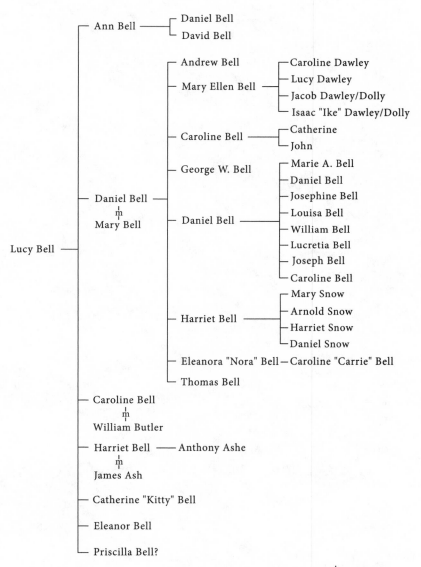

Lucy Bell

- Ann Bell
  - Daniel Bell
  - David Bell
- Daniel Bell
  m
  Mary Bell
  - Andrew Bell
  - Mary Ellen Bell
    - Caroline Dawley
    - Lucy Dawley
    - Jacob Dawley/Dolly
    - Isaac "Ike" Dawley/Dolly
  - Caroline Bell
    - Catherine
    - John
  - George W. Bell
  - Daniel Bell
    - Marie A. Bell
    - Daniel Bell
    - Josephine Bell
    - Louisa Bell
    - William Bell
    - Lucretia Bell
    - Joseph Bell
    - Caroline Bell
  - Harriet Bell
    - Mary Snow
    - Arnold Snow
    - Harriet Snow
    - Daniel Snow
  - Eleanora "Nora" Bell — Caroline "Carrie" Bell
  - Thomas Bell
- Caroline Bell
  m
  William Butler
- Harriet Bell — Anthony Ashe
  m
  James Ash
- Catherine "Kitty" Bell
- Eleanor Bell
- Priscilla Bell?

m
Married

Notes

ABA	Archdiocese of Baltimore Archives, St. Mary's Seminary and University, Baltimore
AOMOL	*Archives of Maryland Online,* http://aomol.msa.maryland.gov
CRCC	Corporation of Roman Catholic Clergymen of Maryland
EPA	English Province Archives, Archives of the British Province of the Society of Jesus, London
GCWS	General Court of the Western Shore
GSA	*Georgetown Slavery Archive,* http://slaveryarchive.georgetown.edu
MPA	Maryland Province Archives of the Society of Jesus, Booth Family Center for Special Collections, Georgetown University Library, Washington, D.C.
MSA	Maryland State Archives, Annapolis, msa.maryland.gov
NA	National Archives, Kew, United Kingdom
NARA	National Archives and Records Administration, Washington, D.C.
OSCYS	*O Say Can You See: Early Washington, D.C., Law & Family,* ed. William G. Thomas III et al., University of Nebraska–Lincoln, http://earlywashingtondc.org
RG	Record Group

PROLOGUE

1. "Liturgy of Remembrance, Contrition, and Hope," Georgetown University, April 18, 2017. Notes and recording in possession of the author. A full recording is available at from Georgetown University at https://www.youtube.com/watch?v=tO4Xsz36kTU, with Sandra Green Thomas's remarks beginning at minute 29:33. Several major research projects have come to the fore around the Georgetown history. First, the *Georgetown Slavery Archive* (slaveryarchive.georgetown.edu, herein abbreviated *GSA*) is a repository of archival materials related to the Maryland Jesuits and Georgetown University. Second, the *Georgetown Memory Project* (www.georgetown memoryproject.org) is an independent nonprofit dedicated to researching, finding, and advocating for the descendants of the 272. The project released its database of descendants in May 2019 with *American Ancestors* by the New England Historic Genealogical Society (see the *GU272 Descendants, 1785–2000,* database www .americanancestors.org/search/databasesearch/2756/gu272-descendants-1785-2000). Third, historian Sharon Leon has undertaken a highly significant digital history-based analysis of the families on the Jesuit plantations. See Sharon Leon, *The Jesuit Plantation Project: An Examination of the Enslaved Persons Owned (and Sold) by the Maryland Province Jesuits, 1717–1838* (https://jesuitplantationproject.org). I have also followed closely the Universities Studying Slavery working group at the University

of Virginia since 2014 (slavery.virginia.edu/universities-studying-slavery) and
other university reports, especially Stephen Mullen and Simon Newman, *Slavery,
Abolition and the University of Glasgow, Report and Recommendations of the
University of Glasgow History of Slavery Steering Committee* (September 2018), and
Princeton Seminary and Slavery: A Report of the Historical Audit Committee (slavery
.ptsem.edu/full-report). Also see Craig Steven Wilder, *Ebony and Ivy: Race, Slavery,
and the Troubled History of America's Universities,* reprint ed. (New York: Bloomsbury, 2014).

2. Robert Emmett Curran, *Shaping American Catholicism: Maryland and New York,
1805–1915* (Washington, D.C.: Catholic University Press, 2012), 36–38. See also
Edward F. Beckett, "Listening to Our History: Inculturation and Jesuit Slaveholding," *Studies in the Spirituality of Jesuits* 28, no. 5 (1996), which explains the Jesuits as
paternalists: "To a certain extent, the plantation formed a kind of domestic parish to
which slaves belonged" (11). Beckett concludes that Jesuits treated slaves "no worse
than" other slaveholders, but following Curran, he emphasizes that the Jesuits
encouraged slaves to gain skills. In the most recent and thorough review of Jesuit
slaveholding in Maryland, Thomas Murphy, S.J., argues that the Jesuits understood
themselves as paternalists and as superior, like all other enslavers in the early
American republic. His account is the most balanced examination of the Jesuit role
in slaveholding, yet his stance is similarly apologetic. As for their decision to sell
supernumerary slaves, Murphy concludes that the Jesuits could not bring themselves to do so and instead sold the physically fit and "missed an opportunity to
develop a morally strong case for making profits out of right motives." See Murphy,
Jesuit Slaveholding in Maryland, 1717–1838 (New York: Routledge, 2001), 72.

3. A central aspect of the approach taken here is historical imagination. This asks
readers to experience a world other than their own and to step outside of themselves
into the characters in this history. Recent examples of narrative imagination include
Imani Perry, *Looking for Lorraine: The Radiant and Radical Life of Lorraine
Hansberry* (Boston: Beacon Press, 2018); Lisa Brooks, *Our Beloved Kin: A New
History of King Philip's War* (New Haven: Yale University Press, 2018); and Saidiya
Hartman, *Wayward Lives, Beautiful Experiments: Intimate Histories of Social
Upheaval* (New York: W. W. Norton, 2019). Each is an inspiration in the form of its
narrative and in its attention to re-creating the voices, situations, and daily
experiences of people left out of the archive. See also Natalie Zemon Davis, *The
Return of Martin Guerre* (Cambridge: Harvard University Press, 1983).

4. This book's narrative draws on the court records and relationships uncovered in an
edited digital collection of all freedom petitions filed in the Circuit Court of the
District of Columbia between 1800 and 1862 and antecedent freedom suits filed in
Maryland and Virginia courts. The collection includes over five hundred freedom
suits with nearly eight hundred enslaved plaintiffs. The collection draws on relevant
court papers and documents from the NARA, MSA, and Library of Virginia. See
William G. Thomas III et al., *O Say Can You See: Early Washington, D.C., Law and
Family* (University of Nebraska–Lincoln, earlywashingtondc.org, herein abbreviated
as *OSCYS*). For other similar approaches to digital legal history, see *Law and History
Review* 34, no. 4, special issue: Digital Law and History (2016), esp. Tim Hitchcock
and William J. Turkel, "The *Old Bailey Proceedings, 1674–1913:* Text Mining for
Evidence of Court Behavior," 929–955.

5. All names throughout this book correspond to the full names used in the freedom suits. The Jesuits referred to Edward Queen only as "Ned," but I use the name he used for himself. Similarly, in 1829 Henry Clay, the outgoing secretary of state and former Speaker of the House, referred to Charlotte Dupee only by the diminutive "Lotty," but I refer to her by the full name she used after her freedom suit.

6. Eric Papenfuse, "From Recompense to Revolution: *Mahoney v. Ashton* and the Transfiguration of Maryland Culture, 1791–1802," *Slavery and Abolition* 15, no. 3 (1994): 39–62. On Maryland, see Patricia Ann Reid, "Between Slavery and Freedom" (Ph.D. diss., University of Iowa, 2006); and Patricia A. Reid, "The Legal Construction of Whiteness and Citizenship in Maryland, 1780–1820," *Law, Culture and the Humanities* (2016), https://doi.org/10.1177/1743872116652886.

7. Every case, the legal scholar Hendrik Hartog has written, "carried with it a buried politics" and was "at most a momentary conclusion to ongoing struggles." See Hartog, "Introduction to Symposium on 'Critical Legal Histories,'" *Law and Social Inquiry* 37, no. 1 (2012): 147–154. On the defining work in critical legal studies and law as constitutive of consciousness, see Robert W. Gordon, "Critical Legal Histories," *Stanford Law Review* 36, no. 1/2 (1984): 57–125.

8. On New York, see David Gellman, *Emancipating New York: The Politics of Slavery and Freedom, 1777–1827* (Baton Rouge: Louisiana State University Press, 2006). Gellman traces the political discourse and the give and take of the political process of emancipation, arguing that although the Revolution did not disrupt slavery, it did plant "the seeds of an enduring antislavery discourse" (27). See also Manisha Sinha, *The Slave's Cause: A History of Abolition* (New Haven: Yale University Press, 2016).

9. Leslie Friedman Goldstein, "Slavery and the Marshall Court: Preventing 'Oppressions of the Minor Party'?" *Maryland Law Review* 67, no. 1 (2007): 166. See also Paul Finkelman, *Supreme Injustice: Slavery in the Nation's Highest Court* (Cambridge: Harvard University Press, 2018); R. Kent Newmyer, *John Marshall and the Heroic Age of the Supreme Court* (Baton Rouge: Louisiana State University Press, 2001), 414–434; and Frances Howell Rudko, "Pause at the Rubicon, John Marshall and Emancipation: Reparations in the Early National Period?" *John Marshall Law Review* 35, no. 1 (2001): 75–89.

10. My purpose is to describe the situation of these legal actors in the freedom suits, free and enslaved, black, white, and mixed families, and to situate them in the context of a specific place and time and to make sense of what they were doing and their experiences. For a cogent assessment of this situational approach, see Sarah Knott, "Narrating the Age of Revolution," *William and Mary Quarterly*, 3rd ser., 73, no. 1 (2016): 3–26. See also Walter Johnson, "On Agency," *Journal of Social History* 37, no. 1 (2003): 113–124. Other examples of a situational approach include Adam Rothman, *Beyond Freedom's Reach: A Kidnapping in the Twilight of Slavery* (Cambridge: Harvard University Press, 2015); Rebecca J. Scott and Jean M. Hébrard, *Freedom Papers: An Atlantic Odyssey in the Age of Emancipation* (Cambridge: Harvard University Press, 2014); Rebecca J. Scott, "Paper Thin: Freedom and Re-Enslavement in the Diaspora of the Haitian Revolution," *Law and History Review* 29, no. 4 (2011): 1061–1087; Walter Johnson, "Resetting the Legal History of Slavery: Divination, Torture, Poisoning, Murder, Revolution, Emancipation, and Re-Enslavement," *Law and History Review* 29, no. 4 (2011): 1089–1095; and Hendrik Hartog, *The Trouble with Minna: A Case of Slavery and Emancipation in the*

Antebellum North (Chapel Hill: University of North Carolina Press, 2018). In the use
of legal records to recover the history of free black families and their world, I am
especially influenced by Melvin Patrick Ely, *Israel on the Appomattox: A Southern
Experiment in Black Freedom from the 1790s Through the Civil War* (New York:
Vintage, 2004).

11. Significantly, the statutes in the 1780s prohibited importation of slaves and otherwise restricted slavery. For statutes in the 1780s that built on colonial acts but did
not authorize slavery a priori, see "An Act to Prohibit the Bringing of Slaves in to
This State" (1783), *Hanson's Laws of Maryland, 1763–1784, AOMOL*, 203:350; "An Act
to Prevent the Inconveniences Arising from Slaves Being Permitted to Act as Free"
(1787), *Laws of Maryland, 1785–1791, AOMOL*, 204:231; and "An Act to Repeal Certain
Parts of an Act, Entitled, An Act to Prevent Disabled and Superannuated Slaves
Being Set Free, or the Manumission of Slaves by Any Last Will and Testament"
(1790), *Laws of Maryland, 1785–1791, AOMOL*, 204:458. On the instability of the law
of slavery in the colonies, see Jonathan A. Bush, "Free to Enslave: The Foundations
of Colonial American Slave Law," *Yale Journal of Law and the Humanities* 5, no. 2
(1993): 417–470. In contrast, Holly Brewer has argued that slavery was never
customary in the law but instead contested and constructed within common-law
legal forms. See Brewer, "Slavery, Sovereignty, and 'Inheritable Blood': Reconsidering John Locke and the Origins of American Slavery," *American Historical Review*
122, no. 4 (2017): 1038–1078. Brewer's forthcoming book, *"Inheritable Blood": Slavery
and Sovereignty in Early America and the British Empire,* promises to develop her
stunning and original thesis situating the development of American slavery in the
legal practices surrounding the divine right of kings. On the importance of the
Somerset decision, the literature is voluminous. For its imperial context and
repercussions, see esp. George William Van Cleve, *A Slaveholder's Union: Slavery,
Politics, and the Constitution in the Early American Republic* (Chicago: University of
Chicago Press, 2010), chap. 1.

12. For the argument of antislavery lawyers, see *The Case of William Chaplin* (Boston:
Chaplin Committee, 1851), 9–11. Other scholars have focused on the lack of founda-
tional law authorizing slavery in the U.S. Constitution, despite its obvious recogni-
tion of slavery. Sean Wilentz, *No Property in Man: Slavery and Antislavery at the
Nation's Founding* (Cambridge: Harvard University Press, 2018), 142–145, argues
that the Constitutional Convention "refused to validate property rights in slaves."
See also James Oakes, *Freedom National: The Destruction of Slavery in the United
States, 1861–1865* (New York: W. W. Norton, 2013), 2–9. In contrast, the legal scholar
Paul Finkelman has argued, more than any other scholar, that the U.S. Constitution
was entirely proslavery in meaning and effect; his voluminous essays and law review
articles on this subject include: "Frederick Douglass's Constitution: From Garriso-
nian Abolitionist to Lincoln Republican," *Missouri Law Review* 81, no. 1 (2016): 2–73;
"The Founders and Slavery: Little Ventured, Little Gained," *Yale Journal of Law and
the Humanities* 13, no. 2 (2001): 413–447; and "How the Proslavery Constitution Led
to the Civil War," *Rutgers Law Journal* 43, no. 3 (2013): 405. A more nuanced
interpretation of slavery as essential to the formation of the American Constitution
can be seen in David Waldstreicher, *Slavery's Constitution: From Revolution to
Ratification* (New York: Hill and Wang, 2009); and Van Cleve, *Slaveholder's Union*.
On the law's possibilities, Annette Gordon-Reed has argued that it was "highly

improbable that the end of chattel slavery in the United States could have been achieved through the reformist operations of the law." See Gordon-Reed, "Logic and Experience: Thomas Jefferson's Life in the Law," in *Slavery and the American South,* ed. Winthrop Jordan (Jackson: University Press of Mississippi, 2003), 4. My approach complements Michael Meranze's in "Hargrave's Nightmare and Taney's Dream," *UC Irvine Law Review* 4, no. 1 (2014): 219–238, who argues, "No one should imagine that the institution of slavery faced an imminent threat of destruction in the 1770s and 1780s. But we need to recognize the possibility that slave owners would lose 'their' property and that slavery might have faced unprecedented political and legal challenge" (226). Meranze points to the landmark significance of the *Somerset* decision in denying common-law support for slavery and creating a "new constitutional and juridical 'problematization' of slavery" (226). He notes the contingent outcomes possible in the 1780s and that federal ratification of the Constitution accomplished "the constitutionalization of slavery itself" (234).

13. Clement Dorsey, *The General Public Statutory Law and Public Local Law of the State of Maryland from the Year 1692 to 1839 Inclusive,* vol. 1 (Baltimore: John D. Toy, 1840), xlviii. The amendment was ratified March 10, 1837: see *Laws Made and Passed by the General Assembly of the State of Maryland* (Annapolis, Md.: Jeremiah Hughes, 1837), chap. 197, sec. 26. "An Act Declaring Domestic Slavery to Be Lawful in This State," passed March 20, 1840, *Session Laws, 1839, AOMOL,* 600:42.

14. For a cogent analysis of the interpretation stressing persistent conflict over the politics of slavery and race from the Revolution to the Civil War, see James Oakes, "Conflict vs. Racial Consensus in the History of Antislavery Politics," in *Contesting Slavery: The Politics of Bondage and Freedom in the New American Nation,* ed. John Craig Hammond and Matthew Mason (Charlottesville: University of Virginia Press, 2011), 291–298.

15. The courts in Maryland separated the freedom suits in their dockets as "Petitions," a distinct form of pleading under the common law. On the inalienable right to petition, see Larry D. Kramer, *The People Themselves: Popular Constitutionalism and Judicial Review* (Oxford: Oxford University Press, 2004), 25. See Loren Schweninger, *Appealing for Liberty: Freedom Suits in the South* (Oxford: Oxford University Press, 2018). The scale of African American use of the legal system defies easy categorization but has only recently been recognized. See esp. Kimberly M. Welch, *Black Litigants in the Antebellum American South* (Chapel Hill: University of North Carolina Press, 2018). In June 2015, the Fairfax Circuit Court Historic Records Center in Fairfax County, Va., began an exhaustive search of all court records to record the names of all African Americans mentioned in that county between 1742 and 1870. They found over 21,000 enslaved and over 3,000 free blacks mentioned. Over 600 manumissions were recorded. In Anne Arundel County, Md., there were over 1,000 manumissions between 1780 and 1830. See John Joseph Condon, "Manumission, Slavery and Family in Post-Revolutionary Rural Chesapeake: Anne Arundel County, Maryland" (Ph.D. diss., University of Minnesota, 2001).

16. Welch, *Black Litigants in the Antebellum American South;* Schweninger, *Appealing for Liberty;* Pedro Jimenez Cantisano and Mariana Armond Dias Paes, "Legal Reasoning in a Slave Society (Brazil, 1860–1888)," *Law and History Review* 36, no. 3 (2018): 471–510; Sarah L. Gronningsater, "'On Behalf of His Race and the Lemmon Slaves': Louis Napoleon, Northern Black Legal Culture, and the Politics of Sectional

Crisis," *Journal of the Civil War Era* 7, no. 2 (2017): 206–241; Ariela Gross and Alejandro de la Fuente, *Becoming Free, Becoming Black: Race, Freedom, and Law in Cuba, Virginia, and Louisiana* (Cambridge: Cambridge University Press, 2020); Kelly M. Kennington, *In the Shadow of Dred Scott: St. Louis Freedom Suits and the Legal Culture of Slavery in Antebellum America* (Athens: University of Georgia Press, 2017); Anne Silverwood Twitty, *Before Dred Scott: Slavery and Legal Culture in the American Confluence, 1787–1857* (New York: Cambridge University Press, 2016); Loren Schweninger, "Freedom Suits, African American Women, and the Genealogy of Slavery," *William and Mary Quarterly*, 3rd ser., 71, no. 1 (2014): 35–62; Ariela Gross and Alejandro de la Fuente, "Slaves, Free Blacks, and Race in the Legal Regimes of Cuba, Louisiana, and Virginia: A Comparison," *North Carolina Law Review* 91, no. 5 (2013): 1699–1756; Honor Sachs, "'Freedom by a Judgment': The Legal History of an Afro-Indian Family," *Law and History Review* 30, no. 1 (2012): 173–203; Jason A. Gillmer, "Suing for Freedom: Interracial Sex, Slave Law, and Racial Identity in the Post-Revolutionary and Antebellum South," *North Carolina Law Review* 82, no. 4 (2004): 535–619. On Massachusetts, see Emily Blanck, "Seventeen-Eighty-Three: The Turning Point in the Law of Slavery and Freedom in Massachusetts," *New England Quarterly* 75, no. 1 (2002): 24–51. On Maryland and the legal and social context of manumission, see T. Stephen Whitman, *The Price of Freedom: Slavery and Manumission in Baltimore and Early National Maryland* (Lexington: University Press of Kentucky, 1997), for the most thorough analysis of manumission and term slavery in the Chesapeake. See also Jessica Millward, *Finding Charity's Folk: Enslaved and Free Black Women in Maryland* (Athens: University of Georgia Press, 2015); and T. Stephen Whitman, *Challenging Slavery in the Chesapeake: Black and White Resistance to Human Bondage, 1775–1865* (Baltimore: Johns Hopkins University Press, 2006).

17. The history of slavery in the law has been dominated by the idea of the law as an instrument of hegemony in Eugene Genovese, *Roll, Jordan, Roll: The World the Slaves Made* (New York: Vintage Books, 1974), 25–49. My views have been shaped by Ariela Gross's "Reflections on Law, Culture, and Slavery" and Laura Edwards's "Commentary," both in *Slavery and the American South: Essays and Commentaries,* ed. Winthrop Jordan (Jackson: University Press of Mississippi, 2003), 57–82, 82–92. Other scholars have also studied the way enslaved and free blacks in the South used the law, including bringing civil suits to protect property. See Melvyn Patrick Ely, *Israel on the Appomattox: A Southern Experiment in Black Freedom from the 1790s Through the Civil War* (New York: Vintage, 2004); Dylan Penningroth, *The Claims of Kinfolk: African American Property and Community in the Nineteenth-Century South* (Chapel Hill: University of North Carolina Press, 2003); Kenneth Aslakson, *Making Race in the Courtroom: The Legal Construction of Three Races in New Orleans* (New York: New York University Press, 2014); and Ariela Gross, *What Blood Won't Tell: A History of Race on Trial in America* (Cambridge: Harvard University Press, 2008). Andrés Reséndez, *The Other Slavery: The Uncovered Story of Indian Enslavement in America* (New York: Houghton Mifflin Harcourt, 2016), suggests that the notion that a slave could sue his or her master to attain freedom "would have been laughable to most southerners during the first half of the nineteenth century" (47–48). Evidence to the contrary can be found in the thousands of petition for freedom suits filed in Washington, D.C., New Orleans, La., and

St. Louis, Mo., courts, as well as in many other jurisdictions. The fights for freedom
Reséndez describes in sixteenth-century Spanish courts resemble those undertaken
in Maryland two centuries later (55–58).

18. See, e.g., the lawsuits filed against William H. Williams in Jeff Forret, *Williams'
Gang: A Notorious Slave Trader and His Cargo of Black Convicts* (Cambridge:
Cambridge University Press, 2020), 109–126, 207–235; Pippa Holloway, "Race and
Law from the Bottom Up in the Nineteenth-Century," *Journal of Southern History*
85, no. 2 (2019): 393–408; and Akhil Reed Amar, *America's Unwritten Constitution*
(New York: Basic Books, 2015), 104–105.

19. On the significant methodological difficulties posed in the recovery of marginalized
subjects in legal proceedings and archives, see esp. Ananya Chakravarti, "Mapping
'Gabriel': Space, Identity and Slavery in the Late Sixteenth-Century Indian Ocean,"
Past and Present 243, no. 1 (2019): 5–34. See also Simon P. Newman, "Hidden in Plain
Sight: Escaped Slaves in Late Eighteenth and Early Nineteenth-Century Jamaica,"
William and Mary Quarterly, 3rd ser., 76, no. 1 (2019): 33–40; and Marisa J. Fuentes,
Dispossessed Lives: Enslaved Women, Violence, and the Archive (Philadelphia:
University of Pennsylvania Press, 2016), 144–146. On reading court dockets as "lies"
and the legal process as creating fictions and "stock figures," see Walter Johnson,
Soul by Soul: Life Inside the Antebellum Slave Market (Cambridge: Harvard
University Press, 1999), 12. I am indebted to the late Joseph C. Miller, mentor,
colleague, and friend, for the pole and tent metaphor and for his detailed written
comments on the methodological issues raised in this study (in possession of the
author).

20. Recent studies of abolition in Anglo-American legal history stress the contradiction
between slavery and liberalism, emphasizing the emergence of an antislavery
constitutionalism. See esp. Dorothy E. Roberts, "Abolition Constitutionalism,"
Harvard Law Review 133, no. 1 (2019): 49–60. See Carole Emberton, "Unwriting the
Freedom Narrative: A Review Essay," *Journal of Southern History* 82, no. 2 (2016):
377–394; and Brewer, "Slavery, Sovereignty, and 'Inheritable Blood.'"

21. Recent scholarship related to freedom suits and the significance of black legal
culture and legal activism is substantial. The 2020 American Historical Association
Conference in New York City included a panel on "Perspectives on Enslaved
Women, Freedom and the Law in the Atlantic World" that featured the latest
scholarship on freedom suits across the Atlantic World, with papers by Randy J.
Sparks, Alexandra Havrylyshyn, and Deirdre Lyons. For recent published work on
freedom suits, see esp. Welch, *Black Litigants in the Antebellum American South;*
Schweninger, *Appealing for Liberty;* Cantisano and Paes, "Legal Reasoning in a Slave
Society"; Gronningsater, "'On Behalf of His Race and the Lemmon Slaves'";
Kennington, *In the Shadow of Dred Scott;* Twitty, *Before Dred Scott;* Schweninger,
"Freedom Suits"; Gross and de la Fuente, "Slaves, Free Blacks, and Race"; Sachs,
"'Freedom by a Judgment'"; Richard S. Newman, "'Lucky to Be Born in Pennsylva-
nia': Free Soil, Fugitive Slaves and the Making of Pennsylvania's Anti-Slavery
Borderland," *Slavery and Abolition* 32, no. 3 (2011): 413–430; Gillmer, "Suing for
Freedom"; Thea K. Hunter, "Publishing Freedom, Winning Arguments: Somerset,
Natural Rights and Massachusetts Freedom Cases, 1772–1836" (Ph.D. diss., Colum-
bia University, 2005); Lea Vandervelde, *Redemption Songs: Suing for Freedom*
(Oxford: Oxford University Press, 2014); Kristen Sword, "Remembering Dinah

Nevil: Strategic Deceptions in Eighteenth-Century Antislavery," *Journal of American History* 97, no. 2 (2010): 315–343; Ariela Gross, *Double Character: Slavery and Mastery in the Antebellum Courtroom* (Princeton: Princeton University Press, 2000); Kelia Grinberg, "Freedom Suits and Civil Law in Brazil and the United States," *Slavery and Abolition* 22, no. 3 (2001): 66–82; Brian P. Owensby, "How Juan and Lenour Won Their Freedom: Litigation and Liberty in Seventeenth-Century Mexico," *Hispanic American Historical Review* 85, no. 1 (2005): 39–80; Edlie L. Wong, *Neither Fugitive nor Free: Atlantic Slavery, Freedom Suits, and the Legal Culture of Travel* (New York: New York University Press, 2009); and Sue Peabody, *"There Are No Slaves in France": The Political Culture of Race and Slavery in the Ancien Régime* (Oxford: Oxford University Press, 1996). For a similar point about the role of procedural battles, see Daniel Farbman, "Resistance Lawyering," *California Law Review* 107, no. 6 (2019): 1877–1953. Of the abolitionist lawyers in the 1850s, Farbman notes, "It was their work against the Law from within its own procedural framework that was most legally and politically effective" (1880). He distinguishes between the "zealous advocate," who "accepts the rules of the game and seeks to play within them to win," and the "resistance lawyer," who "sees the game as rigged and tries to destroy it from within" (1933).

22. Frederick Douglass, "Change of Opinion Announced," *North Star,* May 15, 1851, reprinted in the *Liberator,* May 23, 1851. I consider the freedom suits at the center of an African American–led movement to restrict and challenge slavery, and I argue here that slavery was developed within the framework of English law, rather than customary, and susceptible to legal challenge. James Oakes's book *Freedom National* focuses on the Republican Party's efforts to "denationalize slavery" (15–26), but the legal opposition to slavery came much earlier and derived from the freedom suits more than from Salmon Chase's 1837 arguments in Matilda Lawrence's case and John Quincy Adams's 1841 arguments in the *Creole* case. On slavery's surprising weakness in colonial law, see Bush, "Free to Enslave." On the importance of freedom suits, see Sinha, *Slave's Cause,* 17, 68–70. For a set of observations about the legal development of slavery in New England, arguing that slavery was developed in custom largely outside of law, see Wendy Warren, *New England Bound: Slavery and Colonization in Early America* (New York: W. W. Norton, 2017). On hereditary enslavement and the "indeterminate status of British subjecthood" under common law and constitutionalism in the British colonial empire, see Brooke N. Newman, *A Dark Inheritance: Blood, Race, and Sex in Colonial Jamaica* (New Haven: Yale University Press, 2018), 11. See also the pathbreaking study by Hunter, "Publishing Freedom, Winning Arguments."

23. Note that the Jesuits' White Marsh plantation was located in Prince George's County. There was a contemporaneous "White Marsh Farm" located north of Baltimore in Baltimore County on land held by the Ridgely family. The latter is currently an unincorporated community called White Marsh, Md.

24. Prince George's County, Commissioner of Slave Statistics, 1867–1869, CE404, MSA.

25. The following narratives about different historical forms of complicity and trauma have inspired my approach to personal history: Timothy Garton Ash, *The File: A Personal History* (New York: Vintage, 1998); Edward Ball, *Slaves in the Family* (New York: Farrar, Straus and Giroux, 1999); and Saidiya Hartman, *Lose Your Mother: A Journey Along the Atlantic Slave Route* (New York: Farrar, Straus and Giroux, 2008).

See also the special issue on "Historical Justice" in *Rethinking History: The Journal of Theory and Practice,* esp. Klaus Newman, "Historians and the Yearning for Historical Justice," *Rethinking History: The Journal of Theory and Practice* 18, no. 2 (2014): 145–164.

26. The approach taken here to historical reconciliation has been shaped by my participation in the Duke Divinity School's 2017 Summer Institute for Reconciliation, in particular the seminar on "Narratives" led by Dr. David Anderson Hooker. The structure of the interludes in this book follow the framework of reconciliation described in David Anderson Hooker and Amy Potter Czajkowski, *Transforming Historical Harms* (Harrisonburg, Va.: Coming to the Table and Center for Justice and Peacebuilding, Eastern Mennonite University, 2013). I have also been influenced by Ana Lucia Araujo, *Reparations for Slavery and the Slave Trade: A Transnational and Comparative History* (New York: Bloomsbury, 2017); Ana Lucia Araujo, *Shadows of the Slave Past: Memory, Heritage, and Slavery* (New York: Routledge, 2014); Ta-Nehisi Coates, "The Case for Reparations," *Atlantic,* June 2014, 51–68; Ta-Nehisi Coates, "Are Reparations Due to African Americans?" *New York Times,* June 8, 2014; Ta-Nehisi Coates, *Between the World and Me* (New York: Spiegel and Grau, 2015); Alondra Nelson, *The Social Life of DNA: Race, Reparations, and Reconciliation After the Genome* (Boston: Beacon Press, 2016); Elazar Barkan, "Introduction: Historians and Historical Reconciliation," in the AHR Forum: Truth and Reconciliation in History, *American Historical Review* 114, no. 4 (2009): 899–913; Bryan Stevenson, *Equal Justice Initiative,* http://eji.org; Alon Confino, "Collective Memory and Cultural History: Problems of Method," *American Historical Review* 102, no. 5 (December 1997): 1386–1403; and Stephen Mullen and Simon Newman, *Slavery, Abolition and the University of Glasgow, Report and Recommendations of the University of Glasgow History of Slavery Steering Committee* (University of Glasgow, September 2018), esp. 16–17, recommending a "Programme of reparative justice," https://www.gla.ac.uk/media/media_607547_smxx.pdf. The *Coming to the Table* initiative (http://comingtothetable.org) has been an important beginning point for American families to come to terms with the history of enslavement. See Dionne Ford and Jill Strauss, *Slavery's Descendants: Shared Legacies of Race and Reconciliation* (New Brunswick, N.J.: Rutgers University Press, 2019). On language used throughout this book and editorial decisions about terminology, I have followed the helpful guidance of P. Gabrielle Foreman et al., "Writing About Slavery? Teaching About Slavery? This Might Help," community-sourced document, https://docs.google.com/document/d/1A4TEdDgYslX -hlKezLodMIM71My3KTNozxRvoIQTOQs/mobilebasic. My choices of terminology attempt to recognize the historical particularity of American enslavement and the human beings at the heart of this story. They defied the categories imposed upon them and should not be reduced to a term that denies their humanity. I refer to the historical system and institution as "slavery" and the people and the families who were enslaved as "enslaved." I do not use the term "slaveowner" unless in direct quotations and refer to the enslavers generally as "slaveholders." Throughout I try to make clear that they acted as enslavers and engaged in *slaving.* When referring to specific historical aspects of the law's operations, I have retained the term "slave" for clarity and to present the reader with the historical usage of the term and its consequences.

27. For one of the most important treatments of Southern law in this period, emphasiz-
ing its locally contingent context, see Laura F. Edwards, *The People and Their Peace:
Legal Culture and the Transformation of Inequality in the Post-Revolutionary South*
(Chapel Hill: University of North Carolina Press, 2009). On the role of the law in
everyday life, see Martha S. Jones, *Birthright Citizens: A History of Race and Rights
in Antebellum America* (Cambridge: Cambridge University Press, 2018); and
Martha S. Jones, "Leave of Court: African American Claim-Making in the Era of
Dred Scott v. Sandford," in *Contested Democracy: Freedom, Race, and Power in
American History*, ed. Manisha Sinha and Penny von Eschen (New York: Columbia
University Press, 2007), 54–74. On law and lawyers, see Gordon-Reed, "Logic and
Experience"; and Farbman, "Resistance Lawyering." On Maryland, see Reid,
"Between Slavery and Freedom"; Reid, "Legal Construction of Whiteness"; and
Papenfuse, "From Recompense to Revolution."

28. Important studies placing American families at the center include: Erica Armstrong
Dunbar, *Never Caught: The Washingtons' Relentless Pursuit of Their Runaway Slave,
Ona Judge* (New York: Atria, 2017); Kendra Taira Field, *Growing Up with the
Country: Family, Race, and Nation After the Civil War* (New Haven: Yale University
Press, 2018); Annette Gordon-Reed, *The Hemingses of Monticello: An American
Family* (New York: W. W. Norton, 2008); Sydney Nathans, *To Free a Family: The
Journey of Mary Walker* (Cambridge: Harvard University Press, 2013); Sydney
Nathans, *A Mind to Stay: White Plantation, Black Homeland* (Cambridge: Harvard
University Press, 2017); Rothman, *Beyond Freedom's Reach*; Scott and Hébrard,
Freedom Papers; Lisa A. Lindsay, "Remembering His Country Marks: A Nigerian
American Family and Its 'African' Ancestor," in *Biography and the Black Atlantic*,
ed. Lisa A. Lindsay and John Wood Sweet (Philadelphia: University of Pennsylvania
Press, 2014), 192–206; Andrew Graybill, *The Red and the White: A Family Saga of the
American West* (New York: Liveright, 2013); Carla Peterson, *Black Gotham: A Family
History of African Americans in Nineteenth-Century New York City* (New Haven:
Yale University Press, 2012); Daniel Sharfstein, *The Invisible Line: Three American
Families and the Secret Journey from Black to White* (New York: Penguin, 2011);
Claudio Saunt, *Black, White, and Indian: Race and the Unmaking of an American
Family* (New York: Oxford University Press, 2005); Henry Wiencek, *The Hairstons:
An American Family in Black and White* (New York: St. Martin's, 2000); and T. O.
Madden Jr., *We Were Always Free: The Maddens of Culpeper County, Virginia: A
200-Year Family History* (New York: W. W. Norton, 1992).

29. For a fascinating discussion of how the law creates a "now," see Hartog, *Trouble with
Minna*, who argues that legal instruments, writings, contracts, wills, and other
forms of legal transaction "thrust a present relationship—a 'now'—into the future"
(9). For an analogous "work of recovery" of Nat Turner, see Christopher Tomlins, *In
the Matter of Dred Scott: A Speculative History* (Princeton: Princeton University
Press, 2020).

30. See esp. Hooker and Czajkowski, *Transforming Historical Harms*. I have been
inspired and encouraged by the following literary and historical personal approaches to narrative form: Perry, *Vexy Thing*; Carole Anderson, *White Rage:
The Unspoken Truth of Our Racial Divide* (New York: Bloomsbury, 2016); Leslie
Stainton, "Things Too Sweet to Taste," *American Scholar*, June 5, 2017, https://
theamericanscholar.org/things-sweet-to-taste/; Charles Dew, *The Making of a*

Racist: A Southerner Reflects on Family, History, and the Slave Trade (Charlottesville: University of Virginia Press, 2016); Coates, *Between the World and Me;* Field, *Growing Up with the Country;* and Hartman, *Lose Your Mother.* The literature of the history of whiteness, white identity, and racism is extensive. The following historical and literary works have influenced my approach: Stephanie E. Jones-Rogers, *They Were Her Property: White Women as Slave Owners in the American South* (New Haven: Yale University Press, 2019); Walter Johnson, "To Remake the World: Slavery, Racial Capitalism, and Justice," *Boston Review,* February 20, 2018; Nancy Isenberg, *White Trash: The 400-Year Untold History of Class in America* (New York: Viking, 2016); Stephen Middleton and David R. Roediger, eds., *The Construction of Whiteness: An Interdisciplinary Analysis of Race Formation and the Meaning of White Identity* (Oxford: University Press of Mississippi, 2016); Ibram X. Kendi, *Stamped from the Beginning: The Definitive History of Racist Ideas in America* (New York: Bold Type Books, 2016); Nell Irvin Painter, *The History of White People* (New York: W. W. Norton, 2010); Michelle Alexander, *The New Jim Crow: Mass Incarceration in the Age of Colorblindness* (New York: New Press, 2010); and Grace Elizabeth Hale, *Making Whiteness: The Culture of Segregation in the South, 1890–1940* (New York: Vintage, 1999).

CHAPTER 1. A MEETING AT WHITE MARSH, 1789

1. Lorena S. Walsh, "Plantation Management in the Chesapeake, 1620–1820," *Journal of Economic History* 49, no. 2 (1989): 393–406; Lorena S. Walsh, "Slave Life, Slave Society, and Tobacco Production in the Tidewater Chesapeake, 1620–1820," in *Cultivation and Culture: Labor and the Shaping of Slave Life in the Americas,* ed. Ira Berlin and Philip D. Morgan (Charlottesville: University Press of Virginia, 1993), 171–199; Mary M. Schweitzer, "Economic Regulation and the Colonial Economy: The Maryland Tobacco Inspection Act of 1747," *Journal of Economic History* 40 (1980): 551–569; Carville V. Earle, *The Evolution of a Tidewater Settlement System: All Hallow's Parish, Maryland, 1650–1783* (Chicago: University of Chicago, 1975), 26.

2. Carville Earle, in *Evolution of a Tidewater Settlement System,* the closest study of the region, estimates tobacco yields per laborer on the Western Shore of Maryland in the period at 1,800 pounds (27).

3. Fidelius De Grivel to Nicholas Sewell, May 20, 1832, Maryland—Letters of Ours and of Bishops, 1773–1815, BN/3/1, EPA.

4. The classic work on Maryland is Barbara Jeanne Fields, *Slavery and Freedom on the Middle Ground: Maryland During the Nineteenth Century* (New Haven: Yale University Press, 1987). See also the following by Steven Sarson: "Distribution of Wealth in Prince George's County, Maryland, 1800–1820," *Journal of Economic History* 60, no. 3 (2000): 847–853; "Landlessness and Tenancy in Early National Prince George's County, Maryland," *William and Mary Quarterly,* 3rd ser., 57, no. 3 (2000): 576; and "Yeoman Farmers in a Planter's Republic: Socioeconomic Conditions and Relations in Early National Prince George's County, Maryland," *Journal of the Early Republic* 29, no. 1 (2009): 63–99. In 1800, Prince George's County was nearly 58 percent enslaved. The 1810 census data for Prince George's were incorrect; the number of enslaved was higher than reported. Charles County was 49 percent enslaved in 1800 and 61 percent enslaved in 1810.

5. Edmund S. Morgan, *American Slavery, American Freedom: The Ordeal of Colonial Virginia* (New York: W. W. Norton, 1975). See also Robin Blackburn, *The Making of New World Slavery: From the Baroque to the Modern, 1492–1800* (London: Verso, 1997); Allan Gallay, *The Indian Slave Trade: The Rise of the English Empire in the American South, 1670–1717* (New Haven: Yale University Press, 2003); and David Brion Davis, *Inhuman Bondage: The Rise and Fall of Slavery in the New World* (New York: Oxford University Press, 2006). David Brion Davis, *The Problem of Slavery in the Age of Revolution, 1770–1823* (Ithaca: Cornell University Press, 1975), 167–182, 212, concludes that historians have "underestimated the economic strength of slavery in the Revolutionary period, exaggerated the force of anti-slavery sentiment in the Upper South, and minimized the obstacles that abolitionists faced in the northern states" (256).

6. Fields, *Slavery and Freedom on the Middle Ground.* See also Max Grivno, *Gleanings of Freedom: Free and Slave Labor Along the Mason-Dixon Line* (Urbana: University of Illinois Press, 2011), 37, on slavery as "moribund" in parts of northern Maryland. For an account of the expansion of slavery across borders, including Pennsylvania, see Cory James Young, "From North to Natchez During the Age of Gradual Abolition," *Pennsylvania Magazine of History and Biography* 143, no. 2 (2019): 117–139. Allan Kulikoff, *Tobacco and Slaves: The Development of Southern Cultures in the Chesapeake, 1680–1800* (Chapel Hill: University of North Carolina Press, 1986), 275. Kulikoff notes, "One's family, as well as one's wealth, determined social position" (8). Kulikoff's definitive study emphasizes the shift over the eighteenth century from neighborhood societies to spatially distributed, socially networked clans (160, 283). See also Whitman H. Ridgway, *Community Leadership in Maryland, 1790–1840: A Comparative Analysis of Power in Society* (Chapel Hill: University of North Carolina Press, 1979).

7. For the closest analysis of manumission and its timing, see John Joseph Condon, "Manumission, Slavery, and Family in Post-Revolutionary Rural Chesapeake: Anne Arundel County, Maryland" (Ph.D. diss., University of Minnesota, 2001), 8. Condon argues that the timing of manumission in Maryland came later in the 1800–1820 period and was not directly a product of postrevolutionary ideals or a response to the depression in tobacco prices. Instead, enslaved families experienced less isolation, more spatial mobility, and more independent household formation. Confronted with the slave trade after 1800, they tried to free family members. In Anne Arundel, moreover, manumission differed from the rest of the slaveholding world—rather than favoring lighter-colored women, those manumitted were similar in gender, color, and skill to the whole enslaved population. Condon finds that slaveholders who manumitted in the tobacco region tended to operate farms where tobacco was not being grown or controlled estates where commercial farming was not being undertaken and that they tended to be the owners of a few slaves rather than large slaveholders (114). On the slave trade's early development in the 1790s, Michael Tadman, *Speculators and Slaves: Masters, Traders, and Slaves in the Old South* (Madison: University of Wisconsin Press, 1989), calculates Maryland's 1790s net interregional movement of enslaved as a 22 percent loss and asserts that "a professional domestic traffic in slaves dated back to at least the 1780s" (12); see also Tadman, *Speculators and Slaves,* 15–17. Steven Deyle, *Carry Me Back: The Domestic Slave Trade in American Life* (Oxford: Oxford University Press, 2005), 15–19.

8. Christopher Leslie Brown, "Christianity and the Campaign Against Slavery and the Slave Trade," in *The Cambridge History of Christianity*, vol. 7: *Enlightenment, Reawakening and Revolution, 1600–1815*, ed. Stewart J. Brown and Timothy Tackett (Cambridge: Cambridge University Press, 2006), 517–535; Travis Glasson, *Mastering Christianity: Missionary Anglicanism and Slavery in the Atlantic World* (New York: Oxford University Press, 2012), 145.

9. Thomas Hughes, ed., *History of the Society of Jesus in North America: Colonial and Federal*, 3 vols. in 4 (New York: Longmans, Green, 1908–1917), 1, pt. 1:232–233. Maryland Prerogative Court Will Book 19, 797–799, James Carroll (1729), and Maryland Prerogative Court Inventories 15, 496–505, James Carroll estate (1729), both SR 4333-2, MSA. Mary was valued at £30. Mary's daughter "Nan about 12 years old" is also listed. Transcriptions of Carroll's inventory referred to this girl as Maria, but the original shows the name "Nan." From later court records, we know that Mary had a daughter named Nan, or Nanny, who became Nanny Cooper.

10. George Hunter, "Charity to Negroes," December 20, 1749, box 57, folder 1, MPA.

11. John Lewis Small Book, box 29, folder 2, MPA. Lewis's census is referred to in Edward F. Beckett, "Listening to Our History: Inculturation and Jesuit Slaveholding," *Studies in the Spirituality of Jesuits* 28, no. 5 (1996): 12–13.

12. John Lewis Small Book.

13. John Lewis Small Book. Lewis's census is referred to in Beckett, "Listening to Our History," but Beckett makes no effort to connect the families Lewis listed with other records in the Jesuit archives. Sharon Leon is working on a major effort to piece together the families on the Jesuit estates in *The Jesuit Plantation Project: An Examination of the Enslaved Persons Owned (and Sold) by the Maryland Province Jesuits, 1717–1838* (https://jesuitplantationproject.org).

14. For a comparable account of South American Jesuit slaveholding in Brazil, see Dauril Alden, *The Making of an Enterprise: The Society of Jesus in Portugal, Its Empire, and Beyond, 1540–1750* (Stanford, Calif.: Stanford University Press, 1996), 525. See esp. Caitlin Rosenthal, "Slavery's Scientific Management: Masters and Managers," in *Slavery's Capitalism: A New History of American Economic Development*, ed. Seth Rockman and Sven Beckert (Philadelphia: University of Pennsylvania Press, 2016), 62–87. The recent historiography of slavery stresses the violence of enslavement, forced migration, and labor productivity and their relation to the development of capitalism. The most recent and ambitious works include Edward E. Baptist, *The Half Has Never Been Told: Slavery and the Making of American Capitalism* (New York: Basic Books, 2014); Sven Beckert, *Empire of Cotton: A Global History* (New York: Knopf, 2014); Walter Johnson, *River of Dark Dreams: Slavery and Empire in the Cotton Kingdom* (Cambridge: Harvard University Press, 2013); and Greg Grandin, *The Empire of Necessity: Slavery, Freedom, and Deception in the New World* (New York: Metropolitan Books, 2014).

15. John Carroll to Charles Plowden, February 28, 1787, in *The John Carroll Papers*, ed. Thomas O'Brien Hanley (Notre Dame, Ind.: University of Notre Dame Press, 1976), 240–242.

16. Pope Clement XIV issued a papal brief suppressing the Society of Jesus in July 1773. The society was partially restored in Maryland in 1805 when five former Jesuits joined the Russia Province, where Catherine the Great had ignored the brief and the society continued uninterrupted. Elsewhere in Europe, Pope Pius VII restored the

society in 1814. The Jesuits in Maryland sometimes referred to themselves as "exJesuits," especially in correspondence with Rome or the English Province. See esp. Carroll to Plowden, July 7, 1797, Maryland—Letters of Ours and of Bishops, 1773–1815, BN/3/1, EPA: "The exJesuits formed themselves in 1784 into a body for which they have since obtained a law of incorporation, vesting in themselves & their successors . . . all the estates, real, personal & mixed, which are and have been possessed by the clergy heretofore existing in their states." I have chosen to refer to them as "Jesuits" throughout the period of suppression so as not to confuse readers. The terms "ex-Jesuit" or "former Jesuit" imply to a modern ear that they had renounced their vows or the society. But the Jesuits in Maryland were a tight group who continued to identify as Jesuits well after the 1773 papal brief. They founded a corporation, pooled their interests apart from the "secular priests" (another term I have avoided to reduce confusion), and kept track of who was and who was not a former Jesuit among them.

17. Proceedings of the General Chapter meeting at White Marsh, June 27, 1783, box 2, folder 5, MPA.
18. Proceedings of the General Chapter meeting at White Marsh, June 27, 1783.
19. Proceedings of the General Chapter meeting at White Marsh, June 27, 1783.
20. Proceedings of the General Chapter meeting at White Marsh, June 27, 1783.
21. Proceedings of the General Chapter meeting at White Marsh, May 11, 1789, box 2, folder 6, MPA. No evidence remains indicating that the Jesuits sold enslaved people under these guidelines, but there are large gaps in the historical record and the priests never withdrew the resolution authorizing the sales. Sales could indeed have taken place. Thomas Murphy, S.J., *Jesuit Slaveholding in Maryland, 1717–1838* (New York: Routledge, 2001), conjectures that no sales must have taken place or they would have been recorded.
22. "An Act Concerning Negroes & Other Slaves," *Proceedings and Acts of the General Assembly, January 1637/8–September 1664, AOMOL,* 1:533.
23. Depositions of Joseph Jameson, Thomas Bowling, Edward Edelson, and Samuel Hall, May 27, 1767, Provincial Court, Judgment Record, Liber DD 17, S551-85, MSA.
24. Martha Hodes, *White Women, Black Men: Illicit Sex in the Nineteenth-Century South* (New Haven: Yale University Press, 1997), 31–38. See also T. Stephen Whitman, *Challenging Slavery in the Chesapeake: Black and White Resistance to Human Bondage, 1775–1865* (Baltimore: Johns Hopkins University Press, 2006), 62–65. *Proceedings of the Acts of the General Assembly, January 1637/8–September 1664, AOMOL,* 1:533.
25. The 1681 act was superseded by another act in 1692 that reinstated and refined the miscegenation provisions of the 1664 act. The 1692 act required that a freeborn white woman who married a black man serve for seven years bound to her parish and that her husband, if free, become a slave for life for the parish. Children of mixed marriages would be servants of the parish until age twenty-one. If the couple were not married, the woman received seven years' indenture, the child twenty-one years', and the man, if free, seven years'. Critically, the same penalties for white women extended to white men for having a child with a black woman. *Proceedings of the Council of Maryland, 1687/8–1693, AOMOL,* 8:546-549. See also Ross M. Kimmel, "Blacks Before the Law in Colonial Maryland" (M.A. thesis, University of Maryland, 1974), published by MSA (November 2000).

26. During the seventeen-year period of the 1664 act, white women who were wives of enslaved men were considered by law enslaved. These women sought to pass on evidence of their ethnic identities and status. Mary Davis, on her marriage to Domingo, an enslaved man, inscribed a family Bible ca. 1695 noting that she was "from a Christian race" to indicate that her son was born of a free woman. See Thomas F. Brown and Leah C. Simms, "'To Swear Him Free': Ethnic Memory as Social Capital in Eighteenth-Century Freedom Petitions," in *Colonial Chesapeake: New Perspectives,* ed. Debra Meyers and Melanie Perreault (Lanham, Md.: Rowman and Littlefield, 2006), 81–112.

27. Based on a detailed reading of the court records in the Butler freedom petitions, Kaci Nash's research for *OSCYS* indicates that William was Nell Butler's grandson, descended from Elizabeth "Abigail" Butler. Mary Butler was Nell Butler's great-granddaughter, descended from Catherine "Kate" Butler. Their children were William Lazarus and Mary Butler. Both sued in the 1780s. See deposition of John Hooper Broom, May 29, 1786, *Mary Butler v. Adam Craig,* Judgments, Court of Appeals, S381-52, MSA. Deposition of Samuel Hall, folio 238, May 27, 1767, Provincial Court, Judgment Record, Liber DD 17, S551-85, MSA.

28. *William and Mary Butler v. Richard Boarman,* September 1770, in Thomas Harris and John McHenry, *Maryland Reports, Being a Series of the Most Important Law Cases Argued and Determined in the Provincial Court and Court of Appeals of the Then Province of Maryland,* 4 vols. (New York: I. Riley, 1809–1818), 1:371.

29. See *Eleanor Toogood v. Doctor Upton Scott,* in Harris and McHenry, *Maryland Reports,* 2:26. See also Jessica Millward, "Wombs of Liberation: Petitions, Law, and the Black Woman's Body in Maryland, 1780–1858," in *Sexuality and Slavery: Reclaiming Intimate Histories in the Americas,* ed. Daina Ramey Berry and Leslie M. Harris (Athens: University of Georgia Press, 2018), 93–95. Other early freedom suits immediately before and after the Revolution in Prince George's County include: *Elizabeth Bentley v. Lettice Thomson* (1772), *Rosamond Bentley v. Anthony Addison* (1781), and *Mary Bentley v. William Digges* (1781).

30. Harris and McHenry, *Maryland Reports,* 2:214. Deposition of Mary Butler, May 16, 1792, *Samuel, Flora, and Tracey Butler v. Adam Craig,* May 1792 Term, GCWS, Judgment Record, S497-17, MSA.

31. Thomas How Ridgate and Nicholas Lewis Sewall deed, box 39, folder 8, MPA.

32. See *Mary Butler v. Adam Craig,* June 1791 Term, GCWS, Judgments, Court of Appeals, S381-52 no. 3, MSA. The Butlers filed dozens of cases in the General Court: see *Chloe Butler v. Nicholas L. Sewall* and *Stephen Butler v. Charles Carroll* (of Bellevue), October 1791 Term, GCWS, Judgments, S498-14, MSA.

33. Several other families also brought highly complex suits that followed in this period. See Loren Schweninger, "Freedom Suits, African American Women, and the Genealogy of Slavery," *William and Mary Quarterly,* 3rd ser., 71, no. 1 (2014): 58, for analysis of the Boston family freedom suits in the 1790s.

34. Norman K. Risjord, *Chesapeake Politics, 1781–1800* (New York: Columbia University Press, 1978), 74.

35. Joseph C. Miller, "Domiciled and Dominated: Slaving as a History of Women," in *Women and Slavery,* vol. 2: *The Modern Atlantic,* ed. Gwyn Campbell et al. (Columbus: Ohio State University Press, 2007), 304–305; Anthony E. Kaye, *Joining Places: Slave*

Neighborhoods in the Old South (Chapel Hill: University of North Carolina Press, 2009), 22–26; Kulikoff, *Tobacco and Slaves*, 209, 225; Grivno, *Gleanings of Freedom*.

36. Kulikoff, *Tobacco and Slaves*, 209; Grivno, *Gleanings of Freedom*, 42.

37. See esp. Holly Brewer, "Slavery, Sovereignty, and 'Inheritable Blood'": Reconsidering John Locke and the Origins of American Slavery," *American Historical Review* 122, no. 4 (2017): 1038–1078. For the legal development of slavery in New England as customary rather than statutory, see Wendy Warren, *New England Bound: Slavery and Colonization in Early America* (New York: W. W. Norton, 2017). The most recent studies on the complexity of law and legal process regarding abolition in Anglo-American history stress the contradiction between slavery and liberalism. See Sean Wilentz, *No Property in Man: Slavery and Antislavery at the Nation's Founding* (Cambridge: Harvard University Press, 2018), 44–45. On hereditary enslavement and the "indeterminate status of British subjecthood" under common law and constitutionalism in the British colonial empire, see Brooke N. Newman, *A Dark Inheritance: Blood, Race, and Sex in Colonial Jamaica* (New Haven: Yale University Press, 2018), 11.

38. Jonathan A. Bush points out that "colonial America never developed a systematic law of slavery." For an analysis of how colonists from a "densely legalistic culture . . . erected slavery without direct legal authority" and "maintained slavery without the sanction of a thorough slave law," see Bush, "Free to Enslave: The Foundations of Colonial American Slave Law," *Yale Journal of Law and the Humanities* 5, no. 2 (1993): 417–470. For Maryland's 1715 code, see *Proceedings and Acts of the General Assembly, April 26, 1715–August 10, 1716, AOMOL*, 30:289.

39. Brewer, "Slavery, Sovereignty, and 'Inheritable Blood,'" 1051–1052. The two common-law forms of pleading that slaveholders used in these matters were "trover" and "replevin" (Brewer also explores "detinue"). Trover was a form of trespass, taking a property not lawfully one's own, or a withholding of property from another. Replevin was another action for the return of property seized provisionally to determine the rights of the contesting parties. The case to uphold "trover would lie for a negro" was *Butts v. Penny* (1677), later overruled in *Chamberlayne v. Harvey* (1697) and *Smith v. Gould* (1706), and eventually in *Somerset* (1772). In *Pearne v. Lisle*, Amb. 75, 27 Eng. Rep. 47 (1749), Lord Hardwicke's decision attempted to reaffirm *Butts v. Penny* that trover may "lie for a negro." The ambiguity over slavery and the common law of England in these cases stood at the heart of the initial freedom suits in Maryland and was crucially reprised in *Mahoney v. Ashton* (1802). See Harris and McHenry, *Maryland Reports*, 4:296–303, 312–325, for the opposing arguments before the high court of appeals. Maryland's colonial assembly passed numerous slave codes that presumed slaves were chattel property but never passed a statute explicitly declaring that slaves were chattel. On the 1664, 1692, 1715, 1723, and 1751 acts, see Kimmel, "Blacks Before the Law in Colonial Maryland," MSA. I thank Holly A. Brewer for sharing her forthcoming and pathbreaking research on the common law, slavery, and the Stuarts. Brewer, "Creating a Common Law of Slavery for England and Its New World Empire," Paper presented at the Legal History Colloquium, NYU School of Law, February 26, 2018.

40. *Somerset v. Stewart*, 98 Eng. Rep. 499–510 (King's Bench, June 22, 1772). The arguments were reprinted in *The English Reports: King's Bench Division XXVII* (Edinburgh: William Green and Sons, 1909).

41. The Yorke-Talbot Opinion was cited by the court of appeals in *Mahoney v. Ashton* in June 1802, GCWS, Judgments, S498-220, MSA. See Travis Glasson, "'Baptism Doth Not Bestow Freedom': Missionary Anglicanism, Slavery and the Yorke-Talbot Opinion, 1701–30," *William and Mary Quarterly*, 3rd ser., 67, no. 2 (2010): 279–318. On the Debt Recovery Act of 1732 as a "sweeping" guarantee, see George William Van Cleve, *A Slaveholder's Union: Slavery, Politics, and the Constitution in the Early American Republic* (Chicago: University of Chicago Press, 2010), 20–24. In addition, George Van Cleve, "*Somerset*'s Case and Its Antecedents in Imperial Perspective," *Law and History Review* 24, no. 3 (2006): 619–621, notes that the opinion was quoted in full in *Knight v. Wedderburn*, 8 Fac. Dec. 5, More. 14545 (Scot. Ct. Sess. 1778). Van Cleve argues that there were coherent "broad areas of agreement" on slavery law before *Somerset* as well as a "broad consensus in law and social practice" that sanctioned "near slavery" or what he calls "slavish servants." Van Cleve downplays the conflict within English law over whether slavery was legitimate and emphasizes that the *Somerset* decision was motivated by imperial considerations. "Lord Mansfield's conclusion on the origin of slavery, even if qualified, was inevitably, as he well knew, profoundly destructive of the moral and legal legitimacy of slavery, since it made slave property an artificial creature of statute and deprived slavery of the sanction of the common law," he concludes (644). *Mahoney v. Ashton* (see chapter 3) demonstrated how contested the lines of argument over the common law were after the American Revolution into the late eighteenth century. For an interpretation stressing the common-law contest over the legitimacy of slavery, see esp. Brewer, "Creating a Common Law of Slavery," 31.

42. *Somerset v. Stewart.* William Blackstone, *Commentaries on the Laws of England*, vol. 1 (Oxford: Clarendon Press, 1765), 412. On the American Revolution as a "turning point" in judicial decision-making about freedom suits and slavery, see Jason A. Gillmer, "Suing for Freedom: Interracial Sex, Slave Law, and Racial Identity in the Post-Revolutionary and Antebellum South," *North Carolina Law Review* 82, no. 4 (2004): 535–619. See also the definitive work on *Somerset* as a "turning point": Thea K. Hunter, "Publishing Freedom, Winning Arguments: Somerset, Natural Rights and Massachusetts Freedom Cases, 1772–1836" (Ph.D. diss., Columbia University, 2005), 3, 178–224. On the case as "Mansfeldian Moment," see David Waldstreicher, *Slavery's Constitution: From Revolution to Ratification* (New York: Hill and Wang, 2009), 39–40.

43. *Somerset v. Stewart.* Blackstone, *Commentaries*, 412. For an especially insightful argument about the Somerset case as technically narrow decision, a "marked break from previous cases, not so much because it recognizes the 'rights of man' which enslaved people supposedly had, but because it didn't start out as a property dispute," see Derek Litvak, "The Man Is Here: Somerset's Case and Enslaved Subjecthood in the Anglo-Atlantic World" (manuscript in possession of the author). Litvak argues that enslaved people had "legal personhood" as subjects before *Somerset.* I thank Litvak for sharing his research with me and for our extended discussion about the case.

44. *Somerset v. Stewart.* Blackstone, *Commentaries*, 412. Van Cleve, "*Somerset*'s Case," 644. See also Edward B. Rugemer, *Slave Law and the Politics of Resistance in the Early Atlantic World* (Cambridge: Harvard University Press, 2019), 179–181.

45. The most detailed and authoritative legal analysis of *Somerset* remains William W. Wiecek, "*Somerset*: Lord Mansfield and the Legitimacy of Slavery in the Anglo-American World," *Chicago Law Review* 42, no. 1 (1974): 86–146. Michael Meranze, "Hargrave's Nightmare and Taney's Dream," *UC Irvine Law Review* 4, no. 1 (2014): 219–238, indicates that whatever the intent of its participants, *Somerset* challenged slavery and "established a problematization within which the question of the constitutional status and visibility of slavery, the relationship between the constitutional claims of slavery and local, legal regimes, and the necessity to slavery of the support of the state became unavoidable" (227).

46. I thank Eric Berger for his astute analysis of the potential constitutional and statutory issues in the Queen and Mahoney cases. Within Maryland's constitution, English common law operated as a baseline providing the background rule of law, subject to statutory change. But in the 1790s, which colonial laws applied and which did not, which precedents from English common law were applicable and which were not, remained unclear. The exact constitutional language was: "That the inhabitants of Maryland are entitled to the common law of England, and the trial by Jury, according to the course of that law, and to the benefit of such of the English statutes, as existed at the time of their first emigration, and which, by experience, have been found applicable to their local and other circumstances, and of such others as have been since made in England, or Great Britain, and have been introduced, used and practiced by the courts of law or equity; and also to acts of Assembly, in force on the first of June seventeen hundred and seventy-four, except such as may have since expired, or have been or may be altered by facts of Convention, or this Declaration of Rights—subject, nevertheless, to the revision of, and amendment or repeal by, the Legislature of this State." *Declaration of Rights and Constitution of Maryland, as Adopted by the 9th Convention, August–November, 1776*, in *Hanson's Laws of Maryland* (1787), SC 2221-4-8 1776, MSA.

47. *Maryland Gazette*, May 15, 1783.

48. Mary Sarah Bilder, *Madison's Hand: Revising the Constitutional Convention* (Cambridge: Harvard University Press, 2015), 136–137; Wilentz, *No Property in Man*, 4, 11.

49. Bilder, *Madison's Hand*, 125; Wilentz, *No Property in Man*, 14–15. Wilentz points out, "By 1787, however, with astonishing swiftness, the political and intellectual foundations supporting slavery had come under concerted attack" (14). On the Northwest Ordinance as a link in the chain of constitutional law joining the Articles of Confederation to the Constitution, see Akhil Reed Amar, *America's Unwritten Constitution: The Precedents and Principles We Live By* (New York: Basic Books, 2002), 258–262; and Nicholas Guyatt, *Bind Us Apart: How Enlightened Americans Invented Racial Segregation* (New York: Basic Books, 2016), 3. See also Rugemer, *Slave Law and the Politics of Resistance*, 202–204, 213–242. See, e.g., Mary V. Thompson, *"The Only Unavoidable Subject of Regret": George Washington, Slavery, and the Enslaved Community at Mount Vernon* (Charlottesville: University of Virginia Press, 2019), 293–314.

50. On the concept of an "age" or era of gradual abolition, encompassing the slow movement toward abolition in Northern states after 1780, especially Pennsylvania, New York, and New Jersey, see Young, "North to Natchez in the Age of Gradual Abolition," 118. See also James J. Gigantino II, *The Ragged Road to Abolition: Slavery*

and Freedom in New Jersey, 1775–1865 (Philadelphia: University of Pennsylvania Press, 2015); and Wilentz, *No Property in Man,* 142–152.

51. See George William Van Cleve, "Founding a Slaveholder's Union, 1770–1797," in *Contesting Slavery: The Politics of Bondage and Freedom in the New American Nation,* ed. John Craig Hammond and Matthew Mason (Charlottesville: University of Virginia Press, 2011), 117–137.

52. Bilder, *Madison's Hand,* 108, 114–115, 189. On differing views of the Constitution and slavery, see Don Fehrenbacher, *The Slaveholding Republic: An Account of the United States Government's Reaction to Slavery* (New York: Oxford University Press, 2001); and Paul Finkelman, *Slavery and the Founders: Race and Liberty in the Age of Jefferson,* 2nd ed. (Armonk, N.Y.: M. E. Sharpe, 2001). See also David Waldstreicher, *Slavery's Constitution: From Revolution to Ratification* (New York: Hill and Wang, 2009). The point here is that in 1788–1789, arguments were in wide circulation in Maryland against the slave trade and for the abolition of slavery.

53. On the significant number of Federalists in Maryland who supported emancipation, see Richard Newman, "'Good Communications Corrects Bad Manners': The Banneker-Jefferson Dialogue and the Project of White Uplift," in Hammond and Mason, *Contesting Slavery,* 85–87.

54. *Constitution of the Maryland Society, for Promoting the Abolition of Slavery, and the Relief of Free Negroes, and Others, Unlawfully Held in Bondage* (Baltimore: William Goddard and James Angell, 1789).

55. *Constitution of the Maryland Society.* The two attorneys were Zebulon Hollingsworth, a member of the House of Delegates from Baltimore, and Archibald Robinson. According to James McHenry, one of the Federalist political operators in Maryland, Robinson was a "young lawyer of promising talent." See James McHenry to Alexander Hamilton, August 16, 1792, in *The Papers of Alexander Hamilton,* vol. 12: *July–October 1792,* ed. Harold C. Syrett and Jacob E. Cooke (New York: Columbia University Press, 1967), 212–213.

56. Henry Wharton, *Some Account of the Life, Writings, and Speeches of William Pinkney* (New York: J. W. Palmer, 1826), 6; Rev. William Pinkney, *The Life of William Pinkney* (New York: D. Appleton, 1853), 20.

57. William Pinkney, "For the Relief of Slaves," 1788, reprinted in E. B. Williston, *Eloquence of the United States,* vol. 5 (New York: Jonathan Seymour, 1829), 98.

58. *House of Delegates Journal, November 1789,* 10–14, SC M 3197, MSA.

59. *House of Delegates Journal, November 1789,* 10–14. For the original colonial statutes, see *Proceedings of the Acts of the General Assembly, April 26, 1715–August 10, 1776,* AOMOL, 30:290.

60. William Pinkney, *Speech of William Pinkney, Esq. in the House of Delegates of Maryland, at Their Session in November, 1789* (Philadelphia: Crukshank, 1790), 8–24.

61. On the influence of *Somerset* in the 1780s, especially the important Massachusetts freedom suit of Quock Walker, see Hunter, "Publishing Freedom, Winning Arguments," 148–176. Jeffrey Brackett, *The Negro in Maryland: A Study of the Institution of Slavery* (Baltimore: Johns Hopkins University, 1889), 52–54. *House of Delegates Journal, November 1789,* 10–14, 64–65, and *Senate Journal, 1789,* 5–34, SC M 3197, MSA.

62. Brackett, *Negro in Maryland,* 54. Brackett cites an 1832 letter in *Hazard's Register,* 10:411. The letter dates Carroll's proposed bill in 1797.

63. On the lack of statutory definition of slavery and *partus sequitor ventrem,* see Thomas D. Morris, *Slavery and Southern Law, 1619–1860* (Chapel Hill: University of North Carolina Press, 1996), 47–48.

64. Robert M. Ireland, *The Legal Career of William Pinkney, 1764–1822* (New York: Garland, 1986), 17–18. On "judicial legislation," Ireland cites as the best statement the opinion of Alexander Contee Hanson in *State of Maryland v. Buchanan* (1821), cited in *An Exhibit of the Losses Sustained at the Office of Discount and Deposit Baltimore, Under the Administration of James A. Buchanan, President, and James W. McCulloh, Cashier . . .* appended to *A Report of the Conspiracy Cases, Tried at Harford County Court in Maryland* (Baltimore: Thomas Murphy, 1823), SC 4645-1-8, SC 2221-24-1-7, MSA. *State of Maryland v. Buchanan* records are available at http:// msa.maryland.gov/ecp/45/00029/00002/html/cover.html.

65. See Jessica A. Lowe, *Murder in the Shenandoah: Making Law Sovereign in Revolutionary Virginia* (Cambridge: Cambridge University Press, 2019), 84–89.

66. *David Queen v. Sylvester Boarman* and *Ann Queen v. Sylvester Boarman,* August 1794, folder 32:14—Court Records, County Court Records Collection, Historical Society of Harford County, Md.

67. Julius Scott, *The Common Wind: Afro-American Currents in the Age of the Haitian Revolution* (New York: Verso Books, 2018), 130–131.

Attempting to Poison a Certain Richard Duckett the Younger

1. On the Griffith Thomas family, see *A Guide to the Griffith Thomas Family of Virginia Collection, 1934–1990,* Thomas Balch Library, Leesburg, Va., https://ead.lib.virginia .edu/vivaxtf/view?docId=tbl/viletbl00108.xml. The Griffith Thomas family lived next to multiple free black and mulatto families in Loudoun in 1850. U.S. Census, 1850, Loudoun, Va., roll M432_957, p. 177A, image 3, NARA. The Griffith Thomas family members do not appear in the 1850 or 1860 Slave Schedules, nor do members of the family appear in earlier lists, such as Margaret Lail Hopkins, *Index to the Tithables of Loudoun County, Virginia, and to Slaveholders and Slaves, 1758–1786* (Baltimore: Genealogical Publishing, 1991). On slavery and free black life in Loudoun County, see Brenda K. Stevenson, *Life in Black and White: Family and Community in the Slave South* (Oxford: Oxford University Press, 1997).

2. *Proceedings of the Council of Maryland, 1753—1761,* AOMOL, 31:79–80.

3. See Walter Johnson, "Resetting the Legal History of Slavery: Divination, Torture, Poisoning, Murder, Revolution, Emancipation, and Re-Enslavement," *Law and History Review* 29, no. 4 (2011): 1089–1095; Malick W. Ghachem, "Prosecuting Torture: The Strategic Ethics of Slavery in Pre-Revolutionary Saint-Domingue (Haiti)," *Law and History Review* 29, no. 4 (2011): 985–1029; and Thavolia Glymph, *Out of the House of Bondage: The Transformation of the Plantation Household* (Cambridge: Cambridge University Press, 2008), 10.

4. Paul P. Kreisa et al., "Phase III Archaeological Data Recovery of Site 18PR705 at the Waterford Development, Prince George's County, Maryland," Report prepared by Greenhorne & O'Mara, Inc., for Washington Management & Development Company, Inc., 2007, on file at the Maryland Historical Trust; *What Lies Beneath: The History of Waterford Estates,* Maryland National Capital Park and Planning

Commission, Prince George's County, April 23, 2014, http://www.cfma-md.org
/30%20Jan%202014%20Waterford%20Estates%20Public%20Booklet-4-21-14.pdf.

5. Inventory of Richard Duckett, December 13, 1788, Prince George's County Inventories, 1781, 1790–1795, 7–13, CR-11, 297-2, CM 809, MSA, available at *Probing the Past:
Virginia and Maryland Probate Inventories, 1740–1810,* Roy Rosenzweig Center for
History and New Media, George Mason University, and Gunston Hall Plantation,
http://chnm.gmu.edu/probateinventory/index.php.

6. The turn from indentured servitude in the Chesapeake to racial slavery was once
described as an "unthinking decision," to use historian Winthrop Jordan's famous
phrase, but increasingly, historians have suspected that families like mine decided
to become enslavers with more premeditation and much earlier than the idea of an
"unthinking decision" allows. Jordan considered racism so deeply embedded in
English thought and identity that tobacco planters like Duckett automatically
turned to black chattel slavery after 1705 when presented with the opportunity to
import enslaved Africans. They did so to solve a labor problem in an economic
setting that gave them every incentive to become enslavers; they did so without
thinking very hard about the consequences of their decision. But new research has
called that interpretation into question, emphasizing the highly acquisitive and
aggressive intentions of English colonial planters in the Chesapeake. Instead of a
gradual, almost imperceptible shift to enslaved labor, more purposeful decisions
were taken. Enslavement was just one of many forms of labor in the British
American colonies but one that planters like Duckett chose because its boundaries
of coercion were far less constrained, its abstract qualities as a form of property far
more advantageous. Its premise of racial superiority was already well established in
English society. Winthrop Jordan, *White Over Black: American Attitudes Toward
the Negro, 1550–1812* (Chapel Hill: University of North Carolina Press, 1968), 199–222.
Also relevant is Edmund S. Morgan, *American Slavery, American Freedom: The
Ordeal of Colonial Virginia* (New York: Oxford University Press, 1975). See more
recent work by Anthony S. Parent Jr., *Foul Means: The Formation of a Slave Society
in Virginia, 1660–1740* (Chapel Hill: University of North Carolina Press, 2003);
John C. Coombs, "Beyond the 'Origins Debate': Rethinking the Rise of Virginia
Slavery," in *Early Modern Virginia: Reconsidering the Old Dominion,* ed. Douglas
Bradburn and John C. Coombs (Charlottesville: University of Virginia Press, 2013);
John C. Coombs, "The Phases of Conversion: A New Chronology for the Rise of
Slavery in Virginia," *William and Mary Quarterly,* 3rd ser., 68, no. 3 (2011): 332–360;
and Christopher Tomlins, *Freedom Bound: Law, Labor, and Civic Identity in
Colonizing English America, 1580–1865* (Cambridge: Cambridge University Press,
2010). For one of the most succinct and cogent explorations of this subject, see Karin
Wulf, "Vast Early America: Three Simple Words for a Complex Reality," *Humanities*
40, no. 1 (2019), https://www.neh.gov/article/vast-early-america.

7. At this writing, the *New York Times 1619* project has sparked a much-needed
and widespread conversation among historians and the public about how slavery
shaped American institutions. See esp. Nikole Hannah-Jones's seminal introduction, https://www.nytimes.com/interactive/2019/08/14/magazine/1619-america
-slavery.html. For a cogent assessment of the response, see Adam Serwer,
"The Fight over the 1619 Project Is Not About the Facts," *Atlantic,* December 23,
2019.

CHAPTER 2. OUGHT TO BE FREE

1. See *Basil Shorter v. Henry Rozier,* June 17, 1790, Petition for Freedom, October Term 1794, GCWS, Judgment Record, S497-23, JG 25, MSA.
2. John Carroll to Bernard Diderick, July 17, 1788, Special Correspondence, 9A G2, and Carroll to Diderick, July 25, 1788, Special Correspondence, 9A G1, ABA; "Protestant prejudices" quoted at 53.
3. Carroll to Diderick, July 25, 1788, in *The John Carroll Papers,* ed. Thomas O'Brien Hanley, vol. 1 (Notre Dame, Ind.: University of Notre Dame Press, 1976), 322–325, 240, 272. The original letter (see above) is in the ABA, with the original names crossed out but still visible. Hanley did not print the names. His annotations suggest that Diderick's dispute with Ashton concerned merely "financial claims." Hanley missed the connection of this long letter to Diderick to the series of letters later between Ashton and Carroll regarding Sucky Queen. Carroll claimed that he first heard the rumors about Ashton from a lapsed Jesuit named the Reverend Charles Wharton, an Anglican priest. Wharton apparently told Carroll "in a light manner" about the relationship.
4. Carroll to Diderick, July 25, 1788, and Carroll to Charles Plowden, January 22, 1787, and March 1, 1788, in Hanley, *John Carroll Papers,* 322–325, 240, 272. This point has been overlooked in the limited historiography, and most histories suggest that Ashton was personally the defendant.
5. *Maryland Society for Promoting the Abolition of Slavery; At a meeting the 4th of February, 1792* (Baltimore: Goddard and Angell, 1792).
6. Joseph Hopper Nicholson, *To the Printer of the Maryland Herald* (Easton, Md., October 20, 1792).
7. Nicholson, *To the Printer of the Maryland Herald.*
8. GCWS, Judgment Record, May 1794, S497-24, JG 23, MSA; GCWS, Judgment Record, May 1795, S497-24, JG 27, MSA.
9. GCWS, Judgment Record, May 1794, S497-22, JG 23, MSA.
10. GCWS, Judgment Record, May 1792, S497-17, JG 15, MSA.
11. Isaac Weld, *Travels Through the States of North America* (London: John Stockdale, 1799), 129.
12. "A Description of the State House at Annapolis, the Capital of Maryland," *Columbian Magazine,* February 1789, 78–82.
13. David Ridgely, *Annals of Annapolis* (Baltimore: Cushing, 1841), 232–235.
14. *Hanson's Laws of Maryland, 1763–1784, AOMOL,* vol. 203. "An Act to Limit the Jurisdiction of the General Court in Criminal Cases," *Laws of Maryland, 1785–1791, AOMOL,* 204:517; Constitution of Maryland, November 11, 1776, in William Kilty et al., eds., *The Laws of Maryland from the End of the Year 1799 . . . , AOMOL,* 192:11.
15. *Maryland Gazette,* July 28, 1791.
16. Norman K. Risjord, *Chesapeake Politics, 1781–1800* (New York: Columbia University Press, 1978), 399, 476–478. Also see Dorothy Brown, "Maryland and the Federalist Search for Unity," *Maryland Historical Magazine* 63, no. 4 (1968): 1–21. For a summary of the appointments made in January 1791, see John Thomas Scharf, *History of Maryland from the Earliest Period to the Present Day* (Baltimore: John B. Piet, 1879), 573–574.
17. Jessica A. Lowe, *Murder in the Shenandoah: Making Law Sovereign in Revolutionary Virginia* (Cambridge: Cambridge University Press, 2019), 147–150.

18. *The Slavery Code of the District of Columbia* . . . (Washington, D.C.: L. Towers, 1862), 3–4.

19. Julius Scott, *The Common Wind: Afro-American Currents in the Age of the Haitian Revolution* (New York: Verso Books, 2018), 118–119, 130–131, 138; Ada Ferrer, "Haiti, Free Soil, and Antislavery in the Revolutionary Atlantic," *American Historical Review* 117, no. 1 (2012): 40–66; Laurent Dubois, *Avengers of the New World: The Story of the Haitian Revolution* (Cambridge: Harvard University Press, 2004); Laurent Dubois, *A Colony of Citizens: Revolution and Slave Emancipation in the French Caribbean, 1787–1804* (Chapel Hill: University of North Carolina Press, 2004); Laurent Dubois, "An Enslaved Enlightenment: Rethinking the Intellectual History of the French Atlantic," *Social History* 31, no. 1 (2006): 1–14; Robin Blackburn, "Haiti, Slavery, and the Age of the Democratic Revolution," *William and Mary Quarterly,* 3rd ser., 63, no. 4 (2006): 643–674. On the importance of Haiti as a "turning point," see David Brion Davis, *The Problem of Slavery in the Age of Emancipation* (New York: Vintage Books, 2014), 45–65.

20. Thomas Harris and John McHenry, *Maryland Reports, Being a Series of the Most Important Law Cases Argued and Determined in the General Court and Court of Appeals of the Then Province of Maryland,* 4 vols. (New York: I. Riley, 1809–1818), 3:185–186.

21. Sue Peabody, "'Free upon Higher Ground': Saint-Domingue Slaves' Suits for Freedom in U.S. Courts, 1792–1830," in *The World of the Haitian Revolution,* ed. David Patrick Geggus and Norman Fiering (Bloomington: Indiana University Press, 2009), 261–283.

22. A growing body of studies emphasizes the contingency of these suits and the ways that enslaved people manipulated legal processes. See Ariela Gross, *Double Character: Slavery and Mastery in the Antebellum Southern Courtroom* (Athens: University of Georgia Press, 2006); Ariela Gross, *What Blood Won't Tell: A History of Race on Trial in America* (Cambridge: Harvard University Press, 2010); Ariela Gross, "Reflections on Law, Culture, and Slavery," in *Slavery and the American South,* ed. Winthrop P. Jordan (Oxford: University Press of Mississippi, 2003), 57–82; Mark S. Weiner, *Black Trials: Citizenship from the Beginnings of Slavery to the End of Caste* (New York: Knopf, 2004); Peggy Pasco, *What Comes Naturally: Miscegenation Law and the Making of Race in America* (Oxford: Oxford University Press, 2010); and Kathleen M. Brown, *Good Wives, Nasty Wenches, and Anxious Patriarchs: Gender, Race, and Power in Colonial Virginia* (Chapel Hill: University of North Carolina Press, 1996). See also Forum: Racial Determination and the Law in Comparative Perspective, *Law and History Review* 29, no. 2 (2011): 465–572; and Law, Slavery, and Justice: A Special Issue, *Law and History Review* 29, no. 4 (2011): 915–1095. For a treatment of enslaved use of the law in New Spain, see Sherwin Keith Bryant, "Slavery and the Context of Ethnogenesis: Africans, Afro-Creoles, and the Realities of Bondage in the Kingdom of Quito, 1600–1800" (Ph.D. diss., Ohio State University, 2005).

23. On the law as shaping the mindset of ordinary people, and cases as "buried politics," see Hendrik Hartog, "Introduction to Symposium on 'Critical Legal Histories,'" *Law and Social Inquiry* 37, no. 1 (2012): 147–154.

24. Gabriel Duvall to Benjamin Duvall, November 4, 1781, Duvall Family Papers, Library of Congress, Washington, D.C.

25. Gabriel Duvall to Benjamin Duvall, March 28, 1790, Duvall Family Papers.
26. *Minutes and Proceedings of the 4th Convention of Delegates from the Abolition Societies*, May 1797 (Philadelphia: Zachariah Poulson Jr., 1797), 38. See Annette Gordon-Reed, "Logic and Experience: Thomas Jefferson's Life in the Law," in *Slavery and the American South*, ed. Winthrop Jordan (Jackson: University Press of Mississippi, 2003), 3–20. At twenty-eight, Jefferson took on a similar freedom suit and made his first public argument about natural law, writing "under the law of nature, all men are born free, [and] everyone comes into the world with a right to his own person which includes the liberty of moving and using it at his own will." He argued that the colonial law enslaving the mixed-race children of a white woman was "a violation of the law of nature" and that the purpose of the law was to punish the woman, "not to oppress the offspring" (7–9). See also Timothy S. Huebner, "Roger B. Taney and the Slavery Issue: Looking Beyond—and Before—Dred Scott," *Journal of American History* 97, no. 1 (2010): 17–38. In 1806, Roger B. Taney argued a petition for freedom case. In 1810, Anne Taney, Francis Scott Key's sister, swore an affidavit for a freedom suit that the plaintiff was "freeborn."
27. For the best treatment of Philip Barton Key's career, see Marc Leepson, *What So Proudly We Hailed: Francis Scott Key, A Life* (New York: Palgrave Macmillan, 2014), 4–7; also Kimberly Michelle Nath, "Difficulties in Loyalism After Independence: The Treatment of Loyalists and Nonjurors in Maryland, 1777–1784" (M.A. thesis, University of Maryland, 2009); and "Philip Barton Key," *Biographical Series*, SC 3520-2060, MSA.
28. Deposition of Richard Disney, May 14, 1792, GCWS, Judgments, S498-3, MSA.
29. Deposition of Disney, May 14, 1792.
30. Deposition of Thomas Warfield, October 11, 1792, and deposition of George Davis, May 27, 1793, GCWS, Judgments, S498-3, MSA.
31. Deposition of Caleb Clarke, October 23, 1793, GCWS, Judgments, S498-3, MSA.
32. After the Reverend Ashton, as a young Jesuit, came to the Maryland colony in 1767, he was dispatched in the early 1770s to recover £1,000 in principal and interest from the executors of James Carroll for the Reverend Anthony Carroll in England, also a Jesuit priest. James Carroll willed two enslaved people to Anthony, his nephew, who was also John Ashton's uncle. See Thomas Hughes, ed., *History of the Society of Jesus in North America: Colonial and Federal*, 3 vols. in 4 (New York: Longmans, Green, 1908–1917), 2:251–253. There is no evidence that Anthony Carroll took either Margaret or Henry to England. In *Edward Queen v. John Ashton*, Ashton's attorneys introduced a 1794 copy of Carroll's will into evidence, specifically the provision bequeathing "Mary" to Anthony Carroll. The copies of the 1728 will in the MPA, however, reveal that Carroll bequeathed "Margt" (also spelled "Margaret") and therefore that the later transcription of the will was incorrect. See chap. 5, n. 27. I thank Dr. Lauret Savoy for identifying this discrepancy in the records. See Non-Jesuit Wills-(1725–1850) [95 A1-C6], box 25, folder 6; Will (1728) of James Carroll of Fingall [Ann Arundel County]; and [oversize box 5: (95 C2)-James Carroll Will and Codicil], all MPA. The account books of the EPA and MPA do not indicate whether Anthony held any enslaved people in London. See EPA, 1766–1808, Various Accounts, and Province Accounts, 1751–1793. Will of Anthony Carroll, October 1, 1794, PRO NA, Prob 11/1250, 171. See also Hughes, *History of the Society of Jesus in North America*, 1, pt. 1:252.

33. Robert M. Ireland, *The Legal Career of William Pinkney, 1764–1822* (New York: Garland, 1986), 19. On the limitations of attorneys' fees, see William Kilty et al., *The Laws of Maryland . . .* , vol. 1 (Annapolis, Md.: Frederick Green, 1799), Law of 1715, chap. 48, sec. 7, SC M 3150, 725, MSA. Attorneys in Maryland risked disbarment if they charged more than the rate prescribed by law.

34. *Laws of Maryland, Session Laws, 1793,* chap. 55, *AOMOL,* 645:53–54.

35. Entries for June 16 and August 20, 1794, in the St. Thomas Manor account book list payments made to defend the Jesuits against the Queen family freedom petitions. St. Thomas Manor Account Book, 1793–1825, box 46, folder 2, MPA.

36. Deposition of Jenny Shorter, May 16, 1793, *Stephen Shorter v. John Boarman,* October Term 1795, GCWS, Judgment Record, S497-25, JG 29, MSA.

37. Deposition of Henny Butler, June 6, 1793, *William Butler v. Joseph Neale,* October Term 1794, GCWS, Judgment Record, S497-23, JG 25, MSA.

38. Depositions in the original records were written in the third person. I have edited several of the most significant depositions in the freedom suits into the first person so that we can hear the words deponents spoke and the claims they made. On turning third person to first to "eavesdrop" in depositions, see Emmanuel Le Roy Ladurie, *Montaillou: Cathars and Catholics in a French Village, 1294–1324* (Harmondsworth, U.K.: Penguin, 1978). The original is deposition of William Hill, October 23, 1792, September 2, 1793, and September 2, 1794, *Basil Shorter v. Henry Rozier.*

39. *Basil Shorter v. Henry Rozier.*

40. Deposition of Clement Gardiner, May 22, 1794, *George Shorter v. Henry Neale,* October Term 1794, GCWS, Judgment Record, S497-23, JG 25, MSA.

41. For a successful civil suit for damages based on similar claims of false imprisonment, i.e., enslavement, see W. Caleb McDaniel, *Sweet Taste of Liberty: A True Story of Slavery and Restitution in America* (Oxford: Oxford University Press, 2019).

42. *Maryland Gazette,* May 7, 1795.

43. Dennis Cahill to John Carroll, January 27, 1796, ABA.

44. Cahill to Carroll, January 27, 1796.

45. Cahill to Carroll, March 23, 1796, AB ABPS John Carroll, 8J1-8A-Q7, folder 8AC5, ABA.

46. Carroll to Cahill, June 11, 1796, AB ABPS 9A1-9P6, folder 9M1, ABA. Years later Cahill recanted some of his earlier statements and asked Carroll to "throw a veil of silence and oblivion over it forever." Carroll's handwritten notes called the apology "not satisfactory." See Cahill to Carroll, November 22, 1803, folder Special A-F&G, ABA.

47. *Maryland Gazette,* August 18, 1761. Captain Judson Coolidge and Stephen West announced the arrival of the *Hawk* and its cargo of slaves imported from West Africa. Coolidge was also listed in *the Maryland Gazette* as the commander of the *Wilson,* April 23, 1761, and made merchant voyages from Annapolis to London.

48. Deposition of Benjamin Duvall, September 13, 1794, *Nancy Queen v. Charles Sewell,* Charles County, Md., Court Record Liber IB, 143–153, *Queen v. Sewell* (1796), T3236-1, MSA.

49. See Herbert Brewer, "From Sierra Leone to Annapolis: The 1718 Journey of the *Margaret,* an Eighteenth Century Slave Ship" (2018), in *GSA,* http://slaveryarchive .georgetown.edu/files/show/336. See James Carroll Day Book, box 41, folder 1, MPA.

According to the *Transatlantic Voyages Database,* previous voyages into Maryland (thirty-three in total) brought enslaved people primarily from Senegambia and Bight of Biafra. The *Margaret* was the first from Sierra Leone. For one of the best treatments of these voyages, including the role of sharks and the mortality rate, see Marcus Rediker, *The Slave Ship: A Human History* (New York: Penguin Books, 2007); Sowande M. Mustakeem, *Slavery at Sea: Terror, Sex, and Sickness in the Middle Passage* (Urbana: University of Illinois Press, 2016); and Robert Harms, *The Diligent: A Voyage Through the Worlds of the Slave Trade* (New York: Basic Books, 2008).

50. Prince George's County Court, Docket, April 1796, C1203-43, MSA.

51. Prince George's County Court, Docket, April 1796. Joseph Zwinge, S.J., "Jesuit Farms in Maryland," *Woodstock Letters* 41, no. 2 (1912): 209–212, using Mobberly's figures, estimated that the Jesuit plantation at St. Inigoes produced 12,000 pounds of tobacco annually that fetched approximately $600. The records of production on the Jesuit plantations are inexact in the 1790s. For reference, in the mid-1780s the Jesuits paid a white tenant 3,000 pounds of tobacco for building a new barn at Newtown (see Peter C. Finn, S.J., "The Slaves of the Jesuits of Maryland" [M.A. thesis, Georgetown University, 1974], 17), one of the more substantial single expenditures in the accounts.

52. *Nancy Queen v. Charles Sewell,* Judgment Record, August 1796.

53. Deposition of Fredus Ryland, February 26, 1796, *Charles Queen v. John Ashton,* folder 32:14—Court Records, County Court Records Collection, Historical Society of Harford County, Md. Gabriel Duvall entered the Ryland deposition into the record in Charles Queen's suit in Anne Arundel, and it was subsequently copied into the record of Harford County, where Ann Queen and David Queen had sued the Reverend Sylvester Boarman. The only remaining record of the case is cited above. The Charles Queen listed in this suit could have been the eleven-year-old alleged son of the Reverend John Ashton and Susanna "Sucky" Queen. Only Sucky Queen and her infant daughter, probably Elizabeth, were listed on the Prince George's County court docket for April 1796. The suit for Charles in Anne Arundel could have been because he had been separated from his mother and sister. A petition by a minor would typically be filed by a "next friend" but would not be styled as such in depositions like Ryland's. There is no other record of this important freedom suit because the Anne Arundel County Court Judgment Record for the period 1792 to 1807 is not extant in C9, MSA.

54. *Edward Queen v. John Ashton,* GCWS, Judgments, May 10, 1796, S498-3, MSA.

55. For other later examples of lawsuits that claim some form of restitution for enslavement, see Kirk Savage, "A Personal Act of Reparation: The Long Aftermath of a North Carolina Man's Decision to Deed a Plot of Land to His Former Slaves," *Lapham's Quarterly,* December 15, 2019; McDaniel, *Sweet Taste of Liberty;* Richard Bell, *Stolen: Five Free Boys Kidnapped into Slavery and Their Astonishing Odyssey Home* (New York: Simon and Schuster, 2019); and Melissa Milewski, *Litigating Across the Color Line: Civil Cases Between Black and White Southerners from the End of Slavery to Civil Rights* (Oxford: Oxford University Press, 2017).

56. Virgil Maxcy, *The Laws of Maryland: 1786–1800,* vol. 2 (Baltimore: Philip H. Nicklin, 1811), 359. For the 1752 act, see *Proceedings and Acts of the General Assembly, 1752–1754,* AOMOL, 50:74–78. Jeffrey Brackett, *The Negro in Maryland: A Study of the*

Institution of Slavery (Baltimore: Johns Hopkins University, 1889); T. Stephen Whitman, *The Price of Freedom: Slavery and Manumission in Baltimore and Early National Maryland* (Lexington: University Press of Kentucky, 1997), 93–95; John Joseph Condon, "Manumission, Slavery, and Family in the Post-Revolutionary Rural Chesapeake: Anne Arundel County, Maryland" (Ph.D. diss., University of Minnesota, 2001), 6–8; Peter J. Albert, "The Protean Institution: The Geography, Economy, and Ideology of Slavery in Post-Revolutionary Virginia" (Ph.D. diss., University of Maryland, 1976); and Max Grivno, *Gleanings of Freedom: Free and Slave Labor Along the Mason-Dixon Line* (Urbana: University of Illinois Press, 2011), 46, 216.

57. "An Act Relating to Negroes," November 1796, chap. 67, in Maxcy, *Laws of Maryland,* 352.

58. T. Stephen Whitman, *Challenging Slavery in the Chesapeake: Black and White Resistance to Human Bondage, 1775–1865* (Baltimore: Johns Hopkins University Press, 2006), 54–63.

59. On the status of St. Peter's as the Pro-Cathedral of the Maryland Diocese in Baltimore in the 1790s, see Mary A. Piet, *Early Catholic Church Records in Baltimore, Maryland, 1782 Through 1800, from the Original Records of "Old St. Peter's Pro-Cathedral"* (Baltimore: Family Line Publications, 1991), 193.

The Nine Ninety-Nine

1. Dennis Simms, in Federal Writers' Project, *Slave Narratives: A Folk History of Slavery in the United States from Interviews with Former Slaves,* vol. 8 (Washington, D.C.: Library of Congress, 1941), 68.

2. "Parson" Rezin Williams, in *Slave Narratives,* 68.

3. Silas Jackson, in *Slave Narratives,* 31.

4. Mary James, in *Slave Narratives,* 37.

5. Josiah Henson, *The Life of Josiah Henson, Formerly a Slave, Now an Inhabitant of Canada, as Narrated by Himself* (Boston: Arthur D. Phelps, 1849), 2.

6. Josiah Henson, *Uncle Tom's Story of His Life: An Autobiography of the Rev. Josiah Henson . . .* (London: Christian Age Office, 1877), 14.

7. Frederick Douglass, *Narrative of the Life of Frederick Douglass, an American Slave, Written by Himself* (Boston: Anti-Slavery Office, 1845), 3.

CHAPTER 3. CHARLES MAHONEY IS A FREE MAN

1. *Mahoney v. Ashton,* Judgment Record, May 1799, in OSCYS, http://earlywashingtondc.org/doc/oscys.mdcase.0008.003.

2. Deposition of Peter Harbard, May 25, 1792, GCWS, Judgment Record, May 1799, S497-33, JG 43, MSA.

3. Deposition of Peter Harbard, May 25, 1792. On turning third person to first to "eavesdrop" in depositions, see Emmanuel Le Roy Ladurie, *Montaillou: Cathars and Catholics in a French Village, 1294–1324* (Harmondsworth, U.K.: Penguin, 1978).

4. Deposition of Henry Davis, October 9, 1793, GCWS, Judgment Record, May 1799, S497-33, JG 43, MSA. See also deposition of Ann Hurdle, May 28, 1797, GCWS,

Judgment Record, May 1799, S497-33, JG 43, MSA; and GCWS, Judgments, S498-220, 1799, MSA. Charles Mahoney was present in the courtroom for several depositions.

5. Ronald Hoffman, *Princes of Ireland, Planters of Maryland: A Carroll Saga, 1500–1782* (Chapel Hill: University of North Carolina Press, 2002), 255.

6. The most important and extensive treatment of *Mahoney v. Ashton* is Eric Papenfuse, "From Recompense to Revolution: *Mahoney v. Ashton* and the Transfiguration of Maryland Culture, 1791–1802," *Slavery and Abolition* 15, no. 3 (1994): 39–62. Papenfuse's argument stresses the Haitian Revolution as a primary reason for the consolidation of the planter gentry class and the turn away from manumission and freedom petitions. Papenfuse prioritizes outside forces acting on the gentry, stiffening "resistance to social and institutional change that only a Civil War could alter." The case is also treated briefly in Patricia Ann Reid, "Between Slavery and Freedom" (Ph.D. diss., University of Iowa, 2006); and Letitia Woods Brown, *Free Negroes in the District of Columbia, 1790–1846* (New York: Oxford University Press, 1972). See esp. Thea K. Hunter, "Publishing Freedom, Winning Arguments: *Somerset,* Natural Rights and Massachusetts Freedom Cases, 1772–1836" (Ph.D. diss., Columbia University, 2005). The case is also featured in Patricia Ann Reid, "The Legal Construction of Whiteness and Citizenship in Maryland, 1780–1820," *Law, Culture and the Humanities* 15, no. 3 (2016): 656–683. For Reid's analysis of the Mahoney case, see pp. 672–677. I take a different approach from Reid, who argues the Mahoney family was making a legal claim to "whiteness" based on "non African phenotype" and that the case "tested the courts to define what constituted the boundaries of who could claim white racial identity" (672–673).

7. Thomas Harris and John McHenry, *Maryland Reports, Being a Series of the Most Important Law Cases Argued and Determined in the Provincial Court and Court of Appeals of the Then Province of Maryland,* 4 vols. (New York: I. Riley, 1809–1818), 4:210–215.

8. On special verdicts in civil cases, see Jessica A. Lowe, *Murder in the Shenandoah: Making Law Sovereign in Revolutionary Virginia* (Cambridge: Cambridge University Press, 2019), 145–149.

9. *Maryland Gazette,* January 8, 1798.

10. Harris and McHenry, *Maryland Reports,* 4:210–215.

11. The standard biography of Luther Martin is Paul S. Clarkson and R. Samuel Jett, *Luther Martin of Maryland* (Baltimore: Johns Hopkins University Press, 1970). Clarkson and Jett depict Martin as the "slave's counsel" and an advocate for petitions for freedom, largely on the basis of his service as one of the honorary counselors for the Maryland Society for Promoting the Abolition of Slavery. But few of the cases cited in this biography indicate that Martin served as a lawyer for the enslaved in Maryland. Martin served as the attorney for the Humphreys family who sued for their freedom in the 1790s. Martin's participation in *Mahoney v. Ashton* is unmentioned (164–170). Based on the court records in Maryland in this period, the characterization of Martin as the "slave's counsel" is misleading.

12. Harris and McHenry, *Maryland Reports,* 4:210–215.

13. Harris and McHenry, *Maryland Reports,* 4:210–215.

14. Harris and McHenry, *Maryland Reports,* 4:210–215.

15. Prince George's County Circuit Court, Docket Book, April 1797, C1203-45, MSA.

16. Prince George's Land Records, 1801, Liber JRM 9, folio 104, MSA. Prince George's County Black Court Papers, Deed of sale from Samuel J. Coolidge, March 7, 1799, 50199-3, C1187-1, MSA.

17. Harris and McHenry, *Maryland Reports*, 4:297.

18. Harris and McHenry, *Maryland Reports*, 4:304–305. Holly Brewer, "Creating a Common Law of Slavery for England and Its New World Empire," Paper presented at the Legal History Colloquium, NYU School of Law, February 26, 2018.

19. Harris and McHenry, *Maryland Reports*, 4:299.

20. Harris and McHenry, *Maryland Reports*, 4:311. The cases and reports that Ridgely, Johnson, and Jenings cited were the basis for common-law precedents holding that there could be no property in humans in English law outside of old forms of villeinage that were no longer legitimate: *Chamberlayne v. Harvey* 1 Ld. Raym. 147 (1696), *Smith v. Brown* and *Smith v. Gould* 2 Salk. 666 (1706) and reported in 2 Ld. Raym. 1274, overturning *Butts v. Penny* 2 Lev. 201 (1677). See also these citations in David Thomas Konig and Michael P. Zuckert, eds., *Jefferson's Legal Commonplace Book* (Princeton: Princeton University Press, 2019), 135.

21. See Peter C. Mancall, Joshua L. Rosenbloom, and Thomas Weiss, "Exports and the Economy of the Lower South Region, 1720–1770," in *Research in Economic History,* ed. Alexander J. Field, Gregory Clark, and William Sundstrom, vol. 25 (New York: Elsevier, 2008), 1–69. Mancall and colleagues cite a recalculated figure of $7.51 for tobacco in 1799. This should be per hundred pounds of tobacco. See also Arthur Harrison Cole, *Wholesale Commodity Prices in the United States, 1780–1861: Statistical Supplement* (Cambridge: Harvard University Press, 1938), 89–105. Cole's figures indicate the prevailing price per hundred pounds between $2.75 and $6.33 in this period.

22. See Ronald Hoffman, editor-in-chief, and Mary C. Jeske and Sally D. Mason, eds., *A Patriarch and His Family in the Early Republic: The Papers of Charles Carroll of Carrollton, 1782–1832* (Maryland Historical Society, forthcoming 2020), 181, 489, 511 (unpublished proofs in possession of the author with permission).

23. Prince George's County Circuit Court, Docket, 1797–1804, MSA. Also see manumission of Patience, Liber JRM 5, folio 537, MSA.

24. Lowe, *Murder in the Shenandoah,* 80–88.

25. See David Brion Davis, *The Problem of Slavery in the Age of Emancipation, 1770–1823* (Ithaca: Cornell University Press, 1975), 63–65.

26. David Skillen Bogen, "The Maryland Context of *Dred Scott*: The Decline in the Legal Status of Maryland Free Blacks, 1776–1810," *American Journal of Legal History* 34, no. 4 (1990): 381–411.

27. *Centinel of Liberty,* April 4, 1800.

28. Gabriel Duvall to James Madison, April 28, 1800, James Madison Papers, 1723 to 1859, Digital Collections, Library of Congress, Washington, D.C., http://hdl.loc.gov /loc.mss/mjm.06_0774_0775; Gabriel Duvall, "To the Freemen of the Fifth District of Maryland," *Maryland Gazette,* August 14, 1800; Philip Barton Key, "For the Maryland Gazette," *Maryland Gazette,* September 4, 1800.

29. David S. Bogen, "The Annapolis Poll Books of 1800 and 1804: African American Voting in the Early Republic," *Maryland Historical Magazine* 86, no. 1 (1991): 57–65. See also *Votes and Proceedings of the House of Delegates of the State of Maryland, 1800,* 29, SC M 3198, MSA, for the vote on Philip Barton Key's request to reconsider

the election of Allen Quynn and John Johnson as delegates and 51–52 for the vote on restricting the suffrage to "white" men.

30. Bogen, "Annapolis Poll Books of 1800 and 1804." *Votes and Proceedings in the Senate of Maryland, 1800,* December 19, 1800, 47–48, SC M 3186, MSA; *Votes and Proceedings in the Senate of Maryland, 1801,* December 31, 1801, 56, SC M 3186, MSA.

31. Prince George's County Circuit Court Docket: April 1804, *Mareen Duvall Jr. v. Simon Queen,* and April 1797, *Rev. John Ashton vs. Mareen Duvall Jr.;* Prince George's County Court, Judgment Record, C1231-3, 1806–1813, 1/20/9/18, April 1806, *Mareen Duval v. John Ashton.* Duvall's complaint was filed September 20, 1802. A series of cases were especially expensive: the court resurveyed "The Plaine" in 1806, found that Duvall's claim was "false clamour," and ordered Duvall to pay Ashton 560 pounds of tobacco in compensation for the court expenses. CRCC, May 5, 1801, Minutes Book No. 1, box 24, folder 3, MPA.

32. Ashton to Carroll, June 13, 1801, folder Special A-A1-A5, IB1, ABA. For Ashton's statement that he had not seen Susanna Queen since "the time she got free" until June 1800, when she returned to White Marsh, see Ashton to Carroll, August 7, 1801, folder Special A-A1-A5, IC4, ABA. On the timing of Susanna Queen's marriage as ca. June 1799, see Ashton to Carroll, June 13, 1801, folder Special A-A1-A5, IB1, ABA.

33. Ashton to Carroll, June 13, 1801.

34. Ashton to Carroll, June 13, 1801, folder Special A-A1-A5, IC1, ABA.

35. Ashton to Carroll, June 13, 1801, folder Special A-A1-A5, IC1, ABA.

36. Ashton to Carroll, June 13, 1801, folder Special A-A1-A5, IB1, ABA.

37. On the importance of the fifteenth year for enslaved women and the potential for sexual assault, see [Harriet A. Jacobs], *Incidents in the Life of a Slave Girl; Written by Herself,* ed. L. Maria Child (Boston: Published for the author, 1861), 44. See Annette Gordon-Reed, *Thomas Jefferson and Sally Hemings: An American Controversy* (Charlottesville: University of Virginia Press, 1997); Annette Gordon-Reed, *The Hemingses of Monticello: An American Family* (New York: W. W. Norton, 2008); Amrita Chakribarti Myers, *Forging Freedom: Black Women and the Pursuit of Liberty in Antebellum Charleston* (Chapel Hill: University of North Carolina Press, 2011), 176–199; Hannah Rosen, *Terror in the Heart of Freedom: Citizenship, Sexual Violence, and the Meaning of Race in The Postemancipation South* (Chapel Hill: University of North Carolina Press, 2009); and Maurie D. McInnis and Louis Nelson, *Educated in Tyranny: Slavery at Thomas Jefferson's University* (Charlottesville: University of Virginia Press, 2019). Amrita Chakribarti Myers's forthcoming book, *Remembering Julia: A Tale of Sex, Race, Power, and Place,* focuses on the relationship between Julia Chinn and one-term vice president Richard Mentor Johnson. I am especially grateful for Amrita Chakribarti Myers sharing her thoughts about the Queen-Ashton relationship with me.

38. Thomas Hughes, ed., *History of the Society of Jesus in North America: Colonial and Federal,* 3 vols. in 4 (New York: Longmans, Green, 1908–1917), 1, pt. 1:706, n. 9. The question of what was and was not corporation property bedeviled the trustees throughout the 1780s and 1790s. The Jesuits formed a trust in 1784 through an agreement. In 1792, the Maryland Assembly passed "an act for securing certain estates and property for the support and uses of ministers of the Roman Catholic religion" that allowed property "held and possessed by certain individuals" as legal

proprietors under a "confidential or implied trust" to be transferred to a corporate body. All property held individually had to be declared by August 14, 1796. Presumably Ashton did not declare property he later willed and devised to the Reverend Notley Young for the use of Georgetown College and other property he devised to Charles and Elizabeth Queen. See *Proceedings and Acts of the Assembly, 1792,* SC M, 685, MSA. Also relevant are the General Chapter Constitution, 1784, found in Hughes, *History of the Society of Jesus,* 1, pt. 1:630–631, and the discussion over the conditions attending alienation of real property by the chapter. See also Ashton's objections to Carroll's appointment as a trustee of the corporation in October 1802. Hughes, *History of the Society of Jesus,* 1, pt. 1:708–712.

39. Ashton to Carroll, June 19, 1801, I32, ABA.
40. Ashton to Carroll, July 25, 1801, ID2, ABA.
41. Carroll to Leonard Neale, July 5, 1801, box 57.A, folder 18, MPA.
42. Ashton to Carroll, August 7, 1801, IC4, ABA.
43. Ashton to Carroll, August 7, 1801.
44. CRCC, St. Thomas Manor, November 3, 1801, MPA.
45. Ashton to Carroll, January 6, 1802, folder Special A A10-A15, IC6; Ashton to Carroll, January 31, 1802, IB3; and Ashton to Carroll, March 23, 1802, IC5, ABA.
46. Harris and McHenry, *Maryland Reports,* 4:312.
47. *Mahoney v. Ashton,* June 25, 1802, Court of Appeals, Judgments, S381-2, 1800–1805:A, MSA.
48. Harris and McHenry, *Maryland Reports,* 4:325.
49. Charles Carroll of Carrollton to Robert Goodloe Harper, July 11, 1802. I thank Mary C. Jeske and Sally D. Mason, for sharing their research, and this letter, with me. See Hoffman, Jeske, and Mason, eds., *A Patriarch and His Family in the Early Republic: The Papers of Charles Carroll of Carrollton, 1782-1832,* 188–189.
50. Carroll to Harper, July 11, 1802.
51. Carroll to Harper, July 11, 1802. See also Papenfuse, "From Recompense to Revolution."
52. Carroll to Harper, July 11, 1802.
53. *Minchin v. Docker,* December 1806, in William Cranch, *Reports of Cases Civil and Criminal in the United States Circuit Court of the District of Columbia, from 1801 to 1841,* vol. 1 (Boston: Little, Brown, 1852), 307.
54. Deed of Manumission for John Joice, December 7, 1802, *Anne Arundel County Register of Wills (Certificates of Freedom),* AOMOL, vol. 821, 128-9, MSA. See Deed of Manumission for Jemima and Ann from John Joice, *Anne Arundel County Register of Wills (Certificates of Freedom),* AOMOL, vol. 821, 120, MSA Philip E. Thomas to John Parrish, 1804, Cox-Parish-Wharton Collection, Historical Society of Pennsylvania.
55. Carroll to Neale, November 12, 1805, box 57.1, folder 15, MPA. Note: I am using the online MPA finding aid box number; however, the paper finding aid refers to this box as 57.5 and the box itself is labeled 57.A.

Our Ancestors Are Calling Our Names

1. Rachel Swarns, "272 Slaves Were Sold to Save Georgetown; What Does It Owe Their Descendants?" *New York Times,* April 16, 2016. Mélisande Short-Colomb, Karran

Harper Royal, and Sandra Green Thomas, interview by author, New Orleans, La., April 9, 2017.

CHAPTER 4. A PUBLIC SCANDAL

1. Sexual abuse and misconduct by priests in the late twentieth century has led to a major reckoning in American society for the Catholic Church and the Jesuits at the same time as questions of reparations for, and historical trauma from, American slavery have come forward. In the face of the scandal, the Church has exhibited a pattern of evasion. For an account of current allegations, see Paul Elie, "Acts of Penance," *New Yorker,* April 15, 2019. The seminal investigations include: Michael Resendez, "Church Allowed Abuse by Priest for Years," *Boston Globe,* January 6, 2002; and "The Nature and Scope of Sexual Abuse of Minors by Catholic Priests and Deacons in the United States, 1950–2002" (John Jay College of Criminal Justice, February 2004), http://www.usccb.org/issues-and-action/child-and-youth -protection/upload/the-nature-and-scope-of-sexual-abuse-of-minors-by-catholic -priests-and-deacons-in-the-united-states-1950-2002.pdf.
2. Thomas Hughes, ed., *History of the Society of Jesus in North America: Colonial and Federal,* 3 vols. in 4 (New York: Longmans, Green, 1908–1917), 1, pt. 2:710.
3. *Maryland Gazette,* February 17, 1803.
4. CRCC, May 23, 1803, box 24, folder 3, MPA.
5. Francis Neale to John Carroll, July 22, 1803, 5 O11.5 old Sp. A. A11, ABA.
6. John Ashton to Carroll, August 11, 1803, IC6, ABA.
7. Philip E. Thomas to John Parish, March 24, 1805, Cox-Parish-Wharton Collection, Historical Society of Pennsylvania.
8. CRCC, April 25, 1804, box 24, folder 3, MPA; Ashton to Rev. Gentlemen Trustees of the Corporation, March 2, 1804, John Ashton Papers, box 23, folder 13, MPA.
9. *Anne Arundel County Court, Manumission Record, 1797–1807, AOMOL,* 825:258, 269; Prince George's County Court, Chattel Papers, C1174-7, 1810–1817, 40233-190, -194, MSA. Charles Carroll agreed to liberate twenty-two of the descendants of Ann Joice enslaved at Doughoregan Manor, who were descended from Sukey, Charles Mahoney's grandmother, if they won their freedom in court. In May 1799, he made a list of those "who obtained their freedom" when Charles Mahoney won his case, but in 1802 they were returned to bondage. Two of the Mahoneys, John, a shoemaker, and Daniel, a carpenter (who may not have been the Daniel who sued Ashton), later purchased their freedom, but their brother Rezin, also a carpenter, was still enslaved in 1811. I would like to thank Mary Jeske and Sally D. Mason, editors of a forthcoming edition of *The Charles Carroll of Carrollton Papers,* for sharing their extensive research with me on this important matter.
10. See July 5, 1794, February 1, 21, 1804, and March 1, 1804, St. Thomas Manor Account Book, 1793–1825, box 46, folder 2, MPA. Most Jesuit histories of slaveholding have presented these arrangements as benevolent and humane, ascribing paternalistic motives to the slaveholders that they did not hold. See Peter C. Finn, S.J., "The Slaves of the Jesuits of Maryland" (M.A. thesis, Georgetown University, 1974), 84–87; and Joseph Zwinge, S.J., "Jesuit Farms in Maryland," *Woodstock Letters* 41, no. 2 (1912): 208–209.

11. Charles County Court, Land Records, IB 6, 117–118, MSA; Fanny Queen, Negroes Manumitted, 1806–1811, 1, Baltimore City Freedom Records, Baltimore City Archives.

12. Douglas R. Egerton, *Gabriel's Rebellion: The Virginia Slave Conspiracies of 1800 and 1802* (Chapel Hill: University of North Carolina Press, 1993).

13. Alan Taylor, *The Internal Enemy: Slavery and War in Virginia, 1772–1832* (New York: W. W. Norton, 2013), 97–102.

14. David Brion Davis, *The Problem of Slavery in the Age of Emancipation, 1770–1823* (Ithaca: Cornell University Press, 1975), 52. On the importance of freedom papers, see Rebecca J. Scott and Jean M. Hébrand, *Freedom Papers: An Atlantic Odyssey in the Age of Emancipation* (Cambridge: Harvard University Press, 2012); and W. Caleb McDaniel, *Sweet Taste of Liberty: A True Story of Slavery and Restitution in America* (Oxford: Oxford University Press, 2019), 49–50.

15. "An Act, Entitled, 'An Additional Supplement to an Act Entitled an Act Relating to Negroes, and to Repeal the Acts of Assembly Therein Mentioned,'" November 1805, chap. 96, in Virgil Maxcy, *Laws of Maryland: 1801–1809*, vol. 3 (Baltimore: Philip H. Nicklin, 1811), 233–235.

16. St. George Tucker, *Hudgins v. Wright* Case Material, box 71, Tucker-Coleman Papers, Special Collections Research Center, Swem Library, College of William and Mary; Gillmer, "Suing for Freedom"; *Hudgins v. Wright,* 1 Hen. & M. 134, 11 Va. 134 (1806).

17. Taylor, *Internal Enemy,* 106–110.

18. *Hudgins v. Wright.*

19. For another example of this type of discipline at St. Thomas Manor, when Jesuit priests barred the sacraments of confession and holy communion from enslaved people who ran away and sought intercession, see Fr. John Baptist Carey to Rev. Francis Neale, March 21, 1820, box 59, folder 8, MPA, also at *GSA,* http://slaveryarchive.georgetown.edu/items/show/405.

20. Ashton to Carroll, October 26, 1804, IB8, ABA.

21. Rev. Charles Sewall to Nicholas Sewall, February 5, 1805, Maryland—Letters of Ours and of Bishops, 1773–1815, BN/3/1, EPA.

22. Ashton to Carroll, October 28, 1805, IB6, and Ashton to Carroll, January 10, 1806, D4, ABA. Carroll's reply to Ashton's October 28 letter is handwritten on the back.

23. Ashton to Carroll, November 13, 1805, IC7, ABA.

24. Ashton to Carroll, November 13, 1805.

25. Ashton to Carroll, January 10, 1806, D4, ABA.

26. Ashton to Carroll, January 10, 1806.

27. Ashton to Rev. Mr. Germain B. Bitouzey, February 3, 1806, box 23, folder 13, MPA.

28. The land case went to court in April 1806, but Mareen Duvall's attorneys did not appear. Prince George's County Court resurveyed the Plaine and determined that Duvall had no basis on which to claim damages (see his 1802 suit against Ashton) because the contested property belonged to the White Marsh estate. Simon Queen's testimony for Ashton may have played a role in the successful 1806 result.

29. *American and Commercial Daily Advertiser,* August 16, 1806. See runaway slave ad taken out by Germain B. Bitouzey.

30. Ashton to Messrs. Neale et al. at St. Thomas Manor, December 10, 1806, IC9, folder Special A B1-B5, ABA.

31. Ashton to Carroll, March 2, 1809, IC10, ABA.

32. Ashton to Carroll, March 2, 1809.

33. Ashton to Carroll, July 3, 1809, IC5, ABA.

34. CRCC, June 26, 1809, box 24, folder 1, MPA; also "Resolution to Apprehend Tom," *GSA*, https://slaveryarchive.georgetown.edu/items/show/195. Ashton to Carroll, October 7, 1809, IC 13, ABA; this letter includes a copy of Ashton's affidavit dated October 10, 1809.

35. Leonard Neale to Carroll, August 25, 1809, ABA.

36. Neale to Carroll, September 8, 1809, ABA. See *The History of Enslaved People at Georgetown Visitation* (Washington, D.C.: Georgetown Visitation Preparatory School, 2018), 9–11.

37. Neale to Carroll, September 8, 1809. Carroll to William Strickland, February 21, 1809, reported that no successor to the presidency of Georgetown College had been named in the wake of the Rev. Robert Molyneaux's death, but Charles Neale had been appointed superior. Maryland—Letters of Ours and of Bishops, 1773–1815, BN/3/1, EPA.

38. John Ashton affidavit, October 10, 1809, in Ashton to Carroll, October 7, 1809, IC13, ABA.

39. Ashton to Carroll, October 7, 1809.

40. Petition for freedom, Amey and Daniel Ogleton, September 10, 1810, Prince George's County Court, Black Court Papers, 50199-11, C1187-1, MSA.

41. Rev. John Ashton's Will, February 12, 1810, Charles County Register of Wills, April 1816, 460.

42. I am grateful to Queen descendant Keith Pierce, who is descended from Susanna Queen through her son Charles Queen, the legatee of Ashton's will. His three-times-great-grandmother Catherine Queen Hawkins was Charles's granddaughter. Her branch of the Queen family is using DNA matching and appears to confirm a cluster of distant DNA relatives from Tipperary, Ireland. Further research is under way to determine if there is a direct Carroll or Ashton DNA connection. Keith Pierce, email message to the author, June 28, 2019.

43. Lease, Richard Hopkins to Proteus Queen and James Parker, Leonard Collection, box 1, folder 22, SC 4685, MSA.

44. CRCC, August 20, 1816, Minutes Book No. 2, 1814 to April 1, 1907, folder 2, box 24, MPA; Notley Young to Rev. and Gentlemen, June 19, 1816, John Ashton Papers, box 23, folder 11, MPA. The corporation apparently challenged the will in court. Archbishop John Carroll advised Francis Neale to contest Ashton's will in court: "You must know, that without a minute and circumstantial investigation of the claims of the Corporation, my opinion of any proceedings for recovery of the money supposed to be due from Mr. Ashton's estate would be entitled to no other confidence than the information deserves, on which I should judge." Carroll to Neale, October 3, 1815, box 57.1, folder 15, MPA. Note that this letter was misfiled in the 1805 folder, but a close reading of the letter alongside other correspondence indicates that it was written ten years later, after John Ashton's death. I am using the online MPA finding aid box number; however, the paper finding aid refers to this box as 57.5 and the box itself is labeled 57.A.

45. U.S. Census, 1830, Charles County, Md., Durham, 237 (written), 119 (stamped), line 20 Charles Queen, digital image, *Ancestry.com,* citing M19, roll 56, NARA. See David L. Lightner and Alexander M. Ragan, "Were African American Slaveholders

Benevolent or Exploitative? A Quantitative Approach," *Journal of Southern History* 71, no. 3 (2005): 535–558, who find that "black slaveholding was not rare." They assert that 2 percent of free blacks in 1830 held slaves while 6 percent of whites did. See also Loren Scheweninger, *Black Property Owners in the South, 1790–1915* (Urbana: University of Illinois Press, 1990); Philip J. Schwartz, "Emancipators, Protectors, and Anomalies: Free Black Slaveowners in Virginia," *Virginia Magazine of History and Biography* 95, no. 3 (1987): 317–338; Larry Koger, *Black Slaveowners: Free Black Slavemasters in South Carolina, 1790–1860* (Jefferson, N.C.: McFarland, 1985, reprinted 2011); R. Halliburton, "Free Black Owners of Slaves: A Reappraisal of the Woodson Thesis," *South Carolina Historical Magazine* 76, no. 3 (July 1975): 129–135; and Carter G. Woodson, "Free Negro Owners of Slaves in the United States in 1830," *Journal of Negro History* 9, no. 1 (1924): 41–85. See also Kimberly Welch, "William Johnson's Hypothesis: A Free Black Man and the Problem of Legal Knowledge in the Antebellum United States South," *Law and History Review* 37, no. 1 (2019): 90–124.

46. *Nancy Queen v. Rev. Charles Neale,* Judgment Record, December 1810, GCWS, S420-9, MSA, also at *OSCYS,* http://earlywashingtondc.org/doc/oscys.md-case.0004.001. Also Loren Schweninger, *Appealing for Liberty: Freedom Suits in the South* (Oxford: Oxford University Press, 2018), 243, 394n7.

47. Frederick Douglass, *Narrative of the Life of Frederick Douglass* (Rochester, N.Y.: North Star, 1848), 9.

48. Paul S. Clarkson and R. Samuel Jett, *Luther Martin of Maryland* (Baltimore: Johns Hopkins University Press, 1970), 209–229. Clarkson and Jett point out that Philip Barton Key was appointed chief judge of the Fourth U.S. Circuit Court by Adams in 1800. His seat on that court was abolished when the Jeffersonian Republicans repealed the Judiciary Act in 1802 (220). On Woodley and Key's other property in Montgomery County "Bradford's Retreat," see *Federal Republican for the Country,* October 17, 1815; *Daily National Intelligencer,* August 9, 1815; and *National Intelligencer,* October 14, 1818.

49. Francis Scott Key to Marie West, March 6, 1808, and Key to mother, January 20, 1816, Francis Scott Key Letters, Albert and Shirley Small Special Collections, University of Virginia.

50. *Nancy Queen v. Charles Neale,* December 1810, Judgment Record, Court of Appeals, GCWS, MSA. Thomas Harris and Reverdy Johnson, *Reports of Cases Argued and Determined in the Court of Appeals of Maryland,* vol. 3 (Annapolis, Md.: Jonas Green, 1826), 158.

51. Charles Mahoney Certificate of Freedom, August 18, 1807, Anne Arundel County Court, Certificates of Freedom, C46-2, 425, MSA. Manumission of Ann Mahoney, May 7, 1816, *Anne Arundel County Court, Manumission Record, 1807–1816, AOMOL,* 830:343.

52. Prince George's County Court, Certificates of Freedom, April 5, 1815, C1171-1, entry 2, 61, MSA.

53. U.S. Census, 1820, Washington Ward 3, Washington, D.C., p. 96, roll M33_5, image 103, NARA.

54. Issue preclusion or res judicata, like hearsay, was in flux in the early nineteenth century. The doctrine was not raised to bar the Queens from pursuing a similar line of freedom suits in the D.C. Circuit Court. The parties were different in the freedom

suits, of course. The doctrine was in the early nineteenth century focused on barring the relitigation of particular, narrowly construed facts from earlier cases. Only later did courts and lawyers begin to bar relitigation on the grounds more broadly construed, that "the bar also applies to conclusions not set out in the previous judgment, but necessary to the outcome." Simon Stern, "The Analytical Turn in Nineteenth-Century Legal Thought" (May 31, 2011), http://dx.doi.org/10.2139/ssrn .1856146. Eleanor Joice's daughter Clem filed a freedom suit in the D.C. court in 1808 claiming descent from Ann Joice. A year later at trial her suit was unsuccessful. Francis Scott Key, attorney for the slaveholder, discredited the Joice/Mahoney claim. See *Clem Joice v. Robert Alexander* at *OSCYS,* http://earlywashingtondc.org/cases/ oscys.caseid.0337.

ABD

1. On the appointment of Allen Bowie Duckett, see U.S. Senate, *Executive Journal,* 9th Cong., 1st Sess., February 28, 1806, 25.
2. J. Jefferson Looney and Ruth L. Woodward, *Princetonians, 1791–1794: A Biographical Dictionary* (Princeton: Princeton University Press, 1991), 47–49.
3. *National Intelligencer,* May 13, 1808; James Oakes, *The Ruling Race: A History of American Slaveholders* (New York: W. W. Norton, 1998).
4. *Robert Thomas v. Rev. Henry Pile,* Defendant's Bill of Exceptions, October 31, 1794, GCWS, Judgments, S498-343, MSA.
5. Alexander Scott to James A. Porter and John Law, December 23, 1809; Philip Barton Key to Scott, June 30, 1810; and Motion for Rule to Show Cause, RG 21, entry 6, box 20, folder 217, NARA.
6. Rev. John McElroy Journal, January 22, February 4, and February 23, 1818, MPA. See also "Davy Threatened with Sale, 1818," *GSA,* https://slaveryarchive.georgetown.edu /items/show/29.

CHAPTER 5. *QUEEN V. HEPBURN* — A QUESTION OF FREEDOM

1. On the Capitol and its early repairs, see Glenn Brown, *History of the United States Capitol,* vol. 1: *The Old Capitol, 1792–1850* (Washington, D.C.: Government Printing Office, 1900), 44–46. See also William Allen, "History of Slave Laborers in the Construction of the United States Capitol" (Washington, D.C.: Office of the Architect of the Capitol, June 1, 2005), 8–9.
2. On the court's location see Wilhelmus Bogart Bryan, *History of the National Capital* (New York: Macmillan, 1914–1916), vol. 1: 454–455, and vol. 2: 38. F. Regis Noel and Margaret Brent Downing, *The Court-House of the District of Columbia* (Washington, D.C.: Judd and Detweiler, 1919).
3. See, e.g., *Rezin Ogleton v. Isaac Franklin,* September 15, 1810, in *OSCYS,* http:// earlywashingtondc.org/doc/oscys.case.0015.001. Nineteen members of the Ogleton family sued for their freedom in Prince George's County Court in September 1810. The cases were pending when Rezin Ogleton was sold to the slave trader Isaac Franklin and taken to the District of Columbia. Franklin attempted to deflect the

claim by arguing that he "did not own him at that time the petition was filed" and that Ogelton "had no thought of petitioning until he was sold." The D.C. court required Franklin to post £100 recognizance while it investigated the matter in Prince George's. Prince George's County Court, Court Papers, Blacks, C1187-1, MSA.

4. *Priscilla Queen vs. Rev. Francis Neale,* RG 21, entry 6, June Term 1810, NARA. William Cranch, *Reports of Cases Civil and Criminal in the United States Circuit Court of the District of Columbia, from 1801 to 1841,* vol. 2 (Boston: Little, Brown, 1852), 3. John Carroll to Charles Plowden, March 12, 1802, January 27, 1812, Maryland—Letters of Ours and of Bishops: 1773–1815, BN/3/1, EPA. Also Giovanni Grassi to John Carroll, October 8, 1811, enclosed in Carroll to Plowden, January 27, 1812.

5. For a description of the city and Georgetown, see Charles Ball, *Slavery in the United States: A Narrative of the Life and Adventures of Charles Ball, a Black Man, Who Lived Forty Years in Maryland, South Carolina and Georgia, as a Slave Under Various Masters, and Was One Year in the Navy with Commodore Barney, During the Late War* (New York: John S. Taylor, 1837), 27–29. Letitia Woods Brown, "Residence Patterns of Negroes in the District of Columbia, 1800–1860," *Records of the Columbia Historical Society, Washington, D.C.* 47 (1969–70): 66–79.

6. The congressman was Revolutionary War hero General Daniel Morgan, who averred that although he was in favor of "emancipation," he would not countenance "disorder." See *Alexandria Times,* September 2, 1797, 3.

7. John G. Sharp, "History of African Americans Enslaved and Free on the Washington Navy Yard, 1799–1865" (manuscript in possession of the author); John G. Sharp, *History of the Washington Navy Yard Civilian Workforce, 1799–1962* (Stockton, Calif.: Vindolanda, 2005). Allen B. Slauson, "Curious Customs of the Past as Gleaned from Early Issues of the Newspapers in the District of Columbia," *Records of the Columbia Historical Society, Washington, D.C.* 9 (1906): 88–125. On D.C. and black codes, see Letitia Woods Brown, *Free Negroes in the District of Columbia, 1790–1846* (New York: Oxford University Press, 1972), 10–11; Howard B. Furer, *Washington, a Chronological and Documentary History, 1790–1970* (Dobbs Ferry, N.Y.: Oceana, 1975), 67; and Kenneth Winkle, *Lincoln's Citadel: The Civil War in Washington, D.C.* (New York: W. W. Norton, 2013), 14. See Vernon Valentine Palmer, "The Customs of Slavery: The War Without Arms," *American Journal of Legal History* 48, no. 2 (2006): 177. Also J. D. Dickey, *Empire of Mud: The Secret History of Washington, D.C.* (Guilford, Conn.: Lyons Press, 2014); and Worthington G. Snethen, *The Black Code of the District of Columbia in Force September 1st, 1848* (New York: A. and F. Anti-Slavery Society, 1848), 48, for Georgetown's 1805 code.

8. Wilhelmus B. Bryan, "Hotels of Washington Prior to 1814," *Records of the Columbia Historical Society, Washington, D.C.* 7 (1904): 85–91; James Dudley Morgan, "Robert Brent, First Mayor of Washington City," *Records of the Columbia Historical Society, Washington, D.C.* 2 (1899): 236–251; Fanny Lee Jones, "Walter Jones and His Times," *Records of the Columbia Historical Society, Washington, D.C.* 5 (1902): 146–147.

9. Brown, "Residence Patterns of Negroes in the District of Columbia."

10. J. H. B. Latrobe, son of the architect Benjamin Latrobe, quoted in Glenn Brown, *History of the United States Capitol,* vol. 1: *The Old Capitol, 1792–1850* (Washington, D.C.: Government Printing Office, 1900), 47–48.

11. There is no modern biography of William Cranch, one of the most important judges in American history. See William F. Carne, "Life and Times of William Cranch, Judge of the District Circuit Court, 1801–1855," *Records of the Columbia Historical Society, Washington, D.C.* 5 (1902): 294–310.

12. Caesar Bonesana Marquis Beccaria, *An Essay on Crimes and Punishments* (Philadelphia: R. Bell, 1819), 104–105. See John D. Bessler, "Revisiting Beccaria's Vision: The Enlightenment, America's Death Penalty, and the Abolition Movement," *Northwestern Journal of Law and Social Policy* 4, no. 2 (2009): 209–210, 264; and John D. Bessler, *The Birth of American Law: An Italian Philosopher and the American Revolution* (Durham, N.C.: Carolina Academic Press, 2014).

13. John Hepburn, Prince George's County, March 6, September 20, 1775, Calendar of Wills, 1774–1777, 16:77, 78, MSA; probate in Prerogative Court Abstracts, 1774–1777, 119–126:49–50, MSA; inventory in Prince George's Inventories, 1763–1777, 352–361, C1228-7, MSA, also in *Probing the Past: Virginia and Maryland Probate Inventories, 1740–1810.* John Hepburn (Hepburn's grandfather), a judge of the Provincial Court, died August 14, 1774; see *Maryland Gazette,* August 24, 1774. *Samuel Hamilton v. Samuel Hepburn,* March 10, 1798, Chancery Court, Chancery Papers, S512-3-2505, MSA; Samuel Hamilton lease of John and Mary's Chance, 1796, Anne Arundel County, Land Records, NH no. 7, 288–290, MSA; *Moncky v. John Hepburn* and *Henny v. John Hepburn,* Prince George's County, Court Docket, September Term 1797, C-1203-46, MSA.

14. John Hepburn to George Fenwick, September 19, 1805, and John Stephen to Fenwick, July 22, 1804, box 39, folder 10, MSA.

15. Hepburn may have enslaved two descendants of Mary Queen, named Monica ("Moncky") and Henny in Prince George's County. Both women filed petitions for freedom against Hepburn in 1797. See Prince George's County, Court Docket, September Term 1797, C-1203-46, MSA. Both cases were dismissed in 1798 after the verdict in Charles County in *Nancy Queen v. Rev. Charles Sewell.* Hepburn filed for bankruptcy from Charles County in 1800. See *National Intelligencer,* January 9, 1801. William Hamilton of Charles County served as the trustee for Hepburn, March 9, 1801, chancery record of insolvency. See Chancery Court, Chancery Papers, S512, 2343-1, case 2260D, "John Hepburne," MSA.

16. See Mary Beth Corrigan, "Imaginary Cruelties? A History of the Slave Trade in Washington, D.C.," *Washington History* 13, no. 2 (2001/2002): 4–27.

17. Walter C. Clephane, "The Local Aspect of Slavery in the District of Columbia," *Records of the Columbia Historical Society, Washington, D.C.* 3 (1900): 224–256; "An Act to Amend the Laws Within the District of Columbia," sec. 9, June 24, 1812, in *The Acts of Congress in Relation to the District of Columbia from July 16th, 1790, to March 4th, 1831* (Washington, D.C.: Wm A. Davis, 1831), 265. See the 1794 act for the Potomac Company related to its contracts for the construction of federal buildings; the special act provided that slaves could be employed and that "every slave brought from Virginia to Maryland by virtue of this act, shall be carried back to Virginia within twelve calendar months from the final completion of the public works, either of the said City of Washington or of the said River Potomac, respectively, in which the said slave shall be employed, and that every slave, not carried back as aforesaid, shall be entitled to freedom at the expiration of twelve months." *The Acts of Congress in Relation to the District of Columbia from July 16th, 1790, to March 4th, 1831* (Washington, D.C.: Wm A. Davis, 1831, 90.

18. *National Intelligencer,* January 8, 1810, 4.
19. Richard Fenwick, February 23, 1808, and Francis Neale and John Wiseman, August 3, 1808, box 39, folder 10, MPA; Mary Gardiner to George Fenwick, January 3, 1811, box 39, folder 10, MPA; Corrigan, "Imaginary Cruelties?" 8–10.
20. *The History of Enslaved People at Georgetown Visitation: Learning, Reflecting, and Teaching* (Washington, D.C.: Georgetown Visitation Preparatory School, May 15, 2018), 10–11.
21. Petition for Freedom, January 8, 1810, *Priscilla Queen v. Francis Neale.* Key had little experience with freedom suits. He appeared first for a slaveholder in *John Davis et al. v. Hezekiah Wood,* RG 21, entry 6, January Term 1809, NARA. *Hezekiah Wood v. John Davis et al.,* 11 U.S. (7 Cranch) 271 (1812), 3 L. Ed. 339. His argument exploited a technical flaw in the original petition for freedom.
22. On the common-law origins of the use of depositions as evidence in the absence of witnesses, see Bernadette Meyler, "Common Law Confrontations," *Law and History Review* 37 no. 3 (2019): 763–786. On the development of confrontational trials and witness testimony, see John Langbein, *The Origins of Adversary Criminal Trial* (Oxford: Oxford University Press, 2013).
23. Deposition of Caleb Clark, October 23, 1793, *Edward Queen v. John Ashton,* GCWS, Judgments, 1794–1797, S498-3, MSA.
24. Deposition of Benjamin Duvall, September 13, 1794, *Nancy Queen v. Charles Sewell,* Charles County, Md., Court Record Liber IB, 143–153, *Queen v. Sewell* (1796), T3236-1, MSA.
25. See Laura F. Edwards, *The People and Their Peace: Legal Culture and the Transformation of Inequality in the Post-Revolutionary South* (Chapel Hill: University of North Carolina Press, 2009), 40–53; Larry D. Kramer, *The People Themselves: Popular Constitutionalism and Judicial Review* (Oxford: Oxford University Press, 2005), 162–163; and John Philip Reid, *Legislating the Courts: Judicial Dependence in Early National New Hampshire* (DeKalb: Northern Illinois University Press, 2008).
26. R. Kent Newmyer, *John Marshall and the Heroic Age of the Supreme Court* (Baton Rouge: Louisiana State University Press, 2001), 426, suggests that all of the testimony disallowed as hearsay was "hearsay of hearsay." This was true for Clark's and, as we shall see, Richard Disney's testimony but not for Ryland's. The difference is significant. Newmyer did not have access to the petitioners' bill of exceptions. That document makes clear that the first part of Ryland's deposition was hearsay, not hearsay of hearsay. Duvall's was similar to Ryland's, but Duvall's whole deposition was allowed because Key did not object. See RG 21, entry 6, box 20, folder 207, NARA, in *OSCYS,* http://earlywashingtondc.org/doc/oscys.case.0011.005.
27. See also chap. 2, n. 32, for the preceding case *Edward Queen v. Rev. John Ashton.* In *Edward Queen v. John Ashton,* Ashton's attorneys introduced a 1794 copy of Carroll's will into evidence, specifically the provision bequeathing "Mary" to Anthony Carroll. The copies of the 1728 will in the MPA, however, reveal that Carroll bequeathed "Margt" (also spelled "Margaret") and therefore that the later transcription of the will was incorrect. The incorrect transcription of the will in *Queen v. Ashton* was the copy introduced in *Mima Queen v. John Hepburn* in 1810 by Francis Scott Key. The 1794 excerpt was the only publicly accessible evidence Key had of a "Mary" held by James Carroll. Key may have thought that Mary Queen was sent to London with Anthony Carroll. The discrepancy is significant. I thank Dr. Lauret

Savoy for identifying this discrepancy in the records. See Non-Jesuit Wills—(1725–1850) [95 A1-C6], box 25, folder 6; and Will (1728) of James Carroll of Fingall [Ann Arundel Co.], [oversize box 5: (95 C2)—James Carroll Will and Codicil], MPA. The account books of the EPA and MPA do not indicate whether Anthony held any enslaved people in London; see EPA, 1766–1808 Various Accounts, and Province Accounts, 1751–1793; and Will of Anthony Carroll, October 1, 1794, PRO NA, Prob 11/1250, p. 171. See also Thomas Hughes, ed., *History of the Society of Jesus in North America: Colonial and Federal,* 3 vols. in 4 (New York: Longmans, Green, 1908–1917), 1, pt. 1:252.

28. James Carroll Day Book, 1714–1721, box 41, folder 1, Day Book/Account Ledgers, MPA.

29. *Creagh v. Rogers,* C104/160, C104/61, C104/36-37, NA; E190/1168/3-4 The Port of Bristol: Customer Overseas Inwards, NA.

30. Charles County Circuit Court, Land Records, Liber D 2, 80, MSA.

31. James Carroll Will and Estate Inventory, Maryland Prerogative Court Will Book 19, 797–799, James Carroll (1729), SR 4413-2, MSA.

32. Bohemia Day and Ledger Book, 1735–1761, box 49, folder 1, MPA.

33. Deposition of Fredus Ryland, February 26, 1796, *Winifred Queen v. Solomon Sparrow* and *Charles Queen v. John Ashton* in *Ann Queen v. Sylvester Boarman,* March 1801, folder 32:14—Court Records, County Court Records Collection, Historical Society of Harford County, Md.

34. The full title is Woodes Rogers, *A Cruising Voyage Round the World, First to the South Seas, Thence to the East Indies, and Homeward by the Cape of Good Hope, Begun in 1708 and Finish'd in 1711* (London: A. Bell and B. Lintot, 1712). See also Donald Jones, *Captain Woodes Rogers' Voyage Round the World, 1708–1711* (Bristol, U.K.: Bristol Branch of the Historical Association, 1992). The most recent treatment is Timothy Charles Halden Beattie, "The Cruising Voyages of William Dampier, Woodes Rogers, and George Shelvocke and Their Impact" (Ph.D. diss., University of Exeter, 2013).

35. Deposition of Richard Disney, May 14, 1794, *Edward Queen v. John Ashton,* GCWS, Judgments, 1794–1797, S498-3, MSA. Deposition of Fredus Ryland, February 26, 1796.

36. Daniel Rasmussen, *American Uprising: The Untold Story of America's Largest Slave Revolt* (New York: HarperCollins, 2011); Alan Taylor, *The Internal Enemy: Slavery and War in Virginia, 1772–1832* (New York: W. W. Norton, 2013).

37. Recusal was less common on the early court. John Marshall recused himself in *Martin v. Hunter's Lessee* 14 U.S. 304 (1816) because he had a direct financial interest in the outcome. But lawyers often argued cases before judges to whom they were related. Marshall stayed on the bench in *Marbury v. Madison* (1803) even though his brother James Marshall played an important role in the litigation and as secretary of state he had signed the commissions at issue. See Akhil Reed Amar, *America's Unwritten Constitution: The Precedents and Principles We Live By* (New York: Basic Books, 2002), 7, 21, 522–523.

38. The case is cited as *Mima Queen v. John Hepburn* 11 U.S. (7 Cranch) 290 (1813).

39. *Mima Queen v. Hepburn.* Benjamin Roberts Curtis, *Reports of Decisions in the Supreme Court of the United States,* vol. 2 (Boston: Little, Brown, 1855), in OSCYS, http://earlywashingtondc.org/doc/oscys.report.0002.002.

40. On Marshall's slaveholding, see Paul Finkelman, *Supreme Injustice: Slavery in the Nation's Highest Court* (Cambridge: Harvard University Press, 2018), 31, 36–47.

41. S. March Phillipps and Andrew Amos, *A Treatise on the Law of Evidence*, 8th ed. (London: Saunders and Benning, 1838), 219.

42. Kramer, *People Themselves*, 161–163, describes the division as between "professionals" and "democrats."

43. *Negro John Davis et al. v. Wood* 14 U.S. (1 Wheat.) 6 (1816), in *OSCYS*, http:// earlywashingtondc.org/cases/oscys.caseid.0251. See also Finkelman, *Supreme Injustice*, 60–62.

44. Federalist judges, such as Chancellor James Kent in New York, considered allowing any form of hearsay "a dangerous relaxation of the rules of evidence." Asserting the supremacy of first-person testimony, Kent directed justices this way: "You must go, if you can, to the source of testimony, and not introduce a copy, when the original is to be had, nor undertake to prove what another person has been heard to say, when that person is a good witness, and can be produced." Then in the same opinion, and in violation of his own rule to go to the original source, Kent quoted a source he did not cite: "A person who relates a hearsay is not obliged to enter into any particulars, to answer any questions, to solve any difficulties, to reconcile any contradictions, to explain any obscurities, to remove any ambiguities; he entrenches himself in the simple assertion that he was told so, and leaves the burden entirely on his dead or absent author." Kent fulminated against those who permitted looser interpretations of the rules of evidence. Hearsay was full of doubts "from the very nature of it . . . [and] it cannot clear them up." *Coleman v. Southwick*, 9 Johns 45, 50 (N.Y. Sup. Ct. 1812). *Negro John Davis et al. v. Wood* 14 U.S. (1 Wheat.) 6 (1816).

45. Simon Greenleaf, *A Treatise on the Rules of Evidence*, vol. 1, 16th ed. by John Henry Wigmore (Boston: Little, Brown, 1899), chap. 9, sec. 98–99, pp. 182–183. *Queen v. Hepburn* is the first citation. For a wide review of this literature, see Roger C. Park, "A Subject Matter Approach to Hearsay Reform," *Michigan Law Review* 86 (1987): 51–122, esp. on Jeremy Bentham, *Rationale of Judicial Evidence* (London, 1827), that "no species of evidence whatsoever, willing or unwilling, ought to be excluded: for that although in certain cases it may be right that this or that lot of evidence, though tendered, should not be admitted, yet, in these cases, the reason for the exclusion rests on other grounds; viz. avoidance of vexation, expense, and delay" (1).

46. Newmyer, *John Marshall and the Heroic Age of the Supreme Court*, 430. See Edwards, *People and Their Peace*, 240–244, on the shift in "legal focus" from the enslaved as subjects to the individual property rights of others outside of the parameters of any single case.

47. See note 27, above.

48. CRCC, June 14, 1814, Minutes Book No. 2, 1814 to April 1, 1907, folder 2, box 24, and May 18, September 14, 1813, folder 1, box 24, MPA.

49. Joseph Mobberly to Giovanni Grassi, February 5, 1815, box 58, folder 6, MPA.

50. Mobberly to John Carroll, [November] 1814, and Mobberly to Grassi, November 5, 1814, box 58, folder 8, MPA. For the list of enslaved who left with the British, see *American State Papers*, vol. 6: *Foreign Relations, Executive Papers*, 19th Cong., 1st Sess., Doc. No. 122, March 6, 1826. For another account of the British occupation and looting at St. Inigoes, see the diary of Joseph Mobberly, 86–90, box 2, folder 1, MPA.

51. Marc Leepson, *What So Proudly We Hailed: Francis Scott Key, A Life* (New York: Palgrave Macmillan, 2014), 60–64. *Poems of the Late Francis S. Key, Esq., Author of*

the *"Star Spangled Banner" with an Introductory Letter by Chief Justice Taney* (New York: Robert Carter and Brothers, 1857), 31–33.

52. The original petition and court documents refer to her as "Mina," but later printed court reports as "Mima," probably due to a transcription error. Richard Peters, *Full and Arranged Digest of Cases Decided in the Supreme, Circuit and District Courts of the United States from the Organization of the Government of the United States,* vol. 2 (Philadelphia: Thomas, Cowperthwait, 1839), v, vi, 224, Special Collections, Jacob Burns Law Library, George Washington University. In 1840–1841 Key as U.S. district attorney represented Emanuel Price, a free black who had been kidnapped and held at William H. Williams's Yellow House. Key highlighted the index on evidence forfeiture under the embargo and nonintercourse laws and laws prohibiting the slave trade, as well as the section on hearsay evidence that prominently referred to *Queen v. Hepburn.* Price's freedom suit was one of the last Key tried. See *Emanuel Price v. Thomas N. Davis,* Petition for Freedom, January 20, 1840, in *OSCYS,* http://earlywashingtondc.org/cases/oscys.caseid.0126. Jeff Forret, *Williams' Gang: A Notorious Slave Trader and His Cargo of Black Convicts* (Cambridge: Cambridge University Press, 2020), 130–135, offers a more generous portrayal of Key based largely on Leepson's admiring biography.

53. Carroll to Neale, October 3, 1815, box 57.1, folder 15, MPA. Note that this letter is marked "1805" but refers to events including the estate settlement of the Reverend John Ashton in 1815. See CRCC, June 10, 1818, box 24, MPA.

54. "To James Madison from S. Potter, 7 February 1813," *Founders Online,* https://founders.archives.gov/documents/Madison/03-05-02-0556. See Finkelman, *Supreme Injustice,* 74.

55. See Sean Wilentz, *No Property in Man: Slavery and Antislavery at the Nation's Founding* (Cambridge: Harvard University Press, 2018), 186–187, on the significance of the years around 1815.

Dead but Not Forgotten

1. One of Allen Bowie Duckett's last recorded opinions came in December 1806, when he ruled that a free black man could be a witness in a civil suit against a white man. Duckett said "that persons born free, that is, descended from a white woman, were not, in Maryland, held to be negroes; and were permitted to testify against white persons." But he made sure to clarify how the law defined slavery—"color is *prima facie* evidence of slavery." *Minchin v. Docker,* December 1806, in William Cranch, *Reports of Cases Civil and Criminal in the United States Circuit Court of the District of Columbia, from 1801 to 1841,* vol. 1 (Boston: Little, Brown, 1852), 370. Duckett gave an opinion in only one other case. Loyal partisan, he ruled with another Jefferson appointee that there was probable cause to issue a bench warrant in the treason trial of the men associated with Aaron Burr. See R. Kent Newmyer, *The Treason Trial of Aaron Burr: Law, Politics, and the Character Wars of the New Nation* (Cambridge: Cambridge University Press, 2012), 48–49.

2. My visit to the cemetery was in November 2015. The cemetery at Sacred Heart has since been rearranged. The stone "Dead but not Forgotten" has been moved, along with several others, to a pebble garden on the northeast corner to commemorate the enslaved buried on the grounds.

3. James V. Deane, in Federal Writers' Project, *Slave Narratives: A Folk History of Slavery in the United States from Interviews with Former Slaves,* vol. 8 (Washington,

D.C.: Library of Congress, 1941), 9. John Bates, quoted in Daina Ramey Berry, "'Broad Is de Road Dat Leads ter Death': Human Capital and Enslaved Mortality," in *Slavery's Capitalism: A New History of American Economic Development,* ed. Sven Beckert and Seth Rockman (Philadelphia: University of Pennsylvania Press, 2016), 161.

4. See Zora Neale Hurston, *Barracoon: The Story of the Last "Black Cargo"* (New York: Amistad, 2018), 74–75, 89, for the importance of the "family lot" and grave tending. For a recent account along these lines, see Charmaine A. Nelson, "Black Cemeteries Force Us to Re-Examine Our History with Slavery," *Walrus,* May 28, 2018. See also a beginning effort to collect data on enslaved burials at *The National Burial Database of Enslaved Americans* (Periwinkle Humanities Initiative, 2018).

5. Vincent Brown, *The Reaper's Garden: Death and Power in the World of Atlantic Slavery* (Cambridge: Harvard University Press, 2008), 31, 43.

6. John McElroy, "Persons Received in the Catholic Church, 1819," box 9, folder 1, MPA also at *GSA,* https://slaveryarchive.georgetown.edu/items/show/325. "Soul value" is Daina Ramey Berry's term for the inner, personal value of the lives of enslaved people and how they resisted the dehumanizing forces of the market and enslavement. See Berry, *The Price for Their Pound of Flesh: The Value of the Enslaved, from Womb to Grave, in the Building of a Nation* (Boston: Beacon Press, 2017).

CHAPTER 6. THE TURNING

1. All accounts of Ann "Anna" Williams rely heavily on Jesse Torrey, *A Portraiture of Domestic Slavery, in the United States* (Philadelphia: John Boiken, 1817), and a later account in Ethan Allen Andrews, *Slavery and the Domestic Slave-Trade in the United States* (Boston: Light and Stearns, 1836), 128–133. For treatments of Williams in the literature, see Edward E. Baptist, *The Half Has Never Been Told: Slavery and the Making of American Capitalism* (New York: Basic Books, 2014), 27–28; Terri Snyder, *The Power to Die: Slavery and Suicide in British North America* (Chicago: University of Chicago Press, 2015), 1–6; and Robert H. Gudmestad, "Slave Resistance, Coffles, and the Debates over Slavery in the Nation's Capital," in *The Chattel Principle: Internal Slave Trades in the Americas,* ed. Walter Johnson (New Haven: Yale University Press, 2004), 72–90. Baptist asserts understandably but incorrectly that Anna died of her injuries. Gudmestad notes that she was "known only as Anna" (72). Robert Pierce Forbes, *The Missouri Compromise and Its Aftermath: Slavery and the Meaning of America* (Chapel Hill: University of North Carolina Press, 2007), 33–34, refers to this incident. See also Letitia Woods Brown, *Free Negroes in the District of Columbia, 1790–1846* (Oxford: Oxford University Press, 1972). Richard Bell, *We Shall Be No More: Suicide and Self-Government in the Newly United States* (Cambridge: Harvard University Press, 2012), 217–218, considers Torrey's portrayal of "Anna" to mark "a turning point" in antislavery and suicide literature. Suicide, Bell argues, had been seen as the sole province of men of exceptional character, but Torrey's account placed a wife and mother at the center of his indictment of kidnapping and enslavement. For the most recent assessment of the horrors and violence of slavery, see Baptist, *Half Has Never Been Told.* Andrew Delbanco, *The War Before the War: Fugitive Slaves and the Struggle for America's Soul from the Revolution to the Civil War* (New York: Penguin, 2018), 114, reprises the image of Anna from Torrey. On

kidnapping, see Carole Wilson, *Freedom at Risk: The Kidnapping of Free Blacks in America 1780–1865* (Lexington: University Press of Kentucky, 1994). On the cool reception to Torrey's pamphlet, see Bell, *We Shall Be No More*, 219–220. On rumors about its veracity, see *New England Galaxy and Masonic Magazine*, December 19, 1817. See also Candy Carter, "'I Did Not Want to Go': An Enslaved Woman's Leap into the Capital's Conscience," in *OSCYS*, http://earlywashingtondc.org/stories/enslaved_womans_leap. For a film adaptation of the Ann Williams story, see *Anna*, prod. Kwakiutl Dreher, Michael Burton, and William G. Thomas III (Salt Marsh Productions, LLC, 2018, 11 min., http://annwilliamsfilm.com). I am especially grateful to Professor Maurice Jackson, Georgetown University, and Mélisande Short-Colomb for their discussion of African worldviews about death and dying in this period. See Terri L. Snyder, "Suicide, Slavery, and Memory in North America," *Journal of American History* 97, no. 1 (June 2010): 39–62, for an analysis of flying stories, historical memory, and suicide.

2. Torrey, *Portraiture of Domestic Slavery*, 32–33, 41, 43–44. See also *Rosanna Brown v. Bennett*, Petition for Freedom, December 22, 1815, RG 21, NARA. These cases were not recorded in the Minutes of the Circuit Court of the District of Columbia, 1801–1863, M1021, roll 2, NARA. The outcome of these cases remains unclear. However, Key filed several cases against Thomas Offutt, including *Negro Delia and her children Stacey, Edmund, and Madison v. Thomas Offutt*. Delia's case came to trial January 6, 1816, and the jury returned a verdict for the petitioners. Torrey misidentified Key as "Francis T. Key" and both of the other lawyers as "J. B. Caldwell and J. B. Lear." He probably meant Elias Boudinot Caldwell and Benjamin Lincoln Lear.

3. On slavery and the stealing of women's wombs, see Daina Ramey Berry, *The Price for Their Pound of Flesh: The Value of the Enslaved, from Womb to Grave, in the Building of a Nation* (Boston: Beacon Press, 2017), 10–32. See also Deirdre Cooper Owens, *Medical Bondage: Race, Gender, and the Origins of American Gynecology* (Athens: University of Georgia Press, 2018). For episodes of similar violence, see Richard S. Newman, "'Lucky to Be Born in Pennsylvania': Free Soil, Fugitive Slaves and the Making of Pennsylvania's Anti-Slavery Borderland," *Slavery and Abolition* 32, no. 3 (2011): 413–430.

4. See John Joseph Condon, "Manumission, Slavery, and Family in Post-Revolutionary Rural Chesapeake: Anne Arundel County, Maryland" (Ph.D. diss., University of Minnesota, 2001), 79–81, on rates of manumission. Condon finds that the period of manumission in Maryland came not in the 1780s and 1790s but later in the 1810s and 1820s. There were more manumissions in the 1820s in Anne Arundel than in the twenty-year period 1780–1800. See also T. Stephen Whitman, *The Price of Freedom: Black and White Resistance to Human Bondage, 1775–1865* (Baltimore: Johns Hopkins University Press, 2006), 64–67, 119; and Michael Tadman, *Speculators and Slaves: Masters, Traders, and Slaves in the Old South* (Madison: University of Wisconsin Press, 1989), who finds that the periods of heaviest slave sales in Maryland were not during market collapses but when crop production was successful.

5. See esp. Donald J. Ratcliffe, "The Decline of Antislavery Politics, 1815–1840," in *Contesting Slavery: The Politics of Bondage and Freedom in the New American Nation*, ed. John Craig Hammond and Matthew Mason (Charlottesville: University of Virginia Press, 2011), 267–290.

6. See the excellent treatment of this issue in Maryland in Martha S. Jones, *Birthright Citizens: A History of Race and Rights in Antebellum America* (Cambridge: Cambridge University Press, 2018), 40–44.

7. Francis Scott Key, testimony, April 22, 1816, and Petition of Grand Jurors, July Term, 1816, Select Committee to Inquire into the Existence of an Inhuman and Illegal Traffic in Slaves in the District of Columbia, Committee on the District of Columbia, RG 233, chapter 22.27, 14A-C17-4, NARA.

8. Torrey, *Portraiture of Domestic Slavery*, 43–44. Jesse Torrey, testimony, April 29, 1816, Francis Scott Key, testimony, April 22, 1816, Petition of Grand Jurors, July Term, 1816, in Select Committee to Inquire into the Existence of an Inhuman and Illegal Traffic in Slaves in the District of Columbia. See William T. Laprade, "The Domestic Slave Trade in the District of Columbia," *Journal of Negro History* 11 (1926): 17–34. For recent references, see Robert M. Gudmestad, *A Troublesome Commerce: The Transformation of the Interstate Slave Trade* (Baton Rouge: Louisiana State University Press, 2004); Gutmestad, "Slave Resistance, Coffles, and the Debates over Slavery"; and Mary Beth Corrigan, "Imaginary Cruelties? A History of the Slave Trade in Washington, D.C.," *Washington History* 13, no. 2 (2001/2002): 4–27, esp. 17–18. Charlotte Dupee's last name has been spelled in some modern sources as "Dupuy," but it is unclear in the record how that spelling originated. Her husband and children were consistently referred to by the surname "Dupee" and may have used that surname through the late nineteenth century. See *Salem* (Mass.) *Register*, July 13, 1857; *Opelousas* (La.) *Courier*, July 25, 1857; *Richmond* (Va.) *Whig*, February 20, 1866; *Providence* (R.I.) *Evening Press*, February 20, 1866; *Memphis* (Tenn.) *Daily Avalanche*, February 20, 1866; and U.S. Census, 1860, Lexington, Ky., p. 148, dwelling no. 1060, family no. 1165 (Year: 1860; Census Place: Lexington, Fayette, Ky.; Page: 428; Family History Library Film: 80336). I am indebted to William Kelly for sharing his detailed research on Aaron and Charlotte Dupee in William Kelly, "'She's Been Her Own Mistress . . .': The Long History of Charlotte Dupee v. Henry Clay, 1790–1830," Paper presented at the Washington, D.C., Historical Society Conference, November 2019.

9. Allen C. Clark, "Sketch of Elias Boudinot Caldwell," *Records of the Columbia Historical Society, Washington, D.C.* 24 (1922): 204–213.

10. *Maryland Colonization Journal* 4, no. 1 (1847): 9. Also in Rev. Isaac V. Brown, *Biography of the Rev. Robert Finley, D.D. of Basking Ridge, N.J. . . . with an Account of his Agency as the Author of The American Colonization Society and A Sketch of the Slave Trade . . .* (Philadelphia, 1857), 104, 108. Quoted in Torrey, *Portraiture of Domestic Slavery*, 86–87. Torrey objected to one part of the quotation without giving the full context. Later, William Lloyd Garrison picked up Torrey's account and used the abbreviated quotation.

11. Torrey, *Portraiture of Domestic Slavery*, 88.

12. Speech of Robert Wright, in Brown, *Biography of the Rev. Robert Finley*, 114–115.

13. *A Letter from Gen. Harper, of Maryland, to Elias B. Caldwell, Esq., Secretary of the American Society for Colonizing the Free People of Colour in the United States, with Their Own Consent* (Baltimore: Printed for E. J. Coale by R. J. Matchett, 1818), 6–7.

14. *New York Evening Post*, April 21, 1817.

15. James Forten and Russell Perrott, "An Address to the Humane and Benevolent Inhabitants of the City and County of Philadelphia" (1817), in *The American Debate*

over Slavery, 1760–1865: An Anthology of Sources, ed. Howard L. Lubert, Kevin R. Hardwick, and Scott J. Hammond (Indianapolis, Ind.: Hackett, 2016), 64–67; Nicholas Guyatt, *Bind Us Apart: How Enlightened Americans Invented Racial Segregation* (New York: Basic Books, 2016), 259–267.

16. Thomas Smallwood, *A Narrative of Thomas Smallwood* (Toronto: James Stephens, 1851), 13, 14–16.

17. Frederick Douglass, "Henry Clay and Colonization Cant, Sophistry, and False-hood," address delivered in Rochester, N.Y., February 2, 1851, in *Frederick Douglass Papers,* Series One: *Speeches, Debates, and Interviews,* vol. 2: *1847–1854,* ed. John W. Blassingame (New Haven: Yale University Press, 1982), 311–325; Paul Grosskopf, "A Rhetoric of Redirection: Reframing Discourse and Proponents of Colonization in *Frederick Douglass' Paper,*" Research paper for HIST 845 (unpublished manuscript in possession of the author, 2019). See David Blight, *Frederick Douglass: Prophet of Freedom* (New York: Simon and Schuster, 2018), 239–240.

18. Brown, *Biography of the Rev. Robert Finley,* 113.

19. Timothy S. Huebner, "Roger B. Taney and the Slavery Issue: Looking Beyond—and Before—*Dred Scott,*" *Journal of American History* 97, no. 1 (2010): 17–38.

20. Thomas Jefferson, *Notes on the State of Virginia* (Philadelphia: Prichard and Hall, 1788), 172–174; for Jefferson's 1783 Virginia Constitution proposing gradual abolition, see 232–233. See Francis Scott Key to Benjamin Tappan, October 8, 1838, *African Repository and Colonial Journal* 15, no. 7 (1839): 117. Randolph's views are treated most thoroughly in Nicholas Wood, "John Randolph of Roanoke and the Politics of Slavery in the Early Republic," *Virginia Magazine of History and Biography* 120, no. 2 (2012): 118. On Randolph's depression and frustrations with slavery and an "overseer," see Randolph to Francis Scott Key, September 12, October 17, 1813, and, on his break with the ACS, see Randolph to Dr. John Brockenbrough, February 20, 1826, all in Hugh Garland, *Life of John Randolph of Roanoke,* vol. 2 (Philadelphia: D. Appleton, 1851), 19–22, 26–27, 266–277. On his unease with slavery, see Speech of John Randolph, *Biography of the Rev. Robert Finley,* 114, and in Garland, *Life of John Randolph,* 262–263. On the act to prohibit the slave trade and its political importance between 1807 and 1820, see Mitchell Moylan, "The Act Prohibiting the Importation of Slaves of 1807: A Decade of Ineffectiveness" (Senior thesis, University of Nebraska, 2018; unpublished manuscript in possession of the author). Aaron Scott Crawford, "John Randolph of Roanoke and the Politics of Doom: Slavery, Sectionalism, and Self-Deception, 1773–1821" (Ph.D. diss., University of Tennessee, 2012), 230–232, 258–259. On St. George Tucker, Richard Randolph, and the Randolph family's emancipationist history, see Melvin Patrick Ely, *Israel on the Appomattox: A Southern Experiment in Black Freedom from the 1790s Through the Civil War* (New York: Vintage, 2004).

21. See, e.g., *William Tarlton v. Jacob Horine,* February 1814, St. Louis Circuit Court Records, Case No. 7 (St. Louis, Mo.: Washington University in St. Louis, University Libraries, 2011), http://repository.wustl.edu/concern/texts/mp48sd840.

22. Forbes, *Missouri Compromise,* 35–48. I rely here on Forbes's nuanced account of the Missouri debate and especially his treatment of the way the debates forced the hand of the antislavery humanitarians like Randolph, Key, Jefferson, and William Pinkney. He points out that the conduct of Virginia, and by extension Maryland,

"shook Americans' complacency over slavery. No state had contributed more to the ideas of the Revolution; no state's leaders had more eloquently presented the thesis of freedom. Now, Virginians, with much the same ardor and determination they had shown then, defended its antithesis" (49). Forbes notes that the amendment turned into "nothing less than a referendum on the meaning of America" (43). See also James Oakes, *Freedom National: The Destruction of Slavery in the United States, 1861–1865* (New York: W. W. Norton, 2013), 13–14.

23. Forbes, *Missouri Compromise,* 40–41.

24. Forbes, *Missouri Compromise,* 43–44.

25. *Annals of Congress,* 15th Cong., 2nd Sess., 1204–1205.

26. For the voting on the Tallmadge amendment, see Govtrack, https://www.govtrack .us/congress/votes/15-2/h97. On striking the gradual emancipation clause, one Maryland Federalist cast no vote, but the rest of the Maryland delegation voted in favor; see https://www.govtrack.us/congress/votes/15-2/h96. One Maryland congressman, Pennsylvania-born Samuel Smith, a Baltimore merchant and former officer in the Continental Army, voted for the amendment to insert a gradual abolition plan into the Missouri statehood act; see https://www.govtrack.us /congress/votes/15-2/h90.

27. *Annals of Congress,* 15th Cong., 2nd Sess., 1223–1224.

28. Forbes, *Missouri Compromise,* 109–111; Jones, *Birthright Citizens,* 26–30. Jones considers the 1820s a "turning point" in the debate over free black rights and citizenship.

29. CRCC, August 22, 1820, Minutes Book No. 2, 1814 to April 1907, folder 2, box 24, MPA; *Annals of Congress,* 15th Cong., 2nd Sess., 1215–1216; Joseph Mobberly Diary, 77, box 2, folder 1, MPA.

30. Rev. William Pinkney, *Life of William Pinkney* (New York: D. Appleton, 1853), 301–312. A congressman from New Hampshire heard Pinkney's 1820 address and deemed his oratory "impetuous, theatrical, & overbearing" and "could not help thinking all the time that he [Pinkney] might with equal ease, have argued the other side quite as well, &, I have no doubt, much better." Everett Somerville Brown, ed., *The Missouri Compromises and Presidential Politics, 1820–1825, from the Letters of William Plumer, Junior, Representative from New Hampshire* (St. Louis: Missouri Historical Society, 1926), ix.

31. Forbes, *Missouri Compromise,* 104–106.

32. Thomas Jefferson to John Holmes, April 22, 1820, *Founders Online,* https://founders .archives.gov/documents/Jefferson/98-01-02-1234; Forbes, *Missouri Compromise,* 104–106; Wood, "John Randolph of Roanoke," 127–128.

33. This research is just beginning. See "Slavery, History, Memory, and Reconcilia-tion," *Jesuits Central and Southern,* https://jesuitscentralsouthern.org/slavery _history_reconciliation. See also Gilbert J. Garraghan, S.J., *The Jesuits of the Middle United States,* vol. 1 (New York: America Press, 1938), 230, on the estab-lishment of the mission, and 610–618, for an apologist account of Jesuit slave-holding in Missouri. The forthcoming dissertation of Kelly Schmidt promises to shed important light on the families from Maryland sent to Missouri. I am grateful for an extended conversation with Kelly Schmidt and Laura Weiss about the research under way at St. Louis University and the Jesuits Central and Southern Province archives about the missions and slavery (August 9, 2019).

34. Letter of Thomas Brown, October 21, 1833, box 40, folder 5, MPA. Garraghan, *Jesuits of the Middle United States,* 1:616–617, dismissed the Brown letter as unfounded and inaccurate.

35. *Annals of Congress,* 16th Cong., 1st Sess., 403.

36. *Basil Shorter v. Henry Rozier,* GCWS, Judgment Record, October Term 1794, S497-23, JG 25, MSA.

37. See Daniel Rapine advertisements in the *National Intelligencer,* January 12, 1801, and the *Federalist,* February 3, 1802. For Rapine's obituary, see the *Daily National Journal,* May 23, 1826. He died May 11, 1826, at age fifty-eight. *Kitty Shorter, Nancy Shorter, and William Shorter v. Daniel Rapine,* August 22, 1822, in *OSCYS,* http://earlywashingtondc.org/cases/oscys.caseid.0058.

38. On Pedro (Peter) Casanave, see William W. Warner, *At Peace with All Their Neighbors: Catholics and Catholicism in the National Capital, 1787–1860* (Washington, D.C.: Georgetown University Press, 1994), 69–70. *Rachel Shorter et al. v. Ann Casanave,* July 29, 1822, in *OSCYS,* http://earlywashingtondc.org/cases/oscys.caseid.0444; George C. Henning, "The Mansion and Family of Notley Young," *Records of the Columbia Historical Society, Washington, D.C.* 16 (1913): 6, 16. Ann Casanave's daughter Joanna married Major Park G. Howle, U.S. Marine Corps. They resided at the mansion on Fourteenth and C Streets and in 1850 held over $18,000 in real estate. Ann Casanave lived on the lot to the south near the bridge to Virginia. Her son Peter Casanave resided there through at least 1850. The federal census lists his occupation as wood merchant and his real estate value as $6,587. The Library of Congress photograph of the mansion is available here: https://www.loc.gov/item/2016819419/. For Ann Casanave, U.S. Census, 1800, Formerly part of Prince Georges, Md., Washington, District of Columbia, p. 4, line 1, Anne Cassanave, M32, roll 5, NARA. For Peter Casanave, U.S. Census, 1850, Washington Ward 7, Washington, District of Columbia, p. 91, 181, dwelling 7, family 7, Peter Casanave, M432, roll 57, NARA.

39. Key to Tappan, October 8, 1838, 117. Also see Francis Scott Key's speech, July 1842, *African Repository and Colonial Journal* 18, no. 9 (1842): 204–216.

40. Deposition of Nathan Soper, June 4, 1824, *Rachel Shorter et al. v. Ann Casanave.*

41. *Daniel Wells v. Benjamin F. Lewis,* November 1823, in *OSCYS,* http://earlywashingtondc.org/cases/oscys.caseid.0443.

42. Manifest of the *Isaac Franklin,* December 22, 1838, New Orleans, La., *Slave Manifests of Coastwise Vessels Filed at New Orleans, Louisiana, 1807–1860,* M1895, roll 8, NARA.

43. "Memorial of Inhabitants of the District of Columbia, Praying for the Gradual Abolition of Slavery in the District of Columbia," 23rd Cong., 2nd Sess., H. Rep., Doc. no. 140. The memorial was presented on December 18, 1828, referred to the Committee for the District of Columbia on March 24, 1828, and ordered to be printed on February 9, 1835. We have no evidence that John Hepburn ever freed Mina and Louisa Queen. He died intestate sometime in late 1825. There is a probate record January 12, 1826, but despite extensive searches in the D.C. Archives and NARA, I have been unable to locate an inventory. Wesley E. Pippenger, comp., *District of Columbia Probate Records: Will Books 1 Through 6, 1801–1852, and Estate Files, 1801–1852* (Westminster, Md.: Family Line, 1996), 399. For the Docket/File Number, the Pippenger index cited OS (Old Series) 1302, RG 21, NARA. That file is a

summons to John Hepburn's cousin John M. Hepburn, who was the administrator
de bonis non of John Hepburn's estate. There would have been an original administrator. Hepburn had enslaved property in 1820, including possibly Mina and Louisa
Queen, but I have not been able to locate a probate for the administrator of his
estate. Hepburn may have freed one or more of his slaves in his will. Hepburn's wife
probably survived him, however, and she may have been bequeathed the slaves.
I have not been able to trace a record of her name or the estate records. See Rebecca
Katz, email message to Kaci Nash, December 10, 2015, on the D.C. Archives and the
probate records (in possession of the author).

44. *Thomas Butler et al. v. Gabriel Duvall,* Petition for Freedom, in William Cranch,
    *Reports of Cases Civil and Criminal in the United States Circuit Court of the District
    of Columbia, from 1801 to 1841,* vol. 3 (Boston: Little, Brown, 1852), available at
    OSCYS, http://earlywashingtondc.org/doc/oscys.report.0030.001. See Fanny Lee
    Jones, "Walter Jones and His Times," *Records of the Columbia Historical Society,
    Washington, D.C.* 5 (1902): 139–150. Jones read law under Bushrod C. Washington
    and was admitted to the bar in Virginia in May 1796 at age twenty. President
    Thomas Jefferson appointed Jones U.S. attorney for the District of Columbia in 1804.
    He held that position until 1821. Jones was a founding member of the ACS.

45. U.S. Census, 1820, Vansville, Prince George, Md., p. 185, Gabriel Duvall, M33, roll
    44, NARA; E. W. Duvall to Gabriel Duvall, June 1, 1828, Duvall Family Papers,
    Library of Congress, Washington, D.C.

46. *Thomas Butler et al. v. Gabriel Duvall.*

47. In the late 1820s more freedom suits erupted in Prince George's County. In one
    Samuel West freed two women and most of their large family in his will and to give
    them 62 1/2 acres of land. When he died in 1828, one of his two sons supported the
    provisions, but the other decided to contest the will in court. See *Arthur P. West v.
    Charles H. L. West, negroes Polly, Charlotte and others,* Prince George's County
    Court, Black Court Papers, Orphan's Court, July 28, 1828, 50199-27, October 1, 1828,
    C1187-1, MSA.

48. David Walker, *Walker's Appeal in Four Articles Together with a Preamble to the
    Coloured Citizens of the World,* 3rd ed. (Boston: David Walker, 1830), 56. The first
    edition was published in September 1829.

49. Walker, *Walker's Appeal . . . to the Coloured Citizens of the World,* 51.

50. *Charlotte et al. v. Henry Clay,* Petition for Freedom, February 13, 1829, in *OSCYS,*
    http://earlywashingtondc.org/doc/oscys.case.0348.002. The case has been treated
    briefly in a few studies as a political episode. See James Klotter, *Henry Clay: The
    Man Who Would Be President* (Oxford: Oxford University Press, 2018), 195–197.
    There is no evidence that Clay's political enemies in the Andrew Jackson and Martin
    Van Buren administration fostered, trumped up, or sponsored this freedom suit to
    attack Clay for political reasons. Instead, the lawsuit was Charlotte Dupee's and had
    its origins in the social and legal history of the freedom suits by the enslaved
    families in Maryland and D.C. See esp. Kelly, "'She's Been Her Own Mistress.'"

51. Henry Clay to the Circuit Court for the District of Columbia, February 18, 1829, in
    Papers of Henry Clay, ed. James F. Hopkins and Mary W. M. Hargreaves, vol. 7 (Lex-
    ington: University of Kentucky Press, 1959), 622–625.

52. In over 450 freedom suits in the D.C. court, just eleven slaveholders responded with
    an "Answer" to the claim of freedom. Most of these were perfunctory. Clay's

response is an extensive one, and it is uniquely valuable both as a window into the thinking of a slaveholder defendant and as a measure of how seriously slaveholders took these lawsuits.

53. James Condon to Clay, March 1, 1829, in *Papers of Henry Clay,* 7:630–633.

54. Clay to Philip R. Fendall, August 17, 1830, in *Papers of Henry Clay,* 8:252–253.

55. Clay to Fendall, September 10, 1830, in *Papers of Henry Clay,* 8:260–261.

56. Clay, Deed of Manumission, October 12, 1840, in *Papers of Henry Clay,* 9:52–53. See also Anne Brown Clay Erwin to Clay, January 7, 1832, in *Papers of Henry Clay,* 8:440–442.

57. See Aaron Dupee's obituary, *Providence Evening Press,* February 20, 1866. Aaron Dupee is mentioned in Henry Clay's obituary, *Opelousas Courier,* July 25, 1857. For biographies that downplay Charlotte Dupee's suit or accept Clay's views of its political origins, see David T. Heidler and Jeanne T. Heidler, *Henry Clay: The Essential American* (New York: Penguin, 2010).

58. *National Intelligencer,* August 4, 1833.

59. Daniel Walker Howe, *What Hath God Wrought: The Transformation of America, 1815–1848* (Oxford: Oxford University Press, 2007), 411–446; Michael F. Holt, *The Rise and Fall of the American Whig Party: Jacksonian Politics and the Onset of the Civil War* (Oxford: Oxford University Press, 2003), 2–18; Christopher L. Tomlins, *In the Matter of Nat Turner: A Speculative History* (Princeton: Princeton University Press, 2020), 135–145.

60. On the importance of the early 1830s, especially in Washington, D.C., see David Brion Davis, "The Impact of British Abolitionism on American Sectionalism," in *In the Shadow of Freedom: The Politics of Slavery in the National Capital,* ed. Paul Finkelman and Donald R. Kennon (Athens: Ohio University Press, 2011), 25–28. I am especially influenced by the constitutional and imperial argument of Christopher Leslie Brown, *Moral Capital: Foundations of British Abolitionism* (Chapel Hill: University of North Carolina Press, 2006), 24–30, 456–462. William W. Freehling, *The Road to Disunion: Secessionists at Bay, 1776–1854* (Oxford: Oxford University Press, 1990), 197–210.

61. James Martin Wright, *The Free Negro in Maryland, 1634–1860* (New York: Longmans, Green, 1921), 268–269; Jones, *Birthright Citizens,* 47.

62. "Opinion of Roger B. Taney, Attorney General, South Carolina Law Respecting Colored Mariner, May 28, 1832," is held in Carl Brent Swisher Collection, Manuscript Division, Library of Congress, Washington, D.C., and reprinted with Taney's accompanying notes in H. Jefferson Powell, "Attorney General Taney and the South Carolina Police Bill," *Green Bag* 5 (Autumn 2001): 83–93. See also Timothy S. Huebner, "Roger B. Taney and the Slavery Issue: Looking Beyond—and Before— Dred Scott," *Journal of American History* 97, no. 1 (2010): 17–38. Huebner argues that Taney's harder line on slavery and black rights "reason and act as a representative of the president and his party" (35).

63. Paul Finkelman, *Supreme Injustice: Slavery in the Nation's Highest Court* (Cambridge: Harvard University Press, 2018), 192–193; Jones, *Birthright Citizens,* 48.

64. Amos Phelps, "Various Notes on Slavery, Emancipation, Immediate Abolition of Slavery, etc.," ca. 1834–1842, manuscript, Boston Public Library, https://ark .digitalcommonwealth.org/ark:/50959/m900qr11x.

65. Minutes of the U.S. Circuit Court of the District of Columbia, 1801–1863, M1021, roll 3, NARA. Williams filed her suit in 1828 and enlisted Francis Scott Key as her

attorney. See *Ann Williams et al. v. George Miller and George Miller, Jr.*, May 1832, in *OSCYS*, http://earlywashingtondc.org/cases/oscys.caseid.0105.

66. *Rebecca Hobbs v. Thomas Magruder and Washington Robey*, February 22, 1835, Supplemental Complaint, in *OSCYS*, http://earlywashingtondc.org/doc/oscys.case.0193.005.

67. On the combination of freedom suits and assisted escapes, see Stanley Harrold, *Subversives: Antislavery Community in Washington, D.C., 1828–1865* (Baton Rouge: Louisiana State University Press, 2003), 52–54.

Juneteenth

1. Letitia Clark and Guilford Queen, interview by author, Port Tobacco, Md., June 19, 2018. *Baltimore Sun*, January 15, 18, 1842; *American and Commercial Daily Advertiser*, January 15, 19, 1842. On Duckett, see also *Easton* (Md.) *Gazette*, February 29, 1840, and *American and Commercial Daily Advertiser*, August 22, 1842. Thomas Duckett was Allen Bowie Duckett's son.

2. Torrey was eventually imprisoned in Baltimore for helping enslaved people escape, and he died in prison. See Joseph Lovejoy, *Memoir of Rev. Charles T. Torrey Who Died in the Penitentiary of Maryland* (Boston: John P. Jewett, 1847). The episode is recounted in Stanley Harrold, *Subversives: Antislavery Community in Washington, D.C., 1828–1865* (Baton Rouge: Louisiana State University Press, 2003), 71–72.

CHAPTER 7. MOB LAW

1. Charles Ball, *Slavery in the United States: A Narrative of the Life and Adventures of Charles Ball, a Black Man, Who Lived Forty Years in Maryland, South Carolina and Georgia, as a Slave Under Various Masters, and Was One Year in the Navy with Commodore Barney, During the Late War* (New York: John S. Taylor, 1837), 28. Michael Shiner Diary, Manuscript Division, Library of Congress, Washington, D.C. See Shiner's numerous references to the gate, especially p. 34 in 1828, for incidents of men gathering at the gate and activity at the gate. Robert J. Kapsch, *Building Washington: Engineering and Construction of the New Federal City, 1790–1840* (Baltimore: Johns Hopkins University Press, 2018), 163–164; Main Gate, Washington Navy Yard, *National Register of Historic Places Inventory—Nomination Form*, April 2, 1973.

2. Frederick Douglass, *My Bondage and My Freedom* (New York: Miller, Orton and Mulligan, 1855), 349. On Douglass's ideas about work and its relation to the Republican free labor ideology, see Daniel D. Clausen, "'The Most Noble Employment of Man': Farm Labor and Environment in Nineteenth Century American Literature" (Ph.D. diss., University of Nebraska, 2019).

3. Ball, *Slavery in the United States*, 37.

4. Daniel Walker Howe, *What Hath God Wrought: The Transformation of America, 1815–1848* (Oxford: Oxford University Press, 2007), 431; Paul Gilje, *Rioting in America* (Bloomington: Indiana University Press, 1999); Jack Tager, *Boston Riots: Three Centuries of Social Violence* (Boston: Northeastern University Press, 2001);

and Iver Bernstein, *The New York City Draft Riots: Their Significance for American Society and Politics in the Age of the Civil War* (Oxford: Oxford University Press, 1991). I am indebted to Patrick Hoehne for sharing his research on riots and rioting as political acts of speech and his analysis of the spatial unfolding of riots in the United States, and especially Washington, in the summer of 1835, using Historical Geographic Information Systems (HGIS). Patrick Hoehne, "Rereading the Riot Acts: Race, Labor, Law, and the Snow Riot of 1835," Paper presented at the Organization of American Historians Conference, April 2–5, 2020, Washington, D.C.; Hoehne, "Riot Acts," Research paper for HIST 845, Fall 2019 (unpublished manuscript in possession of the author).

5. See *Patt, Hannah, and Patty v. Gerard T. Greenfield and Thomas Greenfield,* December 7, 1809, Petition for Freedom, in *OSCYS,* http://earlywashingtondc.org/cases/oscys.caseid.0276. The main accounts can be found in: "The Recaptured Fugitives," *North Star,* May 12, 1848; and "Beauties of the Slave System," *North Star,* October 13, 1848.

6. Hoehne, "Rereading the Riot Acts."

7. Michael Shiner Diary, 60, transcription and page images from the Navy Department Library, https://www.history.navy.mil/research/library/online-reading-room/title-list-alphabetically/d/diary-of-michael-shiner.html. I have corrected the spelling in this diary throughout the text to make it more readable and accessible for the reader. The original spelling can be seen at the above link. See Linda M. Maloney, *The Captain from Connecticut: The Life and Naval Times of Isaac Hull* (Annapolis, Md.: Naval Institute Press, 1996), 436–440.

8. Michael Shiner Diary, 1831, 44–45. See Leslie Anderson, "The Life of Freed Slave Michael Shiner," C-SPAN, Washington, D.C., February 4, 2014, https://www.c-span.org/video/?317598-1/life-freed-slave-michael-shiner.

9. R. Kent Newmyer, *John Marshall and the Heroic Age of the Supreme Court* (Baton Rouge: Louisiana State University Press, 2001), 386–388, 466. See also Mark A. Graber, "Federalist or Friends of Adams: The Marshall Court and Party Politics," *Studies in American Political Development* 12, no. 2 (1998): 229–266; and Michael J. Gerhardt, "The Lives of John Marshall," *William and Mary Law Review* 43, no. 4 (2002): 1399–1452.

10. Michael Shiner Diary, 60–61.

11. On the importance of the events of 1835 in the political battle over slavery, including the contest over the judiciary, see Donald J. Ratcliffe, "The Decline of Antislavery Politics," in *Contesting Slavery: The Politics of Bondage and Freedom in the New American Nation,* ed. John Craig Hammond and Matthew Mason (Charlottesville: University of Virginia Press, 2011), 273–276. *Daily National Intelligencer,* August 26, 1835.

12. John G. Sharp, "Washington Navy Yard Pay Rolls of Mechanics and Laborers, July 1811" (manuscript in possession of the author). *Joe Thompson, Nelly Thompson, and Sarah Anne Thompson v. Walter Clarke,* December 1817, in William Cranch, *Reports of Cases Civil and Criminal in the United States Circuit Court of the District of Columbia, from 1801 to 1841,* vol. 2 (Boston: Little, Brown, 1852), in *OSCYS,* http://earlywashingtondc.org/doc/oscys.report.0010.001. Jessica Millward, "'That All Her Increase Shall Be Free': Enslaved Women's Bodies and the Maryland 1809 Law of Manumission," *Women's History Review* 21, no. 3 (2012): 363–378. The jury

returned a verdict for the Thompsons, without excluding Sarah Ann. Crucially, neither the judges nor the counsel for the slaveholders attempted to enforce the 1809 Maryland act that would have enslaved Sarah Ann for life. The entire family was free. In 1809, Maryland passed one of the first laws regarding the status of children born to women who were free "*in futuro*"—the statute allowed slaveholders the legal authority to grant conditional emancipation through a will and to use the terms of a will to determine the status of children born to a woman to be freed in futuro, but crucially, if the slaveholder did not specify the exact terms—his or her intent—then the children would be enslaved for life. In other words, if a slaveholder's will freed an enslaved woman after a term of service but said nothing about the status of her children, then any children she had before the moment of her own freedom would be slaves for life. In the District of Columbia, the 1809 statute might not have been applied because earlier Maryland statutes governed, but the implications of the Maryland act could not be ignored. The legalities of in futuro freedom were not resolved.

13. John Davis of Abel, Blacksmith Foreman, to Thomas Tingey, Marcy 13, 1817, quoted in John G. Sharp, "Washington Navy Yard Pay Rolls of Mechanics and Laborers, July 1811" (manuscript in possession of the author). On Sukey Dean and black women's resistance at the Navy Yard, see Tamika Richeson, "Crimes of Discontent: The Contours of Black Women's Law Breaking in Civil War Era Washington, D.C., 1830–1865," (Ph.D. diss., University of Virginia, 2014) 66–68.

14. In the 1822 city directory, seventeen of ninety-five public buildings in D.C. were within a mile of the Navy Yard, and of these, six were drinking establishments and five were churches. These data and maps are available at *OSCYS*. Michael Shiner Diary, 15–16. The biracial Ebenezer congregation split in 1827 and an African Methodist church began holding services one block south, at Fourth Street and Virginia Avenue. Nina Honemond Clarke, *History of the Nineteenth-Century Black Churches in Maryland and Washington, D.C.* (New York: Vantage, 1983), 18.

15. Within a few years, especially after the founding of the American Anti-Slavery Society in 1833, petitions of this sort flooded the halls of Congress aiming to end slavery in the capital or abolish slavery entirely. In 1837–1838, a decade after the D.C. residents signed their memorial, Congress received approximately 130,000 petitions opposing slavery in the District. Joanne B. Freeman, *The Field of Blood: Violence in Congress and the Road to Civil War* (New York: Farrar, Straus and Giroux, 2018), 112–115, 340n4.

16. Prince Georges County Register of Wills, William Pumphrey, August 12, 1827, Liber TT 1, folio 423, and Archives of the District of Columbia, Orphans Court (Probate) Court, RG 2, Records of the Superior Court, Will of Thomas Howard, 1832, box 11, cited in *The Diary of Michael Shiner Relating to the History of the Washington Navy Yard, 1813–1869, Introduction* (2015), Naval History and Heritage Command, https://www.history.navy.mil/research/library/online-reading-room/title-list -alphabetically/d/diary-of-michael-shiner/introduction.html.

17. Michael Shiner Diary, 1833, 54.

18. *Phillis Shiner, Ann Shiner, Harriet Shiner, and Mary Ann Shiner v. Levi Pumphrey*, Petition for Freedom, June 1, 1833, in *OSCYS*, http://earlywashingtondc.org/cases/ oscys.caseid.0446.

19. District of Columbia Free Negro Registers, 1821–1861, 2:255–256, RG 21, NARA. Michael Shiner Diary, 53–54.

20. *Washington Critic-Record,* September 12, 1873; Michael Shiner obituary, *Washington Evening Star,* January 19, 1880.

21. *Daily National Intelligencer,* August 14, 1835; Jefferson Morley, *Snow-Storm in August: Washington City, Francis Scott Key, and the Forgotten Race Riot of 1835* (New York: Doubleday, 2012), 136–147.

22. *Globe,* August 12, 14, 1835.

23. *Georgetown Metropolitan,* December 11, 1835; Morley, *Snow-Storm in August,* 134, but this quotation is misattributed. Morley cites the *Georgetown Metropolitan,* December 18, 1835 (290).

24. *Mary Bell v. Susan Armistead,* Affidavits from Almshouse, March 31, 1837, in *OSCYS,* http://earlywashingtondc.org/doc/oscys.case.0172.002. The defendant's surname is spelled variably in the court documents, sometimes with an "i," sometimes without. I have chosen for consistency to spell the name "Armstead" in the text. Citations follow the spelling used in the original pleading.

25. Deed of manumission, September 14, 1835, *Mary Bell v. Susan Armistead,* RG 21, entry 6, box 755, folder 376, NARA, in *OSCYS,* http://earlywashingtondc.org/doc/oscys.case.0243.007.

26. Michael Shiner Diary, September 6, 1835, 66–70.

27. James Hoban Jr. held two enslaved people in 1840 and employed two free black people in his household. See U.S. Census, 1840, Washington, D.C., population schedule, p. 32, James Hoban, M704, roll 32, NARA. His antiabolitionism became more public in his National Repeal Association. See Angela F. Murphy, *American Slavery, Irish Freedom: Abolition, Immigrant Citizenship, and the Transatlantic Movement for Irish Repeal* (Baton Rouge: Louisiana State University Press, 2010), 135.

28. Michael Shiner Diary, 1838, 77. On the actions of enslaved as rights-bearing citizens, see Martha S. Jones, *Birthright Citizens: A History of Race and Rights in Antebellum America* (Cambridge: Cambridge University Press, 2018), 10, 52, 67, 126–127.

29. Obituary of Joseph H. Bradley, *Daily Critic,* April 4, 1887, and *Washington Evening Star,* April 4, 1887; American Colonization Society, *Thirty-Eighth Annual Report* (Washington, D.C., 1845); Charles S. Bradley, "The Bradley Family and the Times in Which They Lived," *Records of the Columbia Historical Society, Washington, D.C.* 6 (1903): 123–142. The presiding judge in the case, Buckner Thruston, was related to Bradley by marriage but did not recuse himself. See Maud Burr Morris, "William A. Bradley: Eleventh Mayor of the Corporation of Washington," *Records of the Columbia Historical Society, Washington, D.C.* 25 (1923): 105–139.

30. Maryland Laws, chap. 325, sec. 1, in *Laws Made and Passed by the General Assembly of the State of Maryland* (Annapolis, Md.: Jeremiah Hughes, 1836); Carl Lawrence Paulus, *The Slaveholding Crisis: Fear of Insurrection and the Coming of the Civil War* (Baton Rouge: Louisiana State University Press, 2017); Peter Charles Hoffer, *John Quincy Adams and the Gag Rule, 1835–1850* (Baltimore: Johns Hopkins University Press, 2017); Stanley Harrold, *The Abolitionist and the South, 1831–1861* (Lexington: University Press of Kentucky, 2015); Jennifer Rose Mercieca, "The Culture of Honor: How Slaveholders Responded to the Abolitionist Mail Crisis of 1835," *Rhetoric and Public Affairs* 10, no. 1 (2007): 51–76.

31. William W. Freehling, *The Road to Disunion: Secessionists at Bay, 1776–1854* (Oxford: Oxford University Press, 1990), 308–324; Freeman, *Field of Blood*, 116–141; *United States' Telegraph*, December 22, 31, 1835; David C. Frederick, "John Quincy Adams, Slavery, and the Disappearance of the Right of Petition," *Law and History Review* 9, no. 1 (1991): 113–155.

32. *The Trial of Reuben Crandall, M.D.: Charged with Publishing Seditious Libels, by Circulating the Publications of the American Anti-Slavery Society, before the Circuit Court for the District of Columbia, Held at Washington, in April, 1836, Occupying the Court the Period of Ten Days* (New York: H. R. Piercy, 1836), 6. Another transcript of the trial was produced by a member of the D.C. bar and printed separately—see *The Trial of Reuben Crandall, M.D., Charged with Publishing and Circulating Seditious and Incendiary Papers, &c. in the District of Columbia with the Intent of Exciting Servile Insurrection . . .* (Washington, D.C.: Printed for the Proprietors, 1836). They do not diverge in their accounts in any substantive way. See also Neil S. Kramer, "The Trial of Reuben Crandall," *Records of the Columbia Historical Society, Washington, D.C.* 50 (1980): 123–139. To distinguish between the two, I have added the publication place to the following citations.

33. *Trial of Reuben Crandall, M.D.* (Washington, D.C.), 9.

34. *Daily National Intelligencer,* April 20, 1836.

35. On Thruston's career, see John E. Kleber, ed., *The Kentucky Encyclopedia* (Lexington: University Press of Kentucky, 1992), s.v. "Thruston, Buckner," 883. Thruston's son Charles Mynn Thruston later played a role in Henrietta Wood's petition for freedom case in Kentucky. See W. Caleb McDaniel, *Sweet Taste of Liberty: A True Story of Slavery and Restitution in America* (Oxford: Oxford University Press, 2019), 35, 86–87.

36. *Daily National Intelligencer,* April 20, 1836.

37. Thruston was impeached in 1837 on the basis of a memorial filed by attorneys Richard S. Coxe and William L. Brent. Their memorial accused Thruston of being "grossly and avowedly ignorant and irregardless of the law," "habitually inattentive," "rude, insolent, and undignified," and "quarrelsome" with lawyers. Thruston apparently suffered from a "mental disease" that made for "irrational outbursts." The House Judiciary Committee took hundreds of pages of testimony but did not recommend articles of impeachment and tabled the matter. See *The Case of Judge Thruston,* H.R. Rep. 327, House Committee on the Judiciary, Serial vol. 306, 24th Cong., 2nd Sess. (1836–1837). In much of the testimony Thruston was also accused of impartiality and favoritism in court, especially toward Joseph H. Bradley. Bradley served as Thruston's counsel in the impeachment hearing. Bradley's first cousin, William A. Bradley, was married to Judge Thruston's daughter. None of the dozens of witnesses, including Judge Cranch, James Hoban, and Francis Scott Key, referred directly to the Crandall trial.

38. *The Eleventh Annual Report of the American Society for Colonizing the Free People of Color of the United States, Proceedings of the American Colonization Society at Their Eleventh Annual Meeting* (Georgetown: James Dunn, 1828), 20–21, for Key's address, 25; for George W. P. Custis's address, see *Trial of Reuben Crandall, M.D.* (New York), 30.

39. *Trial of Reuben Crandall, M.D.* (New York), 57.

40. Francis Scott Key, *A Part of a Speech Pronounced by Francis S. Key, Esq. on the Trial of Reuben Crandall, M.D.: Before the Circuit Court of the District of Columbia, at the March Term Thereof, 1836 . . .* (Washington, D.C., 1836), 3.

41. Key, *Part of a Speech,* 9.

42. Key, *Part of a Speech,* 12. For another example of the proslavery myth of black degeneracy and the importance of the mid-1830s, see Melvin Patrick Ely, *Israel on the Appomattox: A Southern Experiment in Black Freedom from the 1790s Through the Civil War* (New York: Vintage, 2004), 196–224.

43. Key, *Part of a Speech,* 12. See also Early Lee Fox, "The American Colonization Society, 1817–1840" (Ph.D. diss. Johns Hopkins University, 1919), 18.

44. Key, *Part of a Speech,* 12.

45. "Correspondence Between Mr. [Benjamin] Tappan and Mr. [Francis Scott] Key," *African Repository and Colonial Journal* 15, no. 7 (1839): 113–125. See also Key, *Part of a Speech.* Key reprised this argument six years after the Crandall trial, in July 1842, in a speech to "The Friends of Colonization," printed in *African Repository and Colonial Journal* 18, no. 9 (1842): 216.

46. Donald E. Williams Jr., *Prudence Crandall's Legacy: The Fight for Equality in the 1830s, Dred Scott, and Brown v. Board of Education* (Middletown, Conn.: Wesleyan University Press, 2014), 230–231.

47. Freehling, *Road to Disunion,* 330–336.

48. See Ratcliffe, "Decline of Antislavery Politics," 275; and Paul Finkelman, *Supreme Injustice: Slavery in the Nation's Highest Court* (Cambridge: Harvard University Press, 2018), 191–201.

49. Clement Dorsey, *The General Public Statutory Law and Public Local Law of the State of Maryland from the Year 1692 to 1839 Inclusive,* vol. 1 (Baltimore: John D. Toy, 1840), xlviii. The amendment was ratified March 10, 1837. See *Laws Made and Passed by the General Assembly of the State of Maryland* (Annapolis, Md.: Jeremiah Hughes, 1837), chap. 197, sec. 26; *Session Laws,* 600:42, in *Laws Made and Passed by the General Assembly of the State of Maryland* (Annapolis, Md.: William M'Neir, 1840), chap. 42, "An Act Declaring Domestic Slavery to Be Lawful in This State," passed March 20, 1840.

50. *The Case of William Chaplin* (Boston: Chaplin Committee, 1851), 50.

51. *Case of William Chaplin,* 52.

52. *Ann Bell, Daniel Bell, and David Bell v. Gerard T. Greenfield,* Petition for Freedom, December 24, 1836, in *OSCYS,* http://earlywashingtondc.org/cases/oscys.caseid.0104. See also Kaci Nash, "Emancipating the Bell Family: An Inquiry into the Strategies of Freedom Making" (June 2018), in *OSCYS,* http://earlywashingtondc.org/stories/emancipating_bells; and Josephine F. Pacheco, *The Pearl: A Failed Slave Escape on the Potomac* (Chapel Hill: University of North Carolina Press, 2005), 49.

Return to Pleasant Prospect

1. "What Lies Beneath: The History of the Waterford Estates," brochure, based on Paul P. Kreisa et al., "Phase III Archaeological Data Recovery of Site 18PR705 at the Waterford Development, Prince George's County, Maryland," Report prepared by Greenhorne & O'Mara, Inc., for Washington Management & Development Company, Inc., 2007, on file at the Maryland Historical Trust.

2. See Corey M. Brooks, "Sculpting Memories of the Slavery Conflict: Commemorating Roger Taney in Washington, D.C., Annapolis, and Baltimore, 1864–1887," *Maryland Historical Magazine* 112, no. 1 (2017): 6–36. See "Confederate Monuments Are Coming Down Across the United States; Here's a List," *New York Times,* updated August 28, 2017, https://www.nytimes.com/interactive/2017/08/16/us/confederate -monuments-removed.html; and Colin Campbell and Luke Broadwater, "Citing 'Safety and Security,' Pugh Has Baltimore Confederate Monuments Taken Down," *Baltimore Sun,* August 16, 2017.

3. In a similar incident in February 2019 at Tuckahoe Plantation, Thomas Jefferson's boyhood home in Goochland County, Va., protesters painted "We profit off slavery" on the entrance gate and issued an anonymous news release condemning the "exploitation" of Virginia's "dark history." See C. Suarez Rojas, "Anonymous New Release Details 'We Profit Off Slavery' Vandalism at Tuckahoe Plantation," *Richmond Times-Dispatch,* February 18, 2019.

4. I made several inquiries with the homeowner's association that controls the exhibit. The Waterford Preserve HOA is a separate entity from the residence, Pleasant Prospect. The current owner of Pleasant Prospect, Zachary Warrender, has set out to refurbish the historic home. His blog on the historic building is https:// pleasantprospect.wordpress.com/blog/. Warrender bought Pleasant Prospect in late 2015.

CHAPTER 8. THE SALE

1. The relevant studies of the expansion of slaveholding and the interstate trade in the early republic include Adam Rothman, *Slave Country: American Expansion and the Origins of the Deep South* (Cambridge: Harvard University Press, 2005), 188; Calvin Schermerhorn, *Money over Mastery, Family over Freedom: Slavery in the Antebellum Upper South* (Baltimore: Johns Hopkins University Press, 2011), 14; Calvin Schermerhorn, *The Business of Slavery and the Rise of American Capitalism, 1815–1860* (New Haven: Yale University Press, 2016); and Steven Deyle, *Carry Me Back: The Domestic Slave Trade in American Life* (Oxford: Oxford University Press, 2006). For the importance of "soul value" and the perpetuation of the interstate slave trade, see Daina Ramey Berry, *The Price for Their Pound of Flesh: The Value of the Enslaved, from Womb to Grave, in the Building of a Nation* (Boston: Beacon Press, 2017).

2. On the largest recorded public sale in American history, of 436 men, women, and children, see Anne C. Bailey, *The Weeping Time: Memory and the Largest Slave Auction in American History* (Cambridge: Cambridge University Press, 2017). See also James Baldwin, "The White Problem," in *The Cross of Redemption: Uncollected Writings,* ed. Randall Kenan (New York: Vintage, 2011), 92–93.

3. Inventory of Nicholas Lewis Sewall, 1802, box 39, folder 8, MPA.

4. *The Antelope,* 23 U.S. (10 Wheat.) 66 (1825). See also R. Kent Newmyer, *John Marshall and the Heroic Age of the Supreme Court* (Baton Rouge: Louisiana State University Press, 2001), 430–433. On the chattel principle, see Walter Johnson and David Brion Davis, eds., *The Chattel Principle: Internal Slave Trade in the Americas* (New Haven: Yale University Press, 2005); and Walter Johnson, *Soul by Soul: Life Inside the Antebellum Slave Market* (Cambridge: Harvard University Press, 1999). On *The Antelope,* see also Paul Finkelman, *Supreme Injustice: Slavery in the Nation's Highest Court* (Cambridge:

Harvard University Press, 2018), 90–102. Arguing for freedom over property rights and on the basis of natural law, Francis Scott Key and William Wirt, the attorney general of the United States, appealed to "the great moral and legal revolution going on in the world" outlawing the slave trade. Newmyer, *John Marshall and the Heroic Age of the Supreme Court,* 432.

5. Judith Schafer, *Slavery, the Civil Law, and the Supreme Court of Louisiana* (Baton Rouge: Louisiana State University Press, 1994); Vernon Valentine Palmer, *Through the Codes Darkly: Slave Law and Civil Law in Louisiana* (Clark, N.J.: Lawbook Exchange, 2012), 141–145; Kimberly M. Welch, *Black Litigants in the Antebellum American South* (Chapel Hill: University of North Carolina Press, 2018), 165–189.

6. CRCC, August 22, October 16, November 20, 1822, Minutes Book No. 2, 1814 to April 1, 1907, box 24, folder 2, MPA. See January 9, 1823, minutes for the Ambrose Marchal attempt to wrest White Marsh's land and slaves from the corporation, and the Neales' protest.

7. On the sale of children, see CRCC, October 16, 1822, September 29, 1824, August 22, 1826, April 21, 1830, Minutes Book No. 2, 1814 to April 1, 1907, box 24, folder 2, MPA. Letter dated January 9, 1826, and Francis Neale to Francis Dzierozynski, January 10, 1826, box 61, folder 9, MPA.

8. See Joseph Mobberly Diary, ca. 1823, box 2, folder 1, 67–83, MPA, defending slavery and Jesuit slaveholding. See also Mobberly to John Grassi, February 5, 1815, box 58, folder 6, MPA, recommending an end to Jesuit slaveholding for economic reasons and to avoid the danger of a slave revolt. Mobberly defended slaveholding on racial and biblical grounds. He was appointed manager of St. Inigoes in 1818 and two years later reassigned by the Jesuit corporation, probably because he despised the "slavery, corn & tobacco" plantation system. Mobberly disparaged the enslaved persons, too. His 1823 diary included long sections on the inefficiencies he attributed to slavery. I have dated the diary to 1823 because of the entry on p. 77 referring to the St. Inigoes' uprising six years earlier in 1817.

9. The Philodemic Society Debate, 1830 or 1831, *GSA,* slaveryarchive.georgetown.edu /items/show/86.

10. Peter Havermans to G. Fenwick, July 17, 1832, box 63, folder 18, MPA, also at *GSA,* http://slaveryarchive.georgetown.edu/items/show/242. P. Kenney to J. McElroy, August 19, 1832, box 63, file 18, item 9, MPA, also at *GSA,* http://slaveryarchive .georgetown.edu/items/show/118.

11. John Carroll to John Rosseter, January 26, 29, 1811, box 57.A, folder 7, MPA; Fidele de Grivel to Nicholas Sewall, May 20, 1832, and Grivel to Joseph Tristram, March 10, 1835[?], Maryland—Letters of Ours and of Bishops, 1773–1815, BN/3/1, EPA.

12. McSherry Reports, 1833, box 26, folder 3, MPA.

13. William McSherry to Fr. Roothann, May 13, 1837, *GSA,* https://slaveryarchive .georgetown.edu/items/show/275; Province Financial Records—Cashbook, 1834– 1839, 29, *GSA,* https://slaveryarchive.georgetown.edu/items/show/400.

14. The Dubuisson Memorandum (1836), *GSA,* https://slaveryarchive.georgetown.edu /items/show/95.

15. Jan Philip Roothaan to William McSherry, December 27, 1836, box 93, folder 9, MPA, also at *GSA,* https://slaveryarchive.georgetown.edu/items/show/94. The conditions Roothaan imposed on the sale included: (1) that the enslaved must have the free exercise of the Catholic religion; (2) that they must not be sold to planters

who afterward might "carelessly separate" them and sell them to others; (3) that husbands and wives must "in no way" be separated, or children and parents as much as possible; (4) that if a spouse were in another slaveholder's possession (not the Jesuits'), then they must be kept together and not sold; and (5) that the money from the sale not be used to pay off the college's or the corporation's debts but be considered "capital" to be invested as endowment. Roothaan urged the Maryland Jesuits that the "survival of this Province depends to a large degree on this being done well."

16. There is little information on Henry Johnson's early life and career. One of the best sources is the long obituary in the *New Orleans Times-Picayune*, October 30, 1864. A short notice appeared in the *Daily True Delta*, September 1, 1864, and noted that Henry and Elizabeth Johnson did not have children. They were married October 1, 1829. See T. J. C. Williams, *History of Frederick County, Maryland, from the Earliest Settlements to the Beginning of the War Between the States*, vol. 1 ([Frederick, Md.]: L. R. Titsworth, 1910), 315. This volume notes that Philip Barton Key Jr. went to Louisiana in 1835. Also see Georgina Pell Curtis, ed., *The American Catholic Who's Who* (St. Louis, Mo.: B. Herder, 1911), 332–333; and Christopher Johnson, "The Key Family," *Maryland Historical Magazine* 5 (1910): 198.

17. *United States Telegraph*, February 16, 1837; *Register of Debates*, 24 Cong., 1st Sess., May 25, 1836, 4029–4031; *Register of Debates*, 24 Cong., 2nd Sess., February 6, 1837, 1587–1590.

18. *Register of Debates*, 24 Cong., 2nd Sess., February 6, 1837, 1599–1600, 1639–1640, 1681.

19. *United States Telegraph*, February 16, 1837.

20. The authoritative treatment of the complicated maneuvering over the gag rule is William Freehling, *The Road to Disunion: Secessionists at Bay, 1776–1854* (Oxford: Oxford University Press, 1990), 343–352. Freehling notes that Adams claimed that the petition from slaves was a petition to remain enslaved. Adams's ploy embarrassed the fire-eaters in the House. Freehling does not deal with the subsequent attempt to address retrospectively the implications of slave petitioning in the defeated resolution against Adams. Freehling explains how and why Maryland's Whig U.S. senator William Cost Johnson led the total gag rule counteroffensive, arguing that tabling petitions was insufficient and that petitions should not be received in the House at all.

21. Irene D. Neu, "Edmond Jean Forstall and Louisiana Banking," *Explorations in Economic History* 7, no. 4 (1970): 303–398; Calvin Schermerhorn, *The Business of Slavery and the Rise of American Capitalism, 1815–1860* (New Haven: Yale University Press, 2015), 99–123; Rashauna Johnson, *Slavery's Metropolis: Unfree Labor in New Orleans During the Age of Revolutions* (Cambridge: Cambridge University Press, 2016), 62.

22. Schermerhorn, *Business of Slavery*, 116.

23. *Bob and Milly et al. v. John Nugent et al.*, Fourth Judicial District Court, No. 1322, April 17, 1833, Parish of Iberville, Civil Cases, Iberville Parish Court House, Plaquemine, La. See also the treatment of this case in Welch, *Black Litigants in the Antebellum American South*, 174. Mississippi allowed such manumissions until 1842. The defendants appealed the case April 27, 1839, but there is no further record in the case file.

24. Bond of David Chambers et al., May 2, 1839, *Bob and Milly et al. v. John Nugent et al.*

25. Jesse Batey advertisement, *Washington Globe,* May 29, 1838, available at *GSA,* http://slaveryarchive.georgetown.edu/items/show/224; McSherry to Roothaan, May 13, 1837, *GSA,* http://slaveryarchive.georgetown.edu/items/show/275; "Articles of Agreement," June 19, 1838, box 40, folder 10, MPA.

26. "Articles of Agreement," June 19, 1838.

27. Henry Johnson to Wade H. Gilbert, September 21, November 24, 1838, March 24, 1839, book 15, 283, 396, 308, Conveyances, Ascension Parish Courthouse, Donaldsonville, La.

28. See note 26, above. See also Johnson, *Soul by Soul.*

29. See Anthony J. Kuzniewski, S.J., "'Our American Champions': The First American Generation of American Jesuit Leaders After the Restoration of the Society," *Studies in the Spirituality of Jesuits* 46, no. 1 (2014): 25, 27–32.

30. Census of Slaves to Be Sold, 1838, oversize box 4, MPA, also at *GSA.* "Bill of sale for 56 slaves," Thomas F. Mulledy to Henry Johnson, November 10, 1838, box 40, folder 10, MPA. "Manifest of the Katherine Jackson," November 13, 1838, *GSA,* https://slaveryarchive.georgetown.edu/items/show/2.

31. This analysis draws on my reading of the original documents in the MPA, the *GSA,* and the conveyances recorded in Terrebonne, Ascension, and Iberville courts. The *Georgetown Memory Project* has compiled an exhaustive analysis of these records and the individuals who remained in Maryland. See "The Lost Jesuit Slaves of Maryland: Searching for 91 People Left Behind in 1838," https://www.georgetownmemoryproject.org/wp-content/uploads/Research-Memo-Lost-Jesuit-Slaves.pdf. See also the *Georgetown Memory Project*'s updated June 19, 2019, memorandum (in possession of the author), asserting that 314 total people were swept up in the sale and that 99 people were not taken to Louisiana but remained in Maryland.

32. Thomas Mulledy (Georgetown) to John McElroy, November 11, 1838, box 66, folder 3, MPA; Joseph Zwinge, S.J., "Jesuit Farms in Maryland," *Woodstock Letters* 41, no. 2 (1912): 195.

33. Letter Book 1, 405–406, *GSA,* https://slaveryarchive.georgetown.edu/items/show/382.

34. Rev. Fidel Grivel to Rev. Charles Lancaster, November 6, 1838, box 66, folder 3, MPA.

35. Grivel to Lancaster, November 6, 1838, postscript.

36. See Grivel to Lancaster, November 6, 1838, and February 3, 1839, box 66, folder 2, MPA.

37. Schermerhorn, *Business of Slavery,* 142, on the *Uncas,* and 147, 158, on Franklin's "fancy girl."

38. On shipping and slave ships, see Schermerhorn, *Business of Slavery,* 135–138, 164. The manifest of the *Katherine Jackson* in 1838 is at the *GSA.* The MPA also hold a census compiled in 1838. See box 4, MPA, also available at the *GSA.* On the *Katherine Jackson,* see advertisements in the *Daily National Intelligencer,* September 30, 1836, October 2, 1838, and November 15, 1839.

39. Schermerhorn, *Business of Slavery,* 158, 164.

40. Thomas Mulledy to John McElroy, November 11, 1838, box 66, folder 3, MPA. See "Lost Jesuit Slaves of Maryland," 57.

41. Contract for fifty-six slaves with Henry Johnson, November 10, 1838, box 40, folder 9, MPA. John McElroy to Jesse Batey, February 18, 1840, box 77, Letter Book 1, MPA, *GSA.*

42. Louis Janin to Georgetown College, August 8, 1843, box 40, folder 8, MPA.

43. Janin to Georgetown College, August 8, 1843.

44. Henry Johnson to Edmond J. Forstall, December 2, 1843, box 40, folder 6, MPA.

45. See Henry Johnson and Elizabeth R. Key, March 12, 1841, mortgage $6,000 to Bank of Louisiana, Conveyances, book 17, pp. 7, 7A, Ascension Parish Courthouse, Donaldsonville, La. Mortgaged twelve people, including several of the husbands exchanged from Maryland, Tom Nolland, Hilary Ford, Clem, Augustus (Gustus, Augusty).

46. Declaration of Henry Johnson, Miscellaneous notes and documents, box 40, folder 6, MPA.

47. February 17, 1844, agreement, Miscellaneous notes and documents, box 40, folder 6, MPA.

48. Johnson to Philip Barton Key, February 15, 1844, and Johnson and Key to John B. Thompson, June 4, 1845, book 19, 7, 266–277, Conveyances, Ascension Parish Courthouse, Donaldsonville, La. See *Robert Sewall v. Henry Johnson et al.*, October 15, 1849, Minute Book, 4th Judicial District Court, 1845–1859, Ascension Parish, Louisiana State Archives, Baton Rouge. Sewall was likely Key's brother-in-law from his first marriage. He was a Maryland-born planter worth $70,000 in Iberville in 1850. See U.S. Census, 1850, Iberville, La., population schedule, p. 326A, dwelling 259, family 292, Robert Sewall, M432, roll 231, NARA. See also Johnson to Lancaster, January 28, 1851, and Thompson to Lancaster, February 22, 1853, and December 31, 1858, box 40, folder 5, MPA.

49. Inventory and appraisement of the property of Dr. Jesse Batey, March 5, 1851, book 2, no. 192, Conveyances 2, Iberville Parish, Iberville Courthouse, Plaquemine, La. Heirs of Jesse Batey to Washington and John Barrow, book 5, no. 201, Conveyances 5, Iberville Parish, Iberville Courthouse, Plaquemine, La. On Austin Woolfolk, see Schermerhorn, *Business of Slavery*, 54–59, 66–68. His wife, Emily Woolfolk, inherited his considerable property after his death in February 1847, including at least five thousand acres near Maringouin and hundreds of enslaved people. The estate was appraised at $422,828. Also *Samuel Batey et al. v. Widow Emily Woolfolk et al.* (1866), Historical Archives of the Supreme Court of Louisiana, University of New Orleans. See also *Sarah and Austin Woolfolk v. Mrs. Emily Woolfolk*, January 1878, in Thomas C. Manning, François-Xavier Martin, and Merritt M. Robinson, *Reports of Cases Argued and Determined in the Supreme Court of Louisiana and in the Superior Court of the Territory of Louisiana*, book 37, vol. 30 (St. Paul, Minn.: West, 1908), 140–148.

50. "Bill of Sale for Land and Slaves from William Patrick and Joseph Woolfolk to Emily Sparks, Widow of Austin Woolfolk," July 16, 1859, in *GSA*, http://slaveryarchive.georgetown.edu/items/show/17.

51. Lawrence T. Kottikoff and Anton J. Rupert, "The Manumission of Slaves in New Orleans, 1827–1846," *Southern Studies* 19 (Summer 1980): 172–181. See Loren Schweninger, *Appealing for Liberty: Freedom Suits in the South* (Oxford: Oxford University Press, 2018), 291.

52. *Mount St. Mary's College to the use of Louisa Mahoney, a woman of color v. Francis B. Jameson and Edmund H. McCabe*, April Term, 1854, St. Louis Circuit Court (St. Louis, Mo.: Washington University in St. Louis, University Libraries), http://repository.wustl.edu/concern/texts/hq37vp57t.

Duckettsville

1. William Still, *The Underground Railroad: A Record of Facts . . .* , rev. ed. (Philadelphia: Porter and Coates, 1872), in Project Gutenburg, http://www.gutenberg.org/files /15263/15263-h/15263-h.htm.
2. Cecilia Queen, email message to the author, June 8, 2019.
3. Cecilia Queen, email message to the author, June 24, 2019.
4. Will of Anne Duckett Hall, Prince George's County Will Book TT 1, 158–159, in Maryland Register of Wills Records, 1629–1999, database and images, FamilySearch .org, Prince George's, Wills 1808, vol. 1, image 88. New York's 1799 act liberated males at age twenty-eight and females at twenty-five. New Jersey's lowered the age to twenty-five for males and twenty-one for females. Pennsylvania's 1780 abolition act indentured the children of enslaved women born after 1780 for twenty-eight years.

CHAPTER 9. THE LAST FREEDOM TRIAL

1. The case citations in the Bell freedom suits refer to "Susan Arm[i]stead" as the defendant. Later documents in the *Pearl* litigation refer to her as "Susanna Arm[i]stead." On her relationship to the Greenfield family, as "the Greenfield widow" in some accounts, see Kaci Nash, "Emancipating the Bell Family: An Inquiry into the Strategies of Freedom Making" (June 2018), in *OSCYS*, http://earlywashingtondc.org/ stories/emancipating_bells. Estate of Robert Armstead, RG 21, entry 115, O.S. case file 1832, NARA. For one of the most detailed accounts of the Bell family's freedom suit, see also Josephine F. Pacheco, *The Pearl: A Failed Slave Escape on the Potomac* (Chapel Hill: University of North Carolina Press, 2005), 46–50.
2. See esp. Stephanie E. Jones-Rogers, *They Were Her Property: White Women as Slave Owners in the American South* (New Haven: Yale University Press, 2019), xi. Jones-Rogers documents white women "who owned enslaved people in their own right." She calls them "mistresses of the market" (xv), subverting the terms to indicate that women took a direct hand in acquiring, governing, disciplining, and selling the enslaved.
3. Harriet Beecher Stowe, *A Key to Uncle Tom's Cabin* (Boston: John P. Jewett, 1853), 171.
4. I consider *Eleanora Bell v. Susan Armistead* one of the last freedom trials because it was among the last freedom suits in the Circuit Court of the District of Columbia to go to a jury trial as part of a multigenerational series of suits. Several pending Bell cases followed—*Louisa Bell v. Lee,* filed in May 1854 and again May 1856, and *Charles Bell v. Luther Jones,* December 1854–January 1859. In the 1850s, summons of the court went unanswered in dozens of freedom cases, including Charles Bell's. Both were represented by Joseph H. Bradley, the attorney for Mary Bell, Ann Bell, and Moses Bell. Less than a handful of other suits went to trial after Eleanora Bell, and most were cases of mistaken identity: the relevant cases are *Mary Vigel v. Robert K. Nevitt* in October 1858, *Primus Garner v. H. R. Maryann* in April 1857, *Andrew Jones v. Joshua Pearce* in November 1854, and *Jesse Nelson v. John Cornwell* in December 1854. *Mary Ann Bond et al. v. Thomas C. Magruder,* April 1854, and *Andrew Jones v. Joshua Pearce,* November 1854. In St. Louis, Mo., the Dred Scott case began earlier in 1846 and, based on residency in a free territory, went to trial in

1847. See Lea Vandervelde, *Redemption Songs: Suing for Freedom* (Oxford: Oxford University Press, 2014), 189–193; and Loren Schweninger, *Appealing for Liberty: Freedom Suits in the South* (Oxford: Oxford University Press, 2018), 167–169. Schweninger counts 347 freedom suits in his county courts dataset in the period 1840–1863 (296–298). He includes the D.C. cases, but the vast majority of them were likely tried before Eleanora Bell's jury trial in December 1851.

5. *Williams v. Ash,* Records of the United States Supreme Court, box 232, folder 2183, RG 21, NARA. See also Jeff Forret, *Williams' Gang: A Notorious Slave Trader and His Cargo of Black Convicts* (Cambridge: Cambridge University Press, 2020), 127.

6. The relevant Maryland law on kidnapping is *Laws of Maryland, Session Laws, 1809,* chap. 138, AOMOL, 570:92.

7. Stanley Harrold, *Subversives: Antislavery Community in Washington, D.C., 1828–1865* (Baton Rouge: Louisiana State University Press, 2003), 52, 82–83; Charles S. Bradley, "The Bradley Family and the Times in Which They Lived," *Records of the Columbia Historical Society, Washington, D.C.* 6 (1903): 123–142. Daniel Farbman has argued, "There is little evidence that any lawyer affirmatively facilitated an escape of one of their clients while representing them. This fact reveals a fascinating dissonance in the practice of even the most radical resistance lawyers. For legal process to work as a tool of delay and confusion, lawyers could not entirely rupture their relationship to the legitimacy of the process." Farbman, "Resistance Lawyering," *California Law Review* 107, no. 6 (2019): 1927.

8. *Williams v. Ash,* 3.

9. Petition for Freedom, December 24, 1836, *Ann Bell, Daniel Bell, and David Bell v. Gerard T. Greenfield,* in *OSCYS,* http://earlywashingtondc.org/cases/oscys.ca-seid.0104.

10. Petition for Freedom, *Ann Bell, Daniel Bell, and David Bell v. Gerard T. Greenfield.* On John H. Goddard, see Harrold, *Subversives,* 46, 79, 83, 146–149.

11. *William H. Williams v. James Ash,* Supreme Court Report, in *OSCYS,* http://earlywashingtondc.org/doc/oscys.report.0027.001.

12. Benjamin C. Howard, *Reports of Cases Argued and Adjudged in the Supreme Court of the United States,* January Term, 1843, vol. 1 (Philadelphia: T. and J. W. Johnson, 1843), in *OSCYS,* http://earlywashingtondc.org/doc/oscys.report.0027.001.

13. *James Ash v. William H. Williams,* in *OSCYS,* http://earlywashingtondc.org/cases/oscys.caseid.0149.

14. Of the D.C. freedom suits, only five others were successful in the U.S. Supreme Court, though several were remanded to the lower court without a judgment: *Ben v. Sabret Scott* (1811), *Sarah Ann Allen et al. v. Joseph Wallingsford* (1836), *Julia Roberts v. Austin L. Adams and Ann C. Harding* (1844), *Moses Bell v. James Rhodes* (1844), and *Susan Vigel v. Henry Naylor* (1860).

15. *Mary Bell v. Susan Armistead,* in *OSCYS,* http://earlywashingtondc.org/cases/oscys.caseid.0174.

16. *Mary Bell v. Susan Armistead,* Motion for a new trial, December 14, 1847, in *OSCYS,* http://earlywashingtondc.org/doc/oscys.case.0172.013.

17. Daniel Drayton, *Personal Memoir of Daniel Drayton, for Four Years and Four Months a Prisoner (for Charity's Sake) in Washington Jail: Including a Narrative of the Voyage and Capture of the Schooner Pearl* (Boston: B. Marsh, 1853), 24–30. Stowe, *Key to Uncle Tom's Cabin,* 171.

18. Stowe, *Key to Uncle Tom's Cabin*, 171; *Letha Duckett, Mary Duckett, Thomas Duckett, Barbara Duckett, Julia Duckett, and Lewis Duckett v. John McCutchen and John H. G. McCutchen*, in *OSCYS*, http://earlywashingtondc.org/cases/oscys.caseid.0163. See also Harrold, *Subversives*, 116–145. Stowe reported that Thomas Ducket's "wife" was on board the *Pearl* but said nothing about their children. The lists of passengers on the *Pearl* were incomplete and contradictory (see note 19, below). There was a woman named "Mary Letha" on board. She was listed in one place as Mary Letha King along with a man named Leonard King, who might have been either her father or her husband. If her husband, then she would not be Ducket's spouse. The timing of Letha and Mary Duckett's freedom suits, however, strongly indicate that they are related to the *Pearl* events and therefore to Thomas Ducket. Within a few weeks her attorney David A. Hall became the one of the lead attorneys for the *Pearl* defendants. See also Harrold, *Subversives*, 118–145.

19. Hillary Russell, "The Operation of the Underground Railroad in Washington, D.C., c. 1800–1860" (Washington, D.C.: Historical Society of Washington, D.C., and National Park Service, July 2001). See also the list published in *Daily Union*, April 19, 1848. The list of W. C. Williams, April 17, 1848, is slightly different, as are the additional individual documents for each charge of larceny (found in *U.S. v. Daniel Drayton*, Criminal Trials, March Term 1849, RG 21, entry 45—The Pearl, folder 9f, NARA). For example, Harriet Queen, age nine, is missing from both of these lists but is listed in an individual larceny charge.

20. *U.S. v. Daniel Drayton*. The ship's cook, Chester English, was also charged. See Harrold, *Subversives*, 116–120.

21. The U.S. district attorney was Philip Barton Key II, the son of Francis Scott Key. For the best account of the slaveholders' reaction, see Josephine Pacheco, *The Pearl: A Failed Slave Escape on the Potomac*, 112–113.

22. John H. Slingerland, a congressman from Albany, N.Y., was a witness and wrote about the scene in "The Recaptured Fugitives," *North Star*, May 12, 1848, and "Beauties of the Slave System," *North Star*, October 13, 1848. See Nash, "Emancipating the Bell Family: An Inquiry into the Strategies of Freedom Making" (June 2018), in *OSCYS*, http://earlywashingtondc.org/stories/emancipating_bells.

23. Thomas Ducket to Jacob Bigelow, February 18, 1852, in Stowe, *Key to Uncle Tom's Cabin*, 171.

24. Eleanora's "next friend" was Mary E. Edwards. She is possibly the daughter of Ann and James Edwards, a government clerk with over $13,500 in real estate in 1850 and over $20,000 in personal property in 1860 (possibly enslaved people, though he does not appear in the slave schedule). Mary Edwards was single, thirty years old in 1850, and born in Massachusetts. The family had two free black women living in the household, Sarah Bayne, age fifty, a cook, and Lucy Bayne, age twenty-five, her daughter.

25. "Obituary," *Baltimore Sun*, August 22, 1887; "Real Estate Supplement—Real Estate Transfers," *Baltimore Sun*, March 14, 1887; Griffith Morgan Hopkins, *Atlas of Fifteen Miles Around Baltimore* (Philadelphia, 1878), Geography and Maps Division, Library of Congress, Washington, D.C.

26. *Susanna Queen v. Arch and Jane Gray et al.*, Charles County, Chancery Court, Equity Papers, 1850–1852, T2154-2, Liber 4, MSA.

27. Charles H. Queen and John E. Queen to David Middleton, January 1, 1857, Charles County Circuit Court, Land Records, Liber JS 2, 65, MSA; William M. Lyon to Susanna Queen, December 28, 1854, Charles County Circuit Court, Land Records, Liber JS 1, 157, MSA.

28. T. Stephen Whitman, *The Price of Freedom: Slavery and Manumission in Baltimore and Early National Maryland* (Lexington: University Press of Kentucky, 1997), offers the most thorough analysis of manumission and term slavery in the Chesapeake region. See also T. Stephen Whitman, *Challenging Slavery in the Chesapeake: Black and White Resistance to Human Bondage, 1775–1865* (Baltimore: Johns Hopkins University Press, 2006).

29. *The Case of William Chaplin* (Boston: Chaplin Committee, 1851), 5–6, 9–11. "Review of the Chaplin Pamphlet," *Liberator,* April 25, 1851. Chaplin skipped bail, remained in New York, withdrew from the antislavery movement, and never returned to Washington for trial. See Harrold, *Subversives,* 161.

30. David Blight, *Frederick Douglass: Prophet of Freedom* (New York: Simon and Schuster, 2018), 213–217. Farbman describes the strategies of abolitionist lawyers in response to the Fugitive Slave Act of "delay, confusion, and obstruction" as "surprisingly successful." Farbman, "Resistance Lawyering," 1905, 1924.

31. Frederick Douglass, "Change of Opinion Announced," *North Star,* May 15, 1851, reprinted in the *Liberator,* May 23, 1851. Dorothy E. Roberts, "Abolition Constitutionalism," *Harvard Law Review* 133, no. 1 (2019): 58–62.

32. From 1790 to 1840 the most common surname of free black household heads in Maryland was Queen. John Joseph Condon, "Manumission, Slavery, and Family in Post-Revolutionary Rural Chesapeake: Ann Arundel County, Maryland" (Ph.D. diss., University of Minnesota, 2001), 211n370. All compiled military service records for men from the Butler, Queen, and Mahoney families born in Maryland were collected from NARA. Twenty-six Queen men served in the army, 4 in the navy. Fifteen of the 26 Queen men (58 percent) were drafted. All pension files for the Queen men in the U.S. Colored Troops from Maryland were collected from NARA. See, e.g., John Queen, Co. H, 29th USCT, Widow Pension, application no. 429171, certificate no. 435257, NARA. On Sarah Queen as "in her early life bound to my young master," see Affidavit of Isaac Ennis, May 19, 1896. On Sarah Queen as "free born," see her affidavit March 21, 1891. Approximately 95 Butler men served in the army, 17 in the navy; of these 15 were drafted. Eight Maryland-born Mahoney men served in the army, 3 in the navy; 1 was drafted. Over 8,700 black men from Maryland served in the USCT. See Barbara Jeanne Fields, *Slavery and Freedom on the Middle Ground: Maryland during the Nineteenth Century* (New Haven: Yale University Press, 1987), 122–125; and John W. Blassingame, "The Recruitment of Negro Troops in Maryland," *Maryland Historical Magazine* 58, no. 1 (1963): 21–28; Edward G. Longacre, *A Regiment of Slaves: The 4th United States Colored Infantry, 1863–1866* (Lincoln: University of Nebraska Press, 2003), 14–16; and Ira Berlin and Leslie S. Rowland, eds., *Families and Freedom: A Documentary History of African-American Kinship in the Civil War Era* (New York: New Press, 1997), 95–96.

33. George Queen, Pvt., Co. E, 1 U.S. Colored Infantry, Compiled Military Service Records of Volunteer Union Soldiers Who Served with the United States Colored Troops: 1st U.S. Colored Infantry, 1st South Carolina Volunteers (Colored) Company A, 1st U.S. Colored Infantry (1 Year), M1819, roll 12; Gabriel Mahoney,

Compiled Military Service Records of Volunteer Union Soldiers Who Served with
the United States Colored Troops: Artillery Organizations, M1818, roll 122; James
Mahoney, Compiled Military Service Records of Volunteer Union Soldiers Who
Served with the United States Colored Troops: Infantry Organizations, 41st through
46th, M1994, roll 104; Daniel Mahoney, Compiled Military Service Records of
Volunteer Union Soldiers Who Served With the United States Colored Troops:
1st U.S. Colored Infantry, 1st South Carolina Volunteers (Colored) Company A,
1st U.S. Colored Infantry (1 Year), M1819, roll 19; all in Records of the Adjutant
General's Office, 1762–1984, RG 94, NARA.

34. On the Crater, see Kevin M. Levin, *Remembering the Battle of the Crater: War as
Murder* (Lexington: University Press of Kentucky, 2012). Noah Queen, Co. I,
29th USCT, Invalid Pension, application no. 80878, certificate no. 63219, NARA.
Affidavit of Eliza Woolford and Nancy Woolford, September 30, 1869, Daniel
Queen, Co. G, 19th USCT, Minor Pension, certificate no. 136012, NARA. Daniel
Queen and Noah Queen, Compiled Military Service Records of Volunteer Union
Soldiers Who Served with the United States Colored Troops: Infantry Organ-
izations, 14th through 19th, M1822, roll 98; Andrew Queen, Compiled Military
Service Records of Volunteer Union Soldiers Who Served with the United States
Colored Troops: Infantry Organizations, 26th through 30th, Including the
29th Connecticut (Colored), M1824, roll 102; George Mahoney and John Mahoney,
Compiled Military Service Records of Volunteer Union Soldiers Who Served With
the United States Colored Troops: Infantry Organizations, 36th through 40th,
M1993, roll 91; Charles H. Butler, Compiled Military Service Records of Volunteer
Union Soldiers Who Served with the United States Colored Troops: Infantry Organ-
izations, 36th through 40th, M1993, roll 81; all in Records of the Adjutant General's
Office, 1762–1984, RG 94, NARA.

35. *Annapolis (Md.) Gazette,* May 19, 1864; *New York Times,* June 25, November 4, 1864.
See also Daniel W. Crofts, "Holding the Line in Maryland," *New York Times,*
October 22, 2013. Ned Queen's enslavement would not have ended with the passage
of the Thirteenth Amendment. The research of Amanda Laury Kleintop promises to
shed light on this important but understudied period when slaveholders sought
compensation and some forms of slavery persisted after the war. Her work, *The
Balance of Freedom: Abolishing Property Rights in Slaves After Emancipation,* is
forthcoming. See Amanda Laury Kleintop, "Life, Liberty, and Property in Slaves:
White Mississippians Seek 'Just Compensation' for Their Freed Slaves in 1865,"
Slavery and Abolition 39, no. 2 (2018): 383–404; and Amanda Laury Kleintop, "The
Balance of Freedom: Abolishing Property Rights in Slaves after the U.S. Civil War"
(Ph.D. diss., Northwestern University, 2018).

Acknowledgments

This book took ten years to research and write, a journey on which I feel fortunate to have made so many friends along the way.

The descendants of the families that sued for freedom generously encouraged me, and without them this book would not have taken the shape that it did. I am profoundly grateful for their friendship, patience, and honesty throughout. Guilford Queen, Letitia Clark, Kristin Hart, Stephen Hart, Mélisande Short-Colomb, Sandra Green Thomas, Melissa Kemp, Karran Harper Royal, Khris Royal, Jeff Tignor, Kemi Ogidan, Lynn Nehemiah, Dante Eubanks, Cecilia Queen, Rhonda Pindell Charles, Amari Jackson, Sandra Braddock, Charisse Carney-Nunes, Harvey Nunes, Renee Thompson, Marlene Colbert, Roger Barnes, Clyde Bernett Jr., Freida Thomas, Felicia Rollins, Wanda Belt, Sherman A. Bernett Sr., Thelma W. Bernett, Keith Peirce, and Joe Bates.

I am especially grateful for the research assistance and dedication of Kaci L. Nash and Gail Blankeneau. They have worked with me on this project from the beginning, spent many days in the archives chasing down court records, and had long conversations with me about the intricate research behind this book. They patiently corrected me when I needed it. Kaci Nash deserves special recognition and thanks. The team at the Center for Digital Research in the Humanities supported the digital collection of the Maryland and D.C. freedom suits (www.earlywashingtondc.org): thanks especially to Laura Weakly, Karin Dalziel, Jessica Dussault, Kay Walter, and Ken Price. Thanks to the team at the University of Maryland's Institute for Technology in the Humanities, especially Trevor Muñoz and Jennifer Guiliano, for their early support.

Archivists, librarians, local historians, and genealogists supported this research at every stage. I would like to thank Susan Pearl of the Prince George's County Historical Society for her enthusiasm, energy, and dedication. Donna Schneider of the Prince George's County Historical Society and Elizabeth Walker, Prince George's County Planning Commission, have each encouraged this work. Thanks to the following archivists who worked with me throughout this project: Maya Davis, Chris Haley, and the staff of the

Maryland State Archives; Karen Wahl of the George Washington University Law Library; Mary Beth Corrigan and the staff at Lauinger Library at Georgetown University Special Collections; Marianne Gill of the Sacred Heart Church; Mary Jeske, Damon Talbot, and the staff of the Maryland Historical Society; Alison Foley and the staff of the Associate Archives at St. Mary's Seminary and University; Jan Graffius, Stonyhurst College; Anna Edwards and the staff of the Archives of the British Province of the Society of Jesus; Amy Sampson and the staff of the National Archives, Kew (U.K.); and Robert Ellis and the staff of the National Archives and Records Administration in Washington, D.C. Thanks to Richard Cellini, Judy Riffel, and Melissa Ruffner of the Georgetown Memory Project for their support and encouragement.

I wrote most of this book while in residence at the Virginia Theological Seminary (VTS) in Alexandria, Va., and as a visiting fellow of the Georgetown Slavery Institute. VTS generously provided me with much needed housing through many years of research and writing. I am especially grateful for the support at VTS of the Reverend Dr. Joseph Thompson, the Very Reverend Dr. Ian Markham, Kathryn Glover, Dr. David Charlton, the Right Reverend Phoebe Roaf, the Reverend Harold Cobb, the Reverend Dr. Mitzi Budde, Christopher Pote, the Reverend Dr. Melody Knowles, and the Reverend Dr. Barney Hawkins IV, who have been tireless supporters. Thanks to friends Mike and Carter Fleming and Elizabeth Porter for housing me many times at a moment's notice.

My wonderful colleagues Michael Burton and Kwakiutl L. Dreher have each inspired me and encouraged me to think creatively about every story we tell. We began our partnership with *Anna* (2018), and it continues with *The Bell Affair*. Our adventure together has been a joy.

The Duke Divinity Summer Institute on Reconciliation colleagues and teachers opened my eyes to models of reconciliation. Special thanks to Dr. David Anderson Hooker, Valerie Hulbert, and Michael Moore.

I owe a special debt of gratitude to Dr. Lauret Savoy, at Mount Holyoke College, who is writing her own memoir history of her family's roots in Washington, D.C., and Maryland. We met early in this journey, and I am forever grateful for her close reading of my first draft of the manuscript and our many long conversations, our friendship, and her warm encouragement of our mutual research and writing.

Generous colleagues and friends read parts of the manuscript, and the book is better for their suggestions: Yoni Appelbaum, Tom Bailey, Eric Berger, Peter Capuano, Mary Beth Corrigan, Andrew Graybill, Hendrik Hartog,

Margaret Jacobs, Katrina Jagodinsky, Jeannette E. Jones, James D. Le Sueur, Tim Mahoney, Kate Masur, Joseph Miller, Daniel Nelson, Richard Newman, Tamika Y. Nunley, Dudley P. Olsson, Marcus Rediker, Leslie Stainton, Joe Starita, Rachel Swarns, Lea Vandervelde, Elizabeth Varon, and Kenneth Winkle. Two scholars of American slavery I admire deeply, Edward L. Ayers and Adam Rothman, read the entire manuscript and offered especially valuable comments. I thank them both.

Thanks to the faculty in the University of Nebraska College of Law Research Seminar who provided insight and comments on chapters related to constitutional questions in *Queen v. Hepburn*. Graduate students at the University of Nebraska in the Nineteenth-Century Studies Seminar read chapters and gave me especially valuable feedback: Patrick Hoehne, William Kelly, Christy Hyman, Donna Devlin, and Paul Grosskopf. Thanks to the faculty and students of the Washington Early American Seminar at the University of Maryland, who read and commented on chapter 3, especially Holly Brewer, Richard Bell, Chris Bonner, Clare Lyons, and Derek Livak. Thanks to the students and faculty of the Georgetown University U.S. History Seminar: Chandra Manning, Maurice Jackson, Adam Rothman, Cory Young, Mélisande Short-Colomb, Luke Frederick, Elsa Barraza Mendoza, Andrew Ross, Erina Nakashima, Maria Zyla, Benjamin Feldman, Rebeckah McGoodwin, and Greg Beaman. Thanks to Mike Reynolds and his students in the History of the South Seminar at Episcopal High School in 2016. Thanks to Lindsay Duvall, Suzanne Duvall, Ian Fagelson, Peter H. Wood, David Plater, Bob Kaplan, Laurence Kaplan, Byron Anway, and J. B. Milliken for support and encouragement.

The John Simon Guggenheim Memorial Foundation fellowship in 2016 gave me the time and creative freedom to write. The National Endowment for the Humanities supported this project with a Collaborative Research grant. My department chair at the University of Nebraska, James D. Le Sueur, gave me consistent support and, at a critical juncture, the time I needed to complete the manuscript. I am deeply thankful for his friendship, kindness, and generosity as a scholar and a chair.

My literary agent, Wendy Strothman, believed in this project at the start and shaped my early drafts. I am grateful for her consistent and patient support. Jessica Hatch edited and proofed the manuscript at a critical stage. Adina Berk, my editor at Yale University Press, worked with me closely for years, sharpened every chapter, and guided this book to completion. Molly Roy produced the maps. Her unmatched cartographic skill and design expertise gave visual life to my vague ideas for a set of narrative maps.

The team at Yale University Press is the best in the business: thanks to Eva Skewes for her expert help in design, Susan Laity for her professional editing and production, and Laura Jones Dooley for her excellent proofing and copy editing. As a team they are without peer.

Family is at the center of everything, and mine supported this journey every step of the way. Thanks to my mother, Suzanne Thomas, and to Margaret Konkel, Brian Konkel, Alexander Y. Thomas, Brigid Thomas, Lawrence Webb, Gerhard Schwabe, Chris Schwabe, and Amray Schwabe.

Heather Thomas, whose love and support make so much possible, and my children, Sarah Thomas, Guy Thomas, and Jane Thomas, lived with the stories of this book for many years and always encouraged me.

This book is dedicated to the memory of my father, who believed in the importance of this story from the beginning and encouraged me to the end.

Index

Page numbers in italics indicate illustrations. Many freedom suits are indexed by the first name of the petitioner instead of the surname.